Turning Right

The Making of the Rehnquist Supreme Court

Turning Right
The Making of the Rehnquist Supreme Court

David G. Savage

John Wiley & Sons, Inc.
New York • Chichester • Brisbane • Toronto • Singapore

For my children:
Manning and Whitley

ISBN 0-471-59553-5

Printed in the United States of America
10 9 8 7 6 5 4 3 2 1

Preface

For a journalist, the Supreme Court can be an odd beat. On most days, there is nothing to see and no one to talk to. The justices as a rule do not speak to reporters, nor do they employ others—special assistants, public information officers, or the like—who can brief journalists on the substance of matters before the Court. The law clerks, who typically spend one year working for a justice, see the inner workings of the Court, but they are told not to discuss cases with reporters, lawyers, or anyone else outside the chambers.

But there is drama aplenty in the cases that come before the Supreme Court. And despite the penchant for secrecy, the Court and its decision-making are not truly mysterious. The justices act only on cases and legal questions that are appealed to them. They hear arguments and question the competing attorneys in open court. And when a decision is made, they issue lengthy opinions explaining their reasons.

In preparing this book, I have relied in large measure on the written work of the Court: opinions and dissents, as well as briefs, past rulings, and the legal history that shaped the cases before the Rehnquist Court. The justices should be judged by how they decide cases. But I have also been helped greatly by a series of interviews with the justices and their clerks, nearly all of whom insisted that they not be cited by name. Most of the members of the Court agreed to speak with me, and they set me straight on many points. I greatly appreciate their help. Dozens of former law clerks recounted the day-to-day workings of the chambers or described the justice they worked for—and without betraying confidences about the handling of specific cases. I thank them for their aid and insights.

Finally, I want to thank two sets of editors. First, at Wiley, Roger Scholl offered astute advice on shaping this manuscript. I owe a special debt to the editors of the Los Angeles Times. The Supreme Court cannot be covered well as an occasional, part-time job. There is simply too much to read, and no good short-cut to spending countless hours at the Court reading. The editors at the Times have always wanted—and insisted—that the Court be covered thoroughly and well, and I thank them for giving me the chance to try.

Contents

Turning Right
The Making of the Rehnquist
Supreme Court

PART ONE
The Summer of 1986

1

The Changing of the Guard

I t was just past noon when the new chief justice of the United States stepped from behind the marble columns of the Supreme Court and out into the bright September sun. A week earlier, on September 17, 1986, Associate Justice William H. Rehnquist had been confirmed by the Senate to become the nation's sixteenth chief justice, after a long, rancorous debate and a divided vote. The senators, exhausted, then quickly approved without opposition the bright and bold Antonin Scalia to fill Rehnquist's seat as the ninth justice.

September 26 was a day for taking oaths and posing for pictures. In the morning, Rehnquist and Scalia went to the White House to stand next to the president as they pledged their allegiance to the U.S. Constitution. Ronald Reagan predicted that Rehnquist "will be a chief justice of historic stature." The justices then traveled back to Capitol Hill and stood at the front of the ornate courtroom, where they swore to "do equal right to the poor and to the rich."

Shortly afterward, like a wedding party, Rehnquist and Scalia moved out into the sunlight and down the long steps toward the waiting photographers. A "photo opportunity" is a rarity at the Supreme Court. Cameras and microphones are barred from the building, and the justices generally refuse to appear on television. Once a year, photographers are allowed inside to snap the formal photo of the Court. There, the justices appear as "nine black-robed figures who look as if their heads are interchangeable," Rehnquist once joked.

The restriction on cameras suited Rehnquist perfectly well. Before crowds or photographers, he looked stiff and uncomfortable. His hands fidgeted awkwardly. As he paused for a moment on the steps during the photo session, the new chief justice hooked his thumbs in his pockets, with his fingers pointed outward. Scalia, on the other hand, delighted in being the focus of attention. Short and stocky, with jet black hair, he had a confident, steady gaze and a jutting lower lip.

Between them stood the retiring chief justice, Warren E. Burger. Though 79 years old and slightly stooped, Burger still looked as though he had been cast by Hollywood for the part of chief justice. His snow-white hair, well-chiseled chin, and deep voice spoke of gravity and somber judgment.

Inside the dark chambers of the Court, however, where law and the Constitution were debated, Burger had not fared as well. He had been long-winded and ponderous, to the irritation of his colleagues. His pompous manner offended them; he could be spiteful and petty to those who disagreed with him.

His 17-year tenure had been considered a failure, especially by conservatives. In 1969, President Richard Nixon had chosen him to lead a conservative counterrevolution at the Court. Three other Nixon appointees soon followed, but the counterrevolution did not. Indeed, the 1970s saw landmark victories for the liberals. The supposedly conservative Court gave a green light to citywide busing for school desegregation, struck down the death penalty, legalized abortion, and upheld "affirmative" preferences for racial minorities. Unable to secure the votes—or even the decent regard—of the majority of his colleagues, Burger presided over a fractured, uncertain Court.

Four months before, in late May of 1986, he had paid a quiet visit to the White House to talk with President Reagan about the upcoming 200th anniversary of the Constitution. It was Burger's favorite topic of conversation, although his enthusiasm was not shared widely. As chair of the commission organizing the celebration, he faced a daunting problem. The Statue of Liberty in New York Harbor had stolen the public spotlight—as well as millions of dollars of corporate support—for its planned 100th birthday bash. On top of that, the nation's bicentennial had been celebrated ten years earlier, to commemorate the 200th anniversary of the Declaration of Independence. Compared to that glowing proclamation, the Con-

stitution read as a dry organization plan for the government—
hugely significant but dull. Its best-known phrases were added
four years later in the Bill of Rights. Nonetheless, Burger had
high hopes for the bicentennial. He wanted the schoolchildren
of the nation to appreciate the significance of the "separation
of powers" concept.

As their conversation drew to a close, Reagan suddenly
became alert. The bicentennial celebration was behind schedule and in deep trouble, Burger said, and it would now require
his full time. He had decided to retire from the Supreme Court
to devote all his efforts to the bicentennial. The President had
had no previous warning of Burger's intentions, but he did not
try to change his mind. Reagan praised his service on the Court
and his devotion to the constitutional celebration and accepted
the resignation. As the outgoing chief was ushered from the
Oval Office, an aide was dispatched to call Attorney General
Edwin Meese III with the news.

At last, the moment had come, a chance finally to change
the complexion of the Supreme Court. After two landslide victories and nearly six years in the White House, the "Reagan
revolution" had swept across most of Washington but had
stopped at the steps of the Court. As a result, the Reagan social
agenda on abortion, school prayer, civil rights, and crime had
remained dormant. So far, Reagan had replaced only one of
the nine justices. In the first six months of his first term, Reagan
picked Sandra Day O'Connor, the first woman to sit on the
high court. The nomination had won praise from all quarters
except from the core of Reagan's conservative constituency. At
the Justice Department, she was known derisively as an "80
percenter." Though generally conservative, she deserted the
Administration at crucial moments. She had cast a vote or two
to permit affirmative action for blacks and women, she had
joined a ruling striking down a voluntary prayer law for the
schools, and even on the abortion issue, her support was in
doubt.

The conservatives had grown frustrated. Year after year,
the Supreme Court had rebuffed Reagan's advances. His Justice
Department attorneys had gone to the Court seeking new restrictions on abortion and affirmative action but came back
empty handed. Now, time was running out. The old liberals,
with fortitude and good health, were determined to hang on.
For a time, it looked as though 1960s-style legal liberalism
might well outlast the Reagan era of the 1980s. Burger's sur-

prise resignation suddenly changed that picture. At the Justice Department, however, Reagan's appointees had long been ready for this.

"When Brad and I went out jogging, we often talked about 'What if?' " said Charles Cooper, a young Alabaman who had risen to the top of the Justice Department. Cooper referred to William Bradford Reynolds, chief of the Civil Rights Division, Meese's closest adviser and the enforcer of the Reagan–Meese legal ideology. At first glance, Cooper and Reynolds made for an odd couple. Athletically built, Cooper sported a broad smile and a hearty handshake. Reynolds was tall, gaunt, and balding, with a stiff, humorless demeanor.

Nonetheless, the two friends shared a common view of the law. An extraordinary cadre of young, bright, and committed conservatives had been drawn to the Reagan Justice Department. Unlike in earlier administrations, where lawyers took positions in the Justice Department to fight crime, defend civil rights, or pad a résumé for a later career in private practice, the Reagan administration attracted attorneys who cared deeply about legal ideology. Simply put, they believed that for a generation, the Supreme Court had abandoned its role as an arbiter of narrow legal issues and had instead become the engine of a liberal social revolution. In their view, the left-leaning Court cared more about protecting pornography in the streets than about prayer in the schools. It enforced busing orders for schoolchildren but refused to enforce the death penalty for murderers. The Court's priorities were those of the liberal left in America, as they saw it, and they meant to change that.

Reagan himself had never understood how the Supreme Court could decide it was unconstitutional to provide a daily moment of prayer for schoolchildren. Meese, a former Oakland prosecutor, never understood why it was unconstitutional to make use of a suspect's voluntary confession, whether or not he had been warned to remain silent. For a later generation of conservatives, the *Roe* v. *Wade* ruling symbolized a Court run amok. They felt that the liberals, rather than abide by the Constitution as written, had created a right to abortion that had not previously existed.

For Cooper, the "crystallizing moment" had come in 1979. As a top graduate of the University of Alabama law school, he had won a Supreme Court clerkship with the most conservative justice, William H. Rehnquist. That term, the Court was called upon to decide whether federal law permitted employers to give preferences to blacks or women—at the expense of white males. The Civil Rights Act of 1964 said that employers may not "discriminate against any individual . . . because of such individual's race, color, religion, sex or national origin." Brian Weber, a white steelworker from Louisiana, brought his case to the Supreme Court, contending that he had lost a promotion because of his race. Fewer than 2 percent of the skilled workers at his Kaiser Steel plant were black, even though 39 percent of the local work force were black. To remedy that imbalance, the company and the steelworkers union negotiated a plan to offer blacks 50 percent of the new apprenticeships for skilled jobs. When Weber lost out to a somewhat less experienced black employee, he filed a reverse discrimination suit against the union.

Rehnquist and his clerk Cooper pored over the congressional debates on the 1964 law and were convinced it meant just what it said: no discrimination against anyone, black or white. Senator Hubert Humphrey, the primary sponsor, had said on the Senate floor, "The truth is that this title forbids discriminating against anyone on account of race." Humphrey sought to put to rest what he called "the bugaboo" that the new law would force employers "to meet a racial quota or to achieve a certain balance."

When the votes were counted in the Supreme Court, though, Justice William J. Brennan, Jr., the leading liberal, had a five-vote majority to uphold "voluntary affirmative action" by employers. He, too, quoted Senator Humphrey as saying that the law was spurred by "the plight of the Negro in our economy." For a century after slavery was abolished, blacks had been denied an equal chance to enter white workplaces. It would be a tragic irony, Brennan wrote, if the landmark law intended to finally give them that chance were interpreted to bar a voluntary effort by an employer or a union to "break down old patterns of racial segregation and hierarchy."

Rehnquist wrote a biting dissent. He called the Brennan opinion "a tour de force reminiscent not of jurists such as Hale, Holmes, or Hughes, but of escape artists such as Houdini." Both the language and the intent of the law could not have been more clear, he said. "Congress outlawed ALL racial discrimination, recognizing that no discrimination based on race is benign, that no action disadvantaging a person because of his color is affirmative," he wrote.

"I had my eyes opened," Cooper said. "Bill Rehnquist had gone over every scrap of evidence. He demonstrated that no one could reasonably believe the law meant what Brennan said it meant. The law was about equal opportunity for all, not about creating a racial spoils system." Cooper also drew a lesson from the experience: The only way to change the law in the Supreme Court was to change the people who served there.

The corollary to Cooper's rule was just as important: Promote judges to the Supreme Court who were reliable—not "80 percenters" or good Republicans whose sole virtue was that they had friends in high places—certainly not those lawyers who were described as "open minded."

After all, the Reagan revolution had been thwarted largely because Richard Nixon and Gerald Ford failed to pick true conservatives. Of Nixon's four appointments, two were outright mistakes in the view of hard-core conservatives: First, Lewis F. Powell, a courtly Virginian, had been picked by Nixon for his law-and-order beliefs. As expected, Powell proved to be generally conservative on crime and the death penalty, but he often sided with the liberals on matters of civil rights, religion, and abortion. The second "mistake," Harry A. Blackmun, a Minnesota Republican, turned out to be even worse, from the conservatives' point of view. After barely two years on the Court, he wrote the *Roe* v. *Wade* opinion giving pregnant women a constitutional right to abortion. Burger, Nixon's chief justice, had been conservative but ineffectual.

Only Rehnquist, among the Nixon appointees, fully lived up to the conservatives' hopes. From his first day, he took up the position on the ideological far right. He fought for the death penalty and against a broad right to appeal, for school prayer but against school desegregation, for equal treatment for white males and against equal rights for women, for government limits on free speech and against the right to abortion. He never wavered or played to the liberal press, nor did he seem fazed by criticism from lawyers or legal academics. On a Court dominated by liberals and moderates, he stood alone on the right. His clerks dubbed him "The Lone Ranger."

As Cooper saw it, no one could be better at leading a Reagan Court than William H. Rehnquist. He had a powerful legal mind, reliably conservative views, the respect of his colleagues, and 14 years of Court experience. Reynolds, Cooper's jogging partner, agreed entirely. In the Nixon Justice Department, Reynolds had an office just down the hall from then-

Assistant Attorney General Rehnquist. He was now a neighbor of Rehnquist's in north Arlington, across the river from Washington.

"But Bill didn't need friendship to get the appointment. He was quite clearly the justice who most represented the judicial views of the Reagan administration," Reynolds said.

Even during its most embarrassing moments, the Administration had had a loyal ally in Rehnquist. In their first year in office, Reynolds and Meese, then the White House counselor, stumbled into a hornet's nest. Since the early 1970s, the Internal Revenue Service (IRS) had denied charitable tax exemptions to private schools and colleges that were racially segregated. Bob Jones University in South Carolina, along with several private academies that practiced segregation, challenged this policy in court, and Reynolds and Meese brought the Reagan Administration into the case on the schools' side. As the new civil rights chief, Reynolds was promoting a new "color-blind" policy—in contrast, he said, to recent favoritism for selected minorities. However, the fight against the IRS policy looked like the old-style conservative blindness to racism of the worst sort. When the Bob Jones University case came before the Supreme Court, Reynolds, Meese, and the segregated academies picked up only one vote: Justice Rehnquist.

Armed with the still-secret news of Burger's retirement, Meese and Reynolds got together to talk over lunch. They quickly settled on a form of the double steal in baseball: Promote Rehnquist to chief justice, and replace him with a younger conservative. Previously, presidents had usually looked outside the Court to find a new chief justice, in part because promoting one of the brethren could sow dissent and jealousy. In 1941, Franklin Roosevelt elevated Justice Harlan Stone to be the chief, and personal jealousies and factional fighting split the Court. When Stone died suddenly of a stroke in 1946, Harry Truman steered clear of the brethren and picked a crony, his treasury secretary, Fred Vinson, to lead the Court. When Vinson succumbed to a heart attack in 1953, Dwight Eisenhower also chose someone outside of the Court, California Governor Earl Warren. When he retired in 1969, Nixon selected another outsider, Warren Burger, a federal appellate judge.

Reagan had his own views on who he wanted to send to the Supreme Court. As governor of California, he had come to distrust politicians as judges. They were unpredictable and unreliable. He made it clear he wanted to promote experienced judges whose views were known. Rehnquist easily passed that test. Like Reagan, Rehnquist had enunciated the same beliefs throughout his career. Indeed, his college friends were convinced that his views were already fully formed when he was an undergraduate at Stanford University and had not shifted since then. Through 14 years as an associate justice, he never seemed to agonize over decisions and never deviated from the conservative side. Regardless of the case that came before the Court, it would be hard to imagine Rehnquist voting to oppose the death penalty or to expand civil rights.

If Rehnquist were the chief justice, could he lead the other justices? Reagan's advisers certainly thought he could. Unlike Burger, Rehnquist had a notably quick, incisive legal mind. No matter how complicated or muddy the legal dispute, he could penetrate to the heart of the matter and distill the key issue at stake. What amazed his colleagues, too, was that Rehnquist did not require the hours of study that they—also experienced and learned in the law—needed to get ready to a hear a case.

"Bill Rehnquist is the quickest lawyer I ever met," said Lewis Powell, who joined him on the high court in 1972, after four decades of private practice. In conference, Rehnquist also had a unique ability to recite phrases from past cases or from literature. "I've probably known people who knew more literature than him, but I don't think I know anyone who recalled more of it," Powell added.

One concern was whether Rehnquist could match wits and charm, as well as brains, with William J. Brennan, the unquestioned leader of the liberal faction of the Court. Brennan, a tiny Irishman with twinkling eyes and a warm handshake, had become a legendary figure among law clerks, civil libertarians, and constitutional scholars. Somehow, year after year, despite a parade of new Republican appointees, Brennan managed to put together liberal majorities to win the big cases. Unknown to the general public, during the 1960s he had been the behind-the-scenes architect for many of the landmark rulings of the Court's liberal era—in desegregation, school prayer, the rights of crime suspects, the freedom of the press, women's rights, and the right to abortion. Since then, the nation had moved to the right, but the Supreme Court had not—in large measure because of William Brennan.

Like Rehnquist, Brennan knew exactly what he believed and never wavered. He was a champion of the underdog, the defender of the minority. Where Rehnquist thought the Court should uphold the will of the majority, Brennan took a nearly opposite approach. He revered the Bill of Rights and held it up as a secular Ten Commandments. He was determined to make these ideals a reality. It was the Court's duty, he preached, to enforce the rights of the lowliest of Americans, regardless of the wishes of the majority. Whether the case involved an inmate on Death Row seeking the right to appeal a conviction, a black child seeking the right to attend an integrated school, a political dissident seeking the right to protest freely, or a woman seeking the right to end her pregnancy, Brennan had taken up their causes. For more than three decades, he had breathed new life into the Constitution and had unalterably changed the law of the land.

He had also exasperated conservatives. In their view, Brennan was less a defender of the Constitution than a liberal activist in black robes. Brennan's style of judging made the Supreme Court all-powerful, they complained. Two Reagan administration attorneys wrote of Brennan in 1984, "There is no individual in this country, on or off the Court, who has had a more profound and sustained impact on public policy in the United States over the past 27 years." Their tone was one of despair. How could a mere judge exercise so much power? they asked.

Certainly, the Supreme Court is a somewhat odd institution in a democratic society. A committee of unelected lawyers, the Court possesses the power to nullify the decisions of elected officials, whether the Congress, the president, or a local school board. The Court sets its own rules, decides what it wants to decide, and proudly ignores the public's reaction once it has decided. Not only are its members not selected by the voters, but also, once seated, they hold their jobs for life.

No doubt the Court's prominence, and the respect in which it is held, reflects a basic ambivalence about government. From the beginning, Americans wanted a government strong enough to preserve order but not so powerful that freedom could be smothered. The Constitution itself reflects this ambivalence. As drawn up in 1787, the original document simply spelled out the powers of the various branches of government. That was not enough, however, to win the document wide approval. It was soon amended by a Bill of Rights, which also spelled out those areas in which the government could not meddle. As one might expect, the words employed in the Constitution were general. Persons were protected in their right

to "liberty" and from "unreasonable searches and seizures."
What do those words mean? Does *liberty* include the right to
abort a pregnancy or to engage in homosexual activity? Is it
unreasonable to be forcibly tested for drugs on the job or to
be stopped on the highway to have your sobriety checked? In
disputes such as this, the Supreme Court is called upon to give
specific meanings to the Constitution's general wordings. The
justices draw the line between the powers of the government
and the rights of the individual. No one had a precise formula
for drawing those lines. No law book supplied the correct answers, and no legal theory always pointed to the correct way.
Much depended on what words such as *liberty* and *equality*
meant to the nine justices. In the end, the Constitution means
what these nine persons say that it means.

Both Rehnquist and Brennan had a practical view of how
the Court worked. Neither sought to portray it as a genuinely
deliberative body, which, after deep thought and intense debate, arrived at the true meaning of the Constitution. They
were both too realistic to hold that view. Each year, Brennan
would ask his new batch of law clerks whether they knew the
most important rule of the Supreme Court. Usually, they were
stumped. After a moment, he would hold up his hand, palm
open and fingers spread wide. "It takes five votes to do anything
in the Supreme Court," he told them.

No one at the Court—lawyers, law clerks, or the justices—
ignored the "rule of five." As lawyers prepared their briefs for
the Court, they often described the process as "counting to
five." They tried to find a set of arguments that would win the
approval of at least five of the nine justices. For the justices,
the rule of five determined not only the outcome of a case, but
also how a new rule of law was to be written in the Court
opinion. If the chief justice had at least four other votes on his
side, he controlled the result and the opinion. However, if
Brennan, the senior liberal, could muster four other votes, he
determined the decision and the opinion.

The voting takes place in secret. From October until the
end of April, the justices hear arguments in as many as 12 cases
per week. On Wednesday afternoons and Friday mornings, they
gather alone in the conference room in the back of the Court
building. Its dark wood-paneled walls are lined with the bound
volumes of 200 years of the Court's decisions. An ornate crystal
chandelier hangs overhead. The long, rectangular wooden table is surrounded by nine leather chairs. At each place are

sharpened pencils, scoring sheets, and a wooden stand to hold papers. Sinking down into one of those chairs, you might think you had wandered into an exclusive men's poker club.

When the justices gather, the chief sits at one end of the table. With each case, he briefly summarizes the issue, explains how he believes it should be decided, and announces his vote: to affirm or reverse the ruling of the lower court. The Supreme Court does not try cases or pronounce defendants innocent or guilty. Rather, it decides legal questions that have arisen in cases previously decided in the lower courts. After the chief justice finishes, the senior justice sitting at the far end of the table speaks next. Brennan occupied that venerated position for 15 years. He would explain his view of the matter and vote next. Then, the discussion moved around the table in order of seniority. Rarely did Brennan and either of the conservative chief justices (Burger or Rehnquist) agree in the major cases. The votes of the others determined the outcome.

During Burger's years, Brennan continued to surprise Court experts. Though he and the liberals had their heyday during the Warren Court of the 1960s, he still won the major battles of the 1970s. Though the Equal Rights Amendment for women died before ratification by three-fourths of the states, Brennan found a five-vote majority to rule that the Constitution's guarantee of the "equal protection of the laws" prohibited nearly all discrimination against women. In 1972, he wrote an opinion in a Massachusetts case involving the sale of contraceptives to unmarried persons, in which he said that the right to privacy in the Constitution means that "the individual, married or single, [is] free from unwarranted governmental intrusion into matters so fundamentally affecting a person as the decision whether to bear or beget a child." Those words served as a springboard the next year for the *Roe* v. *Wade* ruling. In the late 1970s, he found a slim majority to agree that the Constitution and federal civil rights law permit universities and employers to give an edge to minority applicants. Through the first half of the 1980s, he blocked the Reagan administration's moves to roll back abortion rights and affirmative action and to permit a return of school prayer.

"[Brennan] fought one of the greatest rear-guard actions in history," University of Michigan law professor Yale Kamisar said. However, the aging liberal disliked being called a "playmaker" at the Court. "The implication is that . . . you go running about the building talking, shaking hands, putting your arm around everyone," he said in an interview. "Only once did I go around and talk to everybody, and that was on the Nixon tapes case" in 1974. He sought a single, unanimous opinion, such as the Court had given in 1954, in the landmark *Brown* v. *Board of Education* case that outlawed official segregation. Regarding his own lobbying effort, Brennan said, "It was a complete failure. Nobody agreed. Not one."

In Brennan's view, he owed his success more to intellectual persuasion than to arm twisting. "It really isn't very mysterious or complex. You try to get a sense of what will sell, what the others will accept. Will this be rejected by Lewis Powell or Harry Blackmun? Will Thurgood [Marshall] agree with this? Has John Stevens written any cases which may suggest how he is thinking? What does Sandra [O'Connor] think? And you write it that way," he said. Brennan also had the Bill of Rights on his side. Though the Court had been filled with Republican appointees, Brennan could still usually find five who agreed with his generous view of the basic rights and liberties enjoyed by every citizen.

In conversation, the Reagan administration attorneys groused about the little Irishman. How much longer could he survive? Brad Reynolds even took to denouncing him by name in speeches, accusing the aging justice of espousing what he called "radical egalitarianism."

Nonetheless, speeches and denunciations had no impact on Brennan or the Court. Reynolds and the other Reagan attorneys knew they needed a chief justice who could counter Brennan. They felt that Rehnquist was ideal. He not only had the firm views and the quick legal mind of his liberal adversary but also displayed a down-to-earth charm that had endeared him to his colleagues. Even the liberal tandem of Brennan and Marshall spoke well of Rehnquist. "I don't agree with him on much, but he's a great guy," Marshall told a friend.

Many who met Rehnquist for the first time came away surprised. In his writing for the Court, he could be cold and cutting. Certainly no one accused him of being sensitive or unduly compassionate. Yet in person, he was invariably genial and displayed an old-fashioned courtesy. He bowed slightly at the waist to greet newcomers. Unlike Brennan, Rehnquist did not wrap his arm around the shoulder of acquaintances or pump their hands; he was more reserved. Rehnquist, after having met Reagan at a White House reception, observed that the president was a man with "no edges"; he was straightforward and

good-spirited, with no air of superiority; he had no quirks or pomposity. Much the same could be said about Rehnquist.

On May 29, just two days after Burger announced his intention to retire, Meese went by the White House to meet with the President, Chief of Staff Donald Regan, and White House counsel Peter Wallison. They went over a few of Reagan's ground rules. The president wanted to appoint a judge, not a politician, to the Supreme Court vacancy. He also wanted someone who believed in "judicial restraint," a judge who would leave the lawmaking to the elected officials. There was little talk of specific names and no talk of issues, including abortion, nor was there any need for such talk. The views of the leading candidates were already well known. In addition, Chief of Staff Regan stressed the importance of keeping the discussion confined to only a few top advisers. So far, the news of Burger's resignation had not leaked out.

Meese, like the president, barely knew Rehnquist, but Reynolds and Cooper had convinced him that Rehnquist would make the best chief for a Reagan Court. "That turned out to be the easy decision," Reynolds said later. "We thought Rehnquist was a pretty safe bet" for confirmation in the Senate, he added. "He was already on the Court. He was well liked by his colleagues. The only thing they could raise was that old memo he wrote as a clerk in 1952" in which a young Bill Rehnquist questioned the wisdom of overturning the "separate but equal" doctrine, the pillar of Southern segregation.

A few days later, when the White House group met next, Meese strongly recommended that Rehnquist be elevated to chief justice. He was smart, experienced, reliably conservative, and well liked by his colleagues. Meese had only one cautionary warning: He may not want the job. "That was my only real fear—that he would say 'No,' " Cooper said.

At age 61 and with more than 14 years on the Court, Rehnquist was nearing the time when he could retire with a full pension. For years, he had talked openly of doing just that. Often, he was bored and frustrated with the Court. "I've heard all this before," he exclaimed in disgust at the end of one long conference session. Year after year, it seemed to him, the justices squabbled over the same issues and finally compromised with utterly confusing rulings that failed to decide the issues.

One example of these conflicting rulings related to the death penalty. A decade earlier, the Court had ruled that capital punishment was constitutional. Nonetheless, the liberals never gave up trying to ban capital punishment, and each year the Court would "tinker" some more, as Rehnquist put it. New, intricate procedural rules would be announced, which in turn would prompt more litigation in the Supreme Court to define the limits of those new rules. "The ball game never ends in our Court," Rehnquist once observed ruefully.

In addition, his intention to quit went beyond the politics of the Court. He wanted to leave before he was too old. He enjoyed reading and writing history and was interested in teaching. "Do not let the law be too jealous a mistress," he told one law school graduating class. "You must give yourself time not only to do a variety of things, but [also] to allow yourself time to appreciate and enjoy what you are doing."

Rehnquist followed his own advice. He usually left the Court by 3 P.M. In the afternoons, he swam or played tennis. He took up painting, too. Once, as Ronald Reagan delivered his State of the Union address, the cameras panned the assembled dignitaries and showed that only eight members of the Supreme Court were in attendance. Apparently, the White House had scheduled Reagan's speech on the same night as Rehnquist's painting class at the Arlington County adult education center, and Rehnquist had gone to class.

Rehnquist also enjoyed playing practical jokes. Unlike his colleagues, Rehnquist never spoke ill of Burger, but he had been well aware of the chief justice's concern for the dignity of his office. On April Fools' Day in 1985, he asked Burger for a ride to work. As the long black limousine passed in front of the Court, they noted a street photographer holding a life-sized photo of Burger, with a sign that read: "Have your picture taken with the chief justice. $1." Burger was plainly irritated. He might have been even more so had he known that the photographer had been sent there by Associate Justice William Rehnquist.

Though Rehnquist took his legal work seriously, he did not want to die a bitter old man on the Supreme Court. His wife, Nan, had been battling cancer, and Rehnquist wanted to be with her when she needed him. For years, he had been the lone conservative on a Court that congealed in the middle. If nothing changed, he had no desire to stay much longer. Still, Meese and Reynolds figured that the chance to be chief justice might change Rehnquist's mind. Without question, Rehnquist deserved the first offer.

The harder decision for the Administration was, Who should be nominated to fill the vacant ninth seat?

A team of young Justice Department attorneys had spent years preparing for this decision. They had systematically scrutinized the decisions and the records of hundreds of judges and lawyers. Some were recommended as federal trial judges, others to sit on the regional U.S. appellate courts. At least a dozen names were also on the list of potential candidates for the Supreme Court. At the top stood two names: Robert H. Bork and Antonin Scalia.

In legal circles, the two were usually mentioned in the same sentence, as if they were a tag team. Bork and Scalia were Reagan-appointed judges on the U.S. appeals court in Washington, D.C., often considered the nation's second most important court. Public interest lawyers who challenged federal regulations usually filed suit in Washington, and their cases eventually landed in the 12-member U.S. Court of Appeals for the District of Columbia.

Neither Bork nor Scalia aspired to a career of deciding regulatory cases. For both, the appellate court was seen as a stepping-stone to the Supreme Court. Both had academic backgrounds, as well as government experience in the Nixon and Ford administrations. They were conservative, intellectually oriented, and committed to reshaping the role of the federal courts. Bork was 59, and Scalia was 50.

Both were ideal candidates. They were good writers and thought in broad ideological terms. They would not just decide narrow cases; their opinions would change the law. Bork had more experience in government, but Scalia was younger. It was noted, too, that Bork was overweight and a heavy smoker. How many years could he serve? the Administration's lawyers wondered.

Reynolds leaned toward Scalia because he worried that a Rehnquist–Bork combination could provoke a huge confirmation fight in the Senate. Bork had made a cameo appearance during the Watergate scandal as the Justice Department official who carried out Richard Nixon's order to fire Special Prosecutor Archibald Cox. That incident would provide ammunition for his critics. Moreover, he had spent years on the lecture circuit delivering provocatively conservative speeches.

"If we put the two of them [Rehnquist and Bork] up there together, they would have made a big target," Reynolds said. If Scalia were picked now, Bork could be nominated for the next seat, he argued. White House counsel Peter Wallison argued the opposite view. Rehnquist would draw most of the fire and shield Bork, he contended, while the younger Scalia could be selected for the next seat. However, if Bork were picked next, the civil rights groups would gang up on him, he contended.

As Reagan listened to the back-and-forth discussion, he heard something that caught his attention: Scalia would be the first Italian-American to sit on the Supreme Court. He had been assured that Scalia was just as conservative as Bork. Everyone remembered an appointment that was a "first." Lyndon Johnson got credit for naming the first black to the Court in Thurgood Marshall. Reagan had been lauded across the political spectrum for naming the first woman, Sandra Day O'Connor. Why not take advantage of the opportunity to put the first Italian-American on the Court? While his advisers talked on about the confirmation prospects, Reagan seemed to have made up his mind.

Let's get Rehnquist in here to see whether he'll take the job; then, we'll talk to Scalia, Reagan concluded.

Don Regan put in a call to Rehnquist to tell him of the offer. The justice asked for a chance to think it over. The job would entail lots of administrative and ceremonial duties, which Rehnquist tended to view as a waste of time. The Court itself operated as a self-contained institution, with 300 employees. It had a library, a cafeteria, a gym, and a print shop. The curator's office handled exhibits throughout the building, while the police force patrolled the halls and the grounds. The chief justice not only presided over this small bureaucracy but also headed the entire federal judicial system. Burger had relished this aspect of the job, and even his critics conceded that he had been a fine administrator. He had helped move the judiciary from the era of the quill pen to that of the computer.

Rehnquist was bored by administrative chores, but most of those tasks could be delegated to others. He kept his eye on the law. The chief justice could put his stamp on an entire legal era. John Marshall and Roger Taney in the nineteenth century, and Charles Evans Hughes and Earl Warren in this one had influence on the law and the nation that easily surpassed that of the presidents who appointed them. For someone who had stubbornly pressed his view of the Constitution when he stood nearly alone, the opportunity to be chief justice could not be passed up. Rehnquist realized too that if he turned down the job, the White House would go searching for another candidate. Why turn over the job to another, he figured, when he could handle it better than anyone else? He called the White House to make an appointment to see the President.

Reagan tried his usual assortment of jokes and one-liners, but the reticent Rehnquist sat stiffly through most of their meeting. He assured the President that his health was good; his formerly ailing back was now under control. In 1971, he had undergone surgery for a "slipped disc" but continued to suffer pain for a decade. He took a prescribed painkiller in ever-increasing doses until, in late 1981, he was noticed to be slurring his sentences. He briefly checked into a Washington hospital to be weaned from what a hospital official called a "degree of physiological dependence" on the drug. Since then, however, through swimming, tennis, and walking, he kept his back loose and warded off further problems. With his good health restored, he told Reagan he would be honored to accept the president's nomination. A few days later, the irrepressible Scalia drove himself to the White House in his own car and exchanged jokes with Reagan.

No one had leaked the story to the press. Chief of Staff Don Regan delighted in the fact that Burger, Rehnquist, and Scalia had all visited the Oval Office without being spotted by the reporters waiting nearby. No one knew of the impending change on the nation's highest court, other than a handful of Reagan's top aides. At midday on June 17, White House reporters were told to gather in the cramped press room for an important announcement. At the Court, the justices were called to gather in the conference room. There, on a television set, they, along with the rest of the nation, learned of Burger's retirement and Reagan's nominations.

The President, with Burger, Rehnquist, and Scalia standing behind him, delivered a rather bare-bones statement, describing Rehnquist as a justice "noted for his intellectual power and the lucidity of his opinions." Of Scalia, he said, "His great personal energy, the force of his intellect, and the depth of his understanding of our constitutional jurisprudence uniquely qualify him for elevation to our highest court." There was no mention that both men had quite conservative views. After Reagan refused to answer questions, the reporters turned to Rehnquist and Scalia. Both said they would not comment further until the Senate hearings. Only Burger would talk, and what he wanted to talk about was the bicentennial of the Constitution. After a few moments, the press conference was adjourned.

Conservatives did not celebrate too loudly, but they were nonetheless delighted. No one on the right had a record to match Rehnquist's. Of course, the chief's vote counts as only one among nine, as the cliché goes. However, Rehnquist had the intellectual power and the clear-eyed consistency to shape the arguments around the conference table. He also had the personal grace to hold the allegiance of his colleagues. Also, Scalia looked to be a young version of Rehnquist.

For much the same reason, millions of others heard the Reagan announcement with a sense of dread. For a generation, the Supreme Court had stood as the defender of civil rights and civil liberties, the last bastion of justice for the little person. With Reagan's announcement, that era seemed to be coming to an end.

At the White House and the Justice Department, Reagan's advisers were confident Rehnquist would win a comfortable confirmation in the Senate, although not without a struggle. In 1971, 26 Senators, mostly liberal Democrats, had voted against his appointment as an associate justice. His performance on the Court since then certainly had not won over the Democratic left. Nonetheless, the times had changed, too. Rehnquist now went before the Senate with the backing of a hugely popular president. He had also been on the Court for 14 years. No one could quibble over his qualifications. In addition, the Republicans now controlled the Senate majority. The Senate Judiciary Committee was in especially friendly hands. Its chair was the old South Carolinian Strom Thurmond, the long-time segregationist and fervent foe of civil rights laws of the 1960s. By the 1980s, Thurmond had reconstructed himself as a politician of the new South, seeking out black votes as well as white ones, but he never abandoned his conservative heritage. Through the first six years of the Reagan Administration, hundreds of Republican court appointees came before Thurmond's panel for confirmation. Old Strom took them under his wing as if they were sweet, young debutantes who could be flustered by tough-talking Democrats, and he guided them through the sometimes treacherous confirmation process.

Rehnquist and Scalia had a simple strategy: to say as little as possible. Answering questions before the Senate could cost them votes, and it would not gain them any support. During his years in the Nixon administration, Rehnquist had seen plenty of Senate confirmation hearings, several of them disastrous for the nominee. He had become convinced that nominees could lose votes at a Senate hearing, but none could win votes there. It would be better to sit like a mute defendant on trial rather than to pontificate freely from the witness stand.

Their strategy made for a one-sided battle through the summer of 1986. For weeks prior to the Senate hearing, Rehnquist was pummeled in the press for his record of opposing civil rights and civil liberties. The NAACP Legal Defense Fund tallied 83 cases in which a divided Supreme Court, including Rehnquist, was called upon to vote on a civil rights matter affecting racial minorities, women, or the elderly. It found Rehnquist had voted against these plaintiffs 82 times. After the hearing began, it only got worse. Senator Edward Kennedy denounced Rehnquist as "an extremist" who was "out of the mainstream." Other Democrats followed his lead. Republicans Strom Thurmond and Orrin Hatch (of Utah) rose to his defense, but only to argue that the charges were unfair or exaggerated. Curiously missing was any forceful advocate arguing that Rehnquist's conservative views were correct.

Two episodes proved embarrassing: First, the Democrats revealed that the deed to Rehnquist's summer home in Vermont, which he purchased in 1974, included a prohibition on its sale or rental "to any member of the Hebrew race." In addition, the FBI learned that his Phoenix home in the 1960s had a deed restriction barring its sale or rental to "any person not of the white or Caucasian race." Though one of the nation's most prominent lawyers, Rehnquist told the committee he had not examined his deeds and knew nothing of these restrictive covenants.

Meanwhile, a former U.S. attorney joined several Phoenix Democrats to testify that he had seen Rehnquist at polling places in 1962 or 1964 challenging the credentials of black voters. Such challenges were not outlawed until later, but Rehnquist in 1971 had denied that he personally challenged or "harassed" any voter. He repeated that denial during the 1986 hearing. Certainly he had been active in Republican campaigns and had served as a legal adviser to their so-called ballot security teams. Several Republican activists testifying in Rehnquist's defense said he may have visited polling places on election day, but only to advise poll watchers, not to question or harass likely Democratic voters.

The hearings created an unease among many senators, but not enough to peel away many votes from the president's nominee. In early August, the Judiciary Committee approved the nomination on a 13–5 vote. Rehnquist heard the news via a note handed him during a law class in the hills of Malibu, near Los Angeles. Rather than sweat out the confirmation battle in Washington, he had chosen to go ahead with a previous commitment to teach a summer class at the Pepperdine University Law School.

Back in Washington, though, the fight was not over. Usually, a nominee approved by the Judiciary Committee wins routine approval by the full Senate. However, liberal activists were convinced that more damaging information—perhaps suggesting that Rehnquist had not told the full truth to the committee—could still block his confirmation. The Leadership Conference on Civil Rights thought it already had ample evidence to justify rejecting his confirmation. Rehnquist had compiled "a 35-year history of hostility to victims of discrimination," the group said.

When the nomination went to the Senate floor in mid-September, Democrats renewed their attack. Even some Republicans were having second thoughts. Senator Charles Mathias, the second-ranking Republican on the Judiciary Committee, changed his mind and decided to vote against confirmation. Leading the defense, Hatch lambasted the Democrats. "They have left no stone unthrown," he said. Debates on the Senate floor are often deceptive, though. Those who dominate the discussion usually do so because they have not lined up the votes needed to win. When it was time to count the votes on the evening of September 17, the Republicans poured onto the floor and ensured Rehnquist's victory. The final tally was 65 in favor and 33 against, the most votes ever cast against a chief justice.

While Rehnquist had taken a thrashing, Scalia had been mostly ignored. He came to the Senate hearings with an air of confidence that implied, "I'm the smartest fellow in this room." As the Judiciary Committee members questioned him, he lit up a pipe and puffed serenely. Senator Howard Metzenbaum, an Ohio Democrat who rankles witnesses with his versions of "When-did-you-stop-beating-your-wife?", began by noting that Scalia had recently beaten him on the tennis court. "It was a case of my integrity overcoming my judgment, Senator," Scalia jauntily replied.

No one was going to lay a glove on "Nino" Scalia. After several rounds of questioning, Scalia emerged unscathed and won the committee's approval with ease.

Scalia was the only child of an Italian immigrant father, S. Eugene Scalia, who was a professor of Romance languages at Brooklyn College, an authority on Dante, and a translator of Italian works into English. His wife, Catherine Panaro Scalia, was a first-generation Italian-American who taught elementary school. "Nino," their only child, was born March 11, 1936, in Trenton, New Jersey. When Professor Scalia accepted the position at Brooklyn College, the family moved to a middle-class neighborhood in Queens, New York, where Antonin grew up. Antonin attended a Jesuit school in lower Manhattan, St. Francis Xavier Military Academy. "People just competed for second, he was so superior academically," William Stern, a high school friend and later a political adviser to New York governor Mario Cuomo, said of Scalia. "This kid was a conservative when he was 17 years old," he added.

Scalia finished first in his high school class and was the valedictorian. His was a classical education, which included a total of six years of Latin and five years of Greek. He enrolled in Georgetown University in Washington, D.C., and was valedictorian of the class of 1957. From there, he went to the Harvard Law School. Friends remembered him as gregarious and hardworking and, of course, a top student. He was an editor of the *Harvard Law Review* and graduated at the top of the class of 1960. Scalia's classmates included dozens of attorneys who went on to prominent careers in government, academia, and politics, including a friend and the son of Greek immigrants who went on the become the governor of Massachusetts, Michael Dukakis. Upon his graduation, Scalia married Maureen McCarthy, a Radcliffe graduate. He later joked that her parents saw it as a mixed marriage: She was an Irish Catholic, and he was an Italian Catholic.

The young attorney went to work for the Cleveland law firm now known as Jones, Day, Reavis and Pogue, one of the nation's largest. After six years, however, he chose to leave the practice of law—and its big-money salaries—to return to academia. In 1967, he moved his growing family to Charlottesville, Virginia, where he taught law at the University of Virginia. In 1971, he took a job in the Nixon administration as general counsel for the Office of Telecommunications Policy. He developed a special interest in the dry and dense field of government regulatory law. Considering the problems that could befall attorneys in the Nixon administration, it was probably a wise move. In 1974, shortly after Nixon resigned and Gerald Ford became president, Scalia was named as head of the Justice Department's Office of Legal Counsel. He was sworn in by a former holder of the office, Justice William H. Rehnquist.

Three years later, when Jimmy Carter ousted Gerald Ford from the White House, Scalia moved into the nonprofit American Enterprise Institute (AEI), a haven for scholarly conservatives in exile. There, and at a few other conservative think tanks such as the Hoover Institute in Palo Alto, the ideas and policies of the future Reagan administration were being germinated. All the while, Nino Scalia was making friends and gaining a reputation as a bright and feisty conservative. He left AEI to teach at the University of Chicago, where he bought a former fraternity house to accommodate his family of nine children. When the Reagan administration came to Washington, Scalia was immediately tapped as a potential Supreme Court nominee.

Now, that potential was about to be realized. He would be the first true academic to sit on the Court since Felix Frankfurter. On the night of September 17, when the Senate finally gave its approval to Rehnquist's nomination, Scalia's name was brought up quickly and approved unanimously.

After the last votes were cast, Senate Majority Leader Bob Dole left the floor to put in a late-evening call to Reagan to tell him the result. The president had watched some of the debate in his bedroom and said he was grateful his nominees survived. "It looked like they were forming a lynch mob," he told Dole.

Rehnquist indeed had escaped just in time. Two months later, the Republicans were battered at the polls, and the Democrats retook control of the Senate. Later in November, it was revealed that Ronald Reagan had secretly sold arms to the terrorist state of Iran, while his aides funneled the profits to the Contras in Nicaragua in defiance of a congressional ban on such aid. Reagan's endorsement would never again carry the same weight on Capitol Hill.

None of that would matter to Rehnquist and Scalia, though. As they stood on the Court steps on September 26, they had good reason to smile. They possessed a power that was unique to the American system of government. With their colleagues, they would determine the meaning of the Constitution as well as of the laws passed by Congress. It was certainly a power any politician would envy. They need not pay any attention to the public, and this power was theirs for as long as they chose to exercise it.

When they reached the bottom of the steps, Burger quietly stepped aside and walked away. For an uncertain moment, Rehnquist and Scalia stood apart, staring at the assembled photographers. Then, they turned to each other and clasped hands with a broad smile. The Burger Court was now history. The era of the Rehnquist Court had begun.

2

The Court, Past and Present

I n June 1964, the civil rights movement reached a peak. The campaign to end the American apartheid in the South was about to culminate in Congress with a landmark antidiscrimination law. The summer before, Martin Luther King, Jr. had electrified the movement with his "I Have a Dream" speech on the steps of the Lincoln Memorial. Nearly two centuries after the declaration that "all men are created equal," the nation clearly had failed to live up to that promise. In many places, blacks could be refused the right to eat in restaurants, to stay overnight in hotels or motels, to ride on buses or trains—all simply because of their race. They could be relegated to menial jobs or denied work altogether. They could still be barred from public schools and universities. In 16 states, blacks and whites were denied the right even to intermarry.

President John F. Kennedy had proposed to Congress a sweeping civil rights bill, but it took his assassination in November 1963, to finally spur action on Capitol Hill. In February of 1964, the House passed his civil rights measure in a 290–130 vote. In the Senate, southern segregationists had filibustered many previous civil rights bills, but this time the tide could not be stopped. On June 10, 1964, the Senate voted 71 to 29 to halt the debate and determine a final vote. The passage of the bill was now assured. It would, among other things, state that no one could be denied a job or a promotion because of race, sex, religion, or ethnic heritage. The new law also opened "public accommodations" to all: No longer could blacks be denied service in restaurants, gasoline stations, hotels, or motels.

To some historians, all this must have seemed familiar. In fact, Congress had enacted a similar public accommodations law long before. In the decade after the Civil War, Congress was led by northern abolitionists who were determined to ensure equality for the newly freed slaves. Southerners had gone to war believing that the states, not the national government, were sovereign. The states, they had said, determined the rights of their citizens, including their right to own slaves. According to the U.S. Supreme Court of that time, the Bill of Rights in the U.S. Constitution then applied only to the federal government. Because the First Amendment begins, "Congress shall make no law . . . ," the entire Bill of Rights was interpreted to mean that only the federal government was barred from limiting a person's right to free speech, a free press, the free exercise of religion, or a fair trial. The Constitution said nothing about the states, which therefore made their own rules. As historian James McPherson has noted, the United States was then referred to in the plural—that is, the United States *are* a collection of states.

It took the lives of 365,000 Union soldiers to make *United States* a singular noun. In addition, the so-called Radical Republicans in Congress were determined to translate that victory on the battlefield into a fundamentally new arrangement of government. Now, the national government would be supreme, and it would protect the basic civil rights of its citizens. The states had shown that they could not be trusted with that power, certainly not the rebellious southern states.

In 1866, Congress approved what remains today the single most important amendment to the Constitution. It begins: "All persons born or naturalized in the United States . . . are citizens of the United States and of the state wherein they reside. No state shall make or enforce any law which shall abridge the privileges or immunities of citizens of the United States; nor shall any state deprive any person of life, liberty or property without due process of law; nor deny to any person within its jurisdiction the equal protection of the laws." The authors of the amendment stood on the floor of the Senate and the House and said that these "privileges and immunities" include all the "fundamental rights," including specifically those set forth in the Bill of Rights. The last section of the amendment said, "Congress shall have the power to enforce, by appropriate legislation, the provisions of this article." Ratified by the states, this Fourteenth Amendment was added to the Constitution in July 1868.

Relying on this new authority, Congress passed law after law to protect the freed slaves. Blacks were given the same right as whites to buy and sell real estate and to make and enforce contracts. Federal judges were given new powers to enforce these civil rights. The Ku Klux Klan Act of 1871 created a right to bring suits into federal courts against persons who would conspire to deprive blacks of their other civil rights. Finally, the Civil Rights Act of 1875 gave all persons, regardless of color, the right to "the full and equal enjoyment" of public transportation, inns, theaters, and "other places of public amusement."

To be sure, the Reconstruction Congress did not have a flawless record on matters of race. For example, the same Congress that wrote the 14th Amendment also authorized segregated schools for the District of Columbia. But for nearly a decade after the Civil War, Congress sought to assure that the newly freed slaves were accorded equal rights.

Despite the legislators' efforts, nearly as fast as Congress passed these laws, the U.S. Supreme Court rendered them meaningless. Within three decades, the Court turned the abolitionist's vision of equal rights for all into an apartheid system in half of the nation. This dramatic transformation began on April 14, 1873, eight years to the day after Lincoln's assassination. Before an almost empty courtroom in the basement of the Capitol, Justice Samuel F. Miller read a decision for a 5–4 majority, which, for the first time, interpreted the meaning of the phrase "the privileges and immunities" of an American citizen, as written in the Fourteenth Amendment. The case involved, of all things, butchers in New Orleans, who were challenging a citywide monopoly given to one slaughterhouse. The Court concluded that the butchers' rights to "liberty" were not violated, even though this government-created monopoly put them out of business. Why? Because their individual rights were not protected by the Constitution and the Fourteenth Amendment. By a margin of one vote, the Court concluded that the "privileges and immunities of a citizen of the United States" are only those few rights uniquely national in character, such as the right to travel freely on the high seas. Everything else, the Court said, including matters such as free speech, fair trials, and the basic civil rights "are left to the state governments for security and protection and not by this article [the Fourteenth Amendment] placed under the special care of the federal government."

At first, the decision in the "Slaughterhouse cases" was noted only by a few lawyers in Washington, D.C., but its significance soon became apparent. The Court had concluded that Congress and the U.S. Constitution did not protect the fundamental civil rights and civil liberties of its citizens. Only the states had that power. With a stroke of the pen, the Court had essentially overturned the national government's victory over the individual states in the Civil War. To be sure, slavery was gone, outlawed by the Thirteenth Amendment. Nonetheless, as the four dissenters said, the Court had turned the Fourteenth Amendment from a revolutionary guarantee of protection for basic civil rights and civil liberties into "a vain and idle enactment which accomplished nothing." Now, the states were in charge again. It was if the South had won after all.

What is more, that was just the beginning. In some southern states, the Reconstruction governments created by Union forces passed laws of their own to protect blacks. For example, prior to the slaughterhouse decision, the Louisiana legislature had decreed that "common carriers" such as railroads and steamships must accommodate travelers "without distinction or discrimination on account of race and color." A few years later, Mrs. Josephine DeCuir, a light-skinned Negro woman who had lived much of her life in Paris, bought a ticket on a steamship traveling up the Mississippi River from New Orleans to Vicksburg, Mississippi. She planned to disembark at a landing up-river in Louisiana. The captain, however, refused her the berth she had purchased and refused her service in the dining car because of her race. She sued and won a judgment in the Louisiana courts. However, the captain appealed to the U.S. Supreme Court.

Louisiana's law could create "embarrassments" and "inconvenience" for the captain, the Court explained in *Hall* v. *DeCuir* in 1878. If a state such as Louisiana were permitted to ban segregation while another allowed it, "the confusion likely to follow could not but be productive of great inconvenience and unnecessary hardship," it said. Because commerce demands "uniformity in the regulations . . . from one end to the other of his route," Louisiana's nondiscrimination law is "unconstitutional and void," the Court ruled.

Twelve years later, opponents of segregation took this argument back to the Court to challenge a Mississippi law that *required* segregation on railroads crossing into the state. This time, without a blush and with only two dissents, the Court upheld the state's law. Because it applied to traffic only within its borders, the state law was constitutional, the Court said in *Louisville, New Orleans and Texas Railways* v. *Mississippi*. Those two rulings of the Supreme Court did much to create the Jim Crow era of southern segregation. States that sought to ban discrimination, such as Louisiana, were told they were violating the Constitution, while those that segregated were upheld. Given the green light by the nation's highest court, six other southern states quickly enacted segregation laws for their railroads.

In 1896, the Court considered one of these new measures, a Louisiana law requiring separate but equal accommodations for blacks. In *Plessy* v. *Ferguson*, the Court concluded that enforced segregation did not violate a black person's right to the equal protection of the laws. "The object of the [Fourteenth] Amendment was undoubtedly to enforce the absolute equality of the two races before the law, but in the nature of things it could not have been intended to abolish distinctions based upon color," the Court said in one of the most remarkable sentences of its long history. If the former slaves and their heirs believe that a law demanding that they be separated from whites stamps them as second-class citizens, that is so "solely because the colored races choose to put this construction upon it," the Court said.

By then, the ruling surprised no one. The Court had long since made clear that it would not "enforce the absolute equality of the two races" that was envisioned by the Fourteenth Amendment. Moreover, it would block any move by Congress to do so. Its greatest blow had been struck in 1883. Five separate cases were then before the Court. Two involved black couples who bought theater tickets in San Francisco and New York but were then denied their seats. Two others involved a hotel in Missouri and a restaurant in Kansas, each of which refused to serve blacks. The fifth involved a black woman who was excluded from the first-class car on a Tennessee railroad. They sued under the Civil Rights Act of 1875, which gave all Americans the right to the "full and equal enjoyment of the accommodations . . . of inns, public conveyances on land or water, theaters or other places of public amusement." Congress passed the law under the authority in the Thirteenth and Fourteenth Amendments to enact "appropriate legislation" to ensure civil rights.

The Court, however, deemed this legislation inappropriate and ruled the entire act unconstitutional. Congress did not have the power to do anything about the "individual invasion of individual rights," the Court said in the Civil Rights Cases of 1883. The time must come, the justices added, when the black race "ceases to be the special favorite of the laws."

Eighty years later, in 1964, Congress determined to do what it had sought to do long ago: create a structure of federally guaranteed civil rights that would reach into every community in the nation. This time, the civil rights movement was not about to be denied. Because the old Supreme Court ruling of 1883 had never been overturned, the new law of 1964 demanded a little lawyerly sleight of hand. The Civil Rights Act of 1964 was said to be a measure to regulate interstate commerce, rather than a civil rights measure. Otherwise, however, its wording copied much from the post–Civil War measures. On June 19, 1964, with the southern filibuster broken, the landmark civil rights law won final passage in the Senate on a 73–27 vote.

Nonetheless, the measure had its vocal detractors. Arizona Senator Barry Goldwater, soon to be the Republican candidate for president, voted against the measure and said its enforcement would require the "creation of [a] police state." Alabama governor George Wallace echoed that view. "It will take a police state to enforce it," he told reporters.

In California, actor Ronald Reagan was entering the political wars as a speechmaker for Goldwater. He said he strongly opposed the pending Civil Rights Act "on constitutional grounds." In Texas, 40-year-old George Bush was making his first run for office, an unsuccessful challenge to Democratic Senator Ralph Yarborough. Throughout the campaign, Bush stressed that had he been in the Senate rather than Yarborough, he would have fought against the Civil Rights Act. He added that he "emphatically" opposed those provisions guaranteeing blacks the right to be served in hotels, restaurants, and other public accommodations.

However, by the time of the law's passage, the civil rights cause had captured the nation's attention. That summer, hundreds of college students, white as well as black, traveled south to aid in voter registration drives. On June 21, three of those young workers—Michael Schwerner, James Chaney, and Andrew Goodman—were abducted near Philadelphia, Mississippi, and were murdered.

That summer, the civil rights struggle was not limited to the South. States and cities across the nation moved to sweep away discriminatory policies. A few years earlier, the city of Phoenix, Arizona, had been embarrassed when, during a national meeting of attorneys there, it had been revealed that one of the city's premier resort hotels refused to admit Jewish guests. On the night of June 15, the city council intended to put that problem to rest. It had before it a citywide "public accommodations" law that would forbid discrimination against customers based on race, color, or religion. The measure had the support of the entire city council. Some 26 speakers showed up at the meeting to endorse the proposal. Three came to oppose it.

The first to speak was a 39-year-old attorney known to many of the council members. He had been active in Republican politics, including the surging Goldwater-for-president campaign. They knew he had graduated at the top of his Stanford University law class and had clerked at the Supreme Court.

"My name is William Rehnquist. I am a lawyer without a client tonight," he began. He opposed the ordinance, he said, "because I believe that the values it sacrifices are greater than the values which it gives."

He posed the issue as one of the "freedom" of an individual versus heavy-handed government interference. In a subsequent letter to the editor in *The Arizona Republic*, he repeated his view that the so-called public accommodations ordinance was a mistake.

"The Founders of this nation thought of it as the 'land of the free' just as surely as they thought of it as the 'land of the equal,' " he wrote. "By a wave of the legislative wand, . . . the ordinance summarily does away with the historic right of the owner of a drug store, lunch counter, or theater to choose his own customers."

Like Goldwater and Wallace, he suggested that no law could remedy the racial problem because it "stems from the state of mind of the proprietor. . . . Unable to correct the source of the indignity to the Negro, it redresses the situation by placing a separate indignity on the proprietor. It is as barren of accomplishment in what it gives to the Negro as in what it takes from the proprietor. The unwanted customer and the disliked proprietor are left glowering at one another across the lunch counter." He concluded, "It is, I believe, impossible to justify the sacrifice of even a portion of our historic individual freedom for a purpose such as this." His notion of freedom appeared to leave out the black residents of Phoenix who might well also value the freedom to shop in a corner drugstore.

Those who heard Rehnquist that evening recall him as articulate and assured. "Bill spoke his mind and he always spoke well," said Jarrett Jarvis, then a Republican member of the council. "He saw it [as] a matter of fundamental property rights. And we all listened, but he didn't persuade anyone."

The city attorney who had drafted the ordinance had known Rehnquist distantly at Stanford. "He was a smart fellow and stubborn," said the attorney, Melvin J. Mirkin. "He knew it was going to pass, but he was going to make his point anyway. He didn't seem to care whether anyone agreed with him."

Another prominent Phoenix attorney active in Democratic circles, John P. Frank, knew Rehnquist but didn't understand his strongly held views. "Bill was set in concrete long before I met him," Frank said. "I always suspected he hatched from the right side of the egg."

William Hubbs Rehnquist was born October 1, 1924. He grew up in a modest tan stucco home in Shorewood, Wisconsin, a well-to-do suburb of Milwaukee. His father, of Swedish heritage, was a wholesale paper salesman, his mother a University of Wisconsin graduate who was fluent in five languages. He and his younger sister, Jean, grew up in a time when Franklin Delano Roosevelt (FDR) and his New Deal dominated American politics, but the political heroes in the Rehnquist household were Republicans Alf Landon, Wendell Wilkie, and Herbert Hoover.

His high school friends remember him as tall and thin, a bit on the gawky side. He was better at debate and working on the school newspaper than at sports, they said. "He was a neat guy with a dry sense of humor, smart but not exceptional," said one friend. "He grew up in a home with very conservative values. That was his upbringing," said another high school friend. Nearby Milwaukee then had a socialist mayor, but the all-white Shorewood suburb was staunchly Republican. "You worked hard and didn't depend on others. That's how we were taught," another friend said.

He was a 17-year-old high school senior when Pearl Harbor was bombed. "Rennie," as his friends called him, helped organize a school assembly called "Wake Up America." Young Rehnquist quoted Winston Churchill on the need for the nation to rearm. He and several classmates also became block captains in a local civil defense effort in which they were to report to the police "any subversive activities which might lead to sabotaging our national unity."

Though he won a scholarship to Kenyon College in Ohio, he stayed only a year before joining the Army Air Corps as a weather observer in 1943. A tour of duty in North Africa convinced him he wanted to live in a warmer climate, such as California. After the war, he enrolled at Stanford University in Palo Alto, where he earned a political science bachelor's degree in 1948 and then a master's degree the next year. By then, however, no one called him just an ordinary student. "He was very sharp, a brilliant student, but far-out politically," a classmate recalled at the time of his Supreme Court nomination.

Rehnquist also spent a year at Harvard, earning a master's degree in government there. However, after reporting that he "couldn't take Harvard liberalism," he returned to Stanford for law school, graduating at the top of the class of 1952. He was "head and shoulders above all the rest of us in sheer legal talent and ability," recalled classmate Sandra Day O'Connor. "In a class discussion, he could go right to the heart of the matter and extract the key principle. He was definitely the star of our class."

His professors noticed his extraordinary ability too. When Justice Robert H. Jackson, an FDR appointee to the high court, stopped by, a professor set up an interview for Rehnquist. The coveted clerkships at the Supreme Court at that time went mostly to Ivy Leaguers, but Jackson liked to have a westerner on occasion. He also needed a clerk at midyear, and Rehnquist was graduating early. A few weeks after the interview, Rehnquist received a letter from Jackson offering him a clerkship. On February 1, 1952, after a drive across the upper Midwest in an unheated 1941 Studebaker, William Rehnquist walked up the marble steps of the Supreme Court for the first time.

He arrived in Washington, D.C., during the depths of the Cold War. Wisconsin Senator Joseph McCarthy was at the height of his power, ferreting out suspected Communists in the government. Julius and Ethel Rosenberg awaited execution for having smuggled atomic secrets to the Soviet Union. The Supreme Court was struggling with the Jim Crow laws that it had done so much to create. By 1952, no one seriously believed that "separate" was "equal" for the black students, in the South and parts of the Midwest, who were excluded from their state universities and law schools.

In the Court cafeteria, the clerks got together each day to argue the issues of the day over lunch.

Rehnquist "was funny and charming, very bright and quick. He could give you all the good conservative arguments on any issue," said Harvard law professor Donald Trautman, then a clerk to Justice Felix Frankfurter.

"He was bright, very full of himself, a lively guy to argue with," remembers another former clerk.

Unlike most of his young counterparts, Rehnquist thought the Rosenbergs should be executed and soon. In a later note to Justice Jackson, he wondered why the "highest court of the nation must behave like a bunch of old women" when confronted with the death penalty.

"He had no sympathy for criminal defendants. None," said Trautman. "When you talked about the problems of the cities or the poor or blacks, it was clear he had no understanding. It was a universe he didn't comprehend," he said.

Several other clerks from that time echo Trautman's view, although they do not want to be quoted because they still practice law. They recall Rehnquist as a pleasant companion but most notable for his rigid conservatism. "I remember when that year was over, my wife and I sat down and made a list of the ones we thought would make a name for themselves," said a prominent attorney. "We put down about seven names. There were 18 of us in all. Bill Rehnquist's name was not on the list. He was too fixed, too narrow in his views."

Rehnquist certainly made clear that he disagreed with the legal views of his fellow clerks. The liberals seemed to believe the Constitution gave the Court license to meddle everywhere, he maintained. He believed that matters such as the death penalty and civil rights were better left to the states. He soon had a chance to put his beliefs to a test. In June, just four months after he arrived, the justices announced that they would hear arguments in the fall in a school segregation case known as *Brown* v. *Board of Education of Topeka, Kansas.*

For more than 15 years, the NAACP Legal Defense Fund, led by its chief counsel, Thurgood Marshall, had been battling state-imposed segregation in federal courts throughout the South and the Midwest. It was clear that the southern states were not going to abolish segregation on their own. Marshall's strategy called for holding the Fourteenth Amendment in the face of the federal judges. To Marshall, the issue seemed as clear as could be: The Fourteenth Amendment demanded equal treatment for all. Racial discrimination by the government was simply unconstitutional. The NAACP team had won its share of victories, but the biggest barrier remained intact: the *Plessy* v. *Ferguson* ruling upholding the separate but equal doctrine.

By now, however, several justices were ready to strike down *Plessy,* including William O. Douglas and Alabama native Hugo Black. Several others, including Chief Justice Fred Vinson, were wary, fearing a violent reaction from southern whites.

Justice Jackson was undecided. Then 60 years old, he was known worldwide as the U.S. prosecutor during the Nazi war crimes trials at Nuremberg. A distinguished man and a stylish writer, Jackson owned the Hickory Hill estate in suburban McLean, Virginia, later owned by John F. and Robert F. Kennedy. As a justice, he believed in building the law on a framework of precedents. The doctrine of enforced racial segregation seemed wrong, but suddenly overturning *Plessy* after nearly 60 years would look like a political act, not a judicial decision. To prepare for the December 11 argument in the *Brown* case, he asked his two clerks to submit memos on the issue.

The first memo, initialed "DC" for Donald Cronson, was entitled, "A Few Expressed Prejudices on the Segregation Cases." There "is no doubt *Plessy* was wrong" when it was decided, Cronson opined. Overturning it now, however, is quite another matter. Because "a whole way of life has grown up around such a prior error," the Court should not reverse itself now but rather should wait for Congress to act, he said.

The second memo, initialed "WHR," had an assured, even "imperious" tone, in the words of its author. It was entitled "A Random Thought on the Segregation Cases." The memo quickly canvased the Court's history and concluded that the institution worked better as an "arbiter" of disputes between branches of government than as an enforcer of "individual rights." After all, the author noted, the Court had acted on behalf of individuals when it upheld the rights of slave owners in 1857 and struck down minimum wage and child labor laws in the early decades of the twentieth century.

"In these cases now before the Court, the Court is . . . being asked to read its own sociological views into the Constitution. Urging a view palpably at variance with precedent and probably with legislative history, appellants [NAACP] seek to convince the Court of the moral wrongness of the treatment they are receiving. I would suggest that this is a question the Court need never reach; for regardless of the Justice's individual views on the merits of segregation, it quite clearly is not one of those extreme cases which commands intervention. . . .

"If the Court, because its members individually are 'liberal' and dislike segregation, now chooses to strike it down, it differs from the McReynolds Court [of the 1920s] only in the kinds of litigants it favors and the kinds of special claims it protects. . . . To the arguments made by Marshall ['THURGOOD, NOT JOHN,' Rehnquist penciled in] that a majority may not deprive a minority of its constitutional right, the answer must be made that while this is sound in theory, in the long run it is the majority who will determine what the constitutional rights of the minority are. One hundred and fifty years of attempts on the part of this Court to protect minority rights of any kind—whether those of business, slaveholders, or Jehovah's Witnesses—have all met the same fate. One by one the cases establishing such rights have been sloughed off, and crept silently to rest. If the present court is unable to profit by this example, it must be prepared to see its work fade in time, too, as embodying only the sentiments of a transient majority of nine men.

"I realize that it is an unpopular and unhumanitarian position, for which I have been excoriated by 'liberal' colleagues, but I think *Plessy* v. *Ferguson* was right and should be re-affirmed. WHR"

This memo, when revealed in December 1971, nearly derailed Rehnquist's nomination to the Supreme Court. It came to light after the Senate Judiciary Committee had completed its hearings, and the chair, crusty Mississippian James O. Eastland, refused to reopen them. Rehnquist did, however, submit a letter to the Senate maintaining that the memo was intended to express Jackson's views, not his own. To back up this contention, Rehnquist said the "imperious tone" of the memo does not read like a note from a clerk to a justice. It is "extremely informal in style and loosely organized," Rehnquist wrote in 1971. "Justice Jackson not only would not have welcomed such a submission in this form, but he would have quite emphatically rejected it," he concluded.

Still later, however, other Rehnquist memos were found in Jackson's papers, and they, too, had a conversational, argumentative tone. In 1952, NAACP attorneys were challenging the all-white primary elections run by county Democratic organizations in Texas. In the solid South of that time, the Democratic candidates won all the elections, yet blacks were excluded from helping to choose the party candidate. As a result, they were effectively denied the right to vote. As a clerk, Rehnquist's job included reviewing the appeals and submitting memos to Jackson outlining the cases and recommending whether they should be heard by the Court.

"I have a hard time being detached about this case because several . . . clerks began screaming as soon as they saw this that 'Now we can show those damn southerners,' etc.," Rehnquist wrote in his memo to Jackson on the Texas primary case, *Terry* v. *Adams.* "I take a dim view of this pathological search for discrimination . . . and as a result I now have a mental block against the case," he added.

The Court did agree to hear the case, and the majority voted to declare the all-white primaries unconstitutional. In a subsequent memo to Jackson, Rehnquist suggested some ideas for a possible dissent. "It is about time the Court faced the fact that the white people of the South don't like the colored people: the constitution restrains them from effecting this dislike thru [sic] state action, but it most assuredly did not appoint the Court as a sociological watchdog to rear up every time private discrimination raises its admittedly ugly head." The memo concluded, "This is a position that I am sure ought to be stated; but if stated by Vinson, Minton or Reed, it just won't sound the same way as if you state it. WHR."

Justice Jackson ignored the advice. He joined Hugo Black's opinion for an 8–1 majority to outlaw the all-white primaries. In addition, of course, he joined the unanimous Court on May 17, 1954, in striking down the *Plessy* doctrine in *Brown* v. *Board of Education.*

Years later, Rehnquist made two points about the *Brown* and *Plessy* rulings. First, he said, he fully supported the *Brown* decision "from the standpoint of fundamental fairness." He added, however, that there was "a perfectly reasonable argument the other way" to uphold *Plessy* because of *stare decisis,* the Latin term for letting the decision stand as decided. During the 1986 Senate hearings on his nomination to be chief justice, Rehnquist was asked by Senator Charles Mathias whether he knew how he would have voted in the *Brown* case if he had been on the Court then. "I thought the stare decisis argument in *Plessy* was a strong one," he replied.

A number of his long-time acquaintances have observed that Rehnquist's basic views were "flash frozen" during his younger days and have remained unchanged since then, a view he has not sought to rebut. In 1985, an interviewer pressed him on whether his thinking had evolved over the years. "No," he replied. "I can remember arguments we would get into as law clerks in the early 50s. And I don't know that my views have changed much from that time," he said.

In the summer of 1953, with his clerkship finished, Rehnquist left Washington and settled in Phoenix. As a top Stanford law graduate and a Supreme Court clerk, he could have had his pick of elite law firms in the nation's major cities, but New York, Chicago, Boston, and Los Angeles had no appeal for him. Rehnquist chose instead a small firm in the hot, dry, desert town that still offered a sense of the frontier. He married Natalie Cornell and settled in a small tract home, where they raised three children. As a lawyer, he handled wills and divorces as well as courtroom litigation. From a distance, he maintained an interest in the Supreme Court, too. Early in 1954, shortly before Justice Jackson died of a heart attack, Rehnquist sent him a final letter telling him of his new life and offering a few thoughts on the recent appointment of Earl Warren to be the new chief justice.

"Most everyone here was quite disappointed at the nomination of Warren to the Chief Justiceship," he wrote. "Perhaps this is less than fair to the man, since there certainly is no affirmative blot on the record."

Of course, there were soon plenty of "affirmative blots" as Warren led an increasingly liberal Court. In a 1958 article in the *U.S. News and World Report,* Rehnquist blamed the "political cast" of the Court clerks for slanting opinions toward the left and for showing "extreme solicitude for the claims of Communists and other criminal defendants." In a local bar association speech, he also denounced Warren, along with justices Black and Douglas, as "left-wing philosophers" who were rewriting the Constitution. By the late 1950s, Rehnquist saw the Court as dangerously liberal, even before its true liberal era arrived.

Meanwhile, his law practice flourished during the 1960s, and he bought a larger home in the upper-middle-class, in-town neighborhood of Palmcroft. He was not drawn to the stylish, affluent neighborhoods of north Phoenix. Instead, he was drawn to Republican politics. He became a trusted legal adviser to state party chair Richard Kleindienst. Rehnquist later helped organize a controversial poll-watching team which challenged voting credentials in the predominantly black and Hispanic neighborhoods of Phoenix.

He also took to the pages of the Phoenix newspapers again when the city's school superintendent proposed an integration plan. He was especially distressed with the school official's statement that the city "must be concerned with achieving an integrated society." Countered Rehnquist: "I think many would take issue with his statement on the merits and would feel that we are no more dedicated to an 'integrated' society than we are to a 'segregated' society."

The Goldwater presidential campaign in 1964 ended in overwhelming defeat. The Arizona senator won only his home state and five others, all in the Deep South. Nonetheless, the Goldwater Republicans stayed together and threw their support to Richard Nixon in 1968. When Nixon won the White House, several top Arizonans went to Washington, D.C. Kleindienst was offered the number-two job in the Justice Department, under Attorney General John Mitchell. He, in turn, recommended hiring his trusted legal adviser from Phoenix. Rehnquist returned to Washington as the head of the Office of Legal Counsel, the legal think tank within the Justice Department.

As an assistant attorney general, Rehnquist won admirers within the Nixon administration as a man of bold views and mild manners. He had none of the surly, tough-guy quality of some Nixon aides. Rather, he was uniformly gracious, pleasant, and self-deprecating. Nonetheless, whenever the Nixon White House needed someone to justify its use of executive power,

Rehnquist was there. He defended the legality of wire tapping, preventive detentions, and "no-knock searches."

In one speech, he referred to leftist college students and antiwar protesters as the "new barbarians" and suggested that they posed a serious threat to the nation. "The original barbarians—the invaders of the Roman Empire—did not seem to pose a threat to the empire when they first appeared on the banks of the Danube. . . . We must be prepared, if necessary, to devote whatever energies are necessary, at whatever sacrifice to private gain or pleasure, to see that these essential values of our system are maintained," he told a Kiwanis Club audience. "Disobedience cannot be tolerated, whether it be violent or nonviolent disobedience. . . . If force or the threat of force is required in order to enforce the law, we must not shirk from its employment."

He put his ideas to work during the huge march against the Vietnam War in May 1971. Invoking a doctrine of "qualified martial law," Rehnquist said that federal agents and the police had the authority to round up protesters en masse in the streets of Washington and to hold them indefinitely without filing specific charges. The government, he said, has the authority to "protect itself and its citizens against actual violence or a real threat of violence." Later, the May Day arrests were ruled illegal, and the government paid out $3.3 million in court judgments to the protesters.

Rehnquist also provoked the wrath of Senator Sam Ervin by defending the Army's surveillance of antiwar activists and by suggesting that the executive branch could be trusted to "police itself" from abusing constitutional rights. Only a few years before, Rehnquist had stood before the Phoenix city council defending what he called the "freedom" of the individual proprietor against heavy-handed government interference. Now, he no longer seemed as concerned about individual freedom or as troubled by heavy-handed government.

Outside the public eye, he drew up for the White House a proposed constitutional amendment to halt busing for school desegregation. Fearing political reaction, Nixon's aides shelved the proposal. Rehnquist also urged the White House to oppose the Equal Rights Amendment (ERA) for women, opining that it would "turn 'holy wedlock' into 'holy deadlock' " and would "hasten the dissolution of the family." Again, his advice was rejected. Instead, he was sent up to Capitol Hill to voice the Administration's support for the ERA. In the 1986 Senate hearings, before his ERA memo was revealed, Rehnquist cited his testimony in behalf of the ERA as an example of how he sought to further civil rights. In a late-night session, he also drew up the legal papers seeking to block the publication of the so-called Pentagon Papers on the inception of the Vietnam War.

Despite his loyal service to the Administration, Rehnquist was not a Nixon intimate. In fact, the president had trouble remembering his name. On the Watergate tapes of July 24, 1971, Nixon is heard to complain to aide John Ehrlichman, "Nobody follows up on [deleted] thing. Do you remember the meeting we had when I told that group of clowns we had around here, Renchberg and that group—What's his name?"

"Rehnquist," said Ehrlichman.

Nixon had less trouble with his name three months later. Two vacancies had suddenly come open on the Supreme Court, with the deathbed retirements of justices Hugo Black and John Marshall Harlan, the distinguished conservative of the liberal Warren Court. Nixon had settled on Richmond attorney Lewis F. Powell, Jr., for one slot but had not decided on the other. He considered the young Tennessee senator Howard Baker, who soon after made a name for himself at Nixon's expense. Other names, including those of prominent lawyers and politicians, were tossed around as well, but none seemed right.

The Nixon administration, unlike the Reagan administration a decade later, had not employed a team of lawyers to systematically prepare lists of potential Supreme Court candidates, each of whose résumé and legal work had been carefully analyzed. A lawyer by training, Nixon could do his own analysis. The president, however, was preoccupied with other matters. As a result, perhaps, his Supreme Court picks had something of a grab-bag quality. Nixon aides knew what he did *not* want: another Ivy Leaguer. Nixon wanted a bright conservative, an independent thinker, someone who could be confirmed without a messy fight. Richard Moore, an aide, suggested the young assistant attorney general Rehnquist. He was a rather low-ranking official for such a high appointment, but after a few moments, Nixon warmed to the idea. So did Mitchell at the Justice Department. The next day, on October 21, 1971, the two nominations were announced. "I would rate William Rehnquist as having one of the finest legal minds in this whole nation today," Nixon said.

At age 47, Rehnquist was still young to gain a Supreme Court nomination, but the timing of his nomination could not

have been better. Eight months later, after the "third-rate bur-
glary" at the Watergate Hotel, the Nixon administration began
to unravel. The Watergate scandal not only stamped an era and
sent several top Nixon aides to prison, but also stained nearly
everyone at the top of Nixon's Justice Department. Rehnquist
got out just in time.

Rehnquist's confirmation proved to be messier than either
Nixon or his nominee expected, however. Civil rights leaders
denounced the nomination as "an insult." They brought forth
black Arizonans who said Rehnquist had harassed and intimidated nonwhite voters at polling places in 1958, 1962, and
1964. A state senator testified that after the Phoenix city council meeting, Rehnquist had told him, "I oppose all civil rights
laws." Rehnquist admitted that he had worked with Republican
poll watchers on election days but denied that he had ever
harassed or sought to intimidate any voter. He also denied
making such a categorical statement about civil rights.

Senate liberals found themselves in a quandary. They had
defeated two Nixon nominees the year before: Judge Clement
F. Haynsworth, based on the somewhat trumped-up charge that
he had committed an ethical lapse by ruling on cases in which
he had a possible financial interest, and Judge G. Harrold Carswell, on the grounds that he did not meet the intellectual standards of a Supreme Court justice. Rehnquist may have had a
thin official record—just two-and-a-half years of government
service—but he had no financial improprieties, and he certainly
qualified intellectually. How could senators oppose him, except
to say that they disagreed with his conservative philosophy?

For his part, the nominee was not about to give them more
material to work with. In 1959, Rehnquist had criticized the
Senate in the pages of the *Harvard Law Review* for failing to
closely interrogate Supreme Court nominees so as to reveal
publicly their basic philosophies. The public has a right to know
what it is getting, Rehnquist noted, before a nominee is confirmed to a life-tenured position on the Court. Rehnquist made
clear he was upset that several nominees of Republican president Dwight Eisenhower had proven to be more liberal than
advertised.

Not surprisingly, several Judiciary Committee members
in 1971 read back his law review article to nominee Rehnquist
and asked for a fuller explanation of his judicial philosophy. "I
have given it some further thought, Senator," he replied, "and
I would say that I have no reservation at all about what I said

from the point of view of the Senate. I think I did not fully appreciate the difficulty of the position that the nominee is in," he said. The hearing room erupted in laughter. He explained that it was proper for the senators to "probe" for the nominee's basic views, but the nominee could refuse to respond. Divulging his views in such a public forum could threaten his independence and integrity as a judge, Rehnquist contended. The senators did their duty—they asked the questions—and the nominee did his duty by giving minimalist answers.

For Rehnquist, those few weeks under the spotlight in November 1971 were a searing experience. Basically a shy man, he found himself in the glare of intense publicity. In addition, the stories in the press didn't suggest that he had just had a great honor bestowed upon him, but rather that he might be a criminal or a racist, if only the full truth were known. In his short time in Washington, D.C., Rehnquist had already seen the reputations of three Supreme Court figures ruined, two of whom never recovered. Justice Abe Fortas had been forced to resign in May 1969, disgraced by revelations that he had taken money from an accused stock swindler, and both Haynsworth and Carswell had been defeated after a series of damaging news stories. In Washington, D.C., as in other shark-infested areas, a little blood in the water draws a crowd. Allegations, rumors, and so-called facts could be mixed together quickly. For a lawyer, the subtleties of any past statement could become lost. Comments could be distorted or exaggerated.

Rehnquist figured that the best approach was to say little and to ride out the storm. Years later, he still recalled with dismay having to watch his three children head out to school in the morning, their father having been pilloried in the morning papers. On December 10, his ordeal came to an end. On a 68–26 vote, the Senate confirmed his nomination to be the 100th justice of the Supreme Court.

A few weeks later, in early January, he and Powell were sworn in. It had been 20 years since Rehnquist first walked up the Court steps as a young law clerk. Then, he had been awed by the majesty of it. Now, as he donned the black robes of a justice, his thoughts were different. When he walked into the Court building, he felt as if he were entering a monastery. Down its dark and quiet corridors, the nine justices labored alone, largely cut off from the experiences of their fellows on the outside. New justices found that their old friends quit calling. At the same time, they had to avoid new "friends," those lawyers and lobbyists who had a special interest in cases before the Court. It made for an eerie atmosphere. Though public controversy swirled around the Court, and the disputes that came before it were intensely public and political, the justices themselves lived and worked in private, largely removed from the rough and tumble of the political world. It was, as Oliver Wendell Holmes put it, like the "quiet at the center of a storm."

In the nearly two decades Rehnquist had been gone, the Court had provoked more than one storm around the country. Under Earl Warren, the Supreme Court had moved boldly to enforce its vision of the Constitution. It outlawed official prayers and Bible reading in the public schools. It forced an end to segregation in southern colleges and schools and then turned its attention to the North. Just months before Rehnquist and Powell arrived, the Court had paved the way for cross-town busing in cities across the country. Its most controversial rulings, however, came in criminal justice. In scores of cases, the Court strengthened the rights of crime suspects. "Impeach Earl Warren" signs sprouted up across the nation.

The justices saw their decisions as enforcing the Four-teenth Amendment. Lawyers referred to it as the "criminal justice revolution," but legal historians saw it as the Recon-struction era returned. The Supreme Court of the 1960s re-vived the laws of the 1860s. The rights and privileges of an American citizen were to be enforced in every community in the nation.

Average Americans, if asked in 1960, would have said that the Bill of Rights protected their constitutional rights anywhere in the nation, but that wasn't entirely true at that time. The first ten amendments to the Constitution, known as the Bill of Rights, speak of protecting persons from "unreasonable searches and seizures," from forced self-incrimination, from being tried twice for the same crime, or from being subjected to "cruel and unusual punishment." However, as they were set forth in 1791, those rights limited only the federal government and its agents. More than 95 percent of crime cases are investigated by local and state police and prosecuted in state courts. There, the Bill of Rights was not considered to apply specifically in the vast majority of cases. Certainly, every person was entitled to "due process of law," but that did not mean that a local or state crime suspect was due all the rights set forth in the first ten Amendments. The result was that in some parts of the nation, as recently as 1960, the police could knock down a door without a search warrant, roughly question a suspect for hours, try a defendant without a lawyer, and execute a convict for an offense well short of murder—all without violating anyone's constitutional rights.

All that changed in the 1960s with the Warren Court. Hugo Black, the old Alabaman and a devotee of the Constitution, wanted his colleagues simply to declare that the Fourteenth Amendment guaranteed all the individual rights in the Bill of Rights throughout the country. With one declaration, it would be done. Your rights would not differ depending on whether the agent knocking at your door worked for a federal or a state investigating agency. That, however, was too bold a move even for the Warren Court. Instead, over a decade many individual cases accomplished the same result, but in piecemeal fashion. One by one, rights such as freedom from unreasonable searches, the right to a lawyer, the right against self-incrimination, the right to confront the witnesses against you, and the right against double jeopardy were declared fundamental aspects of "liberty" and "due process of law" and, therefore, were protected by the Fourteenth Amendment. By the time Earl Warren retired in 1969, the Fourteenth Amendment had become the federal guarantee of the basic rights of a U.S. citizen.

In the process, however, the Court also had become a major political issue. In 1968, with the nation coming apart at the seams, Richard Nixon ran for the presidency by promising a return to "law and order." Riots had torn apart cities, and violent protests had erupted on college campuses. Martin Luther King, Jr. and Robert F. Kennedy had been felled by assassins. Nixon hammered away at crime, dissent, and lawlessness and found a convenient target to blame. Nixon suggested that throughout the 1960s, the Supreme Court had appeared more interested in shackling the police rather than the criminals. He promised to change the direction of the high court.

The 1968 campaign also saw the beginning of a historic realignment of the political parties. Until then, the Democratic party had as its base of support the white working class in the North and the industrial Midwest, along with the so-called solid South. Ever since the days of the "Radical Republicans" who insisted on equal rights for blacks, the South had voted with the Democratic party. However, as the Democrats in the 1960s led the fight for civil rights in Congress, Republican strategists saw an opportunity in the South. By the 1980s, the South had become a solid base of support for the Republican party. Similarly, Nixon saw an opportunity to appeal to white workers, the "hard-hat vote," as it was then called. They were fed up with the Democratic party's courting of racial minorities and its advocacy of liberal social policies. By the middle of the 1980s, these voters had a new name: "Reagan Democrats."

When Rehnquist donned the judicial black robes in 1972, he shared Nixon's mission of changing the direction of the Supreme Court. As he saw it, the Court had moved dangerously far to the left during the Earl Warren era. It had shown itself to be more sympathetic to criminals than to crime victims, more willing to protect pornographers and protesters than government officials carrying out their duties. It seemed skeptical of religion and unwilling to enforce the death penalty. Moreover, the Court had become an aggressive meddler in the affairs of states and towns, all too willing to strike down laws passed by elected officials. It seemed to him that the Court's opinions reflected the views of neither the average American nor the authors of the Constitution. Rather, they reflected the liberal orthodoxy of the nation's elite lawyers and academics.

"I felt that at the time I came on the Court, the boat was kind of heeling over in one direction," he told one interviewer. "Interpreting my oath as I saw it, I felt that my job was . . . to kind of lean the other way." And lean he did. He pushed hard to block busing for desegregation, to limit the rights of crime suspects, to uphold death sentences, and to bring back religion to the public schools. He dissented with the other Nixon appointees in 1972 when the Court struck down the states' death penalty laws as "arbitrary and capricious." A year later, he dissented when seven members of the Court, including the other three Nixon appointees, voted to strike down all the anti-abortion laws in *Roe* v. *Wade*.

Rehnquist became known for his acerbic dissents. In 1977, for example, when the Court struck down a New York law forbidding the sale of contraceptives to minors, he roasted his colleagues for inventing a constitutional right to contraception. He wrote that it is hard to imagine the reaction of "those who valiantly but vainly defended the heights of Bunker Hill in 1775, [if they] could have lived to know that their efforts had enshrined in the Constitution the right of commercial vendors of contraceptives to peddle them to unmarried minors through vending machines located in the men's room of truck stops."

In his view, the Court's rulings were not just mistaken but grossly wrong. Frequently, he challenged the entire doctrine on which they were based. The Constitution does not demand a "separation of church and state," he said, nor does it require the Court to review writs of habeas corpus from inmates incarcerated in state prisons. The Constitution does not give suspects a right to be warned that a confession will be used against them, nor does it create a "right to privacy" for individuals. All these, he said, were inventions of the liberal majority on the Court.

In those years, Rehnquist sported long sideburns and parted his hair in the middle. He wore rumpled sport coats and Hush Puppies shoes. He walked with a peculiar bobbing stride, his head hunched down on his shoulders. In the marble halls of the Court, he looked more like a refugee from a small college math department than a justice of the Supreme Court. Through the 1970s, he was viewed by most lawyers and law clerks as something of a brilliant eccentric, a man whose views were confined to the past. All along, however, there were bright conservative clerks whose estimate of Rehnquist proved more accurate. They saw him as the voice of the future.

PART TWO
The
1986–1987 Term

3

Sunset for the Brennan Court

F resh from having escaped the "lynch mob" in the Senate, Rehnquist had only two weeks to get ready for the opening of the Court's 1986 term. Over the summer, more than 1,000 appeals had piled up. In addition, 101 cases were already set for argument during the fall.

Once the term officially begins on the first Monday in October, the justices juggle three balls in the air at once. Their first task is complex in itself: They must prepare to hear the oral arguments in cases, then make their decisions, and cast their votes. Typically, 24 cases are argued each month. Within two days after each case's argument, the justices meet in the conference room and cast their votes. Their second major task is to write opinions to explain their decisions. Dividing up the 24 cases, each justice can expect to be assigned two or three majority opinions per month—and as many dissents as he or she wants to write. Third, they and their clerks must read through the new appeals, which arrive at a rate of about 100 per week. Actually, week to week the job of scanning the new appeals is left mostly to the clerks, but any that are being seriously considered for review by the Court are also read by the justices.

Appeals are submitted by a person, company, or government agency that has lost a case in a state supreme court or a federal appeals court; these individuals have a right to file with the justices a *petition for certiorari*—in essence, a plea for the Court's attention. The justices have no obligation to hear these appeals; they pick only those that raise important, disputed issues involving federal law or the U.S. Constitution. Big law firms charge clients, hoping to attract the eye of the justices, as much as $30,000 to prepare a 25-page petition. Few succeed. On average, about three percent of the appeals win a *review*, which means that the cases will be argued before the justices and decided with a written opinion.

The first test of the chief justice comes with the annual fall conference in late September. During July and August, while the justices are away from Washington, appeal petitions continue to pour into the Supreme Court building. The new clerks, most of whom are just one year out of law school and still learning their jobs, are left alone to read through them. For each petition, they are told to draft a concise memo for the justices on the issue raised by the case, the decision of the lower court, and a recommendation on whether the Court should grant a review of it. Typically, the justices themselves also read through the petitions in the most promising cases.

With the first Monday in October fast approaching, the justices get together for what is known as the "long conference." In a few days, they must work through the summer backlog of appeals. The chief justice gets the first chance to set the agenda for the committee of nine. A few days before the meeting, the chief sends his "discuss list" to the chambers of the other justices. These are the appeals he wants discussed. Other justices can add cases to the list. The appealed cases that do not make the final discuss list—the fate of about three cases in four—are consigned to the "dead list." They will be rejected by the Court without getting any mention in the conference room.

At 9:25 in the morning, a buzzer sounds on the first floor. The conference will begin in five minutes. For new justices, the routine of marching to the time of buzzers recalls their high school days. The nine of them meet alone; no clerks, secretaries, or aides are allowed in the meeting. By tradition dating to the nineteenth century, they begin by shaking hands and greeting each other. Then, over Danish pastries and tea, they get to the business at hand.

During Warren Burger's tenure, these sessions, especially the first conference of the fall, became a painful ritual. His ill-focused presentations left the justices restless and irritated. At times, Burger seemed to have the poorest grasp of the cases when compared to anyone else in the room.

Rehnquist made an instant hit; he absolutely hated to waste time. In his view, meetings should start on time and end early. Rehnquist moved through the cases briskly. He distilled the key issue raised by an appeal and described the lower court ruling. Did the decision jibe with the Court's precedents? Were judges around the country confused on this point of law? Was the issue important enough for the Court to hear the case and resolve the problem?

One justice described Rehnquist's presentations as "honest." The new chief did not slant his comments or leave out key facts so as to put a conservative spin on the issue. The cases were discussed at a rapid pace, without wasted words or pointless diatribes. Under Burger, the fall conference often dragged on for five days. Under Rehnquist, it was completed in two. Under Rehnquist, the Court moved quickly, with minimal discussion and no haggling.

On October 6, 1986, the first Monday of October, the Court announced the results. A thick "orders list" told lawyers in 23 cases that they had won a full hearing before the justices. In about 90 days, they would have to file briefs and appear to argue their cases. Meanwhile, the attorneys in 917 cases were told their appeals were rejected without comment.

As the fall term began, the justices had a full schedule of cases. These had been granted a review in the spring before Burger's resignation. Now, they would provide an early test of whether the "Rehnquist Court" would tilt the law to the right. The key issues that divide the Court can be ticked off quickly: civil rights, abortion, free speech, religion, the rights of crime defendants, and the death penalty. For Rehnquist, the fall lineup of cases offered a chance to change the law on civil rights and religion as well as to clear away a major challenge to the death penalty.

The stories in the press that fall suggested that the Court was ready to lurch to the right. Affirmative action was said to be doomed and the right to abortion threatened. Rehnquist and Scalia added brainpower and youth on the right, it was said. Both were personable as well as persuasive. Brennan had heard all this before. He was hardly mentioned in the accounts of the new Court, as if he were a relic from the past. Like Mark Twain, he had read before these "greatly exaggerated" reports of his demise. He also had a ready reply: Wait until the votes are counted.

That fall, the Court had two affirmative action cases before it. One replayed a now-familiar theme. A judge had found an employer guilty of refusing to hire blacks. Could the judge now order that more blacks be hired—or impose a "quota"— to make up for the past discrimination? The Court had grappled with this question in a series of cases in the early 1980s, most of which involved white police officers and firefighters challenging the judge's order. On November 12, the Court would consider a judge's effort to remedy the blatant exclusion of blacks from the Alabama state troopers.

The second affirmative action case broke new ground. It could have arisen in practically any office or job site in the nation. It did not concern gross discrimination or quotas, but rather, giving an edge to a woman seeking a job traditionally held by men. By 1986, few employers blatantly excluded blacks, Hispanics, or women. Still, many offices and work sites remained the domain of white males. Now, however, many employers were uncomfortable with an all-white, all-male work force. It was not good for business. It left the employer vulnerable to accusations—from customers as well as from the courts—that the work force did not reflect the community. The result was that most companies and public agencies sought to give an edge, subtle or otherwise, to black and female applicants who wanted jobs presently held mostly by white males.

Among top executives who ordered the new preferential hiring, as well as those employees who benefited from it, this seemed a wise and just policy. After being discouraged for so long, blacks and women now found an open door. However, millions of white males tended to see it differently. In their view, they had won their jobs through merit and hard work, not *because* they were white and male. Now, they could be passed over for a job or a promotion simply because of their color or gender.

In American politics, the backlash against affirmative action helped create an electoral phenomenon of the 1980s—the "Reagan Democrat." In their 1984 platform, the Republicans lambasted "quotas" as "insidious." Reagan's opponent, former U.S. Senator and Vice President Walter Mondale, had been a strong supporter of civil rights and of using "goals" and "timetables" to force employers to hire more minorities and women. As the Democratic presidential nominee, he did more than preach affirmative action. He chose a woman, Representative Geraldine Ferraro, as his running mate. In the November presidential elections, however, Reagan and his mate, George Bush, won 49 of the 50 states.

In the fall of 1986, Reagan could claim as his own two members of the high court: justices O'Connor and Scalia. They sat at opposite ends of the bench and had, if not opposite, quite differing views of affirmative action. Sandra O'Connor had been both a victim of discrimination and a beneficiary of affirmative action. In 1953, she graduated third in her class from the Stanford University Law School but was unable to land a job with any of California's prominent law firms. On the other hand, she now sat on the Supreme Court largely because she was a woman.

Antonin Scalia was the first Italian-American to earn a seat on the high court, a fact Reagan often noted. Scalia, however, had no reason to believe he was nominated *because* he was an Italian-American. As a student in New York City, at Georgetown University, and at Harvard Law, Scalia was stellar. As a lawyer, law professor, government official, and federal appellate judge, he was brilliant, intense, hardworking, and passionately devoted to the law. Of course, in the 1980s it helped to be an outspoken conservative, and Scalia excelled there, too. When he donned his black robe in 1986, he had good reason to think he had made it on his own.

Nino Scalia absolutely despised affirmative action. It struck him as all wrong—legally, morally, and personally. "He grew up with the merit system in the New York schools and the 'melting pot' ethic," says one friend. With brains and hard work, any young person could rise to the top, as Scalia did. So, why couldn't others do the same?

In a 1979 law school talk, Professor Antonin Scalia delivered a scornful attack on the Supreme Court for having upheld affirmative action. In particular, he vented his wrath on what he called the "Aryan" judges and justices who supported the idea. Judge John Minor Wisdom, a prominent liberal from Louisiana, had written that federal law encouraged "restorative justice" for blacks and other disadvantaged persons.

That phrase, Scalia said, "may explain why I feel a bit differently about these issues than, for example, Judge Wisdom or Justice Powell or Justice White." It reminded him, he said, of the old story of the Lone Ranger and his faithful American Indian companion, Tonto. When the two come upon a band of Mohawks in war dress, the Lone Ranger turns to Tonto for advice. "Ugh, ride um west," Tonto says, but they run into another band of Indian warriors in that direction. "Ride um south," Tonto says—but they have no luck there either. They try going east but again are stopped in their tracks. The Lone Ranger, now worried, turns to his companion and says, "What do we do now?" Tonto replies, "Ugh, what do you mean 'we,' white man," said Scalia, recounting the tale.

"I have somewhat the same feeling when John Minor Wisdom talks of the evils that 'we' whites have done to blacks and that 'we' must now make restoration for," Scalia continued. "My father came to this country when he was a teenager. Not only had he never profited from the sweat of any black man's brow, I don't think he had ever seen a black man." The same can be said for many other white ethnics, he added. "Yet curiously enough, we find that in the system of restorative justice established by the Wisdoms and the Powells and the Whites, it is precisely these groups that do most of the restoring," he said. If affirmative action was driven by white liberal guilt, Scalia did not feel guilty.

He added, however, that he was "entirely in favor of according the poor inner-city child, who happens to be black, advantages and preferences not given to my own children because they don't need them. But I am not willing to prefer the son of a prosperous and well-educated black doctor or lawyer— solely because of his race—to the son of a recent refugee from Eastern Europe who is working as a manual laborer to get his family ahead." The so-called "affirmative action" now practiced in America must be condemned, he said, "because it is based upon concepts of racial indebtedness and racial entitlement, rather than individual worth and individual need, and that is to say, because it is racist."

The year after Scalia's 1979 speech, Ronald Reagan was elected president, and Reagan soon made Professor Antonin Scalia a judge on the federal appeals court in Washington, D.C. By the fall of 1986, Scalia was sitting alongside "the Powells and the Whites," with a chance to reverse the Court's stance on affirmative action.

Brennan and Rehnquist had clashed over affirmative action before, but now the balance looked as if it might tilt toward Rehnquist. Most Court observers were certain that Scalia would join a ruling that would halt affirmative action. In addition, the bow-tied John Paul Stevens was a potential ally. He had sat out the Brian Weber case in 1979 because he had done work for Kaiser Steel as a Chicago lawyer, but he had said he believed that the 1964 Civil Rights Act did not permit race or gender discrimination of any sort. Byron White, whom Scalia had attacked in 1979, had also grown skeptical of affirmative action. If Rehnquist could just bring along O'Connor, he would have five votes.

Unfortunately for Rehnquist, however, his first opportunity to halt affirmative action came in a case involving, of all things, a woman who had sought to enter an all-male work force in Santa Clara County, California, just a few miles down the freeway from Stanford University and the San Mateo County Courthouse, where young Sandra Day had found her first job.

Diane Joyce was a 42-year-old widow with two children. For nearly ten years, she had worked for the Santa Clara County Transportation Agency, first as a clerk and then as a road maintenance worker. When a road dispatcher's job opened up in December 1979, Joyce applied.

Unlike the road crews, whose work is hot and dirty, the dispatcher sits in a small office equipped with a radio and sends equipment and crews around the county. The county considered the dispatcher job to be a skilled position. A few years earlier, Joyce had tried to get a dispatcher's job but was told she needed more experience working on the roads. She had done her time and, on occasion, had filled in as a substitute dispatcher. She easily met all the qualifications to be a dispatcher.

However, 54-year-old Paul Johnson wanted the same job and thought he had an even better claim to it. He had worked for the county longer than Joyce. Previously, he had been a dispatcher and supervisor for a cement company in San Jose for 17 years. As a county employee, he had worked on the roads, in the equipment yards, and as a part-time dispatcher. He knew the ins and outs of heavy equipment. He knew the crews, and he knew the county.

To no one's surprise, when the applicants were tested and interviewed, Johnson ranked first, with a score of 75 points. Diane Joyce was ranked fourth, with a score of 72.5. Under the scoring system, an applicant who scored above 70 was qualified for the job. Nonetheless, the two interviewers—both men—believed Johnson's experience and knowledge were superior. They recommended him for the job.

Normally, that would have been the end of the matter, but Joyce was not about to give up. For years, she had put up with sexist jokes and comments about her dress. The walls of the maintenance hall featured calendars of nearly nude females. "They always try to embarrass you, even the supervisors," she said. The men acted as if women were good for one thing, and it was not repairing roads. Joyce didn't trust the two male interviewers, so she called the Santa Clara County women's coordinator, who in turn contacted the agency's affirmative action coordinator. The year before, the county board of supervisors directed the agency to develop an affirmative action plan. Its "goal" was to "attain an agency work force whose composition reflects the ethnic and sexual makeup of the area work force." That meant, according to the plan, that females should hold "36.4 percent" of the jobs in each category.

Under the plan, Joyce was a member of a "protected class." Johnson, a white male, was not. Moreover, none of the 237 skilled positions in the transportation agency was then held by a woman. The county affirmative action coordinator recommended that Joyce get the dispatcher's job, and James Graebner, the agency director, agreed.

So Joyce got the job, Johnson got a disappointment, and the county got itself a lawsuit. Johnson charged in federal court that he had been denied a job based on sex, in violation of Title VII of the Civil Rights Act. It is "unlawful," the act says, for an employer "to discriminate against any individual . . . because of such individual's race, color, religion, sex or national origin."

A federal judge who heard the evidence ruled for Johnson because gender was "the determining factor" in the selection of Joyce over Johnson. He ordered that Johnson be awarded the job and given back pay. However, this decision was reversed by the U.S. Ninth Circuit Court of Appeals on a 2-1 vote. Two Jimmy Carter appointees made up the majority, with a Republican appointee in dissent. Lawyers for the Mountain States Legal Foundation, a conservative advocacy group, then took Johnson's appeal to the U.S. Supreme Court.

For the justices, the case of *Johnson* v. *Transportation Agency of Santa Clara County* raised a new version of the question first raised in the *Weber* case in 1979. Unlike the *Weber* case, there was no hint here that the county had actually discriminated against women road workers before. On the other hand, Paul Johnson did not lose the promotion because of a strict quota, but rather because the county chose to give an edge to a qualified woman. The case then raised a question that could affect workplaces nationwide: Could an employer give a preference based on race or gender to some individuals over others simply to correct a statistical imbalance in its work force?

Before, justices Powell and O'Connor, the swing votes, had said affirmative action was justified only as a "remedy" for actual past discrimination by an employer, not a way to make up for 200 years of American history. In the *Weber* case, the Court could have assumed that no blacks were employed in a Louisiana plant because of past racial discrimination. What was Santa Clara County seeking to remedy?

The Reagan administration filed a brief supporting Johnson, which was signed by Solicitor General Charles Fried and civil rights chief William Bradford Reynolds. It called the Santa Clara affirmative action plan "a rather extreme example of casual social engineering heedless of individual rights." If employers can hire and promote based simply on statistical quotas, the Administration said, white males will have no civil rights on the job.

A ruling against the county could tie the hands of employers nationwide, however, corporate lawyers countered. Both Joyce and Johnson were, after all, judged to be "well qualified" for the job. If companies can be sued every time they hire or promote one individual over a marginally better qualified one, they will spend a lot of time in federal court. No wonder then that corporate groups and government employers lined up on the side of Santa Clara County.

The case was argued November 12. The county's attorney, Steven Woodside, was making his first visit to the Supreme Court. He had, of course, seen countless photos of the Court building and had read even more about what transpires there. Nonetheless, for any lawyer, a first visit to the marble temple of the law can be inspiring.

The Court is best known for its façade—the long steps and the columns of Italian marble that jut out from the main building. Above its front entrance are engraved the words "Equal Justice Under Law." This phrase, one of the best known in American law, was not plucked from the U.S. Constitution, the Declaration of Independence, or any of the Court's decisions. Instead, the words came from an architect, Cass Gilbert, who designed and built the structure in the early 1930s. He needed a concise message, and these words fit nicely.

Before 1935, the justices worked mostly at home and met in a small chamber in the Capitol. At first, the justices derided the grandeur of their official edifice. With the nation mired in the Great Depression, the justices sounded embarrassed by the magnificence of their marble palace. Justice Harlan Stone said he felt "like a beetle entering the temple of Karnak." In time, however, the Court's grand edifice and Cass Gilbert's slogan came to symbolize American justice.

From the top of the steps, a visitor enters through thick, bronze doors and walks down the Great Hall. It is cool and dark, and words echo from the high ceiling. At the far end is the courtroom. A visitor enters through a parted red curtain. Inside, the words of justices, even if spoken in a near whisper, are picked up by the microphone and boom throughout the high-ceilinged room. For a first-time visitor, the effect is like entering the chamber of the Wizard of Oz.

Woodside, the attorney for Santa Clara County, had been warned to expect a barrage of questions from Justice Scalia. The warnings proved accurate. As is usual for Court cases, Woodside had 30 minutes to defend the county's plan; however, most of his time was spent fending off Scalia.

Why did the county decide that 36.4 percent of jobs in each job category should be held by women? Scalia wondered.

Woodside: "One would ordinarily expect in jobs throughout the agency that they would be comprised, absent discrimination, of roughly the numbers that exist in the general labor pool."

Scalia looked amazed: "Is that right?"

Woodside: "Yes."

Scalia: "You mean it is statistically reasonable to expect as many women to be working on road crews and to believe that if there aren't that proportion, there must be discrimination?"

Woodside: "I think that there would be an inference of discrimination drawn from that factor alone."

Scalia: "What is that based on? Human experience or some governmental policy?"

Woodside: "I think it is based on both human experience and governmental policy."

Scalia: "On human experience?"

Woodside: "Yes, Your Honor."

Scalia: "In this country?"

Woodside: "Yes."

Flabbergasted, Scalia sat back in his leather seat.

When it was time to present Johnson's argument, Constance Brooks, the Mountain States attorney representing Johnson, said the Santa Clara plan was unlawful because it was not a "remedy" for discrimination.

In contrast to Scalia's jab-jab-jab style of interrogation, O'Connor usually asked one pointed question and then sat back to listen to the answer. "Well, if a statistical imbalance in the work force is evident and they adopt an affirmative action plan," O'Connor said, "isn't it apparent on its face that it is remedial?"

No, Brooks argued, because there was no discrimination against women. O'Connor had good reason to believe otherwise.

When voting time came, Rehnquist and Brennan, as usual, took the opposing sides. The chief justice argued that the Civil Rights Act clearly forbids race or gender discrimination against anyone, including Paul Johnson. To Brennan, it was just as clear that Congress wanted to break down the vestiges of earlier discrimination, which is exactly what Santa Clara County was trying to do, he maintained.

White now lined up with Rehnquist. He had once been a solid vote for the liberals in civil rights cases. In the late 1970s, however, when the issues changed from racial exclusions to racial preferences, White got off the civil rights bandwagon. In general, he was a stickler for following precedent, but Brennan was trying to stretch the *Weber* precedent past its breaking point.

"My understanding of Weber was, and is, that the employer's plan . . . was designed to remedy intentional and systematic exclusion of blacks," White said. In a Louisiana steel plant with a nearly all-white work force, old-fashioned racial discrimination was surely at work, but what does that have to do with women seeking jobs on a road crew? White wondered. Brennan was now suggesting that race and gender preferences could be based on "nothing more than a manifest imbalance" in the numbers of blacks and women on the job, he continued. If that was to be the new rule, White wanted no part of it. "I would overrule Weber and reverse the judgment below" in favor of Santa Clara County, he said.

Nonetheless, White dissented against Brennan's opinion. Brennan had the votes of fellow liberals Thurgood Marshall and Harry Blackmun. Powell, the usual swing vote, saw Santa Clara's plan not as a hard and fast quota, but as a reasonable means of bringing more women into the workplace. In the 1978 *Bakke* case, the Court's first and most famous ruling on affirmative action, Powell set forth a unique middle position that became the law: Quotas are illegal, but universities may give some preference to underrepresented minorities to bring about "diversity" in their classrooms. As Brennan argued, Santa Clara had not used a quota but rather gave a slight edge to a qualified female. Powell signed on to the Brennan opinion.

Brennan also picked up a new convert in Stevens. With his white hair, bow tie, and kindly manner, Stevens looked like a college physics professor. Certainly, he had the intellect for that or any job. For pure brainpower, Stevens had no match on the Court except, perhaps, for Scalia. One legal academic described Stevens as "flat-out brilliant." An admiring law clerk observed, "For pure intellect, you can't match him." He also won plaudits for being one of the kindest and gentlest persons in the building. "If Stevens ran a gas station, it would be a wonderful place to work," one clerk observed.

Yet this exceptionally bright and likeable justice usually rated as the least significant of the nine justices. In the Court's major cases, Stevens had been nearly invisible. He rarely was given a chance to write an important opinion. Even when he dissented, he often spoke only for himself. The other dissenters—liberal or conservative—usually would draft a separate dissent.

Why did Stevens have so little impact on the Court? In 1975, President Gerald Ford had chosen the professorial Stevens to replace William O. Douglas, the fiery liberal. By comparison with Douglas, Stevens had moderate to conservative views, but the two shared a fierce individualism. Exceedingly bright and apolitical, Stevens liked to devise a unique position on nearly every legal issue. He also steadfastly refused to adopt the thinking of his colleagues. He shunned chances to be a power broker. Even when he could sway the outcome of a case by joining either a liberal or a conservative coalition, Stevens often refused and wrote a separate opinion for himself. The clerks would joke that a particular upcoming case "looks to be 4, 4, and Stevens" or "5, 3, and Stevens." Though he wrote the most dissents and separate concurrences, his views were usually ignored. As Stevens conceded in a 1986 speech, "The audience that I most frequently address does not always seem to be listening to what I have to say."

His colleagues have found him to be quirky and so unpredictable as to be irritating. "With each term, his jurisprudence begins anew," one justice commented sarcastically.

Still, as the Court's maverick, Stevens challenged his colleagues with new ideas and new perspectives. "His memos are either brilliant or off the wall," said a former clerk.

Stevens was born in Chicago on April 20, 1920, and had grown up in an atmosphere of affluence and intellectual intensity. His father owned and managed the Stevens Hotel, a grand edifice on Michigan Avenue, which once was the world's largest hotel. It later became the Conrad Hilton Hotel. Raised in Hyde Park, Stevens attended private schools run by the University of Chicago. During the Great Depression, his family suffered a sharp financial reversal, but young Stevens was not held back by it. In 1941, he graduated Phi Beta Kappa from the University of Chicago and then served four years as a U.S. Naval intelligence officer. Returning to Chicago, he enrolled in the Northwestern University Law School and graduated at the top of the 1947 class, with the highest grade point average in the school's history. He took a Supreme Court clerkship with Justice Wiley Rutledge and spent a second year in Washington, D.C., as counsel for the House antitrust subcommittee.

He then went back to Chicago, where he practiced law for 22 years, gaining a national reputation as an antitrust expert. He also taught antitrust law at Northwestern and Chicago. In 1970, Richard Nixon appointed him to the highly regarded U.S. Seventh Circuit Court of Appeals in Chicago. Five years later, President Ford had a chance to fill the Supreme Court vacancy created by Douglas's retirement after his record 36 years on the bench. Ironically, when Ford served as a member of the House of Representatives, he had sought to have Douglas impeached. In choosing Douglas's successor, the president had to tread gingerly. Ford faced a yearlong reelection battle and did not want to get bogged down in a fight over the Supreme Court. Therefore, he turned over the search for a new justice to Attorney General Edward Levi, the former president of the University of Chicago and dean of its law school. Levi's—and Ford's—choice was Judge John Paul Stevens. Stevens won a unanimous confirmation from the Senate on December 17, 1975.

The new justice found the Court to be mildly disappointing. He expected his colleagues to engage in an intellectual and principled search for the right solution in each case. Instead, they seemed to be more interested in fitting cases into a liberal or a conservative box. Once labeled, they knew how to vote.

Stevens works alone and works hard. Up at 5:30 in the morning, he likes to draft opinions at home and then take a break to play tennis. He also likes to go his own way and at his own high rate of speed. For years, he had flown his own private plane. Where several of the older justices are driven to work in Court limousines, Stevens speeds to the Court in his own car, impatiently changing lanes and darting between cars as he crosses the Potomac River bridges. Where other justices use four law clerks, he uses two. Where others are happy to delegate much of the writing to others, Stevens wants to do most of it himself. For a man in his 70s, he is buoyantly energetic. Whether on the bench or talking law with his clerks, his mind moves quickly.

He was once invited to American University, along with Brennan and Blackmun, to hear arguments and then to "decide" an important literary question: Did William Shakespeare write his plays, or was the true author the worldly and well-educated Edward DeVere, the Earl of Oxford? Each of the seventeenth-century writers was represented by an attorney, and Shakespeare's counsel chose to attack DeVere. It is preposterous to think that this courtier could have written the plays, the attorney said. After all, he said, DeVere was known as a drunk, a brawler, a conniver, and a lecher.

"Sounds like a playwright," Stevens interjected.

After hearing the arguments, the justices gave the nod to Shakespeare, but predictably, Stevens issued a partial dissent: If there were another author, DeVere is probably the true author, he contended.

The other justices at the Court would have found the scene familiar. They have found Stevens dismaying at times because he has refused to join the reasoning favored by the majority. As Rehnquist once observed, if there were any possible way to find a different approach to deciding a case, Stevens would find it.

For his part, Stevens is dismayed by the political nature of many of the Court's decisions. "I'm the most conservative justice up here," he likes to say. Characteristically though, he means something different by the word *conservative*. In his view, a conservative judge is one who decides the narrow issue presented by a case and relies on precedent. Increasingly in the 1980s, Stevens felt surrounded by conservative "judicial activists" who would bend the law to enunciate right-wing political principles.

In the late 1970s, Stevens had agreed with Rehnquist that the federal antidiscrimination laws did not allow "affirmative" preferences for minorities and women. In 1986, however, in the first test of affirmative action in the Rehnquist Court, Stevens switched sides and supplied Brennan with a fifth vote. Ironically, he did so by relying on the 1979 precedent he had originally opposed.

"The only problem for me" in the *Santa Clara* case "is whether to adhere to an authoritative construction of the Act that is at odds with my understanding of the actual intent of the authors of the legislation. I conclude without hesitation that I must answer the question in the affirmative," he wrote. In 1979, Stevens thought the ruling in the Weber case was flatly wrong. Nonetheless, the Court majority had concluded otherwise, and Stevens said he accepted that conclusion. In the years since then, many employers had adopted affirmative action plans relying on the Court's decision. Moreover, Congress seemed quite content with the outcome. There had been no move to overturn the *Weber* decision. In the *Santa Clara* case, he not only joined Brennan's opinion but also wrote a separate opinion to give an open-ended endorsement to affirmative action. In this case, Stevens took the most liberal position of the nine.

O'Connor, as usual, was torn. On her right were natural allies Rehnquist and Scalia, but they wanted to go too far. Scalia had drafted a dissent calling for *Weber* to be reversed. That was too rash for O'Connor. She dismissed Scalia's opinion as nothing more than "a useful point of academic discussion."

On her left, however, were the liberals who wanted to push what they called "race-conscious" preferences far beyond what the law, or the country, would accept. Brennan's opinion did not limit affirmative action to being a remedy for actual discrimination. Even if no one was discriminated against in the past, employers could give preferences in the future to make up for an "imbalance" in the work force. This went way too far in the other direction for O'Connor. She struggled to find a middle ground.

To O'Connor, the key fact was a statistic: 0 women in 237 skilled jobs in the county transportation department. Employ-

ers must have "a firm basis," she said, for believing that discrimination against women and minorities has occurred before
they can undertake a preference scheme to remedy it. "There
were no women in skilled craft positions," she said, so "I am
satisfied that the [county] had a firm basis for adopting an affirmative action program." She voted with Brennan to uphold
the county and Diane Joyce but refused to join his "expansive
and ill-defined" opinion in favor of affirmative action.

An irritated Scalia sat at his computer terminal and hammered out his dissent. Affirmative action was wrong, it violated
the law, and *Weber* should be overruled, he wrote. He also
kicked aside O'Connor's "firm basis" notion, calling it "something of a half-way house between leaving employers scot-free
to discriminate against disfavored groups, as the majority opinion does, and prohibiting discrimination, as do the words of
Title VII [of the Civil Rights Act]."

Scalia made three arguments: First, the Civil Rights Act
clearly forbids discrimination; it does not "give each protected
racial and sexual group a governmentally determined 'proper'
proportion of each job category." Second, he mocked the notion that this was a "discrimination" case. "It is absurd to think
that the nationwide failure of road maintenance crews, for example, to achieve the agency's ambition of 36.4 percent female
representation is attributable primarily, if even substantially,
to the systematic exclusion of women eager to shoulder pick
and shovel," he said.

Third, Scalia concluded by turning the tables on the liberals and their concern for justice for the powerless. "The only
losers in the process [of affirmative action] are the Johnsons of
the country, for whom Title VII has been not merely repealed
but actually inverted. The irony is that these individuals—predominantly unknown, unaffluent, unorganized—suffer this injustice at the hands of a Court fond of thinking itself the champion of the politically impotent."

The opinions were released on March 25, 1987. The
6-3 vote surprised many commentators. So did the Court's
open-ended endorsement of affirmative action, even where no
discrimination had been charged or proven. Bruce Fein, a conservative legal analyst and former Reagan administration official, called the ruling "the most significant affirmative action
case" yet in upholding the concept. Diane Joyce called it "a
giant victory for womanhood." Paul Johnson, bitter over his
lost promotion, had taken an early retirement and moved to

Sequim, Washington. "To put it mildly, I think it stinks," he said in reaction to the Court's decision.

A month before the *Johnson* ruling, the Court had handed down a decision in the other pending affirmative action case. By a 5–4 ruling, again with Brennan writing the majority opinion, the Court upheld a federal judge's order requiring the Alabama state police to hire and promote one black for each white hired or promoted. In 1972, the state had been found guilty of "blatant" and deliberate discrimination against blacks. Not a single black trooper had even been hired. By 1984, despite the judge's pressure, there were still no blacks in any rank above the entry level. Exasperated, the judge then imposed the one-for-one hiring-and-promotion order.

The Reagan administration appealed the case, in *U.S.* v. *Paradise*, but came one vote short of getting its desired result. Brennan, Marshall, Blackmun, Stevens, and Powell voted to uphold the judge's order as a necessary remedy for the "pervasive, systematic and obstinate" exclusion of blacks. Rehnquist, White, O'Connor, and Scalia dissented, calling it an illegal quota.

The two rulings marked a surprise beginning for what had been heralded as a new, more conservative Supreme Court.

The other major civil rights case heard in the fall of 1986 raised an issue that the Court had stumbled over before—the rights of pregnant workers. In 1976, female workers had challenged the General Electric Company (GE) for refusing to pay temporary disability benefits to its pregnant employees, while providing such benefits for other medical conditions. The Civil Rights Act of 1964 had stated that employers may not discriminate based on race, gender, religion, or national origin "with respect to . . . compensation, terms, conditions or privileges of employment." The U.S. Equal Employment Opportunity Commission (EEOC) said that GE's policy violated the law; so did the judge who heard the women's complaint, as did several U.S. appeals courts who decided similar cases. However, the Supreme Court disagreed. Then Justice Rehnquist, writing for a 6–3 majority, said that GE's plan does not violate the law because it treats men and women in the same way.

"There is no risk from which men are protected and women are not. Likewise, there is no risk from which women are protected and men are not," Rehnquist wrote in 1976. The dissenters—justices Brennan, Marshall, and Stevens—pointed

out the obvious. Only women suffer the "risk" of pregnancy.
Therefore, a company plan that leaves women financially vulnerable in a way that men are not is unfair and illegal, they
asserted.

The Court's decision in *General Electric* v. *Gilbert* set off
an uproar in Congress, and in short order it was reversed. The
Pregnancy Discrimination Act of 1978 added a new clause to
the 1964 law, to expressly outlaw discrimination "on the basis
of pregnancy, childbirth or related medical conditions." Pregnant women "shall be treated the same for all employment
related purposes, including the receipt of benefits," the law
said. Sponsors of the measure said it would end a "major source
of discrimination unjustly afflicting working women."

That same year, the California state legislature considered
the same problem but took a somewhat different tack. It said
that employers must allow pregnant workers an unpaid disability leave, up to four months, so they can recover from childbirth without the fear of losing their jobs. In January 1982,
Lillian Garland was a receptionist at a savings and loan (S&L)
office in west Los Angeles when she took a leave to have a
baby. Three months later, when she wanted to return to work,
she was told her job had been filled.

"They just told me, 'If something comes up, we'll give
you a call,' " Garland said.

She gave a call instead to the California Department of
Fair Employment and Housing, the agency charged with enforcing the state's pregnancy-leave law. Garland's employer,
California Federal Savings and Loan (Cal Fed), said it tried to
accommodate employees such as Garland, but it "reserved the
right to terminate an employee on leave of absence if a similar
and suitable position is not available." In November, after Garland had filed her complaint, the S&L reinstated her to a receptionist's job. Cal Fed, however, joined by the California
Chamber of Commerce and the Merchants and Manufacturers
Association, decided to challenge the state law in federal court.

Their attack was simple and literal: The 1978 federal law
says that men and women employees "shall be treated the
same," without regard to pregnancy. Yet, the state law requires
a "special preference" for women employees. Only they are
guaranteed the right to take a leave and hold their jobs. Because the state law conflicts with the federal law, it should be
struck down as invalid, they maintained.

A U.S. judge in Los Angeles agreed and ruled that the federal law mandating the "same" treatment of men and women nullified the state law giving "special" treatment to women. However, three judges of the U.S. Ninth Circuit Court of Appeals—all of whom happened to be appointees of President Jimmy Carter—voted to overrule the judge and to reinstate the law. It "defies common sense," they said, to use a law designed to protect pregnant employees as the basis for striking down a state law designed to protect pregnant employees. Cal Fed appealed to the Supreme Court, which, in the spring of 1986, agreed to hear the dispute the following fall.

The case came up for oral argument in the first week of the new Rehnquist Court. It raised at least three intriguing questions. First, as a philosophical matter, what is *equal?* Does *equal* mean "identical treatment," or in some instances must employers make special arrangements to foster equal opportunity? For example, if a company refused to build a ramp into its building, it could not be said to provide equal opportunities for a handicapped person in a wheelchair, even though it was treating everyone identically.

Are women sufficiently different from men to require a special accommodation? That issue divided the nation's women's rights groups. The National Organization for Women, the NOW Legal Defense Fund, and the Women's Rights Project of the American Civil Liberties Union (ACLU) filed briefs with the Court, saying that the California law should not be permitted to stand as it is. For centuries, women had been denied equality in the workplace because they were viewed as mothers and childbearers. Now, women wanted full equality, not special benefits, they contended. Other women's rights groups, however, sided with the California law. They said that the law did not give women a special preference. It "merely ensures that no women lose their jobs because of an employment disadvantage no men ever face—pregnancy disability," as California Deputy Attorney General Marian Johnston told the Court. Nationwide, more than 47 million women were in the work force, and 85 percent of them will get pregnant at least once during their working years, she added.

For the justices, the case raised two other questions. Should they rely on the strict, narrow language of the 1978 federal law, or should they instead consider its intent? The law clearly said that women "shall be treated the same." However, its Congressional sponsors made just as clear that they intended to outlaw discrimination against pregnant women, not ban a law in their favor.

Finally, how would a conservative Court grapple with a liberal state law? President Reagan had stressed the virtues of "judicial restraint." Courts should avoid striking down laws passed by elected legislators, he said. Rehnquist, in particular, insisted on the need to uphold state laws. However, in most instances, conservatives such as Reagan or Rehnquist were speaking up for conservative or traditional state laws that had been struck down by a liberal-dominated Court. Now that the conservatives seemed to be in the majority, how would they react?

The Reagan Justice Department filed a brief with the Court urging it to nullify the California law. Because the state law "singles out pregnant female employees for special treatment," it clearly violates the federal Pregnancy Discrimination Act, the department said in a brief signed by Assistant Attorney General William Bradford Reynolds.

On October 8, the courtroom was packed to hear arguments in the case of *California Federal Savings and Loan* v. *Mark Guerra, Director of Fair Employment and Housing.* Theodore Olson, a Justice Department official who came to Washington with Ronald Reagan but was now in private practice, argued for the S&L company.

A key moment in the oral argument came early. Olson began by stating that "the federal mandate of equal protection must prevail over the state policy of special protection." In California, employers were trapped, Olson posited. If they complied with the federal law, they violated the state law. Because the U.S. Constitution makes federal law supreme, the state law must be preempted, he said.

Justice Sandra Day O'Connor leaned forward to her microphone. On the bench, she has a stiff, businesslike manner. She is well-prepared for the arguments. For each case, her clerks write 20- to 30-page memos, spelling out the key issues and the weak points in the arguments presented on both sides. On Saturday mornings, O'Connor and her clerks get together in her chambers to talk over the cases that will be heard in the coming week.

Given her preparedness, quite often an argument has just begun when O'Connor jabs a gaping hole in a lawyer's argument: "Well, Mr. Olson," she began, "I guess in theory an employer could comply with the California law by offering female employees a pregnancy leave and comply with Title VII [the federal law] by offering a comparable leave to other disabled employees. If that is the case, how is the California law preempted?"

Olson was forced to concede "it is theoretically possible, as you suggest," for California employers to comply with both laws by giving disabled men up to four months of unpaid leave. However, he called that solution "an end run" around the issue because the state lawmakers did not intend to give a new benefit to men. Nonetheless, O'Connor's question took much of the steam out of Cal Fed's argument. It also suggested that the challengers had already lost one key vote—O'Connor's.

Still, it was not clear how the rest of the justices would vote. Would they uphold the California law because it was in the spirit of the federal law aiding pregnant women, or would they strike it down based on the strict *same treatment* language of the federal act?

Rehnquist, in his 1987 book *The Supreme Court: How It Was, How It Is,* said that when he leaves the bench after an oral argument, he believes he is in the best position he will ever be to decide the case. He has (a) read the briefs on both sides, (b) read how lower-court judges have decided the same case, (c) looked back at previous Court rulings that could provide a precedent, and (d) heard two half-hour-long arguments on the issue. Rehnquist then mused that in an ideal world, perhaps, the justices could sit and contemplate their decision for weeks, or even months. They could have long, roundtable talks on the issue and its ramifications. Certainly, they could read more briefs and law review articles. Rehnquist said, "It is much easier to read what someone else has said about a particular legal problem than to figure out what YOU think about it."

The actual demands of the Supreme Court, however, require the justices to decide what they think rather quickly. Two days after the *Cal Fed* arguments, at 9:30 on Friday morning, October 10, 1986, the justices gathered alone in the conference room to vote on that case and seven others.

Rehnquist had been much criticized for his 1976 opinion in the GE case. Congressional Democrats said that it showed the Court to be out of touch with the intent of Congress. Women's rights groups said it showed his insensitivity to women. Over the years on the Court, however, Rehnquist had turned a deaf ear to criticism from the left. As chief justice, he was not about to change.

Rehnquist led off the discussion by casting his vote with Cal Fed to strike down the state's pregnancy law because it violated the language of the federal statute. Justice Brennan, at the opposite end of the table, as usual, took the opposite position. Congress sought to prevent discrimination that would hurt working women, not to prevent extra measures that would protect women. When the discussion moved around the table, it was clear that Brennan had the majority. Only justices White and Powell sided with Rehnquist.

The real surprise came last. Justice Scalia, the new conservative, voted to uphold the California law, but for quite a different reason than the liberals. Court liberals Brennan, Marshall, and Blackmun said that the Court could study what members of Congress said in 1978 to discern the meaning of the federal act. Because these legislators spoke of wanting to help pregnant women, not restricting their benefits, the Court could uphold the California law, the liberals reasoned. They took the same approach on "affirmative action." Because the 1964 Civil Rights Act was intended to aid blacks, the Court was justified in reading it to allow employers to give preferences to blacks.

Scalia wanted no part of this. He believed Brennan's approach was too subjective, too political. Judges, if they were so inclined, could read whatever they wanted into the "legislative history." On any complex piece of legislation, the *Congressional Record* displays a series of vague, even contradictory statements by members of the House and Senate on the meaning of the law. Scalia, like many other conservatives, could grow livid recounting the history of the 1964 Civil Rights Act. It clearly barred racial discrimination against "any individual"—black or white, male or female. Yet by the late 1970s, the Supreme Court read this law to permit "affirmative" preferences for some persons because of their race or gender.

All that counts, Scalia maintained, was the language of the law itself, *not* its "intent" or its "spirit." Scalia's father, the professor of Romance languages, had made a career of translating texts. Words and their precise meanings were his life. Now his son, Justice Antonin Scalia, followed the same approach. It did not matter to him what the legislators were thinking of. What did the words of the law say?

By this approach, Scalia might have been inclined to join Rehnquist. After all, the 1978 Pregnancy Discrimination Act said women should get the "same treatment" as men. However, in Scalia's view, the chief justice had not read enough of the law. The 1978 law was attached to Title VII of the 1964 law, which says quite clearly that it is not intended to preempt state laws. "Nothing in this subchapter shall be deemed to exempt or relieve any person from any liability, duty, penalty or punishment [provided] by any present or future law of any *state* or political subdivision of the state," the federal law says. Moreover, "Nothing contained in any title of this Act shall be construed as indicating an intent on the part of Congress to occupy the field . . . to the exclusion of *state* laws on the same subject."

For Scalia, this language settled the matter. If the federal law said it did *not* preempt related state laws, Cal Fed could not go to a federal court and use it as a basis to be exempted from a state law. "Nothing more is needed to decide this case," Scalia wrote in a short concurring opinion issued on January 13, 1987.

Somewhat unexpectedly, Brennan assigned the majority opinion to Marshall. It was rare for Marshall, then 78, to be asked to write the opinion in a significant case. His colleagues realized that this assignment meant that the Court would be speaking through the voice of a 25-year-old law clerk. Marshall took a hands-off approach to the opinion writing. He was old, overweight, and short of breath, and his eyesight was failing. In fact, in one sense, Marshall had much in common with his nemesis Ronald Reagan: Both focused on the big picture. They knew what they believed but chose to leave the details to their aides.

"He didn't write anything my year, but I still think he could," said one clerk. A clerk from the following year said the same thing. In fact, Marshall practiced only an extreme version of the common pattern at the Court. The clerks draft most of the majority and dissenting opinions for most of the justices. Some justices heavily edit or substantially rewrite the clerks' writings, but only a few justices—notably Scalia and Stevens—turn out opinions that feature their own characteristic style.

In addition, it is a well-known but little-discussed Washington phenomenon that the nation's premier political personalities—from the president and candidates for the presidency to Cabinet secretaries and members of Congress—speak to the public in words written for them by anonymous young speechwriters. Defenders of the practice make two points: First, the politicians are saying what they want to communicate, not what a young speechwriter thinks or believes. For example, though Ronald Reagan and Ted Kennedy have each employed many speechwriters over many years, each seems to express his same ideas over and over; no one would mistake a Reagan speech for a Kennedy speech, or vice versa. Second, writers are better at writing than are politicians.

The justices say much the same when asked about law clerks writing Court opinions. "The law clerk is not off on a frolic of his own" when he or she drafts a Court opinion, Rehnquist once said. Rather, the justice tells the clerk the conclusion the opinion must reach, as well as the legal rationale for getting there. The clerks have some freedom, but not much. Their discretion is rather like Brennan's invitation to his clerks to help him with choosing new carpets and curtains for his chambers. "You can pick any color," he said, "so long as it's green."

Rehnquist gives his clerks ten days to draft an opinion for him to review. In large part, the opinions merely recount the facts of a case, with the decisions of the lower courts that heard it, and then string together snippets of language of Court precedents to justify the new ruling. These are decidedly not essays on the law.

In the early years of the twentieth century, the Court opinions of Oliver Wendell Holmes made him an international figure. Each morning, he arose at his Washington, D.C., townhouse and spent the morning writing at his desk. His secretary typed the opinions, and they were issued by the Court as he wrote them. These days, a Court opinion is probably put together by a clerk, relying mostly on language from earlier opinions. The justices whose names go on it may contribute a few paragraphs, but these days no one confuses Court opinions with literature. Usually, they are bland and bloodless works. Even in a 20-page opinion, it can be hard to find a single fresh word or thought.

Marshall's chambers were still unique in one sense: While the other justices focused on hard details of the legal analysis—and especially on the key words that stated the ruling—Marshall left that work to his clerks. When assigned an opinion, he gave the clerks a few words of guidance and sent them to work. "It's the best job in the building. You have enormous discretion and no authority," said one clerk.

Still, Thurgood Marshall had a powerful presence on the Court and around the nation, one that went far beyond legal opinions or legal theories. He was, in the view of many law experts, the greatest American lawyer of the twentieth century. As lead counsel for the NAACP Legal Defense Fund, he had led a legal revolution that swept away government-sanctioned segregation. He had argued 32 cases before the Supreme Court and won 29 of them, including *Brown* v. *Board of Education.*

"In three decades he has probably done as much to transform the life of his people as any Negro alive today, including Nobel laureate Martin Luther King, Jr.," *Newsweek* magazine observed in 1967, upon Marshall's appointment to the Supreme Court. In the 1950s and early 1960s, King led the civil rights revolution in the streets of the South while Marshall fought in the federal courts. It is not clear that one could have succeeded without the other.

To white Americans, Marshall today is known, if at all, as the first black person to sit on the Supreme Court. In newspaper clippings, he was usually counted as a dissenting liberal, a voice from the past. In an occasional television appearance, he appeared to be an old, overweight fellow who mumbles.

To African-Americans, however, Marshall is held in extraordinary esteem, not only as having been one of the nation's most powerful blacks, but as one who used his life and power to win legal equality for all. In a magazine profile of him, *Washington Post* writer Juan Williams recounted Marshall's trudging walk into a Washington hotel to give a speech. "Black bellhops and maids and doormen freeze in place, pointing. Black waiters and waitresses begin streaming out of the kitchen for a glimpse of the man. Elderly black people, some with tears in their eyes, stand on tiptoes to see better and wave."

Marshall had grown up just 40 miles away from that Washington, D.C., hotel, but several eras away in American social history. Born July 2, 1908, as Thoroughgood Marshall, he was raised in a comfortable middle-class home in the Druid Hill neighborhood of Baltimore. Though his great-grandfather began life as a slave, both of his grandfathers owned grocery stores in Baltimore. His father worked as the head steward at an exclusive yacht club on the Chesapeake Bay, and his mother taught elementary school. No one claims that young Thoroughgood was thoroughly good. He is invariably described as having been ornery as a child, not a true troublemaker but a class cutup. His misbehavior in class gave him his first encounter with the U.S. Constitution. As punishment, he was required to stay after school and memorize a portion of the document. "Before I left that school, I knew the whole thing by heart," he said years later. Before leaving elementary school, he also shortened his name to something more manageable: Thurgood.

Though young Marshall grew up in a secure and happy home, much of Baltimore was off-limits to him. The downtown department stores excluded blacks, as did many of the city's restaurants and hotels. Marshall could attend only a "colored school" in the city. He could not go to the University of Maryland or its law school in Baltimore, as only whites were admitted then. "The only thing different between the South and Baltimore was trolley cars," Marshall recalled in an interview. "They weren't segregated. Everything else was segregated."

After graduating from high school in 1925, he enrolled in Lincoln University, a highly regarded black college just above the Mason-Dixon line in Oxford, Pennsylvania. His fellow students included the dancer Cab Calloway and the writer Langston Hughes, who later described Marshall as "the loudest individual in the dormitory, good natured, rough, ready and uncouth." As a college student, Marshall played lots of card games, according to his own account. "He posted a B average in his academic work while encouraging the firm conviction among his classmates that he never cracked a book," author Richard Kluger says of Marshall in Simple Justice, his monumental history of the Brown case. In his senior year, Marshall married and was forced to settle down. The new graduate and his wife, Vivian, returned to his parents' home in Baltimore the next year. Because the Maryland law school was closed to him, he enrolled instead in the Howard University Law School, an hour's train ride away in Washington, D.C.

Howard University changed Marshall's life—and ultimately the law of the land. Until then, segregation had been simply a fact of life to him. However, the new Harvard-educated dean, Charles H. Houston, trained his students to believe that it was not a fact they should accept. Segregation was wrong, unequal, and unconstitutional under the Fourteenth Amendment, he said. His students—the best and brightest among young black attorneys—would have to end it through the courts.

Houston recognized that if his students were to be effective, he first must prepare them to be good lawyers. For young Marshall, it demanded a killer regimen. Up at dawn, he took a train to Washington to be there for 8 A.M. classes. Because of a job in the law library, he couldn't leave the campus until 8 in the evening. According to Marshall, simply due to the strain and the long hours he lost 30 pounds in his first year at Howard. Nonetheless, he survived and eventually graduated first in his class. He began a law practice during the depths of the depression. Marshall operated a none-too-successful, one-man law firm near downtown Baltimore, but his Howard training had inspired him to use his legal skills to battle segregation and racial inequality. Finally, he got his chance, thanks to his Howard University mentor.

In 1933, Houston set up the NAACP Legal Defense Fund in New York. In 1936, when he decided to return to Washington, he picked Marshall to take his place. For the next 25 years, Marshall traveled the country representing blacks in the courts for the NAACP. Usually, he confronted a white prosecutor, a white judge, and an all-white jury sitting in the Deep South. A victory, he said later, often meant that his client was sentenced only to life in prison. Often as not, the conviction of a black man for rape was followed by an execution. His acquaintances and law clerks say that Marshall never got over these experiences of the late 1930s and 1940s. Day after day, he confronted racism of the worst sort. By comparison, the segregated Baltimore of his youth was almost benign. Traveling as a black lawyer in the South, he and his clients heard themselves referred to as "nigger" routinely. Blacks were presumed guilty until proven innocent. Those years stamped on Marshall's mind two views that he never lost: (1) that a death sentence imposed by a court is inherently arbitrary and cruel, and (2) that white America is hopelessly imbued with racism.

Certainly, as his Supreme Court colleagues attest, those years furnished him with a lifetime supply of stories. Around the conference table, Marshall displayed no interest in legal theories. He cared about people and the impact of the law on their lives. Like Ronald Reagan, he always had a story to illustrate his point. "It was a hell of a treat just to listen to him," said one law clerk. "He had seen a world that none of us have known or ever will."

Though he told of good times, such as partying in Harlem with boxing great Joe Louis or bandleader Duke Ellington, most of his stories dealt with legal work in the South. In one story, Marshall arrived in town only to learn that his client had been lynched that afternoon. Another told of a woman's last-minute recantation of a rape charge that spared another client a similar fate. Still another recounted a southern sheriff standing on a train platform and telling the black attorney in no uncertain terms: "The sun never set on a nigger in this town." Marshall said he could take a hint. He boarded the next train.

Some of his clerks say Marshall's personal history was both a strength and a weakness. He had seen racism and injustice and could talk of it as if it happened yesterday. "He is the only one of them who could tell stories about a man about to be lynched," one clerk said. Indeed, Marshall was the only one of his colleagues with real trial experience in criminal cases. "But that world no longer exists," the clerk added. "It left him as a relic of the world that is gone."

By 1986, a half century after Marshall began his pioneering work for the NAACP Legal Defense Fund, he looked to be a relic of a once-dynamic lawyer. Badly overweight, he walked with a painfully slow gait. His eyes looked watery and blurred; he could read only large type. Each morning, he gasped for breath as the justices mounted the few steps to take their seats. His questions to attorneys often came out as an inaudible gurgle. When called upon to read an opinion, he frequently stumbled over the words. In one tax case, he struggled with the word *subsidiary* for an embarrassing moment: "subs . . . subs . . . subsidary [*sic*]."

In his chambers, Marshall had what one clerk called a "drop-dead sense of humor" that some found roguish and others considered rude. For example, a clerk who hailed from Georgia was referred to as "boy"—just a little dig to keep a white southerner in his place. At one reception, Marshall recounted the details of a pornographic movie he had seen. In the cafeteria or at receptions, he would turn grouchy if a stranger tried to take his photograph or shake his hand. "One shake for you, a hundred for me," he groused. A friend recounted seeing a man approach Marshall and say, "You remember me, don't you?" Without pausing even to look at him, Marshall replied, "Of course I don't."

Even the justices were not spared. Marshall enjoyed irritating the pompous Burger. "What's shakin', chief baby," he said to him on one occasion.

The clerks were particularly amused to hear reports of the hallway encounters between a grouchy Marshall and the courtly Lewis Powell. For most of his life, Marshall had diligently avoided any form of exercise, but in 1986 his doctors ordered him to make an effort to keep moving. So, each morning he would trudge along the carpeted hallway until he had completed a lap or two around the building. Often he would encounter the dignified and soft-spoken Powell taking his morning walk in the opposite direction.

"Good morning, Thurgood," Powell said.

"What's so good about it?" Marshall grumbled.

The next time around, as the two nearly 80-year-old gentlemen converged, Marshall's mood had improved.

"I'm gaining on you," he warned.

On the bench, Marshall often looked bored, his mind elsewhere, as the justices heard arguments on an arcane question of maritime or administrative law. Once, during an argument in a tax case, Marshall leaned over to Powell and whispered, "I'll trade you my vote in this case for a future draft pick."

When confronted with a case involving an injustice against a poor and ordinary American, however, Marshall was alert and alive—and downright angry. Lillian Garland's complaint against the California S&L had Marshall riled up. Here was a young black mother who wanted to have a baby and then get her job back, and the S&L industry had hired a posse of high-priced lawyers to argue that the federal law designed to protect the rights of pregnant workers actually forbids giving a pregnant woman a few weeks of unpaid leave to recover from the birth. Marshall was furious.

On January 22, Marshall announced the Court's ruling from the bench. The California law would stand, and the S&L lawyers had lost. The 18-page opinion emphasized that nothing in the 1978 law could be read to "prohibit preferential treatment" for pregnant women. Justices Brennan, Blackmun, Stevens, and O'Connor joined in signing Marshall's majority opinion. Scalia filed his short, separate statement, agreeing with the outcome but not joining Marshall's opinion. Rehnquist assigned the dissent to White. He insisted that the clear language of the 1978 law gave ample reason to strike down what he called the "preferential" state law.

The Court's 6–3 ruling in *Cal Fed* v. *Guerra* had the effect of upholding similar laws in eight other states. It also gave a green light to lawmakers in other states to insist that young mothers not lose their jobs.

For Lillian Garland, the ruling had no immediate impact. She had since left Cal Fed and gone to work for a real estate firm. Nonetheless, she said she was proud of what her case had wrought for young mothers of the future. "I didn't think you should be penalized or lose your job just because you want to have a baby," she said.

Each year during the 1980s, an average of more than 20,000 persons were murdered in the United States. In slightly less than half of those murder cases, a suspect was convicted of the murder. Each year, a dozen or so of those convicted killers were put to death, nearly all of them in the Deep South.

Such is the strange world of crime and capital punishment. Most Americans have two notions about the death penalty. Callous killers, indifferent to their victims, should face the ultimate punishment of death. At the same time, no suspected murderers should be executed until they have been tried, convicted, and sentenced in a way that is entirely fair and just. The Supreme Court, in dozens of cases each year, tries to reconcile those notions. How can the justices assure themselves that the ultimate punishment is given to only the most depraved killers?

In 1972, the Court threw up its hands in despair. Getting a death sentence in the United States seemed akin to being struck by lightning, the Court concluded, more a matter of bad luck than deserved punishment. Even within the same state, a rapist in one county would get a death sentence, while a convicted multiple murderer in a different county would not. Because the system of capital punishment was "irrational and arbitrary," the Court voted 5–4 to strike down all of the nation's capital punishment laws in the case of *Furman* v. *Georgia.*

Two moderate conservatives—Byron White and Potter Stewart—cast the key votes. They were joined by three liberals—Brennan, Marshall, and William O. Douglas—who believed the death penalty was absolutely unconstitutional. The four Nixon appointees—Rehnquist, Powell, Blackmun, and Burger—dissented.

Four years later, the states had changed their laws. Judges and juries were given guidance to pick out the worst of the murderers: the calculated killers rather than the barroom brawlers, for example. The Court had changed too. Gone was Douglas, replaced by Gerald Ford's appointee, John Paul Stevens. In addition, Stewart and White had changed their minds, as the death penalty no longer appeared to be random. On a 6–3 vote in the case of *Gregg* v. *Georgia,* the Court reinstated capital punishment in 1976.

Nonetheless, the questions continued. Ensuring fairness in each case appeared to be a never-ending task. In a typical year, the Court issued written opinions in about 150 cases, and about a dozen of them concerned capital punishment. No detail seemed too small to consider if the end of the case meant an execution.

Take, for example, a case heard in December 1986. Under California law, the jurors who must decide whether to send a convicted killer to prison or the gas chamber were told, among other things, not to "be swayed by mere sentiment, conjecture, sympathy, passion, [or] prejudice." Do those words stack the deck against the defendant? Yes, said the liberal California State Supreme Court. The U.S. Constitution requires that jurors be permitted to feel sympathy for the accused, it ruled.

True enough, said Rehnquist, but "mere sympathy" is another matter. On January 27, 1987, Rehnquist read an opinion for a 5–4 majority reversing the decision of the California court and upholding the state's death penalty law. The "reasonable juror" would understand, Rehnquist said, that he or she is being told to "ignore emotional responses" to the case, but not to ignore "sympathy" based on the evidence.

Rehnquist had long been fed up with the nit-picking and handwringing over the death penalty. Liberal judges insisted on finding reasons to block the death sentences, not because the Constitution demanded it but because they opposed the death penalty. The Constitution itself mentions "capital" crimes and says no one may be "deprived of life . . . without due process of law." Therefore, once given "due process of law" in the courts, a killer may be "deprived of life," Rehnquist maintained. In his view, the Constitution requires that the accused have a fair trial—but nothing more. It is up to the people and their legislators—not the Supreme Court—to decide whether the death penalty should be used.

Nonetheless, the fight went on, year in and year out. Brennan and Marshall pressed and cajoled in hopes of abolishing capital punishment. They simply refused to abide by the Court's precedents upholding capital punishment as constitutional. Instead, they filed a pro forma dissent in each case, restating their view that capital punishment was unconstitutional. On occasion, Stevens, Blackmun, Powell, and White would join them in a particular case. Rehnquist could always be counted on to give the thumbs down.

All the while, the Court also struggled with questions of race and discrimination. Many looked back on the *Brown* v. *Board of Education* ruling outlawing official segregation as the Court's proudest moment in the twentieth century. Even so, that ruling, too, spurred more questions, and nearly every year the Court agreed to consider disputes over alleged racial discrimination in schools, housing, voting, and jobs.

Finally, in the 1986 term, those two core concerns of the Court came together in one case: Was the death penalty infected with racial discrimination? Appropriately enough, the case of *McCleskey* v. *Kemp* came from Georgia, one of the big four states in executions. Thirty-six states authorized the death penalty and shipped convicts to Death Row, but executions remained a phenomenon of the South. By 1990, 120 persons had been put to death since the Gregg ruling restored capital punishment, and 86 of them, or nearly three-fourths of the total, had been executed in four southern states: Texas, Florida, Louisiana, and Georgia.

The death penalty was enormously popular—as Massachusetts governor Michael Dukakis was to learn during the 1988 campaign—but it was especially so in the South. It was hard to get elected as governor, state legislator, or district attorney if you were unduly squeamish about capital punishment.

On the other side of the battle lines was the NAACP Legal Defense Fund. In the 1950s and 1960s, the fund and its attorneys had used the federal courts to dismantle segregation in the South. Ever since then, they had been trying to do the same to the death penalty. For these modern-day "abolitionists," optimism over ending capital punishment waxed in the late 1960s and early 1970s but waned as conservative appointees replaced aging liberals. By the Reagan years of the 1980s, the death penalty had faded as a national issue, pushed aside by abortion and affirmative action.

Nonetheless, the Legal Defense Fund (LDF) attorneys had not given up. Their last, best hope for abolishing the death penalty, they figured, was a direct attack in the Supreme Court, focused on racial discrimination. Even the justices with conservative instincts on crime, such as White, Blackmun, Powell, and O'Connor, were clearly troubled by allegations of racial bias. They knew that in a nation whose history and laws had been tainted by race, the possibility of racial bias could not be ignored.

Just a year earlier, the Court had overturned a long-standing precedent and ruled that prosecutors may not systematically exclude blacks from juries. Now, the stakes were even bigger.

"Around the building, I think everyone saw *McCleskey* as the biggest case of the year," said a clerk who served in the 1986 term. "It was an all-or-nothing case."

John Charles Boger, the LDF attorney leading the attack on the death penalty, says he was shocked when the Court agreed to hear the case. "It was such a clear-cut challenge to the death penalty that I thought they would duck it," he said.

The case had been staged and managed by the LDF, but not everything had gone entirely according to plan. Boger had succeeded in forcing the Court to look at the big picture of capital punishment in the South, but the Death Row inmate appealing his sentence was the most unsympathetic of characters: a cold-blooded cop killer.

The case developed in this way. The LDF employed University of Iowa law professor David Baldus, along with sociologists and statisticians, to compile detailed data on how Georgia prosecuted and punished murderers. Between 1974 and 1979, 2,484 homicides took place in Georgia in which a suspect was arrested. About two-thirds of those murders involved blacks—as victims and as perpetrators. However, the murder cases that resulted in death sentences stood out from the rest, and not just because the crime was more heinous. Usually the victim was white, and quite often the perpetrator was black. The contrast in punishment between black and white victims was stark.

The data did not show a bias against black defendants. Rather, the raw numbers showed that four percent of the blacks who committed murder received death sentences, compared to seven percent of the whites.

Baldus then analyzed the data using 39 factors that measured the severity of the crime—such as whether a gun was used, whether a robbery occurred, whether the killer knew the victim, and whether the defendant had a criminal record. His intent was to compare similar crimes, but including the many factors did not change the conclusion shown by the raw numbers: Killers of whites were punished more severely than killers of blacks. In Georgia, the murderer of a white was 4.3 times more likely to get a death sentence than one who murders a black, he concluded.

Race of Killer/Victim	Number with Death Sentence			Percentage
Black/White	50	of	223	22%
White/White	58	of	748	8%
Black/Black	18	of	1,443	1%
White/Black	2	of	60	3%

Totals by Victim	Numbers of Death Sentences	Percentage
White victim	108 of 981	11%
Black victim	20 of 1,503	1%

Of course, the LDF could not simply put the Baldus study in an envelope and mail it to the Supreme Court. First, they needed a case that had been fully considered and ruled upon by a judge, then appealed up through the system. So, the LDF went shopping for a judge.

When murderers are convicted and sentenced to death, they have an automatic right to appeal up to the state supreme court and on to the U.S. Supreme Court. That is not the end of the road, however. Under the Habeas Corpus Act of 1867, state prison inmates can file a petition in a federal court contending that they are being held in violation of their constitutional rights. Typically, when an execution date draws near, lawyers for Death Row inmates deluge the nearest federal judge with a series of "habeas corpus petitions," claiming that their clients' rights were violated somewhere during their arrest, trial, conviction, or sentence. If a claim appears to have some validity, the U.S. judge can stay the execution order and conduct a triallike hearing to consider the evidence.

Armed with the Baldus study, attorney Boger filed petitions with judges in 30 different cases, contending that the statistics showed Georgia's capital punishment system to be racially biased. Finally, a new Reagan appointee, Judge Owen Forrester, agreed to consider the evidence. The inmate's name on the petition happened to be Warren McCleskey. For Boger and the LDF, that turned out to be a bad break.

On May 13, 1978, McCleskey and three accomplices drove around Marietta, Georgia, outside of Atlanta, looking for someone or something to rob. They settled on the Dixie Furniture Store. Armed with a stolen .38-caliber revolver, Mc-

Cleskey and his friends entered the store, rounded up the employees, and tied them up with tape—but not before a silent alarm was sounded. Officer Frank Schlatt pulled his patrol car up to the front of the store and came walking down its main aisle. Suddenly, two shots rang out. Bullets from a .38-caliber revolver struck Officer Schlatt in the chest and in the face, and he died. A few weeks later, McCleskey was arrested during another robbery, and in his Fulton County jail cell, he told a fellow inmate of shooting the police officer.

On October 12, 1978, McCleskey was convicted of two counts of armed robbery and one count of murder and was sentenced to death. His three accomplices received sentences of life in prison. If it were not for attorney Boger and Judge Forrester, McCleskey would not have been heard from again, but for a brief mention on the day of his execution.

Now, like Linda Brown in the case of *Brown* v. *Board of Education* or Ernesto Miranda in the case of *Miranda* v. *Arizona*, Warren McCleskey would, through no effort of his own, get his name on a landmark Supreme Court case.

The briefs submitted to the Court supported not one conclusion, but two. Warren McCleskey was a cop killer, properly convicted. If anyone was a good candidate for the death penalty, he was. At the same time, racial bias appeared to be at work in Georgia. The Baldus study did not *prove* that death sentences were handed out according to race; no statistical study could prove that. Similarly, no medical study had *proven* that smoking cigarettes caused lung cancer; rather, the studies show only a statistical correlation between smoking and cancer. Smoking cigarettes increases your risk of dying of lung cancer. The Baldus study showed a statistical correlation between your race, your victim's race, and your likelihood of getting a death sentence. In Georgia, killing a white person increases your risk of dying in the electric chair, at least when compared to killing a black person. Even McCleskey's own case illustrated that point. Between 1973 and 1979, 17 persons were charged with killing a police officer in Fulton County. Most of them were serving long prison terms. Only one, McCleskey, had received a death sentence.

Boger theorized that local district attorneys (DAs) were the main source of bias. If a middle-class white home owner were robbed and murdered, a local DA would see the crime as a major one—no plea bargains, no reduced charges for a guilty plea. The prosecutor would seek the death penalty—that is, if the DA wanted to keep public support and remain the DA. However, if the home owner were black, a plea bargain might be arranged. The defendant would plead guilty in exchange for a 20-year prison term.

Boger, in his brief to the Court, also urged the justices to look at history. Before the Civil War, blacks in Georgia could be beaten, even murdered, by whites and the crimes would go unpunished. At the same time, blacks could be hung for any assault on a white. In the days following the Civil War, Union officers patrolled the South and found that little had changed. In late 1865, Congress's Joint Committee on Reconstruction heard testimony regarding how crimes against blacks went unpunished. One example, cited in the court record, came from Major General George A. Custer, who, 11 years before his "last stand" in Montana, was part of the occupying Union Army in Texas. "It is of weekly, if not of daily, occurrence that freedmen are murdered," Custer testified. "Sometimes it is not known who the perpetrators are; but when that is known, no action is taken against them. I believe a white man has never been hung for murder in Texas, although it is the law."

That sort of testimony spurred the Congress to amend the Constitution to ensure that no state "deny to any person within its jurisdiction the equal protection of the laws." That is why Georgia's capital punishment system should be found unconstitutional, Boger contended. Crimes against blacks were not being treated equally with crimes against whites. Until Georgia officials can explain a constitutionally valid reason for the discrepancy, the system should be presumed unconstitutional, Boger said.

Representing Georgia was the state's assistant attorney general, Mary Beth Westmoreland. (In keeping with the formal practice, Rehnquist introduced her at the argument as "General Westmoreland.") She argued that the justices should look at the trees, not at the forest. McCleskey was a killer, properly tried and convicted, under procedures that were almost identical to those drawn up by the Supreme Court. "Although statistics are a useful tool in many contexts," her brief stated, "in the situation presented involving the application of the death penalty, there are simply too many unique factors relevant to each individual case to allow statistics to be an effective tool in proving intentional discrimination."

In several friend-of-the-court briefs, sociologists and statisticians showed that the same pattern of unequal punishments evident in Georgia was also apparent in Florida, Texas, and other southern states. The briefs were intended to bolster Boger's attack on Georgia, but they also made clear to the several wavering justices that a ruling against Georgia probably meant the end of the death penalty in America.

Brennan thought the LDF attorneys had presented a powerful case. Who could deny that racial discrimination played a role in capital punishment? The numbers compiled by Professor Baldus told a tale of blatant bias, and the Georgia state attorneys had not even bothered to rebut the statistics as inaccurate. In Brennan's view, the death penalty was abominable in any situation, but it was especially so when it was tinged with racism. In his early years, blacks in Georgia were lynched for crimes that would have earned a white man a few years behind bars. Certainly, the nation had made progress since then, but how could the Court stop now and turn away from such a blatantly biased method of meting out punishment?

Brennan sent his clerks scouting out the views of the others around the building. Though the justices rarely talk among themselves about the cases before they come up for decision, the clerks do. "The clerks serve as the grapevine around here," said one justice.

Brennan began with one sure vote—Marshall's—and could be reasonably certain of two more. Blackmun and Stevens, the two midwestern Republicans, did not want to be seen as "liberals" on crime cases, but they would not ignore the strong whiff of race discrimination at work here. That is what the Fourteenth Amendment was intended to halt.

Figuring out how White would vote was more difficult, however. As usual, White's clerks had no idea of what he was thinking. He met with them to go over cases, but the justice never tipped his hand. He mostly listened and said little. He had been hurt by *The Brethren,* Bob Woodward and Scott Armstrong's book about the inner workings of the Court—not by what was said about him, but because his personal comments in chambers had found their way into print. Normally a reserved man, White had been particularly sphinxlike around his clerks ever since.

For a fifth vote for Brennan in the McCleskey case, Powell looked like the best prospect, and O'Connor was not beyond hope either. Both voted regularly to uphold the death penalty and took a hard line on crime, but on civil rights matters both had also joined Brennan before. Just the year before, Powell

wrote an opinion overturning a 20-year precedent and ruling
that a criminal conviction can be overturned if the prosecutor
showed a pattern of racial bias in selecting jurors. White and
O'Connor had joined Powell's opinion. For Brennan, this precedent gave a solid basis for overturning Georgia's system. If
the Court, with near unanimity, could act in the face of evidence that prosecutors showed bias in choosing jurors, how
could it ignore even more powerful evidence showing that
prosecutors were displaying bias in choosing candidates for the
electric chair?

Also, as the oral argument approached, Boger, the LDF
attorney, had not even given up on Scalia. "I figured he was a
quick study on the statistics. He knew the numbers were solid,"
Boger said. Boger's optimism would have been dashed, however, had he spoken to the old warrior of the NAACP LDF,
Thurgood Marshall.

Marshall "never thought McCleskey was going anywhere.
He didn't think the white guys would buy the statistics," a
former clerk said.

At 10 A.M. on October 15, 1986, the chief justice intoned,
"We will hear arguments first this morning in No. 84–6811,
Warren McCleskey v. *Ralph Kemp* (a Georgia prison director).
Mr. Boger, you may proceed when you are ready."

Boger hadn't proceeded far into his argument when Byron
White interrupted, seeking to know who put together the studies. After several questions and answers, it turned out that
White wanted to put on the record a small point. Young law
students had gone through the court records in Georgia and
had charted the information.

"Were any of them law graduates?" White asked. Yes,
Boger said, citing a name or two. "Sooner or later," White
grumbled. It was an odd line of questioning, considering that
the Supreme Court justices rely on young people fresh out of
law school to handle much of their work. That is, it was odd,
but not unusual for White.

For years, White has butted heads with the attorneys who
have appeared before the Court. His questions are gruff and
intimidating, just like White himself. He had come to the Court
in 1962, the first appointee of John F. Kennedy. He certainly
fit the New Frontier image of the Kennedy administration: He
was smart, young, and tough, a scholar and an athlete, the ideal

combination of brains and brawn. He was no legal academic or scholarly judge, but he had "seen life," Kennedy said in announcing the appointment. "He has excelled in everything he has attempted—in his academic life, in his military service, in his career before the bar and in the federal government—and I know that he will excel on the highest court in the land," Kennedy said.

Now, more than a quarter of a century after the Kennedy administration passed into history, leaving behind an image of grace and eloquence and a budding commitment to civil rights, who would recognize Byron White as the last representative of the Kennedy years in government? Perhaps it is unfair to hang the Kennedy legacy on White's shoulders, especially since JFK's image as a liberal glowed most brightly after his death. Nonetheless, by the mid-1980s, no one labeled White a liberal. He had become an opponent of affirmative action, a fierce critic of the right to abortion, and a reliable vote with Rehnquist in criminal cases. On the bench and around the Court, White looked to be more of a product of his early years than of his brief tenure in the Kennedy administration.

When he was 20 years old, Byron Raymond White had a name known throughout the nation, although it was a name he despised. In 1937, "Whizzer" White was simply the nation's best college football player. He was tough and mean, with thick forearms and a bull-like neck. As a 6-foot-1-inch halfback for the University of Colorado, he had the speed to run around defenders but preferred to run over them.

"The guy had the strongest forearms and chest development I ever saw. He was hard as iron all over," recalled Frank Potts, an assistant football coach during White's years at Boulder. "He could blast tacklers out of the way with the forearm and get away with it. He was just plain mean and ornery and tenacious. But he wasn't dirty. Just mean."

He was an all-around talent too. He punted, kicked field goals, threw passes, and returned kicks, including a 95-yard runback that beat Utah in his senior year. He led the nation in rushing, scoring, and total offense. He also excelled in basketball, although the game resembled football when he played it. "He was a bruiser," a *Denver Post* writer said of White the basketball player. "There was nothing skillful about it. He was all elbows."

Though undeniably a star, White hardly resembled today's football heroes. No one could imagine Byron White dancing in the end zone or spiking a ball to highlight a touchdown. Modest and shy, White actually resented all the attention given his football exploits. He had gone to the university on an academic scholarship. Football was only a pastime. He went to college to get a degree, not to earn stardom on the gridiron. He did not like adoring sports writers and certainly did not like being dubbed "Whizzer." At the end of an undefeated season, White shocked the university and the entire state of Colorado by leading a move within the team to refuse an invitation to play in the Cotton Bowl. Preparing for a New Year's Day game would interfere with studying for final exams, White had asserted.

He was born June 8, 1917, and grew up poor in Wellington, Colorado, a sugar-beet-growing community. His father, a staunch Republican, ran a lumber-supply business. Young Byron worked picking beets, which he said gave him his strong arms, and also worked on a rail crew. As a college student, he took a variety of odd jobs to make ends meet, including serving tables and pulling weeds at the stadium. His mother had stressed the importance of education for him and for his older brother, who became a doctor and a medical researcher.

White's response to the Cotton Bowl seemed natural. With White, academics came first. It took a visit from the governor and university officials before White and his teammates relented. They would go to the Cotton Bowl, they said, but only with the understanding that there would be no team practices until they finished with finals. Colorado lost to Rice in the bowl game, but the star halfback graduated first in his class of 1938. He had had only two B grades: in public speaking and sociology. As a stellar student and school leader, he won a Rhodes scholarship to study at Oxford University. At the same time, the professional Pittsburgh Pirates (soon to be renamed the "Steelers") team offered him $15,800 to play football for them in the fall, the highest amount paid to any player in the league. When Oxford agreed to delay his arrival, White signed the contract. "How can I refuse an offer like that? It will pay my way through law school," he said. Naturally enough, the rookie White led the National Football League in rushing.

When the season ended, he went off to Oxford, but his studies were cut short when England went to war in September 1939. He did, however, make one very important contact. In London, he met and became friends with the American ambassador's son, John F. Kennedy. When he returned to the states, he entered the Yale Law School, but he also played football on weekends for the Detroit Lions in 1940 and 1941. To Yale students, White resembled Superman. On weekdays, he played Clark Kent, a quiet, studious figure in steel-rimmed glasses. On weekends, he changed into a brutish and glamorous football star.

In 1941, he tried to join the U.S. Marines but was turned down because of his color blindness. The next year, he joined the Navy and became an intelligence officer based in the Solomon Islands. There, he again met up with Jack Kennedy and wrote the official report on the sinking of Kennedy's PT 109. After returning to civilian life, White completed his law degree in 1946 and won a clerkship at the Supreme Court with Chief Justice Fred Vinson. Just a block away was the office of the newly elected Massachusetts representative, John F. Kennedy (JFK).

White could have gone to any elite law firm in the country after his year at the Court, but none of the New York and Washington firms would guarantee him a partnership within two years. So he returned to Denver with his new wife, Marion Stearns, the daughter of the University of Colorado president. In Denver, he worked for 13 years as a lawyer, handling everything from personal bankruptcies to million-dollar oil and gas disputes. His coworkers described him as intense and hardworking, not given to small talk. Then, as now, White would turn and walk out of the room if someone brought up his football career. He "tended to gravitate toward subjects that required hard concentration and long preparation such as bankruptcy and taxation," two Denver attorneys wrote of their former partner. As a trial lawyer, no one accused White of being "flamboyant, dramatic or even eloquent," they recalled, but he was "effective and professional."

Why didn't White go into politics? Certainly, had anyone seen him with JFK in 1939 and wondered which one could be a future president of the United States, White would have been the obvious choice. He had a national reputation as a sports hero and academic star. He was honest, hardworking, and of humble origins—a true self-made man. By comparison, Kennedy looked to be a callow millionaire's son. White's Colorado friends tried to get him to run for office, as governor or attorney general, but White demurred. He took a job as a district captain in the Democratic party organization, a behind-the-scenes position of registering voters and getting them to the polls. Although they never gave up entirely, White's friends came to realize he was not cut out for politics. He was not warm or engaging and was certainly not a backslapper. At cocktail receptions, he often looked pained and uncomfortable. As a public speaker, he could be dreadful: bland and platitudinous.

Throughout his life, White was more a man of action than a man of words, more a doer than a thinker. He could have led a company of Marines into heavy fire. He organized Citizens for Kennedy in 1960, a group of political independents who backed the Democratic candidate. When JFK's new administration was being formed, JFK offered White an array of jobs. White wanted to go to the Justice Department, so the president made him the number-two man under Attorney General Robert F. Kennedy, his brother. As the deputy attorney general, White reorganized the department and drew together a team of top attorneys. In May 1961, White led a contingent of 600 National Guardsmen sent to Alabama to protect the "Freedom Riders" who were seeking to integrate the interstate buses. As a leader, he was calm, organized, and definitely in charge. "You could give him any job and he would do it and do it well," said a long-time friend. After his appointment to the high court, he was frequently rumored to be in line to take over the FBI or to become the commissioner of baseball.

White never did get a chance to lead an organization. At the age of only 44, White was appointed by JFK to the Supreme Court. He had been at the Justice Department only a year when Justice Charles Whittaker, suffering from nervous exhaustion, announced his retirement. The Kennedys had talked over a dozen names as potential Supreme Court nominees, including the eminent Harvard law professor Paul Freund and several state supreme court judges, but neither brother really knew those individuals the way they knew White and Arthur Goldberg, JFK's second pick. Legal views apparently played no part in the decision. White and Goldberg were "his kind of people," Bobby Kennedy said later in explanation of JFK's Supreme Court selections. Two weeks after the president's announcement, the Senate held a brief hearing and unanimously confirmed White on a voice vote.

Over the years, White has defied labeling. Early on, he voted with the liberal bloc on civil rights and school desegregation but with conservatives on crime. In the landmark criminal rulings of the Warren era, White often dissented, as he did in the Miranda case. Along with Rehnquist, he cast a dissenting vote in *Roe* v. *Wade* and has made clear he will overturn the right to abortion if the opportunity arises. Unlike Rehnquist or Brennan, however, he has never set forth a broad view of the Constitution or of the Court's role in interpreting it. White has a quick, penetrating mind but avoids philosophy or broader principles of law. He decides cases and no more.

Even the justices who have served with him for years say they don't understand White or his views. "No one knows what Byron is thinking," said one colleague. As mentioned, the justices cannot even rely on the network of clerks to learn about White's view of an upcoming case. "The grapevine doesn't work with [White] because even his clerks don't know what he's thinking," he said.

His written opinions don't give many clues either. The typical White opinion is terse and conclusionary. When law clerks draft an opinion that explains the reasons for the decision, White often edits out the reasoning, leaving simply the conclusion. That's what counts, he insists. Lawyers who have closely followed White's career over nearly three decades are hard-pressed to recall one line from any of his hundreds of opinions. A 1986 White opinion became infamous among gay groups. He spoke for a 5–4 majority, which upheld the state laws making sodomy between homosexuals a crime. It "is, at best, facetious," White wrote, to suggest the Constitution's protection of liberty includes sexual intercourse between gay men. His opinion displayed the scornful tone of a locker-room conversation. It was joined by Burger, Rehnquist, Powell, and O'Connor. The four dissenters—Brennan, Marshall, Blackmun and Stevens—said the case, *Bowers* v. *Hardwick,* actually involved the "right most valued by civilized men: the right to be let alone."

His clerks admire White as smart and exceptionally hardworking. Though now in his mid-70s, he is at his desk by 7 A.M. and often works through the dinner hour. "I tried beating him into work in the morning," said one clerk, "but I finally figured it was like trying to open the refrigerator door in the morning before the light comes on. It can't be done."

Though most of his clerks develop a warm regard for White, most of them say it takes a while. Most recount stories of an intimidating first encounter. One said he first had a pleasant half-hour talk about law school with one justice but found no such casual amiability in White's chamber. "I hadn't sat down yet when he said, 'What's the worst decision the Supreme

Court made last year?' " he recalled. Clerks soon discover that
no answer will suffice. Each reply prompts only a further, more
penetrating question. "The line of questions only stops when
you finally say, 'I don't know,' " he said. Still another clerk
recalled White clipping his fingernails throughout the interview. "Every time I would begin to make a point," he said, "a
fingernail would go flying by."

In the hallways, White looks like the old warrior of the
gridiron. He walks slowly, bent forward at the waist, as if pushing into a heavy gale. His colleagues say that he has not mel-
lowed; those who disagree with him around the conference
table are treated to a "frozen glare," one said. He still possesses
a crushing grip, which he enjoys exercising during handshakes.

The attorneys before the Court, though, are subjected to
White at his gruffest. A question from him usually demands an
immediate answer, not an explanation.

"Well, Your Honor, we contend that . . . ," one lawyer
began his reply.

"Yes or no? What's your answer?" White snapped.

Boger, the LDF attorney, sweating now before the barrage of questions from White, finally shook himself free, convinced that he had lost White's vote in the *McCleskey* case. If
he was going to find a fifth vote to overturn the death penalty
as racially discriminating, it would not come from Byron White.

Unfortunately for Boger, things only got worse from there.
Scalia said he was not surprised that a study could find unfairness in the criminal justice system. Life was unfair, but what
could be done about it? What if a study found that juries are
more likely to convict defendants "because they're ugly or
because they're shifty-eyed. Does that make the criminal process unlawful?" Scalia asked.

No, Boger replied, but the Fourteenth Amendment tells
the court system to be especially concerned about racial bias.
About midway through his argument, Boger was explaining his
response to an earlier question when a faint voice interrupted.
"Mr. Boger. Mr. Boger . . . Mr. Boger." Finally, the attorney
looked to his left. "Yes, Mr. Justice Powell. I'm sorry," he said.
At age 79, pale and razor-thin, Powell had neither the energy
nor the inclination to butt heads with attorneys, as White and
Scalia liked to do. However, a question from the gentlemanly,
soft-spoken Powell also drew the attention of the entire courtroom. In close cases, Powell usually cast the deciding vote.

"What were the aggravating circumstances in this case?" Powell asked. It was a simple but ominous question for Boger. He had to explain that during the course of the robbery, McCleskey shot and killed a police officer.

"You have to accept the jury verdict that the defendant shot the police officer, don't you," Powell continued.

"Well, of course, we contended below that . . . ," Boger said.

"Right, I understand that," said Powell. "But here you are bound by that." The Supreme Court decides only legal questions, not factual disputes. If a jury hears the evidence and concludes that a person committed a crime, the justices will not reconsider that factual conclusion.

"So this defendant was guilty of shooting a police officer while he was in the process of committing a felony," Powell continued.

"That's correct. It's no doubt, Justice Powell, that's a serious offense," Boger said.

Before the moment could pass, Scalia at the other end of the bench chimed in that the officer was shot in the head at close range, "indicating there was a conscious attempt to kill the man."

For Powell, it was the worst sort of murder: an unprovoked and deliberate killing of a police officer. If the justices looked at Georgia's capital punishment system as a whole, the case was a difficult one. The evidence of discrimination, even if unintended, was overwhelming. However, if they cast their eyes only at Warren McCleskey, the case was easy.

Powell was not a legal theoretician. He cared more for doing justice than devising broad theories. He honed in on the facts of the case before him. This case-by-case approach made him among the least predictable members of the Court, as well as one of its most admired figures. However, his refusal to look beyond the facts of McCleskey's case seemed to ensure a victory for the state.

O'Connor, along with Powell, had agonized over the issue for several weeks before the argument, but both had made up their minds. They were not going to overturn the death penalty in America based on a professor's statistical study. Powell distrusted statistics. In his view, there was something to the cliché about "lies, damn lies, and statistics. Our system of justice is based on individuals," he said. Powell was not about to put every judge in the nation to the task of interviewing sociologists and statisticians to see whether the criminal sentences were being handed out fairly.

In the end, thanks to Powell, Rehnquist had a bare majority of five. White, Scalia, and O'Connor also voted to reject the challenge to Georgia's death penalty system. The chief justice gratefully assigned the most important opinion of the term to Powell, whose vote was the shakiest of the five. A year earlier, Powell had first cast his vote with Brennan to strike down as unconstitutional the Georgia antisodomy law. However, he later changed his mind because the police had dropped charges against Michael Hardwick, the homosexual who had been arrested. Instead, Powell signed on to the Byron White opinion upholding the law. This time, Rehnquist wanted to make sure Powell would not change his mind. Giving him the opinion was the best way to ensure that.

Justice Stevens tried to argue that *McCleskey* was not an all-or-nothing case for the death penalty. The Court could simply rule that the Baldus statistics raised an inference of discrimination and then send the case back to the Georgia courts to allow prosecutors to explain their procedures and prove that they are not biased. The best precedent for that approach was freshly printed in the Supreme Court records, the 7–2 opinion in the case of *Batson* v. *Kentucky* written the year before by Powell. In that case, a prosecutor had rejected the only four blacks in a jury pool for the trial of a black robbery suspect. That move creates an inference of discrimination, Powell said, so the judge must hold a hearing to have the prosecutor prove legitimate, unbiased reasons for rejecting the potential black jurors—a neat solution to the problem.

Powell saw no similar solution in the Georgia death penalty. The jury case involved the procedures used in a single trial. If the Court ruled in favor of McCleskey, statistics would be used to undermine the entire criminal justice system. The opinions, for the majority and the dissenters, went back and forth among the chambers, but on April 22, 1987, they were finally ready to be released.

"At most, the Baldus study indicates a discrepancy that appears to correlate with race," Powell wrote. "Apparent discrepancies in sentencing are an inevitable part of our criminal justice system. If we accept McCleskey's claim that racial bias has impermissibly tainted the capital sentencing decision, we could soon be faced with similar claims as to other types of penalty."

To Brennan, this argument sounded like a fear of "too much justice." If it could be shown that black burglars got more severe sentences than white burglars, that is reason for examining the sentencing system, not for ignoring the problem because it is too widespread.

For Brennan, it was a crushing defeat. He had fought capital punishment with a missionary zeal. Nothing could be more inhumane or more unjust in his view than putting another human to death, and no case in a decade had offered a better prospect for halting capital punishment, but Powell's decision closed the door. Brennan drafted a long and eloquent dissent. He laid out the nation's long history of racial discrimination, as well as the Supreme Court's long history of ignoring it. "In more recent times, we have sought to free ourselves from the burden of this history. Yet it has been scarcely a generation since the Court's first decision striking down racial segregation, and barely two decades since the legislative prohibition of racial discrimination in major domains of national life," Brennan wrote. "These have been honorable steps, but we cannot pretend that in three decades we have completely escaped the historical legacy spanning centuries. Warren McCleskey's evidence confronts us with the subtle and persistent influence of the past. . . . We ignore him at our peril, for we remain imprisoned by the past as long as we deny its influence in the present."

Blackmun, in a separate dissent, also showed how the Reconstruction Congress that wrote the Fourteenth Amendment was most concerned about unequal criminal punishments for blacks and whites. Conservatives such as Judge Robert Bork and Attorney General Edwin Meese liked to make speeches about how the Court should adhere to the "original intent" of the Constitution. Blackmun liked to help the conservatives hoist themselves on their own petards.

Blackmun also wondered why discrimination in capital punishment was being treated differently than other bias cases. When presented with statistical evidence of discrimination in housing, juries, or jobs, the Court had said that the other side then bears the burden of proving that no discrimination has taken place. In the Santa Clara County affirmative action case, O'Connor focused on one statistic—no women in 237 skilled jobs—and opined that it offered a "firm basis" for believing discrimination had occurred there. In the *McCleskey* case, however, O'Connor silently signed on to Powell's majority opinion discounting the statistics. "The Court today gives new meaning to our recognition that death is different," Blackmun wrote.

The 5–4 ruling in the *McCleskey* case sent out a clear message that the Rehnquist Court was not going to overturn the death penalty. In fact, just the day before, the Court had actually expanded the grounds for the death penalty. Before, the Court had reserved the ultimate punishment for actual murderers. However, faced with the gruesome murder of an Arizona family by a convict whose two sons helped him escape from prison, the Court set down a new rule. The two sons could be executed because they were "major participants" in the murder, even though they did not pull the trigger and, in fact, had urged their father not to harm the family. The majority was the same: Rehnquist, White, Powell, O'Connor, and Scalia.

Nonetheless, even the conservatives were not ready to put their stamp of approval on every death sentence. On the same day the *McCleskey* decision was handed down, the Court unanimously overturned a death sentence given to a Florida man who had murdered his niece. Because the trial judge had prevented the defendant from telling the sentencing jury of his miserable childhood, the convicted murderer had been denied the "due process of law" guaranteed by the Constitution, the Court ruled. The state may try again to sentence James Ernest Hitchcock to death, the justices said, but it must allow him and his lawyer the opportunity to tell the jurors about any "mitigating evidence" on his behalf.

Powell, in particular, was personally troubled by the unfairness of the capital punishment system. He had deeply conflicted views on the subject. "We are not dealing with innocent people," he said; these criminals deserved to be behind bars, and the Constitution clearly allowed for capital punishment. However, over the years he had come to question whether capital punishment can be administered fairly. As a form of punishment, the death penalty was constitutional but troubling nonetheless, he maintained.

In the spring of 1987, about the time the *McCleskey* opinion was ready to be released, the justices were confronted with the question of whether prosecutors could tell a sentencing jury of how a murder had devastated the family victimized by the murder. The prosecutors' argument had appeal. Why shouldn't the victims of a crime—in this instance, the survivors—have a right to describe the true impact of the crime?

This time, Powell balked. He worried that this sort of testimony would inject more unfairness into the system. The sentencing jury must focus on the crime and the killer, not the unforeseeable impact on survivors, he said. If this sort of testimony became routine, crimes against the socially prominent would be treated differently than the murder of a convenience-store clerk who happened to be single and lived alone. Thus, Powell voted with Brennan in the case of *Booth* v. *Maryland*, to disallow "victim impact" testimony in a death penalty case. For Rehnquist, that 5–4 ruling marked his one significant loss in his fall 1986 and spring 1987 parade of victories in crime cases.

In the spring of 1987, the justices considered the rights of a minority group that gets little attention. The case itself was not seen as a major one, even though it would determine whether this group had any rights under the Constitution. How the Court handled the issue proved revealing of the justices, especially of Scalia and O'Connor. This peculiar group of Americans whose rights were in doubt were those who fight to protect all other Americans—the men and women in the armed forces. Their constitutional rights were raised by the case of former Army Master Sergeant James B. Stanley.

In February 1959, Stanley was 22 years old and stationed at Fort Knox when he saw a note on the military bulletin board seeking volunteers. The Army wanted to test the effectiveness of gas masks and other protective clothing that would be used in the event of chemical warfare. The young sergeant saw a chance to advance his career and volunteered. However, the testing was not as he expected. Sergeant Stanley spent most of his time in a hospital unit at the Aberdeen Proving Grounds in Maryland. For hours on end, he was interviewed by a psychologist.

"We talked about my family and my background. He offered me a drink of water and then we talked some more," Stanley recalled in an interview. "No one explained anything."

The explanation apparently lay with the Central Intelligence Agency (CIA), the Soviet Union, and the Cold War. The intelligence agency had received reports that the Soviets had stockpiled a mysterious drug: lysergic acid diethylamide. By the late 1960s, it would be known everywhere by its initials—LSD. The U.S. Army wanted to know whether this mind-altering drug could be used against its soldiers in a war. Sergeant

Stanley and as many as 1,000 unwitting volunteers were going to supply the answer.

At Aberdeen, Stanley's behavior became erratic, for reasons he could not fathom. One moment, he would find himself giggling uncontrollably over a thumbtack stuck in a bulletin board. At another moment, he would try to choke a doctor at his bedside. "I really wanted to kill the rascal," he recalled. After four weeks in Maryland, he returned to Fort Knox, but his life did not return to normal.

He was late for his morning formations but could not recall where he had been after leaving his home. He would break down into sobs in front of his men. On occasion, he would awake during the night, beat his wife and children, and then go back to sleep. In the morning, he could recall none of it. Not surprisingly, his military career, as well as his marriage, went into retreat. In 1969, Stanley was finally discharged from the U.S. Army. The next year, he was divorced.

More than 17 years after the LSD experiment in Maryland, Stanley learned what had happened. On December 10, 1975, he received a special-delivery letter from the U.S. Army. "We earnestly solicit your cooperation," the letter began, for a follow-up study of the volunteers who were given LSD in 1959. Researchers wanted to examine the "long-term medical and psychological effects" of the LSD.

Stanley was stunned. "After all those years, I figured out what my government had done to me. Being mad would be putting it mildly," he said. He agreed to participate in the follow-up study, but he also went to see a lawyer. "I wanted my day in court. I wanted the government to have to answer for what they did to me," he said.

His lawsuit had two claims. First, he filed a claim under the Federal Tort Claims Act (FTCA) of 1946, in which Congress allowed citizens to seek damages "for injury or loss of property, or personal injury or death caused by the negligent or wrongful act or omission of any employee of the government."

Second, he sought damages from the government for violating his constitutional rights. The Supreme Court would not decide whether Stanley's claims were valid or whether he deserved any money. As in any such lawsuit, that would be a matter for a judge and a jury. However, the Court *would* decide whether Stanley, or any claimants like him, would ever get their day in court.

Stanley's suit cited a series of U.S. Defense Department and CIA officials who were responsible for the LSD experiments and charged them with violating his constitutional rights. He also sought an unspecified amount of damages under the FTCA of 1946.

For several years, Stanley's suit had bounced around in the lower courts. The judges who looked at it seemed to want to do something for him but were not sure what to do. A federal judge in Fort Lauderdale initially dismissed the suit, but the appeals court in Atlanta sent it back so that it could be revised and sharpened. On the second try, Judge José A. Gonzalez, a Carter appointee, again threw out the FTCA complaint under the so-called Feres doctrine. In a 1950 ruling in *Feres* v. *U.S.*, the Supreme Court said that service personnel may not seek damages under the 1946 law for any injury that was "incident to service" in the military.

However, Judge Gonzalez ruled that Stanley did have a right to a trial on his constitutional claims. "By donning a uniform, a member of the Army does not volunteer himself to be duped and deceived into becoming a guinea pig for his superiors," Gonzalez wrote. "The acts alleged to have been committed by the officers and agents named as defendants in this case are insidious to the most fundamental rights protected by our Constitution: the right of an individual to control his mind, his private thoughts and his bodily integrity."

Government attorneys appealed to the Eleventh Circuit Court of Appeals in Atlanta, arguing that a damage suit such as Stanley's threatens military discipline. The three appeals court judges, all Democratic appointees, disagreed. They noted that Stanley was suing civilian and high Defense Department officials, not his direct superiors at Fort Knox. They upheld Judge Gonzalez and ordered that the suit go to trial on whether his constitutional rights were violated.

But the Justice Department, anxious to get rid of Sergeant Stanley and his lawsuit, played its trump card. The same government that had secretly tested LSD on him would now fight in its highest court to prevent his case from going to trial.

"There is no doubt that permitting [Stanley] to go forward with his claim would involve the judiciary in sensitive military matters," the government maintained in its brief to the Supreme Court, "since a central issue in [his] case would be whether the Army erred in administering LSD to volunteers in the 1950s."

At least, the government lawyers and Stanley agreed on the key issue: the accountability of U.S. officials. Sergeant Stanley said his main purpose in making his allegations was to force military officials to explain their conduct, to be held accountable for secretly administering the LSD. The government lawyers said Stanley's suit should be dismissed because it could force the military to admit that it had "erred" in administering its LSD tests.

The case of *U.S.* v. *Stanley* was set for argument on April 21. However, unknown to Stanley, his lawyers, or the Justice Department that opposed him, the justices were locked in a dispute over the other issue raised by Stanley's case—whether an injured serviceperson can seek damages under the FTCA of 1946. That issue had been considered settled because of the Court's 1950 *Feres* decision. Indeed, Judge Gonzalez dismissed that part of Stanley's suit, and it had not been raised again. However, the issue had been raised instead in an entirely separate case, and suddenly the outcome was in doubt—because of Ronald Reagan's new appointee, Antonin Scalia.

Scalia had a bold, literalist approach to the law that scared many liberals. For example, because the Constitution did not mention "abortion" or "privacy," Scalia thought the *Roe* v. *Wade* ruling was flatly wrong and should be immediately overturned. Sometimes, however, his bold literalism shocked conservatives, too. Scalia intended to follow the language of the law, even if it riled conservatives. When he examined the FTCA of 1946, he saw no exception for damage suits by servicepersons, except in times of war.

The 1946 law said "the United States shall be liable . . . in the same manner and to the same extent as a private individual under like circumstances." If, for example, Sergeant Stanley's private doctor gave him a dangerous drug, without his knowledge or permission, and simply to test its effect, Stanley could certainly go to court and file a damage claim against the doctor.

The FTCA did include several exceptions. No one could sue the government for "any claim arising out of the combatant activities of the military or naval forces, or the Coast Guard, during time of war." The experiments at Aberdeen were not "combatant activities . . . during time of war," so that exception would not cover Stanley.

Nonetheless, the language of the law and the Supreme Court's interpretation of it are not always the same. In 1950, the Court took a look at the relatively new FTCA and decided that it could not mean what it said. Before the Court were three suits filed by servicepersons or their survivors: (1) Bernice Feres had filed a negligence suit against the government after her husband, Rudolph, died in a fire that swept through his army barracks. (2) Arthur K. Jefferson had undergone abdominal surgery while he was in the army. After leaving the service, he underwent a second operation. Doctors found in his abdomen, according to the Supreme Court record, "a towel 30 inches long by 18 inches wide marked 'Medical Department U.S. Army.' " He sued the army for negligence. (3) The third case involved a soldier who died allegedly because of a bungled operation.

The law said nothing about a general exception for service personnel, so the Supreme Court invented one. It threw out the three suits, commenting that they could "prove depleting of the public treasury." Instead, the justices adopted a new rule: Any accident or injury that was "incident to [military] service" put the government off-limits to a damage claim. Ever since then, the so-called Feres doctrine has been much criticized but never overturned. The rule meant, among other things, that service personnel who were the victims of medical malpractice could not sue their doctors or the military hospitals for their injuries.

The issue had come before the justices again in February 1987, two months before Stanley's case was heard. The case involved a serviceman whose wife said he died because of negligence by federal civilian officials. On the foggy morning of January 7, 1982, a Coast Guard station in Hawaii received a distress call from a boat in the area. Lieutenant Commander Horton W. Johnson was sent out in a helicopter to search for it. In the dense fog, Johnson sought radar guidance from the Federal Aviation Administration, a civilian agency. Under FAA radar control, Johnson flew his copter into the side of a mountain on the island of Molakai and was killed.

Johnson's wife, Frieda, received benefits from the Veterans Administration but also filed an FTCA damage claim against the government, charging negligence by the FAA. A judge in Miami threw out the suit because of the Feres doctrine. Commander Johnson was a serviceman and his death was "incident to service." However, the U.S. Eleventh Circuit Court of Appeals in Atlanta reinstated the suit. In its view, the Feres doctrine concerned "military discipline," and this case involved a suit against a civilian agency.

When the Justice Department appealed, the Court agreed to hear the case of *U.S.* v. *Johnson*. It looked to be an easy win for the government, as it is a rare day when the military loses one before the Supreme Court. Instead, the *Johnson* case split the Court.

Scalia may have been a rookie, but he was neither quiet nor unsure of himself. In 1950, the Court got it wrong, he said, and it was time to correct the mistake. He sent around an opinion calling for the Feres doctrine to be reversed. The *Feres* case, he said, saw the Court "ignoring what Congress wrote and imagining what it should have written. *Feres* was wrongly decided and heartily deserves the widespread, almost universal criticism it has received." Scalia had no special sympathy for service personnel; his job was to read the law and apply it as it was written, he insisted. The 1946 law said nothing about forbidding service personnel from suing the government.

Nonetheless, Rehnquist managed four votes, besides his own, to rule for the government and throw out Frieda Johnson's lawsuit. White and Blackmun saw no need to tamper with a 36-year-old precedent. O'Connor and Powell agreed. If Congress thought the Feres doctrine was wrong, it could amend the law and change it. The draft opinions in the *Johnson* case were still circulating on April 21 when the Court heard arguments in the case of *U.S.* v. *Stanley*.

While Johnson's case dealt only with the 1946 law, Stanley's case concerned only the Constitution and whether it allowed damage suits by service personnel. Unlike a law passed by Congress, the words of the Constitution are broad and often vague. The Fifth Amendment says that no person may be "deprived of life, liberty or property without due process of law" by federal officials. Stanley's lawyers contended that, by giving him a dangerous drug without his permission, U.S. Army officials deprived him of "liberty . . . without due process of law."

Brennan and Rehnquist regularly clashed over whether citizens should be able to sue government officials for violating their constitutional rights. In Brennan's view, the Constitution made the government accountable to the people. When officials deliberately violate the rights of a citizen, they should be called to account for their actions. Brennan had voted to uphold suits against welfare officials, prison directors, police officers, and all manner of public employees who were accused of trampling on a constitutional right.

Rehnquist had the opposite view. The Constitution set up government—local, state, and federal—to be run by elected officials and their subordinates. Government cannot operate, he believed, if federal officials, school board members, police officers, or welfare agents can be hauled into court any time citizens can claim that their rights were violated. Under such a regime, judges—not elected officials—would be running the country.

On April 21, Jim Stanley had a good seat in the courtroom to hear the arguments in the case of *U.S.* v. *Stanley.* "I sat there with the hair raised on the back of my neck. It was awesome to see the nine most powerful people in the United States right there talking about my case," he said.

Actually, the justices did little talking as the Justice Department attorney argued for dismissing his suit prior to a trial. They rocked in their high-back leather seats and listened. When Stanley's lawyer, Robert Kupfer, moved to the lecturn, though, the rapid-fire questioning began. Didn't Stanley volunteer for this? After all, what did he think the experiments were about? How does he know that the U.S. Army is responsible? Perhaps some other agency ran the experiments.

At one point, Kupfer pointed out that the Nuremberg Code was drawn up by the U.S. military shortly after World War II in reaction to Nazi experiments on humans. It says, among others things, that "the voluntary consent of the human subject is absolutely essential." No sooner had Kupfer raised this point than the chief justice cut him off.

"Does the Nuremberg Code have the effect of law, civil, positive law in the United States?" Rehnquist asked.

Of course, he knew the answer, too: No. The Nuremberg Code pledged the military to a code of conduct, but there was no legal way to force the U.S. Army to abide by it—that is, unless the Supreme Court allowed Sergeant Stanley to sue the U.S. Army officials for having violated it.

Rehnquist was determined to block these suits. At conference, he argued that the Constitution did not create a general right to sue the government, and the Court should not create such a right for service personnel. White agreed. These days, Blackmun usually voted with Brennan and griped about "the conservatives taking over here," but he also did not want the word *liberal* attached to his name. He saw himself as a midwestern middle-of-the-roader. As his clerks noted, Blackmun trusted the institutions of America: schools, hospitals, prisons, and, of course, the military. He voted again with Rehnquist. Powell, an old military man himself, did the same. At the end of the table, however, came a surprise defection.

O'Connor was appalled by how Stanley had been treated. "In my view, the conduct of the type alleged in this case," she said, "is beyond the bounds of human decency."

For generations, students had debated whether the Supreme Court was a court of law or a court of justice. It was an easy question for most conservatives. It was a court of law because following the law, as written by the people's representatives, was the just way, the only just way. However, O'Connor did not always follow a doctrinaire conservative approach. She was swayed by a sense of justice and fairness. Sometimes the law was not clear, but the facts were. Certainly the military was different, and the Court was correct to prohibit lawsuits concerning strictly military matters. Stanley's case cried out for a different rule, though. The Court must not, she said, "insulate [government officials] from liability for deliberate and calculated exposure of otherwise healthy military personnel to experimentation without their consent, outside of any combat, combat training, or military exigency, and for no other reason than to gather information on the effect of LSD on human beings."

O'Connor's vote could have tipped the majority to Brennan. The aging liberal leader was also appalled by the case. If the Constitution gave citizens a club to fight back against their own government, what better example than this. Here "the government of the United States has treated thousands of its own citizens as laboratory animals," Brennan said. Marshall and Stevens agreed.

Scalia, casting the decisive ninth vote, sided with the government. If Congress wanted to allow suits against the government it should write such a law, and he would uphold it, but Scalia was not about to interpret the Constitution in a way that would allow judges to second-guess military decisions.

"I think he feels very strongly about keeping judges out of the military's affairs," said a former Scalia clerk.

For Scalia, the law was an intellectual exercise, requiring him to figure out what the words meant or how conflicting provisions should be reconciled. A sense of justice had almost nothing to do with it. He was surprised that the old liberals such as Brennan and Blackmun still talked of being deeply troubled over cases. Sometimes the justices received a late-night phone call asking whether they would agree to allow a pending execution to proceed. None of that fazed Scalia. His business was the law, not justice. He boasted to friends that he never had problems sleeping at night.

When the decision in the *Johnson* case was announced in early May, Scalia dissented and condemned the Feres doctrine and its "incident to service" rule because it was not taken from the law passed by Congress. The 5–4 ruling meant that service personnel and their families could not file damage suits against the government under the FTCA, even if they were suing a civilian agency.

Scalia saw Stanley's case as quite different, though. It required the justices to make "an analytic judgement" about the Constitution. On June 25, 1987, Scalia spoke for the 5–4 majority that ruled for the government in *U.S.* v. *Stanley*. In his opinion, Scalia adopted, of all things, the "incident to service" rule that he had roundly condemned in the *Johnson* case.

Because of the "unique disciplinary structure of the Military Establishment," Scalia wrote, servicepersons may not sue any official of the government for any violations of their constitutional rights that were "incident to service." Thus, the Constitution of the United States did not protect the rights of one group of citizens: the men and women who served in the military of the United States.

The two 5–4 rulings, in the *Johnson* and *Stanley* cases, were major victories for the government. The *Johnson* case made clear that service personnel, unlike other citizens, cannot file claims against the government. Stanley would not get his trial to force officials to explain their LSD testing, and the ruling in *U.S.* v. *Stanley* closed the courthouse door to all other service personnel who wanted to sue for damages because their rights under the Constitution had been violated.

The two decisions effectively created a separate class of Americans without the normal legal rights and remedies. Fifteen months earlier, on January 28, 1986, the space shuttle *Challenger* took off from Cape Canaveral on an unusually cold morning and blew up 74 seconds later. On board were NASA scientists, civilian researchers, and a schoolteacher. Their families were entitled to file claims against the government for their deaths, and eventually, to be awarded settlements. At the controls was Navy Commander Michael J. Smith. His wife filed

a $15 million claim against the government, accusing NASA of
negligence and wrongful death, but the claim was later thrown
out of court. The Supreme Court had left the judge who handled Mrs. Smith's lawsuit no other choice. Her husband's death
was "incident to service." The Rehnquist Court had assured
that military service on behalf of the United States government
continued to be "unique."

Ronald Reagan's election in 1980 had put a new spotlight
on a powerful, old bloc of voters: fundamentalist Christians.
For too long, they said, their values and beliefs have been shut
out—mocked even—by Washington, D.C., and Hollywood, by
the news media, and by the public schools. They were not going
to take it quietly any longer.

As usual, the schools became the first point of attack. Fundamentalist parents in Hawkins County, Tennessee, pressed
demands for new textbooks for their children. The current
school curriculum had become infected with "secular human-
ism," they said, where there was no right and wrong, no absolute values. In Alabama, fundamentalists sought a return to
prayer in the schools. In Arkansas and Louisiana, they wanted
to replace godless evolution with God's story of creation.

The surge of fundamentalism forced the Court to reconsider one of its most intractable problems: how to draw a line
between religion and the government. The notion of a separation between church and state had behind it a venerable
tradition in American law, but its origin was little known.

On the first day of 1802, the third President of the United
States sat down at his desk and wrote a brief New Year's greeting to the Baptist congregation of Danbury, Connecticut.
Thomas Jefferson is less known for his presidency than for the
declaration in 1776 that "all men are created equal" and are
"endowed by their Creator with certain unalienable rights,"
including "life, liberty, and the pursuit of happiness."

Jefferson had no direct role in the making of the Constitution and the Bill of Rights, except as a correspondent. He
was then in Paris, serving as America's ambassador. In a series
of letters, though, he urged his protégé James Madison to add
the declaration of individual rights to the new Constitution.
Two years after the Constitution became law, Congress—at
Madison's insistence—approved a Bill of Rights. Two years after
that, these amendments were ratified by the states and added
to the Constitution.

Despite these valuable contributions to twentieth-century constitutional law, Jefferson's most enduring can be found in the brief New Year's Day letter he wrote more than a decade after the Bill of Rights became law: "Believing with you that religion is a matter which lies solely between Man and his God," he wrote, "I contemplate with sovereign reverence that act of the whole American people which declared that their legislature should 'make no law respecting an establishment of religion, or prohibiting the free exercise thereof,' thus building a wall of separation between church and state."

He referred to the first phrase of the First Amendment: "Congress shall make no law respecting an establishment of religion." For most of American history, this restriction meant little. Congress was not inclined to legislate on religion. By the 1940s, however, the Court had concluded that the First Amendment also applied to state and local governments, via the so-called "incorporation doctrine." The Fourteenth Amendment said no state may deny any person "life, liberty or property without due process of law," and the Court concluded this guarantee of "liberty" incorporated the basic liberties set forth in the original Bill of Rights.

Suddenly, the ban on an "establishment of religion" meant something—but what? Searching for a definition, the Court plucked from obscurity Jefferson's metaphor. The First Amendment demands, the Court said, a "wall of separation between church and state." Both religion and free government flourished in America because the two are kept apart, the Court reasoned. Government must not meddle in the affairs of the church, nor the church in the affairs of government.

The true impact of the "separation" idea hit the headlines in 1962 when the Supreme Court outlawed official prayer in public schools. The next year, official public-school Bible reading was banned. Over the next 25 years, the "wall of separation" stood, although it was uneven and crumbling in spots. The Court's decisions on religion grew ever more confused and confusing. In 1984, the Court abandoned the "separation" notion and ruled that a city may use tax dollars to erect during the Christmas season a display of Christ's birth. This was a matter of history and tradition, not religion, Chief Justice Burger opined. The next year, though, the Court returned to strict separation, ruling that public-school tutors may no longer tutor needy pupils in parochial schools. Their presence there for an hour or so per day fostered "an excessive entanglement" between church and state, the Court said.

To many Americans, Ronald Reagan among them, none of this made sense. The liberal Court seemed hostile to religion, he thought. As president, Reagan vowed to bring prayer back to the schools. Reagan's education secretary, William J. Bennett, angry about the school ruling, said that the Court appeared to view "excessive entanglement" with religion as akin to "excessive entanglement with an infectious disease." On the Court, Rehnquist, too, thought the recent decisions made no sense. The problem was Jefferson's metaphor, he said. It was based on "bad history," and it made for bad law.

Reagan first took the religion fight to Congress. In 1984, the President lobbied hard for an amendment to the Constitution that would allow "group prayer in the public schools." He won a majority of 56 Senators, but he was still 11 votes short of the needed two-thirds majority. There, the amendment died.

The next year, the Administration turned its attention to the Supreme Court. There, the Constitution can be "amended" with just five votes. The Court had before it an Alabama law that called for a daily moment of "voluntary prayer" in the schools. The Administration went before the justices to voice support for the prayer law, but again Reagan was rebuffed. On a 6–3 vote, the law was struck down as unconstitutional. Burger, Rehnquist, and White dissented.

Brennan, though a Roman Catholic, saw no place for religion in the public schools. In 1963 he had written one of the key opinions forbidding daily Bible readings in the schools; he saw no need to refight these old battles. In his view, the case of *George Wallace, Governor of Alabama* v. *Ishmael Jaffree* (a parent) was an easy one. The state legislators crafted and passed the law for religious reasons—to encourage prayer in schools. That made it unconstitutional. However, Brennan's views on the decision in the Alabama case were not the most memorable; the case is most noted among attorneys for the opinions rendered by Reagan's two favorite justices: Sandra O'Connor and William Rehnquist.

O'Connor had fashioned her own views on religion, an approach that differed from both her liberal and her conservative colleagues'. She said that a law or government policy was an "establishment of religion" if it appeared to "endorse" a religion. She did not insist on strict separation—such as forbidding public-school tutors from entering parochial schools. However, she would bar "government from conveying or attempting to convey that religion or a particular religious belief is favored or preferred."

O'Connor did not possess the quick mind or verbal agility of Scalia and John Paul Stevens. Nor did she fashion the broad vision of the Constitution of a Rehnquist or a Brennan. Rather, like Byron White and Harry Blackmun, she had made her mark as a hard worker, devoted to detail and intensely committed to the job.

Hard work came naturally to her. Sandra Day had grown up on a ranch straddling the New Mexico–Arizona border. When she was young, the ranch house had no electricity or running water, and the nearest town was 25 miles of dry brush and dirt roads away. She was born in an El Paso hospital on March 26, 1930, the first child of Harry and Ada Mae Day. They raised cattle on a 300-square-mile spread. By age ten years, Sandra could drive a tractor and a truck, could brand a steer, could repair a fence or a windmill, and could shoot a rifle. To add rooms onto their house, she and her parents made adobe bricks out of mud and built the walls themselves. As the nation's most prominent female jurist, O'Connor is called upon to give lectures on all manner of legal and social topics, but if asked, she can also talk at length on the process of making adobe bricks by hand.

As a young girl, she admired her father tremendously. He had wanted to go to Stanford, but when Harry was 18 years old his own father's death forced him, instead, to take control of the ranch. He was resourceful and indomitable, she said, always interested in new ideas and new things. To give the ranch hot water, he devised and built his own solar water heater. He taught his daughter that work was a seven-day-a-week affair. He also despised lawyers and Franklin Roosevelt, family friends said. Her mother was the cultured, well-dressed college-graduate daughter of an El Paso merchant. Despite the ranch's isolation, the Day house had plenty of reading material; her parents subscribed to several distant newspapers and to *Time* magazine, the *New Yorker*, and the Book-of-the-Month Club.

Sandra the cowgirl is also portrayed by some friends and family members who knew her then as Sandra the introverted schoolgirl. Because there were no schools near the Lazy B ranch, her parents sent her away at age six years to attend a

private school in El Paso, where she lived with her grandmother. Though she spent her summers and vacations at the
ranch, her time at school was a heartbreaking experience. "I
was always homesick," she said. At age 16, she graduated from
high school and did something her father had longed to do:
enroll at Stanford. In just five years, she raced through her
undergraduate studies and the law school. While working on
the law review, she met John O'Connor, whose nonstop jokes
kept the sometimes dour, driven Sandra Day laughing. She also
learned a lesson from the experience of dating a fellow law
review editor that she passed on to a recent Stanford class:
"Beware of proofreading over a glass of beer."

O'Connor also remembers going to parties where law students would gather to tell stories or to play cards. There, she
got to know the brightest student in the class: Bill Rehnquist.
In 1952, she married O'Connor and graduated just a few places
behind Rehnquist.

Unfortunately, her stellar academic credentials did not
impress the major law firms of San Francisco and Los Angeles.
They had their standards, which included hiring only men.
"None had ever hired a woman as a lawyer, and they were not
prepared to do so," she said. She *was* offered jobs, though—
as a legal secretary. Among the firms rejecting her application
was the venerable Los Angeles firm of Gibson, Dunn and
Crutcher, the partners of which included William French
Smith. Nearly 30 years later, as Ronald Reagan's attorney general, he was to get a chance to rectify the mistake.

Turned down by the big private firms, Ms. O'Connor took
a job as a deputy county counsel in San Mateo, California.
When her husband took a three-year job with the Army's Judge
Advocate General Corps in West Germany, she worked there
as a civilian lawyer. Upon their return to the United States, in
1957, they settled in Phoenix. He joined a local law firm, and
she became a housewife and a mother of three sons. She described herself as a "joiner" during those years in Paradise
Valley, an affluent suburb of Phoenix. She joined the Junior
League, helped at the Salvation Army, volunteered at a school
for blacks and Hispanics, and played tennis and golf at the local
country club.

Finally, in 1965, she decided she needed a paying job "so
that my life would be more orderly," so she became one of
Arizona's assistant attorney generals. In 1969, the Maricopa
County Board of Supervisors appointed her to fill a vacant seat

in the state senate. Three years later, after two successful re-election campaigns, her fellow Republicans chose her as the state senate majority leader, the first woman in the nation to hold such a job. She was not known for taking strong ideological stands but rather for outworking and outsmarting her foes. "She worked interminable hours and read everything there was," Democratic state senator Alfredo Gutierrez said at the time of her nomination. "We'd go to the floor with a few facts and let rhetoric do the rest. Not Sandy. She would overwhelm you with her knowledge."

Despite her success, she was not entirely comfortable with politics. At political events, she looked stiff and prim, colleagues said, too reserved to warm a crowd. She could have stayed put in the state senate but chose instead to run for a spot as a state trial judge, a move that was seen as a step down. She won, of course, and ran a tight ship as a judge. Attorneys who were late or unprepared got dressed down by Judge O'Connor. She was stern where the law called for it. Once, a Scottsdale mother of two young children came before her to plead guilty to passing bad checks totaling $3,500. She asked for mercy for the children's sake. The judge calmly sentenced her to ten years in prison and then returned to her chambers and wept.

State Republicans sought to bring her back into politics, but she demurred. In 1979, Democratic governor Bruce Babbitt elevated her to the state appeals court. She was there just two years when Ronald Reagan's aides went looking for female candidates for the Supreme Court.

In the 1980 campaign, Reagan pledged to appoint the first woman to the Court, and his chance came sooner than he expected. In April, just three months into his term and with Reagan still recovering from the nearly fatal shot fired by John Hinckley, Justice Potter Stewart told his neighbor, Vice President George Bush, that he planned to retire at the end of the term. An Eisenhower Republican, Stewart had become one of the best-respected and best-liked justices. A moderate, he helped form a stable middle position on the Court as the majority first moved left in the 1960s and then right in the 1970s. In 1981, however, after 22 years on the bench, he was ready to step down.

When told of the impending vacancy, Reagan recalled his campaign pledge and told his advisers he wanted women to be on the list of candidates to be considered. But who? Attorney

General Smith and White House counselor Ed Meese knew plenty of smart conservatives who could be tapped for the Court, but they all shared one common trait: They were white males. With a dearth of women who had high-level experience as judges, several candidates on Reagan's list were Democrats and quite liberal.

Amidst such competition, Judge O'Connor's stock rose quickly. A solid Republican with a law-and-order reputation, she had the strong backing of her Paradise Valley neighbor Senator Barry Goldwater and her former Stanford classmate Justice William H. Rehnquist. "She was the most conservative woman we could find," said one Justice Department official. The more Reagan's aides examined her background, the more they liked her. She had a superb academic record and experience as a trial judge and an appellate judge. She had worked for both county and state governments and knew the inner workings of a legislature. And she was a woman. On July 7, 1981, after only a 45-minute meeting with her, Reagan announced the nomination. Sandra Day O'Connor, who once could not get a job because she was a woman, now got a job on the Supreme Court for much the same reason.

The nomination was greeted with outrage by the Christian right. The Moral Majority leader, Reverend Jerry Falwell, called it a "disaster," and John Wilkie, head of the National Right to Life Committee, denounced it as a "betrayal" of their cause. As a candidate, Reagan had also pledged to appoint judges who would respect "the sanctity of innocent human life," and O'Connor was not one of those judges, or so they said. In 1970, she had voted in a committee to repeal the state law making abortion a crime. She told Reagan's advisers that she didn't recall the vote—the bill never made it to the floor— and that she "had never been a leader or outspoken advocate on behalf of the pro-life or abortion-rights organizations." As a personal matter, she opposed abortion, she said. In her meeting with Reagan, O'Connor said she found abortion "personally repugnant" and the practice "an appropriate subject for state regulation."

She repeated much the same before the Senate Judiciary Committee. "I'm opposed to it, as a matter of birth control or otherwise," she said of abortion. Nonetheless, her personal opposition to abortion did not answer the key question. Would she vote to overturn *Roe* v. *Wade* and allow abortion to be made a crime again? She gave no answer to that question. She won confirmation on a 99–0 vote.

She became a celebrity the day she joined the Court. As the first female admitted to the nation's most exclusive all-male club, she instantly became its best-known member, its most sought-after public speaker, the recipient of bags full of mail. At restaurants, at airports, and in movie lines, she was recognized. When she danced and partied with husband John, the social pages of the Washington newspapers took notice. With the approach of each election cycle, rumors circulated that the Republicans might want her on the ticket as a vice-presidential candidate.

In 1981, however, she was not particularly well prepared for the high-court job. She certainly had the basic qualifications, as well as much experience in state government. She was also the only member of the Court who had run for and been elected to a public office. However, in the state courts she had not grappled with the most intricate issues of federal law and the U.S. Constitution. Suddenly, she was called upon to decide dozens of those issues each month, and the stakes were high. As she once commented, the Supreme Court does not decide the easy cases. Those are handled quietly in the lower courts. Only when judges around the country are divided does the Supreme Court step in.

To compensate for her inexperience, she worked relentlessly. "There's no 'Miller Time' with Sandra O'Connor," a friend once said of her. In addition, she is, by nature, well organized and well prepared. Her son Brian once told of casually asking his mother what she planned to do during the summer. "And I get in the mail a few weeks later, before the summer starts, an itinerary—June through August—to the hour, what she will be doing and my dad will be doing."

In her work she is, if anything, even more organized. She exercises at 7 A.M., is at her desk at 8, and takes briefs home at the end of the day. Saturday mornings are spent with her clerks, in her chambers, going over the coming week's cases. Her chambers in the front of the Court building give a grand view across the Capitol grounds toward the Senate. Even when out of the Court building, a skiing trip to the West has meant packing legal briefs along with the skis.

All her hard work has paid off, though. She has made herself into one of the best-respected members of the Court: thoughtful, precise, and cautious. On issues such as affirmative action, abortion, and religion, she has worked to fashion a responsible and distinct middle position. She avoids the ideological extremes of either the right or the left.

That was evident in her separate opinion in the Alabama school prayer case. Brennan's view that the Constitution required a strict separation of church and state seemed to make all displays of religion suspect. By his standard, even a Christmas tree in a public square was illegal. That went too far. Nonetheless, she was also unwilling to blithely join Rehnquist in the march to the right and allow the government to promote the mainstream religions. That would strip the "establishment" clause of all meaning, she maintained. As usual, Sandra O'Connor made up her own mind.

If schoolchildren want to bow their heads to meditate or pray, they may, O'Connor wrote. Nothing in the Constitution forbids that sort of prayer in schools. However, "the Alabama legislature has intentionally crossed the line between creating a quiet moment . . . and affirmatively endorsing the particular religious practice of prayer," she wrote in her separate opinion. "This line may be a fine one, but our precedents and the principles of liberty require that we draw it," she wrote in *Wallace v. Jaffree.*

Rehnquist followed the majority opinion with a scathing dissent. He first attacked Thomas Jefferson and his "misleading metaphor" and then the justices who had been foolish to follow it for so many years. Because Jefferson was in Paris when the Constitution was written, "he would seem to any detached observer as a less than ideal source of contemporary history as to the meaning of the Religion Clauses of the First Amendment," Rehnquist wrote. "The 'wall of separation between church and state' is a metaphor based on . . . bad history. It should be frankly and explicitly abandoned," he wrote.

Rehnquist then laid out his view of the history of the First Amendment and drew two conclusions from it. The "establishment" clause was intended to prevent the official creation of a "national religion." Second, it prohibited official preferences among religions. However, it does not "require government neutrality between religion and irreligion," nor does it prevent government "from providing nondiscriminatory aid to religion," Rehnquist wrote.

With a five-vote majority, Rehnquist would allow group prayers in public schools as well as tax aid for parochial schools. This is not to say that the schools *must* have prayer, only that they *may*. If the majority of the people want prayer in their public schools, or to give tax credits to parochial schools, that is their decision to make, not the Court's, Rehnquist argues.

In his first term as chief justice, the religion issue was back before the Court, and again in a case from the Deep South. The case began with a Louisiana's schoolboy's talk with his teacher, or so said the sponsor of the creation-science law.

"I first got interested in this subject when my 12-year-old son went into his science class and the teacher asked, 'Richard, how did the world come about and how was man formed?'" said Louisiana's state senator Bill Keith in 1980. "My son answered, 'God created the world and God created man.' And she said, 'No, Richard. Did you study your assignments?' "

Inspired by that exchange, state senator Keith set out to learn more about evolution and creation. He contacted the Institute for Creation Research in San Diego, California, read its literature, and came away with a revelation. Evolution had become "a twentieth-century myth," he concluded, a "symbol of something that is more than just a scientific explanation of the way something happens. A great deal of philosophy is taught through the teaching of evolution," Keith told a Louisiana state senate hearing. It is the philosophy that human life is not special or divine, but rather the result of happenstance. By this theory, humans were not the divine creation of God but the accidental offshoot of some slimy creatures who emerged from the sea.

State senator Keith disclaimed any intention to put religion into the school curriculum. If evolution was a theory, so was creationism. His was a search for "scientific truth," balance, and academic freedom, he said. Even Clarence Darrow, in the famous 1925 "monkey trial" in Tennessee, said it was "bigotry" to teach only one view, Keith said. He proposed equal time for evolution and creationism.

"Public schools within this state shall give balanced treatment to creation-science and to evolution science," said Keith's bill, which passed both houses of the Louisiana legislature and was signed into law as the Balanced Treatment Act. "Creation-science means the scientific evidences for creation and inferences from those scientific evidences," the law said. Textbooks, lectures, and library materials were required to give balanced treatment to both "theories," and discrimination against "creation-scientists" was forbidden.

That was virtually the total text of the new law. Was it unconstitutional? Was it a law "respecting an establishment of religion"? Was this sort of law an end run around the Court's no-religion-in-school rulings?

A federal judge, acting on a lawsuit filed by teachers and parents, ruled that it was and declared the law invalid. The decision provoked a bitter split in the 15-member U.S. Fifth Circuit Court of Appeals, which covers Texas, Mississippi, and Louisiana. Eight judges agreed the law was unconstitutional because its purpose was "to promote a religious belief." The seven dissenters included two of the Reagan and Bush administration's top candidates for the Supreme Court: Patrick Higginbotham and Edith Jones. The dissenters said the Louisiana law simply required teaching "the whole truth," not just a one-sided endorsement of evolution as an "established fact."

The Court scheduled an argument in the case of *Governor Edwin Edwards* v. *Don Aguillard* (a teacher) on December 2, 1986. This would not be Clarence Darrow versus William Jennings Bryan revisited. Arguments before the Court, unlike those before a jury, are not dominated by lawyers. Each lawyer gets 30 minutes to present his or her case, but the justices want facts and arguments, not an oration. Rehnquist, in particular, would cut short a lawyer who began to deliver a speech to the choir.

During the argument opposing "creationism," New York attorney Jay Topkis, representing the Louisiana teachers, rose to a rhetorical peak at one point. Comparing his opponent to a character in Alice in Wonderland, Topkis said he hoped "this honorable Court" will not be "fooled like Alice" by the misleading use of words.

"Don't overestimate us," Rehnquist interrupted dryly.

Once again, Scalia dominated the questioning during the argument. He had already proven himself the most adept and persistent questioner. A devout Catholic as well as a believer in upholding state law, Scalia sounded genuinely irked that the Louisiana law had been struck down simply because a judge thought it had a religious purpose. The law, after all, never mentioned God or a "divine" creation, he noted.

Couldn't the law simply require the teaching of "a first cause that may be quite impersonal, or a giant slug, for all we know"? Scalia asked. "What about Aristotle's view of the first cause, an unmoved mover? I don't think Aristotle considered himself a theologian as opposed to a philosopher," he said.

Leaning forward in his seat, rubbing his black hair back in frustration, Scalia was unrelenting. Why should the Court presume, even without a trial on the issue, that creationism was necessarily a religious view? On a bench lined with solemn gray figures who often sat as silently as pigeons on a railing, Scalia stood out like a talking parrot. One minute, he would look amazed and angry, his hand rubbing his hair. The next minute, he would be joking and gesturing. Scalia never failed to enliven the argument. The *American Lawyer* magazine observed that if Supreme Court sessions were televised, "Nino Scalia" would be a household name nationwide.

Nonetheless, Scalia's show did not always play well with the other justices. Several said they wished he would be quiet for a change. On occasion, Byron White would glare down the bench with a look that suggested he would like to put the newest justice into a headlock if it would shut him up. Sandra O'Connor would harrumph slightly when he interrupted one of her questions.

Lewis Powell, always soft-spoken and reserved, was once asked to comment on his new colleague, Scalia. "I think it is quite apparent," Powell said with a faint smile, "that he had been a law professor. They get to talk for the full hour."

During the creationism argument, Powell interrupted Scalia's series of questions to ask whether "we may come to a lower level of discourse and not talk about philosophy." He then asked several practical questions. Does the law apply to state colleges? No, said attorney Wendell Bird, representing the state. Is it possible to monitor this law in every classroom? Yes, he said.

Scalia was not ready to quit. "Let's assume that there was an ancient history professor in a state high school who has been teaching that the Roman Empire did not extend to the southern shore of the Mediterranean in the first century A.D.," he began. "And let's assume a group of Protestants are concerned about that fact, inasmuch as it makes it seem the Biblical story of the crucifixion has things a bit wrong. . . . So they go to the principal of the school and say, 'This history professor is teaching what is just falsehood.' And the principal says, 'Gee, you're right.' And he goes in and directs the teacher to teach that Rome was on the southern shore of the Mediterranean in the first century A.D."

"Clearly a religious motivation," Scalia continued. "The only reason the people were concerned . . . was the fact that it contradicted their religious view. Now," Scalia asked, "would it be unconstitutional for the principal to listen to them, and on the basis of that religious motivation, to make the change in the high school?"

Topkis brushed off the question. Where Scalia thought the issue profound, Topkis viewed it as simple, almost silly. No, "the principal wouldn't be acting out of religious motivation. He would be acting of out of the scholar's interest in truth," he said.

"Do we know the state is acting out of religious motivation [and not a search for scientific truth]?" Scalia countered.

Of course we do, Topkis countered. The Louisiana lawmakers "talk about how terrible evolution is. Why? Because it's godless evolution, and what we got to do is bring God into balance with evolution. We got to give God equal time," Topkis said sarcastically.

Given the five minutes left for a rebuttal, attorney Wendell Bird stressed the purpose of the state law. It was not intended to advance religion. It was intended to further "academic freedom," he said. With that, however, he quickly ran into trouble with John Paul Stevens.

If there is one member of the Court who can match wits with Scalia, or any attorney appearing before the Court, it is the bow-tied Stevens. His manner is mild, but Stevens generally knows how to pull the one string that can unravel the fabric of an attorney's argument right before the attorney's eyes. Always polite, Stevens began, "May I ask about academic freedom for a moment? Would you say it would advance academic freedom if the school was told [that] you cannot teach a student the German language unless he's also willing to study French?"

Bird tried to wriggle away. "If they were within the same subject area, such as conversational German versus formal German, it . . ."

"No. No, just German. They didn't particularly like Germans and they do like French. So they say you can't study German unless you study French," Stevens said.

"Well, of course, that's not the wording of that statute," Bird replied.

"Well, it's pretty close. It says you can't teach evolution unless you teach this other subject," said Stevens.

Bird tried to move on, but Stevens was not about to let him go. "I'm just asking, would it advance academic freedom [to require the teaching of French when teaching German]?"

Unable to escape, Bird was forced into a nonsensical reply. "Yes, it would," he said.

On that note, Rehnquist interrupted. The time was up.

The conference did not go well for the chief justice. By enacting its Balanced Treatment Act, Louisiana had not established an official religion, at least in Rehnquist's view. Scalia certainly agreed. However, that argument persuaded no one else.

Brennan said the Louisiana lawmakers were engaged in an apparent "sham." State senator Keith and his colleagues had no deep interest in science instruction. They wanted to undercut the theory of evolution only because it conflicted with the Bible's story of creation. Who would be willing to say, with a straight face, that "creationism" is a "scientific" concept rather than a "religious belief"?

Marshall, Stevens, and Blackmun agreed with Brennan that the Constitution demands a clear separation of church and state. In a dispute between Thomas Jefferson and William Rehnquist on the meaning of the First Amendment, they sided with Jefferson.

Even those justices who favored more religion in schools were turned away by "creationism." William Jennings Bryan, a three-time presidential candidate, became something of a national joke in 1925 when he clashed with Clarence Darrow and sought to defend Tennessee's antievolution law based on the creation story in the Bible. Justices White, Powell, and O'Connor were not willing to follow Bryan's example—or the chief justice—on this one. White dodged the issue neatly. He noted that the Court usually relies on the definition of a law as put forth by a state supreme court or the appeals court in the area. Because the appeals court in New Orleans had said that "creation science" is a "religious belief," White said he would abide by their view.

Powell and O'Connor had developed a special affinity during their five years together on the Court. They had a similar approach to the work. Neither was an ideologue or an academic. Alone among the justices, Powell and O'Connor had some experience with the give-and-take of a political job: Powell as a school board member in Virginia, and O'Connor as a state legislator in Arizona. During her first years on the Court, O'Connor came to admire Powell's struggle to find a fair solution for each case. Unlike some of the others, the gentlemanly

Virginian had no interest in manipulating O'Connor in hopes of attracting her vote. Powell did not work that way. Rehnquist had been friends with Sandra Day since their years at Stanford, and Brennan was unmatched at endearing himself to newcomers, yet the clerks noticed that O'Connor spent more time talking with Lewis Powell than with any other justice.

A Richmond aristocrat and an Episcopalian, Powell was certainly not hostile to religion. Nonetheless, the Court had set a clear line, and Louisiana had crossed it. Brennan took the majority opinion for himself in the creationism case, but Powell wrote a separate opinion to explain his commonsense view. O'Connor joined it in full.

Schools may teach about religion so long as they do not teach a religion, Powell argued. "As a matter of history, schoolchildren can and should properly be informed of all aspects of this nation's religious heritage," he wrote. They can be taught comparative religion and shown "how religion permeates our history." Even the Bible can be used "in an appropriate study of history, civilization, ethics, comparative religion or the like." The establishment clause in the Constitution puts only one obvious limit: The state and its public schools may not "advance a particular religious belief," Powell concluded.

Usually it takes about three or four months for the Court to make public a decision in a major case. First, a majority opinion is written and passed around the building. Then, the dissenters get to say why the majority is all wrong. Usually—but not always—the justices who voted in the majority in the conference room sign on to the majority opinion, and then it is released to the public.

The Louisiana case, though argued in December 1986, was not released until June 19, 1987. It was not that the ruling hung on one wavering or undecided justice. Rather, Scalia had spent months working up a dissent. Like Louisiana state senator Keith, he called the Court judgment "Scopes-in-reverse." Instead of letting schoolchildren consider all the evidence about the origins of life, the Court was insisting that only one view be presented. He was especially upset that a law should be struck down simply because the lawmakers had a "religious motivation" when enacting it.

"We surely would not strike down a law providing money to feed the hungry or shelter the homeless if it could be demonstrated that, but for the religious beliefs of the legislators, the funds would not have been approved," he wrote. "Today's religious activism may give us the Balanced Treatment Act, but yesterday's resulted in the abolition of slavery, and tomorrow's may bring relief for famine victims." Still, Scalia's mighty effort convinced no one. Only Rehnquist joined the dissent. The creationism dissent did not do much for Scalia's reputation off the Court either. Conservative columnist George Will mocked his opinion in a column entitled "Good Grief, Scalia!"

The 7–2 ruling marked another embarrassing setback for Rehnquist. For conservatives, the fall 1986 term had begun with high hopes. With a truly conservative chief justice, joined by the irrepressible Scalia, conservatives thought they could finally break the Court's liberal logjam, which had blocked so much of the Reagan revolution. By late spring, however, a series of setbacks had turned into a full-scale rout.

"It's been a disaster so far," said conservative activist Pat McGuigan. Bruce Fein, a conservative legal commentator, said Rehnquist was proving "incompetent" as a chief justice, as Brennan outmaneuvered him.

The first term of the Rehnquist Court had proven to be a stellar one for the 81-year-old liberal. In the two affirmative action cases, Brennan told employers and judges they can give an edge to blacks or women in jobs. In January, he had given his ally Thurgood Marshall the opinion upholding the California law allowing women workers a leave for pregnancies. In early March, Brennan spoke for the Court again in ruling that a public employee suffering from a contagious disease is "handicapped" and therefore protected from discrimination by federal law. The case concerned a Florida schoolteacher with tuberculosis, but it was widely viewed as a test of the rights of an AIDS patient. The Reagan administration had argued that such diseases are not covered by antidiscrimination laws, but only Rehnquist and Scalia accepted that view.

It had now been a full 30 years since Brennan had come to the Court, and nearly two decades since the Republicans had vowed to push him into a lonely liberal corner, powerless to affect the decisions of the Court. Somehow through the years, though, he had managed to hold sway, and no term had been more surprisingly triumphant than this one.

"It is more appropriate to say this is the Brennan Court" than the Rehnquist Court, said Harvard law professor Laurence H. Tribe as the term came to a close in June 1987.

Who could have guessed the impact on American law when Dwight Eisenhower, in the midst of his 1956 reelection campaign, selected the little-known New Jersey state judge to sit on the Supreme Court? Eisenhower was favored to beat Democrat Adlai Stevenson in a rematch of their race four years earlier, but the president had had a recent heart attack. The polls showed that many Americans were concerned about the thought of Vice President Richard Nixon moving into the White House. In a close race, Eisenhower advisers worried that Nixon could drag down the ticket. They thought that the President particularly needed help with the Catholic and labor vote in the Northeast.

Attorney General Herbert Brownell had been searching for a Supreme Court replacement for Justice Sherman Minton, who had announced plans to retire in October. A few months earlier, the New Jersey Supreme Court's renowned chief justice, Arthur Vanderbilt, had been scheduled to address a conference of U.S. attorneys on congestion in the courts. When he fell ill at the last minute, he asked his younger colleague Brennan to take his place. Brennan's speech on streamlining the courts impressed Brownell. A check around the country found that the New Jersey judge was highly regarded as thoughtful and moderate. Plus, he was an Irish Catholic and a Democrat, just what Eisenhower needed to shore up his vote in the Northeast.

William Joseph Brennan, Jr., was born April 25, 1906, the second of eight children. His father, an Irish immigrant, started out as a coal shoveler at the Ballantine Brewery in Newark but worked his way up to become a labor leader and an elected city commissioner of Newark. "He was quite a disciplinarian, and his absolute determination was that each of us would get everything in the way of an education," Brennan said of his father.

The son proved to be a superb student, earning a bachelor's degree at the University of Pennsylvania and graduating near the top of his Harvard law class. He emerged from school in 1931, during the low point of the depression, and became a labor lawyer. In 1949, New Jersey's Republican governor appointed the Democrat Brennan to be a superior court judge, and Vanderbilt persuaded the governor to elevate him to the state supreme court three years later.

Brennan was at work in his chambers on a Friday evening, September 29, when U.S. Attorney General Brownell called and asked him to come to Washington for a meeting the next morning. Brownell offered no explanation except to say it was important. At 1 A.M., Brennan boarded the night train; he was surprised to find the attorney general himself at Union Station at 5:30 A.M. to greet him. Only on the drive across town did Brennan learn the purpose of his visit.

"I was utterly in a daze," he recalled recently. He says he never suspected that he was a candidate for the Court nomination, assuming that it would go to a prominent Republican or a friend of Eisenhower's. He had never met Ike and was certainly not a Republican. Nonetheless, after a 30-minute meeting, the nomination was his. "I never saw a man say 'yes' so fast," said press secretary James Hagerty.

Eisenhower never gave a detailed explanation for the nomination, although Brennan was quite satisfied with Ike's public statement that he was "the best man available" for the job.

"I was willing to stop the inquiries right there," Brennan joked.

He came to the Supreme Court for the first time during the early days of October in 1956. That week, the Brooklyn Dodgers were playing the New York Yankees in the World Series, the last "subway series." Game six saw a perfect game pitched by Yankee Don Larsen. When Chief Justice Warren, a bearlike figure, took the diminutive Brennan on a tour of the building, they stopped by the justices' private lounge. When Warren flipped on the lights, they discovered the brethren gathered around the TV set watching the series. Before the chief justice could complete the introductions, someone called out, "Shut out the lights."

In the Senate, Joseph McCarthy's star was setting, although he took to the floor to cast the lone vote against Brennan. Otherwise, the new justice drew little attention. *Time* magazine reported his nomination in a five-paragraph story entitled "A Happy Irishman." No one foresaw the legal revolution to come or the part that would be played by the little Irishman. Certainly, Brennan's own comments gave no clue. He characterized himself as "the mule entered in the Kentucky Derby—I don't expect to distinguish myself, but I do expect to benefit from the association."

Soon after his arrival, however, Brennan formed a unique relationship with Earl Warren. A large man and a politician by trade, Warren led the Court by force of personality, but he was no one's idea of a brilliant lawyer. However, he soon had one working with him in Brennan. Each week, they met before the

Court's conference to go over cases. Together, they set the agenda for the liberal Court of the 1960s. To the general public, Hugo Black and William O. Douglas, along with Warren, stood out as the leaders of the liberal Court. Later, they were joined by Arthur Goldberg, Abe Fortas, and Thurgood Marshall. Through it all, however, according to scholars of the Court, Brennan stands out as the key member of the Warren Court. He had the ability to write opinions that would mesh the views of a half dozen stubborn and strong-willed lawyers. His 1962 opinion in *Baker* v. *Carr* led to the "one person, one vote" principle that reshaped the state legislatures. His 1964 opinion in *New York Times* v. *Sullivan* reshaped libel law. He also wrote landmarks in areas as diverse as school desegregation, obscenity, freedom of religion, criminal law, and the rights of welfare recipients.

His daughter Nancy, then a teenager and now the director of Baltimore's City Life Museum, remembers her father sitting at a green cardtable propped up in the living room of their Georgetown home. It was invariably covered with legal briefs. The justice would come home for a family dinner at 6 P.M. but then work in the living room until 10 P.M. On Saturday mornings, he would cook breakfast, she said, and then work in the living room for the rest of the day. "I think his energy is simply explained by the love of what he does," she said.

For generations of law clerks and Court employees, Brennan radiated a warmth that few forgot. Though a towering figure in the law, the diminutive justice always had time to stop in the hall to ask a Court employee about his family. When clerks were forced to work late, Brennan would call their spouses to apologize for the late hours. His warm handshake and twinkling eyes charmed even those who found his legal views repugnant. Charles Cooper, the one-time Rehnquist clerk and Reagan administration official, prides himself on his hard-nosed conservatism, but he still recalls warmly a lunch with Justice Brennan. When he and another clerk joined the justice, Brennan locked arms with the two of them and went bouncing down the Court steps. "He is who everyone ought to have as a grandfather," Cooper said.

Brennan was a fighter, too, committed to his view of the law. He could be genuinely irked upon hearing one of the Court's criminal law rulings referred to as a "technicality." Brennan held up the Bill of Rights as a shining set of ideals. In the 1970s and 1980s, long after Warren, Douglas, and Black had departed, Brennan still carried the liberal torch. He fought for civil rights, to enforce desegregation, to preserve the right to choose an abortion, and to stop the death penalty.

In his personal life, he went through several trying periods. In 1978, Brennan underwent radiation treatment for a cancerous tumor in his throat, and he later suffered what was called a "small stroke" that caused a weakness in his right arm. Worst of all, however, he watched as his wife Marjorie died of cancer. "I came close, very close to crumbling under the strain," he said in an interview. On several occasions, Brennan said he was convinced he could not carry on with his life or his work on the Court.

In the year after his wife finally died, however, Brennan began dating his long-time secretary, Mary Fowler. On March 9, 1983, the 76-year-old justice and his 68-year-old secretary eloped. They left behind a brief memo for the justices.

"Mary Fowler and I were married yesterday, and we have gone to Bermuda," it read.

Upon his return, his colleagues noted that Brennan's enthusiasm had returned. He plunged back into the Court battles with the vigor they had come to expect of him.

In the spring of 1987, as the first term of the Rehnquist Court came to an end, Brennan finished his thirtieth term in high style. On June 19, he read aloud his opinion in Louisiana's creationism case. Combined with victories on affirmative action, free speech, and religion, Brennan had had an outstanding year.

By the same token, it had been a frustrating term for Rehnquist. He had prevailed in dozens of cases involving crime and the death penalty, but that only highlighted the fact that nothing much had changed during the 1986–1987 term. Indeed, the Court displayed the same split personality it had shown through the 17 years of the Burger Court: conservative on crime, but liberal on civil rights and civil liberties. So far, the elevation of Rehnquist and the addition of Scalia had changed nothing of significance.

The key figure remained 79-year-old Lewis Powell. In criminal cases, Powell usually sided with the conservatives to uphold the police and prosecutors, but in most other areas, Powell was moderate to liberal. He was not about to push the Court to the right. He provided a solid fifth vote in support of the *Roe* v. *Wade* ruling and the right to abortion. He believed in the separation of church and state and in the importance of free speech and freedom of the press, and on most occasions he cast his vote with Brennan to uphold affirmative action.

A week after the creationism ruling, the Court was set to release the last 5 of the term's 150 written opinions on Friday, June 26, and then adjourn for the summer. For the justices, their clerks, and the Court staff, the annual "rush to judgment" in June is draining. Toward the end of the month, the Court often issues four or five decisions daily—hundreds of pages of opinions and dissents. For reporters, those weeks are akin to final exam periods in college. Suddenly, a semester's worth of study must be regurgitated on demand.

That morning, however, the press room was abuzz, and not over a pending decision. There were rumors that one of the aging justices was about to resign. At 10 A.M., when the gavel sounded, the nine black-robed justices stepped from behind their red velvet curtain to the customary greeting from the marshal: "The honorable the Chief Justice and the Associate Justices of the Supreme Court of the United States. Oyez! Oyez! Oyez! All persons having business before the honorable, the Supreme Court of the United States, are admonished to draw near and give their attention, for the Court is now sitting. God save the United States and this honorable Court."

Lewis Powell, always a frail figure, looked especially fragile that morning. He glanced toward the assembled attorneys and then looked down in despair, as if overcome by emotion. This would be the last morning he would stand before the bench as a justice of the nation's highest court. Just the day before, Powell had made his decision to retire and told Rehnquist of his plans. A few minutes before the justices took the bench on Friday, the chief justice placed a call to the president's chief of staff, Howard Baker, to tell him of the impending vacancy. The Reagan White House, though battered by the Iran–Contra scandal, would get one more chance to remake the Supreme Court.

After the five opinions were announced, Rehnquist made official Powell's resignation.

"Before we turn to the final announcement on today's calendar, we wish to note with great regret the retirement of Justice Lewis F. Powell as a member of the Court," Rehnquist said. The announcement was brief and delivered in a monotone. "We shall miss his wise counsel in our deliberations," the chief justice concluded, "but we look forward to being the continuing beneficiaries of his friendship."

With that, the gavel sounded, and the marshal announced the Court would be in recess until the first Monday in October. The justices quietly slipped back through the curtain and into their summer recess.

The battle for the Court had begun.

PART THREE

The Summer of 1987

4

Robert Bork and the Intellectual Feast

Powell's resignation sent a surge of energy through the Justice Department. The Rehnquist and Scalia appointments may have raised the intellectual level at the Court, but they hadn't changed the results much. The conservatives were still one vote short of controlling the Supreme Court, the one vote that had been held by Lewis Powell. His replacement could tilt the Court decidedly to the right.

At the White House, the reaction was more subdued. The Iran–Contra scandal had thoroughly shaken Ronald Reagan and forced many of his top aides, including Chief of Staff Donald Regan, to resign. The new chief of staff, former Tennessee senator Howard Baker, had been considering a run for the presidency in 1988 but put aside his ambitions to help save Reagan's presidency. For a time, the revelations of the secret arms deals and the diversion of money to the Nicaraguan Contras threatened to ruin Reagan the way that the Watergate scandal had destroyed Richard Nixon. Baker wanted to restore stability to the White House and to calm the political waters; he did not want a major political fight over the Supreme Court.

Among the organized liberal groups in Washington, the news of Powell's retirement set off alarms, far more so even than with the Rehnquist and Scalia nominations the year before. Without Powell, the right to abortion, the legality of affirmative action, and the separation of church and state were in real jeopardy. Kate Michelman, executive director of the National

Abortion Rights Action League (NARAL), was about to deliver a speech to a group of women attorneys when she received a hand-delivered note reporting word of Powell's resignation.

"Our worst fears have just been realized," she began.

Michelman, as well as the leaders of the civil rights organizations, anticipated what would come next. The year before, Justice Department officials had made it clear that Scalia and Robert H. Bork were their two top candidates for the high court. Attorney General Edwin Meese and Assistant Attorney General William Bradford Reynolds certainly had not changed their views since then. On Capitol Hill, Democrats tried to warn Howard Baker that a Bork nomination meant a major fight, but Reagan was not deterred. An apostle of the true conservative faith, Bork had deserved such a nomination for years, Reagan believed. Five days after Powell's resignation, the nomination was his.

Robert Bork was an angry man. For years, he had taught antitrust law, a field that he said was riddled with "intellectual errors." Most economists feared *monopolies*, giant corporations that could fix prices. In the antitrust laws, Congress sought to protect competition among a variety of small firms. Bork believed they had it all wrong. Big was often better, he said. Giant firms could be "more efficient," he said. At the Yale Law School, students dubbed his class "Pro-Trust."

He moved on to constitutional law but discovered disturbing developments there, too. The Supreme Court's landmark decisions in recent decades were "unprincipled" and "illegitimate," Bork announced. They were based more on liberal politics than on a fair reading of the Constitution, he said.

With his scraggly beard and scowling visage, Bork became a provocative figure on the lecture circuit. To the delight of conservative audiences, he heaped scorn on the Supreme Court for "creating" a new "right to privacy," for protecting the free speech rights of pornographers and Communists, and for giving blacks preferences over whites in the name of equal opportunity.

Despite a public reputation as a constitutional scholar, Bork did little scholarly writing. In his speeches, Bork maintained that the courts should rely on the "original intent" of the framers of the Constitution. Historians were deeply divided on what the framers of 1789 intended to convey by phrases such as "the establishment of religion" or "freedom of speech" or what the Reconstruction Congress meant to achieve with the Fourteenth Amendment. Bork, however, didn't explain his opinions with historical research and rarely quoted historians. To him, the answers were obvious.

Bork made a name for himself as a speechmaker and a writer of newspaper opinion pieces. He also paid his political dues. Like Rehnquist, he had written position papers for Barry Goldwater in the 1964 campaign and had organized a professors group in support of Richard Nixon in 1968. When Nixon was under attack in Congress for extending the Vietnam War into Cambodia, Bork opined that the Constitution gave the President "the inherent power" to make such a military move, even in defiance of Congress. The next year, the White House was having a hard time finding any legal authority to support its proposal to forbid judges from ordering busing for school desegregation. Most lawyers thought the courts had the duty to protect constitutional rights and the power to remedy wrongs based on violations of the Constitution, but Bork came forward to testify in Congress in favor of the ill-fated bill.

Nixon had picked four members of the Supreme Court, but Professor Bork was passed over in each instance. Finally, in 1973, with Nixon reeling from the Watergate scandal, he picked Bork to be the Administration's solicitor general, the government's top attorney before the Supreme Court. The job has been dubbed "the tenth justice" because the Court relies on the solicitor general's office for expertise and advice. Also, for many past appointees, it has been a stepping-stone to the Supreme Court.

For Bork, the job became a stepping-stone to Watergate notoriety. Just four months into his new job, Bork became an executioner of sorts in the so-called Saturday Night Massacre. Under pressure, Nixon had appointed Archibald Cox as the Watergate special prosecutor. However, when Cox demanded that the president turn over his tapes of White House conversations, Nixon refused and ordered Attorney General Elliot Richardson to fire Cox. Richardson in turn refused and resigned. His deputy, William Ruckelshaus, did the same. Third in the chain of power at the Justice Department was the solicitor general.

Bork faced a difficult choice. He could follow his colleagues and resign on principle, possibly deepening the constitutional crisis, or he could carry out the White House order and possibly be stained forever for having done so. Bork chose the latter course. He fired Cox, became the acting attorney general, appointed a new special prosecutor, and went on about his duties. By most accounts, Bork was neither a villain of the Watergate era nor one of its heroes. He continued in office as solicitor general under Gerald Ford. Nonetheless, when Justice William O. Douglas finally retired in 1975, Bork was once again passed over for the Supreme Court seat. The Watergate memories were too fresh. John Paul Stevens, a nonpolitical appeals court judge from Chicago, was tapped for the job instead. In January 1977, Robert Bork packed his bags and went back to New Haven and the Yale Law School.

Even at Yale, a dark cloud continued to hang over him. His best friend and colleague at Yale, Professor Alexander Bickel, had recently died of cancer, and Bork's beloved wife, Claire, was desperately ill, also dying of cancer. Bork had to maintain his teaching job while caring for his wife as well as earning extra money through legal work to pay for the soaring medical bills. His speeches during the late 1970s had an even more ominous and angry tone. He decried the spread of liberal "egalitarianism" and "moral relativism." He worried about the "decline of our institutions" because of a loss of standards. He fired off a sharp note to his Yale colleagues when the law school proposed to ban recruiters who discriminated against homosexuals. Public tolerance of homosexuality was a mistake, he believed. "Societies can have very small or very great amounts of homosexual behavior, depending upon the degrees of moral disapproval or tolerance shown," he said in a memo to the faculty.

In December 1980, a month after Ronald Reagan was elected president, Claire Bork died. New Haven became, for Bork, a place with an empty home and sad memories. He jumped at a partnership offer with a Washington, D.C., law firm. No sooner had he settled into the new job and a new home in the same neighborhood with Vice President George Bush and Supreme Court Justice Potter Stewart than officials of the Reagan administration came calling. They, too, had an offer, one he could not refuse. If Bork took a judgeship on the U.S. Court of Appeals in Washington, D.C., his name would be on the short list of potential nominees to the Supreme Court.

The appeals court in the District of Columbia was often called "the nation's second-highest court." The law governing federal programs and regulations was often decided there. Bork found it a bore. He once recalled to reporters the last lines of

Heart of Darkness, the Joseph Conrad novel. " 'The horror, the horror!' I often kid my friends that my last words will be 'The trivia, the trivia.' "

Still, Bork's legal opinions were neither trivial nor boring. They read like the work of a restless intellectual trapped into deciding mundane matters. Where other judges engaged in a drab dissection of a technical legal issue, Bork wrote essays on the law and pronouncements on the Constitution. Among the relatively small circle of lawyers, academics, and journalists who closely follow the courts, Bork's fame grew—as did his frustration.

In 1981, when his friend Potter Stewart resigned from the Court, Reagan passed over Bork to pick the first woman justice: Sandra Day O'Connor. In 1986, when Chief Justice Burger stepped down, Bork could have been made chief justice, or appointed an associate justice to fill Rehnquist's seat, but the phone call from the White House never came. This was an especially crushing blow.

"Bob was known everywhere as the conservative intellectual leader. If we put up both of them [Rehnquist and Bork] together, that would have been a lot of heft, a big target," Brad Reynolds, Meese's chief deputy, said in a later interview. "We were confident that Bork would be better received on his own."

To make matters worse, when Scalia got the nod, word went around Washington that Bork was passed over in part for what sounded like New Age reasons: He was overweight, out of shape, and a heavy smoker. He was also nine years older than Scalia. For this to be a factor was more proof that life was not fair. In the Nixon years, Professor Bork had been passed over in part because he was too young. Now, though established as the nation's most prominent legal conservative, he was passed over in 1986 because he was too old.

Nonetheless, one man had not forgotten Bork: Ronald Reagan. He, too, had been passed over for the presidency on several occasions and was thought to be too old, but he held fast to his conservative principles, and eventually the country came calling for him. Reagan admired a man who stood his ground. On the day Lewis Powell resigned, Reagan had his mind made up. Meese and Reynolds stood with the president. They knew this was probably their last chance to put a Reagan stamp on the Supreme Court. It was not time to pick someone the liberals would welcome.

Still, the nomination Reagan bestowed on Bork on July 1, 1987, was not the same as the one he could have given him a year earlier. That was so because Ronald Reagan was not the same politician he had been a year earlier. The Iran–Contra scandal had knocked Reagan down a notch or two in the public's esteem. His fall was felt on Capitol Hill, too. The Democrats had retaken control of the Senate in large measure because in November 1986, a handful of southern Democrats— solidly backed by black voters—ousted a series of Republican incumbents.

One other calculation had changed over the year—and again, to Bork's detriment. When Burger, a conservative, retired in 1986, he was going to be replaced by a Reagan conservative, leaving the balance on the Court unchanged. The replacement of Lewis Powell was quite another matter. The situation was made to order for a cartoonist: The eight black-robed justices would be perched on a seesaw, four on the left side and four on the right. Then along comes rotund Robert Bork, ready to plop his considerable bulk on the far right end.

That image was a scary one for many, especially for those who valued the right to abortion. A 1986 abortion case from Pennsylvania had revealed that the *Roe* v. *Wade* ruling had only five supporters left: Brennan, Marshall, Blackmun, Stevens, and Powell. On abortion, Bork was surely no Lewis Powell. In a 1981 appearance before a congressional committee, Bork called *Roe* v. *Wade* "an unconstitutional decision, a serious and wholly unjustifiable usurpation of state legislative authority." Thus, the stakes were clear, and the battle was joined. The best known, most acerbic critic of the Supreme Court would get a chance to reverse three decades of liberalism.

From the start, the Bork battle was a mismatch. The stiff, awkward scene in the White House pressroom on July 1 set the tone. Reagan read a brief statement while Bork stood by silently. No questions were taken. The judge was not even permitted to offer the customary "thank you" to the president for having bestowed such a high honor on the nominee. The White House handlers treated him as the proverbial 300-pound gorilla whose every move would cause alarm.

Baker's team at the White House knew they needed to win over the moderates in the Senate, so they decided to highlight Bork's qualifications but play down his conservative views. No one could question that Bork was exceedingly qualified to serve on the Court. He was an intelligent, serious-minded man, devoted to the law, a good writer, and honest. He had been a law professor, a corporate lawyer, a government attorney, and an appeals court judge. As a sportswriter might have put it, he had played the game in the big leagues, studied it, lectured on it, even umpired. What more can you do?

All observers realized, however, that Bork was not nominated by Ronald Reagan just because he was qualified to sit on the Supreme Court. The same could be said of thousands of lawyers in America. Bork rose to the top because he was the most prominent and assertive critic of the liberal drift on the high court.

The White House stealth strategy, combined with Bork's sense of propriety, made for a strange scene in the summer of 1987. For years, Bork had pummeled the Supreme Court in print and in speeches. He called the liberals "unprincipled." He portrayed them as politicians in black robes. The justices harrumphed in private but said nothing in public. Now, Bork suffered the same treatment. Day after day, he was slammed in the press and on airwaves as a dangerous reactionary, a man who cared more for conservative politics than the law. Through it all, though, Bork stood mute. Pilloried in public, grumbling in private, Bork grew more frustrated.

The civil rights activists, abortion rights supporters, and other liberal groups had sounded the alarm. For years, they had read what Bork said. Thanks to the Voting Rights Act of 1965, blacks in the South had mustered considerable political clout; they now mobilized and organized to defeat Bork.

To their surprise, the liberal groups met little resistance. If there was a conservative, pro-Bork movement around the country, it was nearly invisible. On several occasions, Reagan offered the rather lame admonition that "politics" should be kept out of the process, but the Senate Democrats thought Reagan had picked the most conservative nominee possible; they were not about to ignore politics when it came to judging him.

By the time of the televised hearings in mid-September, Bork was in deep trouble, his nomination already perhaps fatally wounded. Unlike Rehnquist and Scalia, Bork could not simply refuse to answer questions. He would have to defend himself, and do it well, if he wanted to win confirmation.

Finally, millions of TV viewers got a chance to see the man who had been portrayed as an ogre. They saw instead a thoughtful, stern professor who refused to offer the politically correct responses. While senators huffed out sound bites of indignation, the law professor tried to explain—and explain, and explain. Others saw a cold, unsmiling man who could extemporize on abstract theories of the law, but who appeared unable to grasp simple notions of justice and fairness. Bork himself put the finishing touch on this portrait of himself when asked why he wanted to serve on the Supreme Court. The job, he said, would be "an intellectual feast."

Watching at home, several justices came away with a third view. They thought television had cheapened the process. It encouraged the senators to posture and pontificate rather than engage in a serious debate. When Burger, a notorious TV-hater, retired in 1986, most of the justices assumed it was only a matter of time before they joined Congress in letting their sessions be televised. After the Bork hearings, however, the sentiment changed. They were not about to let television cheapen the Supreme Court.

Still, despite it all, the summer of 1987 saw an unusual national debate on the meaning of the Constitution. It was, as many remarked, an entirely fitting way to celebrate the charter's 200th anniversary. To his credit, Bork laid out clear principles of how to interpret the Constitution. He encouraged a debate on fundamentals. Like many a critic, however, he proved to be better on the attack than on defending his own views.

He set forth two general principles as guides for the Court in interpreting the Constitution. First, justices should rely on the "original intent" of a particular clause. This is, indeed, a powerful and profound argument: The Constitution was written as the fundamental law of the land and was ratified by the citizens of the day. Its words meant something to those who approved them. If five unelected justices of the Supreme Court could invent an entirely new meaning for those words and use this interpretation to strike down laws, both the Constitution and democracy would be dead. The nation would be governed not by what the people believed then, or what they believe now, but what five life-tenured lawyers believe.

Of course, discerning the "original intent" of the Constitution is somewhat like discerning the "true meaning" of the Bible. The many Christian sects, for example, read the same Scriptures and take a different meaning from them, at least to some extent. Each sect also believes that only its view is correct. Some read the words literally; others draw a general message from the overall text. Where the Constitution was concerned, Bork and Scalia were more in the former camp. They were, in other words, fundamentalists.

Bork's second principle was also Reagan's favorite: "judicial restraint." Simply put, the hard decisions should be made by elected officials, not judges. When in doubt, the Supreme Court should uphold laws passed by Congress, a state legislature, or a city council, as well as regulations put out by the president, a police department, or a school board. This was, of course, the philosophy espoused by Rehnquist and opposed by Brennan, the champion of individual rights.

In Brennan's view, Bork's first point was simplistic, his second hogwash. Who could discern the "original intent" of the Constitution's framers today? he wondered. Also, why should the Court ignore individual rights so as to defer to the other branches of government? The people insisted on a Bill of Rights in the Constitution, and it was the Court's duty to enforce rights such as freedom of speech and freedom of religion. In Brennan's view, if the Court blithely upheld the decisions of other branches of government, it was simply abdicating its responsibility.

Not surprisingly, the Senate Democrats were not about to fight Bork over these abstract principles. They wanted to get to the meat of the matter. Three issues became the focus of the Bork battle: civil rights, free speech, and privacy.

On civil rights, Bork had been remarkably consistent over the years. In 1963, Bork, like Rehnquist, had opposed new laws giving blacks the right to be served in restaurants, to stay in hotels, and to enjoy other such "public accommodations." In the *New Republic* magazine in 1963, Bork condemned the then-pending federal Civil Rights Act, concluding it was based on "a principle of unsurpassed ugliness." The offensive principle was "coercion" by the state, he said. He fretted about the "cost in freedom" and the "morality of enforcing morals through the law." He cited as examples of these costs a white "barber [told] that he must deal with all who come to him" or "a chiropodist [who] cannot refuse a Negro patient."

Black Americans should take no offense at his remarks, Professor Bork made clear later, dismissing his 1963 article as mere intellectual musings. In his 1990 book, *The Tempting of America*, Bork explained that the *New Republic* article was in "the liberal tradition" and "the argument proceeded from a concern with the civil rights of all persons." Of course, Bork's version of "civil rights" and "freedom," like Rehnquist's, seemed to ignore the possibility that blacks might also be interested in the right and freedom to eat dinner in a restaurant open to the public, to get a haircut in a barbershop, or to be treated by a chiropodist.

Bork had also condemned the Court for striking down as unconstitutional racially restrictive deed covenants. These were once the common device employed to keep blacks, Jews, or other minorities out of white Christian neighborhoods. A deed might say the property could be sold only to "Caucasians" or that it may not be sold to "non-Caucasians" or to "Jews." Because these deed restrictions were enforced by state courts, the justices said unanimously in 1948 that they violated the Fourteenth Amendment's ban on any state action that deprives blacks of "the enjoyment of property rights." Bork said these deeds were a private matter, not covered by the Constitution.

Bork also said the Court was wrong in 1966 to strike down as unconstitutional a state poll tax that had kept the poor of all races, which included many blacks, from voting. Because these taxes screened out voters because they were poor, not because they were black, they were not covered by the Fourteenth or Fifteenth Amendments, he said. Meanwhile, Bork also criticized the Court for upholding the Voting Rights Act, passed by Congress, which prevented states from using literacy tests that screened out black voters. Congress had exceeded its constitutional authority, he maintained.

Civil rights lawyers saw a pattern in Bork's opinions, one that did not have much to do with "original intent" or "judicial restraint." When Congress acted to ensure equality for blacks, Bork objected. When the Supreme Court acted to ensure equality for blacks, Bork objected. Bork did support the *Brown* v. *Board of Education* ruling: No nominee to any high federal job in the 1980s could oppose that landmark decision. For Bork, however, supporting the ruling required some fancy footwork. The historical evidence strongly suggests that the Reconstruction Congress that drew up the Fourteenth Amendment in 1866 approved of segregated schools for blacks. The District of Columbia, for example, had continued to have segregated schools under the control of Congress. How then could a strict devotee of "original intent" accept the *Brown* decision? If you believe that the Court must rely on the "original intent" of the Fourteenth Amendment, the Court should have upheld segregation, not struck it down. Bork tiptoed around this mud puddle by asserting that the Fourteenth Amendment was generally intended to further "black equality," and the *Brown* decision was in line with this intent, he said.

One final complication arose with affirmative action. In the *Bakke* case of 1978, the Court said that the University of California may give a preference to black candidates who are seeking admission to its medical school. Predictably, Bork took to the editorial pages of the *Wall Street Journal* to denounce the decision. He labeled the supporters of the university plan as "the hard-core racists of reverse discrimination." The Fourteenth Amendment demands equal treatment for all, Bork asserted, whites as well as blacks.

Bork's viewpoint on the *Bakke* case is held by many, if not most, Americans. Still, it is a hard argument to make if you believe in "original intent" and "judicial restraint." After all, as Bork said, the Fourteenth Amendment was intended to further "black equality." The University of California governing board also aimed to further "black equality." Because the state had an extremely low percentage of black doctors, the physicians who would serve poor black neighborhoods, university officials wanted to give an edge to the few black candidates trying to enter the medical school at the Davis campus. Usually, Robert Bork argued that the Court should defer to the decisions of state officials, but not this time. The same Robert Bork who said the Fourteenth Amendment did not forbid deeds that kept blacks from buying a house or a state poll tax that prevented them from voting concluded that—yes, indeed—it does bar the University of California from giving an edge to black students.

Bork also put forth a quite distinct view of the First Amendment. The ban on laws "abridging the freedom of speech" may be the most cherished of American rights. At least since the early 1960s, the Supreme Court had taken the view that Americans could speak, write, or read whatever they chose, with but a few exceptions—such as printing "obscenity" or malicious lies. It was not always so. In 1919, for example, the Supreme Court upheld a ten-year prison term for Socialist presidential candidate Eugene Debs for having made a speech that obliquely criticized the military draft. In the modern Court, however, the principle of freedom of speech stood as solidly as one of the marble pillars in the courtroom.

Bork asserted that the old view was better. In a 1971 *Indiana Law Review* article, Bork said that the Court should protect only "speech that is explicitly political." Left unprotected would be "other forms of expression, be it scientific, literary or that variety of expression we call obscene or pornographic." (Notice how Bork's view of government "coercion" changed in eight years. In 1963 he worried about giving the government the power to limit the "freedom" of white store owners to keep out blacks, but by 1971 he supported giving the government the power to limit the freedom of what Americans may choose to read.)

If adopted, Bork's view would have entailed a radical rewriting of our notion of free speech. Salman Rushdie's controversial novel *Satanic Verses*, for example, which won the author international notoriety and a death sentence from the Ayatollah Khomeini, could, under Bork's view, simply be banned by the government to avoid the controversy and potential offense to Muslims. In his view, a city or town could also choose to ban controversial movies, such as *The Last Temptation of Christ*.

The same is true of a scientific dispute. Many scientists contend that industrial pollution is causing a dangerous global warming. Some think electromagnetic fields cause cancer. The Bush administration has disputed both assertions. Could the White House simply order a ban on the publication of scientific papers that dispute the Administration's view? According to Bork's view, the Administration could.

Bork also disputed the constitutional protection given radical dissenters. "There should be no constitutional obstruction to laws making criminal any speech that advocates forcible overthrow of the government or the violation of any law," he wrote in the 1971 article. The soapbox orator who says that George Bush should be dumped in the Potomac or the radical pamphleteer who calls for the extermination of "Imperial Amerika" could be arrested and jailed under Bork's view. Under prevailing Court doctrine, speechmakers or pamphleteers, no matter how obnoxious, cannot be punished unless their message poses a danger to incite "imminent lawless action."

In the 1987 hearings, Bork backed away from many of his earlier positions on free speech. The current Court stand on protecting radical dissenters "is okay," he told Senator Patrick Leahy. He also said he had come to the view that other speech involving "moral and scientific debate" should be protected because it is "central to a democratic government." He did not say whether he had changed his mind on literary and artistic works. Bork's opponents used his modified stands as evidence against him, calling it a "confirmation conversion."

The third area was probably the most controversial of all. Do Americans have a constitutional "right to privacy"? Though the word "abortion" was hardly uttered during the Bork hearings, that was what the debate was all about. Bork, the constitutional fundamentalist, stood his ground. The Constitution says nothing about a right to "privacy," a right to abortion, or even a right to buy contraceptives. The Court, as an unelected elite, should not strike down laws based on rights it has "created," he said. If Americans want to buy contraceptives or permit abortions, they should take that message to the ballot box, Bork said, and not wait for the Court to act.

The Supreme Court, of course, had acted many times before to announce rights that are not spelled out in the Constitution. Americans have a fundamental right to marry, to travel where they choose, and to send their children to parochial schools, the Court had said. Though these decisions grew out of the justices' view of the constitutional right to "liberty," the Court has always struggled with these cases.

In 1965, for example, the justices heard a challenge to a Connecticut law that forbade the sale of contraceptives, even to married couples. Everyone agreed that the law was archaic and silly, and it also went unenforced. Was it unconstitutional? Yes, the Court said in *Griswold* v. *Connecticut.* Justice William O. Douglas dashed off an opinion conceding that no particular provision in the Bill of Rights covered this case. Nonetheless, Douglas wrote, these individual rights "have penumbras, formed by emanations" given off by these rights. The result is that the whole is larger than the sum of its parts. Looked at in this way, the Bill of Rights creates a "zone of privacy" where the government cannot intrude, Douglas concluded. Because Connecticut's law intrudes into the marital bedroom, he said, it is unconstitutional.

Douglas's vaporizing about "emanations" and "penumbras" became the standard fare for mocking the Court. What does the right to privacy mean? wondered Bork. It does not mean that couples have a right to use heroin in their bedroom, or to make child pornography, or to beat each other up. In 1986, it became clear this right did not even apply to all couples. In *Bowers* v. *Hardwick,* the Court upheld on a 5–4 vote a Georgia law that made it a crime for homosexuals to engage in sexual intercourse. Byron White, who voted with the majority in the *Griswold* case, saying that married couples have a right to privacy, wrote the opposite majority opinion in the

Bowers case, saying it was "facetious at best" to suggest homosexuals have the same rights.

Of course, it was *Roe* v. *Wade* that made the constitutional "right to privacy" the focus of enormous attention. For the millions of Americans who believe that human life begins at conception, the *Roe* decision was morally wrong and a constitutional abomination. Robert Bork agreed. Throughout the hearings, Committee Chair Joseph R. Biden pushed and prodded him. He talked of a married couple's right to privacy. Didn't the Constitution protect that fundamental right? the Senator asked. Bork would not budge. No, he replied, knowing that his answer might cost him his chance to sit on the Supreme Court.

On October 1, Senator Arlen Specter, a Pennsylvania Republican who had closely questioned Bork during the hearings, announced he would vote against the nominee. Day by day then, conservative Democrats from the South, reacting to pressure from black constituents, joined in repudiating Bork. On October 6, the Judiciary Committee rejected the nomination on a 9–5 vote. Bork refused to quit, and his nomination was sent to the Senate floor. The final vote, on October 23, was 58–42, the largest margin of defeat ever for a Supreme Court nominee.

In the end, fittingly, everyone had a theory, firmly held, on why Bork lost. He blamed "lies and distortions" by his critics. Reagan said the Democrats had "politicized" the nomination. Others pointed to the November 1986 elections—the Democrats simply had the votes. Quite a few armchair analysts blamed Bork's scraggly beard. He looked scary on television, they hypothesized.

The liberals had a simple explanation and a good one. Robert Bork said that the Court was wrong to uphold civil rights so forcefully, wrong to protect freedom of speech so broadly, and wrong to create a right to privacy. Most Americans disagreed with him. They supported those stands and agreed with the Court.

For decades, too, Bork had been saying that the nation's most divisive disputes should be settled in the political arena, not behind closed doors and not by unelected officials. He got his wish in a perverse sort of way. The summer of 1987 offered a view of politics at its roughest, and the loser was Professor Bork.

PART FOUR
The
1987–1988 Term

5

Waiting for the Fifth Vote

On Monday, October 5, the day before the Senate Judiciary Committee was to vote on the Bork nomination, the eight justices of the Supreme Court quietly began the 1987 term. Across First Street, in the Senate chamber, the battle over Bork's nomination still raged, but Rehnquist and Scalia, Bork's friends on the Court, knew by then that he would not be joining them. They also realized that the Court would have a vacant seat for weeks, possibly months.

Rehnquist and Scalia had watched with dismay as Bork's nomination unraveled. Since the early 1970s, the three had been friends. They had joined the government through the Nixon administration and shared conservative legal views that were decidedly out of fashion in academia and most of the legal profession. Being out of favor seemed to bring conservative judges closer together. Rehnquist and Scalia joined several like-minded friends each month for a poker game. Both played true to form, friends said. Scalia talked too much; Rehnquist, subdued and businesslike, would look up on occasion and say, "Let's get on with it"—as always, he hated to waste time. On occasion, Bork came, too. Though a terrible poker player, he sat in a haze of cigarette smoke and kept the others entertained with his pointed sarcasm.

Bork's defeat was more than a personal loss for Rehnquist and Scalia. Both realized that, but for good timing, they too could have been pilloried in public and defeated in the Senate. Rehnquist's views differed little from Bork's over the years, but he benefited in 1986 from being a sitting justice. Even if defeated for confirmation as chief justice, he would have continued to sit on the Court. He also had the good fortune to have come before a Republican-controlled Senate.

In private, however, Rehnquist did not complain about "politics" infecting the process of selecting and confirming Supreme Court justices. In his view, the Court was not a pristine institution that stood above politics, nor were the justices learned men who could "discover" the correct meaning of the Constitution. He asserted that there was no indisputably "right answer" to the questions that come before the Court. The answers inevitably depended on the philosophy—legal and political—that a judge brought to the bench.

Rehnquist liked to go out for lunch with law clerks and reporters, within a few blocks of the Court. His tastes were simple: a cheeseburger, pink in the middle, with a light beer. Though he had cut down on his smoking, he usually had a cigarette or two at lunch. Sometimes, the clerks were surprised, too, by what they saw as his simple and political view of the Court. Rehnquist rarely gave much credence to broad theories as to how the Court should judge cases, even ones favored by conservatives. For example, Attorney General Meese, in a series of speeches, suggested that the justices should look to the "original intent" of the framers of the Constitution. This hardly answered the hard questions, according to the chief justice. He and Brennan could look at the history and "original intent" of the First Amendment, for example, and come to opposite conclusions.

Rehnquist had espoused these same views in law school speeches. "There is no reason in the world" for a president not to try to "pack" the Supreme Court, he said. Usually, they do not succeed, however, because justices come "one at a time" and rarely agree entirely with the justices appointed by the same president. By the same token, he said, the Senate had a right to reject nominees for political reasons. He was not happy with how Bork was treated, but he did not suggest that the Democratic-controlled Senate had no right to reject the president's nominee because they disagreed with his views.

Rehnquist often brought up Franklin Roosevelt's 1937 "court packing" plan. This legislative proposal is often cited as one of FDR's most spectacular failures. Congress, despite its overwhelming loyalty to Roosevelt, refused to pass his bill to expand the Supreme Court's membership and thereby allow the president to pack the Court. Nonetheless, FDR succeeded,

Rehnquist pointed out. Within six years, from 1937 to 1943, he transformed the Court entirely. The "nine old men" who had blocked the New Deal retired in those years and were replaced by liberal Roosevelt appointees.

Of course, it could happen again, Rehnquist noted. If one president makes four or five appointments, the Court and the law can be transformed dramatically, he commented.

For now, however, the chief justice hoped to get one more like-minded justice. Among the cases to be argued in the fall were a half-dozen that figured to evenly split the eight-member Court.

For example, Illinois lawmakers had passed a bill that required a pregnant teenager to tell both of her parents of a planned abortion and then to wait 24 hours before getting an abortion. Lawyers representing a Chicago obstetrician and several of his patients sued, contending the law violated the right to abortion set forth in *Roe* v. *Wade*. A federal appeals court in Chicago agreed and struck down the law as unconstitutional. In the spring, before Powell's resignation, the Court agreed to hear the state's appeal. Without a ninth justice, however, the justices could not decide the case of *Hartigan* v. *Zbaraz*. They heard arguments in the case, but the votes split evenly in the conference room. Rehnquist, White, O'Connor, and Scalia voted to uphold the law; Brennan, Marshall, Blackmun, and Stevens voted to strike it down. On December 14, the Court issued a terse order announcing the deadlock. In the case of *Hartigan* v. *Zbaraz*, "the judgment below is affirmed by an equally divided Court." That meant that the federal appeals court ruling from Chicago would stand as the law in this case, as if the Supreme Court didn't exist.

During the fall, the justices issued similar orders dismissing major cases: one involving a white police officer's attempt to challenge a city affirmative action plan and another addressing the Reagan administration's policy of denying visitors' visas to European officials who had ties to a Communist party. If nothing else, the 4–4 deadlocks made clear to both the Democratic Senate and the Republican White House the importance of the ninth justice.

The deadlock on abortion and civil rights did not necessarily extend to matters of free speech and freedom of the press, however. The First Amendment and particularly freedom of speech stood as a pillar, not just because of its history, but because it crossed political and ideological lines. Conservatives, especially young conservatives, were as devoted to free speech and the "marketplace of ideas" as liberals. After all, the better ideas were theirs, or so they thought.

It was not always so. In the 1960s, when the civil rights activists and Vietnam War protesters stirred the political pot, the banner of free speech was carried by the left. Conservatives voiced support for "law and order." In the 1980s, however, when picketers and marchers in the United States were probably carrying antiabortion banners, while abroad they were calling for the downfall of Communist regimes, conservatives took up the free speech banner. Meanwhile, on college campuses, political leftists more often supported the so-called speech codes that would punish those who utter offending comments about race or gender.

Rehnquist, like Bork, was a conservative from the earlier era, more inclined to uphold limits on free speech. In the 1987 term, the justices had three First Amendment cases that would test how far the Rehnquist Court would go to protect free expression.

No one in America could test the outer limits of free speech better than Larry C. Flynt. He had become a millionaire because of his outrageousness. A poor kid from eastern Kentucky, Flynt went into business running strip-joint bars in Ohio. An entrepreneur of sleaze, Flynt founded a newsletter and then turned it into the glossy sex magazine *Hustler*.

In the 1950s, Hugh Hefner had made a fortune for himself and his *Playboy* magazine by printing air-brushed photos of nude women modestly posed. In the 1970s, Robert Guccione did away with the modest poses in his *Penthouse* magazine. He photographed women posing in sexually explicit ways and talking about—what else?—sex.

Larry Flynt went much further yet. Each month, *Hustler* served up a nauseating concoction of explicit sex, bestiality, mutilation, and raunchy humor. No topic was too disgusting for Flynt. More retching than arousing, his magazine demanded a strong stomach even to flip through its pages. One of its milder monthly features was known as "The Asshole of the Month." A politician or public figure would be lampooned. The person's photo would appear at the top of the column, superimposed on the tail end of a donkey.

Flynt's magazine became an extraordinary success. By the early 1980s, *Hustler* claimed to be selling more than 2 million copies a month. H. L. Mencken, the reigning cynic of the 1920s, once commented that no one ever went broke underestimating the taste of the American people. In one sense, Flynt proved Mencken right again. Even the sage of Baltimore could hardly have imagined a porno king such as Larry Flynt, though. The *Hustler* publisher had broken through the subflooring of American tastes and discovered loot down in a basement no one knew existed.

Mencken could have imagined Jerry Falwell, however. In his time, Mencken relished a chance to heap scorn on Bible-thumping evangelists. Falwell was simply the latest incarnation of an old story. He started small, as a Baptist preacher in a one-room, cinder-block church on Thomas Road in Lynchburg, Virginia. He became a national figure with his *Old Time Gospel Hour,* carried via radio and then television. Where Flynt found a new market in raunch and sleaze, Falwell tapped a much older vein of God, country, and family. As Falwell's New York lawyer, Roy Grutman, wrote of Flynt and Falwell, "One sold sex, the other salvation, and each claimed 25 million satisfied customers."

In 1979, Falwell moved his pulpit into the political arena as president of the Moral Majority. Saving souls one at a time was not good enough. It was time, Falwell believed, to save the soul of America. He attacked abortion, pornography, drugs, and homosexuality as forces that were destroying the nation.

Of course, the preacher and the pornographer viewed each other with contempt. Flynt saw Falwell as an American ayatollah, a righteous right-winger trying to force everyone into line. Falwell saw Flynt as smut peddler who was tearing apart the nation's moral fabric.

Characteristically, Flynt got in the first low blow. He had a clever idea, at least by *Hustler*'s normal standards. It was a takeoff on an ad for Campari liqueur, which had introduced itself to American consumers with its own unquestionably clever promotion. In magazine ads, celebrities talked of their "first time"—drinking Campari, that is. In its November 1983 issue, *Hustler* published what looked to be a Campari ad featuring the Reverend Jerry Falwell. In the upper-left corner was an official looking photo of Falwell. Next to it ran the headline: "Jerry Falwell Talks About His First Time." The lower corner featured the bottle of Campari, exactly as it appears in the company ads. Nonetheless, clever parody or light humor did not fit Flynt's style. He preferred the grotesque. The first line of the supposed interview reads, "Falwell: My first time was in an outhouse outside Lynchburg, Virginia." The interview degenerates from there. The talk is of an incestuous sexual encounter, with an audience of "flies" and "goats." Asked whether he had ever drunk Campari, Falwell concludes by saying: "Oh yeah. I always get sloshed before I go out to the pulpit. You don't think I could lay down all that bullshit sober, do you?" At the bottom of the page, the editors printed a line that was unnecessary even for the most mindless of *Hustler* readers: "Ad Parody—Not To Be Taken Seriously."

The Falwell interview was tasteless and disgusting, typical of *Hustler*. Yet no one could take it seriously as an actual interview with the nation's best-known Baptist preacher. Falwell, however, took it seriously—as a malicious and sordid attack on him. A reporter had pointed out the ad to the Moral Majority president shortly after it appeared. Angry and outraged, Falwell determined to take action. He filed a $45 million damage suit against Larry Flynt and *Hustler* magazine. His lawsuit charged Flynt with libel and intentional infliction of emotional distress.

Libel law is of ancient vintage. For centuries, English and American courts have upheld damage verdicts for someone whose reputation has been falsely stained. *Libel* is, in effect, a hurtful lie that appears in print. A newspaper story reporting, "Mayor Smith stole $50,000 from the city treasury" would be libelous if, in fact, Smith was honest and never stole a dime.

However, poor Mayor Smith could not necessarily win damages from the newspaper that printed such a false story. Since 1964, the Court has protected the press from being punished for honest mistakes made in reporting the news. If the reporters simply made an error—for example, by relying on an auditor who misinformed them—the newspaper may be able to defeat the mayor's libel claim. However, if the reporters had reason to believe their story was false and they printed it anyway, they and their newspaper would probably have to pay the mayor for damaging his reputation.

This doctrine, the *New York Times* v. *Sullivan* rule, did not grow out of a classic free-press struggle, such as the Pentagon Papers case, but rather was another offshoot of the civil rights movement in the South. In 1960, the NAACP and the Committee to Defend Martin Luther King took out a paid ad in the *New York Times*, seeking contributions. The committee said it was fighting racism and police brutality in Alabama. Though not mentioned in the ad, Montgomery police commissioner L. B. Sullivan contended he had been libeled by the comments about police brutality. An Alabama jury agreed and awarded him $500,000 in damages against the newspaper. The Alabama Supreme Court upheld the verdict.

When the *Times* appealed, however, the Supreme Court not only threw out the damage verdict but rewrote the law of libel as well. Justice Brennan said that because the First Amendment explicitly protects the "freedom of the press," the Court was obliged to set constitutional standards to protect that freedom. From now on, Brennan wrote in his opinion, public figures who say they are libeled must not only prove that the statement was factually false and defamatory but also prove it was published with "actual malice." A publication cannot be punished for a false statement, he said, unless the journalists printed it with a "reckless disregard" for the truth. In the case of *Flynt* v. *Falwell*, the "press" had fallen quite a few notches, from a distinguished newspaper down to a porno publication, which proudly proclaimed itself "the magazine nobody quotes." Still, the *New York Times* v. *Sullivan* rule applied all the same.

The other charge in Falwell's lawsuit—"intentional infliction of emotional distress"—was a more recent innovation in state law. This was something of a grab bag, a charge that covered an outrageous wrong that did not fit anywhere else. Examples have included a bill collector who unmercifully harassed a debtor and a hospital that showed a family member a mutilated corpse. Virginia judges had upheld damage verdicts for "emotional distress" if the wrongful act was deliberate and outrageous and if it had a devastating impact on the victim. In the view of Falwell's lawyers, those words described Flynt's deed exactly.

One might question whether Falwell was indeed devastated by the phony Campari ad. He testified that he "felt like weeping" when he first saw the phony ad. Apparently, however, he wanted to share his feelings widely. Within two weeks after the *Hustler* ad appeared, Falwell had sent copies of it in a mass mailing to thousands of his supporters. More than 26,000 copies went to "major donors" of the Moral Majority, with a request for contributions to fight pornography. Another 1.2 million persons on the mailing list of the *Old Time Gospel Hour* and the Moral Majority were sent solicitations that described Flynt's attack and asked for money to fight him.

The trial was held in Roanoke, Virginia, and Flynt proved to be his own worst enemy. In a videotaped deposition that was played for the jury, Flynt ranted and raved. He was angry and profane. Among the milder comments, he called Falwell a "liar, . . . a hypocrite, [and] a glutton." In 1977, Flynt had been shot outside a Georgia courthouse and permanently paralyzed. His assailant had never been captured. During the deposition, Flynt made the wild accusation that Falwell was involved in the shooting. He was asked if he sought to destroy Falwell's integrity. "To assassinate it," Flynt replied.

The jury in Roanoke returned a partial verdict for Falwell. It concluded that Flynt was not guilty of libel because the ad did not contain *factual* statements, but it said that Flynt was guilty of "intentional infliction of emotional distress" and awarded the minister $200,000 in damages. Flynt's attorneys appealed the verdict to the U.S. appeals court based in Richmond but lost there, too. Citing Brennan's opinion in the *New York Times* v. *Sullivan* case, the appeals court said that Flynt's attack on Falwell was a deliberate falsehood published with "actual malice." Flynt's lawyers filed a petition with the Supreme Court, and the justices agreed to hear the case.

For the justices, the case of *Larry Flynt* v. *Jerry Falwell*—the porno peddler versus the preacher—posed two stark alternatives:

On the one hand, if Flynt could get away with this, all public figures would be left unprotected from the most sordid of attacks. If a Baptist minister could be portrayed as a drunk who committed incest, what could be said about George Bush, Dan Quayle, or any other public person? Were there no limits? Did the so-called marketplace of ideas protected by the First Amendment have to include the gutter?

On the other hand, if a public figure could sue and win damages because he was subjected to "emotional distress," no cartoonist or comic would be safe. They deliberately inflicted emotional distress daily. As vice president, Bush once said he was made a "basket case for the rest of the day" after seeing a "Doonesbury" cartoon portraying him as a wimp. Bush's vice president, Dan Quayle, was regularly portrayed as a baby in a high chair, silver spoon in his hand, calling out for Dad. If "freedom of the press" protected cartoonists, how could the Court draw a line between a caricature of the vice president sucking his thumb and a porno magazine caricature of a preacher in an outhouse?

On a cold December 2, Beverly Hills attorney Alan Isaacman, Flynt's lawyer, arrived at the Supreme Court with a decided disadvantage—in addition, that is, to his client. Because Flynt was appealing the judgment from Virginia, he would need five votes to win. A 4–4 tie would mean a victory for Falwell. Isaacman could not even count on the four liberals. Stevens was particularly quirky on the First Amendment, and Blackmun was often more swayed by the facts of a case than by dogma. Even for a First Amendment stalwart, it was hard to muster enthusiasm to defend a false accusation of incest in an outhouse.

Isaacman also needed at least one vote on the conservative side, and the pickings looked slim. O'Connor, cautious and inclined to stick with precedents, seemed his best chance. Scalia, during his years on the appeals court in Washington, had been branded as an enemy of the press. He had upheld libel judgments against the *Washington Post* and against syndicated columnists Evans and Novak (both of which were later overturned). Scalia had made it clear that he did not think being a public official meant you had to meekly accept a pounding from the press. He once joked, however, that he had adopted for himself Muhammed Ali's famous "rope-a-dope" style of fighting to handle the press: Lay on the ropes and let the other guy hit you until he wears himself out.

From there, things got worse for Isaacman. Byron White had a particular contempt for the press. His friends and clerks had no explanation because since his college days, White has led a hero's life in the press.

"Everyone has to hate some profession," offered one clerk. "A lot of people hate lawyers. With him, it's the press." Some said his attitude toward "those SOBs" went all the way back to his days as a college football star when a *Denver Post* sports writer stuck him with the nickname "Whizzer White." In nearly three decades on the Supreme Court, White never entirely rid himself of the nickname or his disdain for the kind of people who stuck it on him.

Then there was the chief justice. Rehnquist displayed no personal animosity toward reporters, even though he had been roughly treated in the press. Since coming to Washington, D.C., in 1969, Rehnquist had been friendly with dozens of journalists. Over lunch, he was well-informed, witty, and sarcastic, the ideal companion for any journalist. He once asked a reporter still new to the beat how he liked covering the Supreme Court. The Court beat was one of the best in town, the reporter said, because compared to, say, the White House or Congress, the stories involved "substance" rather than flash and fluff. Yes, "more substance opportunities," Rehnquist dryly responded, a reference to "photo opportunities."

On another occasion, at a luncheon with journalists who did not cover the Court, Rehnquist was asked in a rather loud voice by one writer whether the Court was swayed by public opinion. "No," the chief justice said patiently, "if you are referring to opinion polls or marches on the Court." The reporter continued, "Well, what about an editorial or a column that states a strong, persuasive argument for deciding a case a particular way." Rehnquist replied that the justices are always interested "in clear, logical, and persuasive arguments, no matter how unlikely the source."

Under Burger, the press at the Court had been treated as the enemy or, at best, a nuisance. As chief justice, Burger shared many traits of the man who appointed him, Richard Nixon. He worried excessively about leaks and about his own image. To prevent stray comments being overheard during lunch, Burger assigned the law clerks to a separate, drab dining room on the Court's ground floor. Many clerks, having listened to Burger lecture on the need to maintain absolute secrecy, came away with a different message: The chief justice worried mostly about derogatory comments about the chief justice.

Under Rehnquist, the atmosphere improved, although veteran Court reporters still describe the beat as comparable to covering the College of Cardinals in Rome or the Kremlin in Moscow, pre-*glasnost*.

Lewis Powell, the now-retired "swing vote" justice, used to say that the Supreme Court was in fact the most open branch of the government. Every action taken by the Court is released to the public. No secret orders are sent out to lawyers or judges. Moreover, nearly every true decision is accompanied by a lengthy opinion, some 50 pages long, explaining the reasons for the Court's action. The pressroom, on the ground floor of the Court, is promptly supplied with copies of all the paper that flows in or out of the building—petitions, briefs, orders, and opinions.

However, the reporters see very little of the justices themselves. The hallways where justices have their chambers are off-limits to the public. The Court police make sure no uninvited guest strolls down the carpeted corridors. For congressional reporters who are used to talking to Senators in the hallways or on the phones, or White House reporters who get to chat occasionally with the president, the Supreme Court comes as a shock. The justices generally do not talk with reporters anywhere—in the hallways, on the phones, or on the streets. At lunches or social gatherings, the conversations are steered away from the pending business of the Court.

Trying to break the ice a bit, Rehnquist has had several evening receptions with scores of legal journalists, and an occasional meeting with the dozen or so reporters who cover the Court full-time. Toni House, the Court's public information officer, opened one reception by noting that the June date was chosen because it marked the anniversary of the congressional passage of the Bill of Rights in 1789. Taking the podium next, Rehnquist remarked that he had actually favored a different date in June, one "marking the anniversary of the Alien and Sedition Acts of 1798."

With his unpretentious manner and dry humor, Rehnquist came as a welcome change from Burger. The relationship between reporters and the justices now is cordial, though distant. Rehnquist got one reception off to a rather leaden start by turning to several reporters and commenting matter-of-factly: "We're the one branch of government that doesn't need you people." It was true enough. The justices do not have to run for reelection or seek reappointment, and their decisions and opinions have the force of law whether or not they are reported in the press, Rehnquist noted.

Close students of Rehnquist's writing counted him a sure vote for Falwell. Rarely did Rehnquist vote for anyone asserting a constitutional right. A criminal defendant claiming to have been illegally searched in violation of the Fourth Amendment probably would not get Rehnquist's vote. Business attorneys usually got the same treatment. When corporations challenged state taxes as discriminating against interstate commerce, Rehnquist usually upheld the taxes. When property owners said a city regulation unconstitutionally limited their development rights, Rehnquist tended to side with the city. "When it comes to constitutional claims, he's a hard sell," said Chuck Cooper, the former Rehnquist clerk.

Attorneys for Flynt asserted that his free-press right under the First Amendment required the Court to nullify the jury verdict from Roanoke. Rehnquist had been especially consistent in press cases. Rodney A. Smolla, a First Amendment scholar at the law school of the College of William and Mary, wrote a complete account of the Falwell case (*Jerry Falwell vs. Larry Flynt: The First Amendment on Trial*, St. Martin's Press, 1988). He tallied 20 earlier cases in which Rehnquist voted on matters of libel and invasion of privacy that involved the press. Rehnquist had voted against the press every time. Did reporters have a right to keep sources confidential? No, Rehnquist said. A right to attend trials? No, not necessarily, he said. A right to print whatever they heard in court? No, not if the judge issued a "gag order," he said.

All the calculations and analyses overlooked one fact, though: Rehnquist absolutely delighted in political cartoons and satires. Deflating pompous politicians seemed to him an entirely worthy calling. As a high school journalist, Rehnquist had mocked the self-important tone used by the eminent radio commentators of the day. On the bench, he became irked quickly by an attorney who adopted a high-blown tone with the Court.

The Association of Editorial Cartoonists supplied the Court with a particularly effective friend-of-the-Court brief, which tickled Rehnquist's soft spot. The text of the brief laid out America's history of political satire. None of the nation's luminaries escaped unscathed. George Washington was once portrayed riding a donkey as the onlookers wondered which one was "the ass." Included also was a series of political cartoons from recent years. There were House Ways and Means Committee chair Wilbur Mills carrying a party girl over his shoulder, Interior Secretary James Watt with a deer head labeled "Bambi" on his office wall, and former president Jimmy Carter scowling as aide Bert Lance grabs a few dollar bills out of a church collection plate. Democrats and Republicans took an equal share of the shots. One cartoon referred to the pending case. *Los Angeles Times* cartoonist Paul Conrad drew Ronald and Nancy Reagan sitting at the breakfast table holding a newspaper with a headline that read "Falwell Wins Damages." Nancy is quoted as saying: "Let's nail all those editorial cartoonists." The message was clear: This nation has a long tradition of sharp, even malicious satire, a tradition that is threatened by the Falwell verdict.

Perhaps Falwell should have countered by mailing the justices a personal copy of *Hustler* magazine. As part of the court record, the justices saw the parody of the Campari ad, which certainly hinted at how low Flynt could stoop. The clerks had picked up a newsstand copy of *Hustler*, but fearing that its wretched raunchiness might offend the justices, they passed it among themselves but kept it away from the justices.

At the oral argument in December, O'Connor and White honed in on the key legal point: The jury had concluded that the *Hustler* parody of Falwell did not contain a *factual* statement. The parody was certainly false and hurtful to Falwell, and it was published with "actual malice." Flynt himself admitted as much by saying he wanted to "assassinate" Falwell's reputation. However, no reader could conclude that the *Hustler* parody was an actual interview with the Baptist minister. The jurors in Roanoke specifically concluded that *Hustler* had not made a *factual* allegation about Falwell. Rehnquist also tipped his hand by asking the attorneys how the case would affect a cartoonist who wanted to portray a political candidate as "just a big windbag, a pompous turkey."

In the end, the case of *Flynt* v. *Falwell* boiled down to a simple question: Could the press be punished for printing a malicious, outrageous satire? Rehnquist led off the discussion by arguing for a reversal of the Virginia verdict. The First Amendment protected sharp satire, and there was no way to draw a line between malicious legal satire and outrageous illegal satire. Trying to do so would plunge the Court back into another swamp like the "obscenity" rulings. Justice Potter Stewart had famously remarked of obscenity that "I know it when I see it," but the Court had failed to define *it* in words that judges and juries could follow. It was clear that words such as "outrageous" or "offensive" were too vague.

In the end, all the justices agreed. Scalia found it troubling to overturn such a verdict, but he also wanted the law to draw clear lines. Had the Court upheld this verdict as an exception to the First Amendment because the parody was "outrageous," judges all around the country would soon find themselves trying to define what is meant by "outrageous." Because of the people involved, the case of *Flynt* v. *Falwell* had looked at first to be a difficult one, but the decision was unanimous to reverse the lower court's verdict for Falwell.

Rehnquist assigned the opinion to himself and had his clerks include all the standard lines from past decisions stressing the importance of free speech and a free press. There were quotes from Oliver Wendell Holmes, Felix Frankfurter, and, more recently, from Brennan and Powell. Rehnquist prefers to dictate opinions at home during the evening. He briefly set forth his view of the case:

"Lincoln's tall, gangling posture, Teddy Roosevelt's glasses and teeth and Franklin D. Roosevelt's jutting jaw and cigarette holder have been memorialized by political cartoons," Rehnquist wrote. "From the viewpoint of history, it is clear that our political discourse would have been considerably poorer without them.

"There is no doubt that the caricature of [Falwell] is at best a distant cousin of the political cartoons described above, and a poor relation at that. If it were possible by laying down a principled standard to separate the one from the other, public discourse would probably suffer little or no harm. But we doubt that there is any such standard, and we are quite sure that the pejorative description 'outrageous' does not supply one," he wrote.

He explained that jurors cannot be permitted to award damages based on a hopelessly vague standard. The law demands clear rules if someone is going to be punished for violating them. One jury might find a satire or cartoon outrageous, while a second set of jurors might find it amusing. The press must be protected against such arbitrary judgments, he said, particularly when it lampoons public figures. All but White signed on to the opinion. Instead, he added a two-line concurring statement in which he said only that he agreed that "publication of the parody" cannot be punished. White wanted no part of the glowing comments about the vital role played by the nation's press.

For weeks after the opinion was released, First Amendment lawyers in Washington walked around shaking their heads in amazement—not because of the outcome, but because the decision was unanimous and Rehnquist wrote a strong opinion. Is this a new Rehnquist? they asked.

The unanimous decision, though something of a surprise, surely did not mean that the chief justice had changed his stripes. From the beginning, Flynt's attorneys had two points in their favor. The first was Rehnquist's penchant for political cartoons and satire. No doubt his fondness for satire affected his view of the case. In addition, Flynt was challenging only a civil court judgment, not a law or a government policy. Rehnquist is a pro-government conservative. In most constitutional cases, an individual comes to the Court challenging the government, and in those cases, Rehnquist can be counted as a near-certain vote for the government. Falwell, however, did not represent the government. He was merely a private citizen who had gone to court to win damages for himself. Had the porno publisher been convicted of violating a Virginia law—perhaps on obscenity grounds—Rehnquist probably would not have cast a vote to overturn that verdict.

Still, Jerry Falwell was amazed. "No sleaze merchant like Larry Flynt should be able to use the First Amendment as an excuse for maliciously attacking public figures," he said in a statement issued by Grutman. "The Supreme Court has given the green light to Flynt and his ilk."

Clearly though, the justices had no fondness for Flynt and his "ilk." Several years earlier, in an earlier suit involving *Hustler*, Flynt had yelled out profanities in the courtroom as the marshals dragged him away. However, the lawsuit against the porn peddler starkly demonstrated that the Supreme Court decides cases of principle, not people.

A second case tested the freedom of speech on the sidewalks of the nation's capital. Several young conservative activists challenged a District of Columbia law that prohibited protests near foreign embassies in Washington. The law made it a crime to "display any flag, banner, placard or device designed to . . . bring into public odium" any foreign government or brings its policies "into public dispute." A second part of the law said persons may not "congregate within 500 feet" of an embassy. Michael Boos, one of the activists who filed the suit, said his protest would not threaten or harass any official. Such behavior was already banned by federal law. He said he wanted to carry protest signs in front of the embassies of the Soviet Union and Nicaragua, urging the Soviets to "Release Sakharov" and the Nicaraguans to "Stop the Killing." Boos had not been arrested for his protest, but rather went to federal court seeking to have the law struck down as unconstitutional so he could carry his sign without fear of arrest.

Despite Boos's petition, a federal judge upheld the law, and so did the U.S. court of appeals in a 2–1 opinion written by Judge Robert H. Bork. The law, he said several months before his Court nomination, was "primarily intended to avoid affronts to the dignity of foreign governments and their diplomatic personnel." Starting from there, Bork wrote a long dissertation on the "law of nations." Since the nation's founding, he asserted, the United States had been pledged to uphold its commitments under international law. Bork had very little

to say about the First Amendment and the American tradition
of free speech.

The Supreme Court disagreed. The two younger con-
servatives—O'Connor and Scalia—joined with Brennan, Mar-
shall, and Stevens to toss out Bork's decision on a 5-3 vote.
O'Connor's opinion in the case of *Boos* v. *Barry* described political protest as being "at the core of the First Amendment."
Under the D.C. law, a sign carrier could walk on Sixteenth
Street in front of the Soviet embassy if his banner read "Hail
Gorbachev," but not if it said "Free Sakharov," she noted. The
First Amendment does not permit the government to punish
people simply because they advocate the wrong message,
O'Connor opined. Rehnquist, White, and Blackmun dissented,
agreeing with Bork that an American citizen could be arrested
for carrying a sign on the wrong sidewalk.

A third case forced the justices to confront a question they
had dodged for years: Did the First Amendment's guarantee
of freedom of the press cover high school newspapers? In the
spring of 1983, Cathy Kuhlmeier was an editor of the *Spectrum*,
the school paper at Hazelwood East High near St. Louis. She
and the other editors decided to publish two stories on subjects
that concerned the real-life problems of teenagers: pregnancy
and parental divorce. Principal Robert Reynolds thought the
news stories were a bit too realistic. Though the quoted students were given false names, he suspected that their friends
could pick them out anyway. Reynolds only came to see the
stories because the journalism instructor had quit a few weeks
before. Lacking a full-time adviser to oversee the journalism
class, Reynolds took on the duties and made a hasty decision.
Before the final spring issue of the *Spectrum* would be printed,
the stories on pregnancy and divorce must be deleted, he ordered.

The students had filed a lawsuit contending the principal
had violated their rights under the First Amendment, but a
federal judge in St. Louis dismissed it. An appeals court disagreed. On a 2-1 vote, it ruled that the First Amendment's
protection of the free press includes high school newspapers.
School officials cannot censor these newspapers unless their
articles would cause "substantial disorder in the school," the
appeals court said.

For the justices, the case known as *Hazelwood School District* v. *Kuhlmeier* raised several important questions. Do high

school students have constitutional rights that are the same as those of adults? In the late 1960s, the Court may well have answered "yes." In response to a Vietnam War protest where students wore black armbands, the Court in 1969 said that high school students do not "shed their constitutional rights . . . at the school house gate." That line was still recycled periodically, but the Court majority no longer believed it. In 1985, the Court said that school officials can search the lockers and purses of students based only on a hunch, even though the Fourth Amendment would prohibit such searches of adults. The next year, the Court ruled that a student could be punished for a speech that contained a veiled sexual allusion, even though no adult could be punished for the same offense. The Court seemed to be saying what teenagers, to their dismay, already knew: High school was indeed a special place.

Even if the high school students had been adults, could they win a First Amendment ruling because an article was deleted from the paper? Certainly professional news reporters could not. If an editor decides that a reporter's story is dull, redundant, misleading, or otherwise unworthy of being published, it gets spiked, and that's the end of the matter. Similarly, if a publisher orders an editor not to print a story, it does not get printed. Journalists have no First Amendment right to sue their superiors. The First Amendment limits only the government. The mayor or the police chief could not order a story killed, but the publisher certainly can.

However, the students had a claim because in a public school system, the principal and the teachers are the "government." Then the question becomes, whose newspaper is it? The students said that it was theirs because they wrote and edited it. They did not, however, sell subscriptions and advertising, which would make it financially independent. School officials said that the paper was part of a journalism class and was under the control of school advisers.

Attorneys for the students said that the principal had engaged in "censorship." During the argument, Rehnquist questioned that use of that word. No doubt the principal considered his decision an act of "editing." When the justices met, Rehnquist, White, O'Connor, Scalia, and Stevens voted to uphold the principal.

White was assigned the 5–3 opinion and turned out his usual terse, workmanlike effort, making three points. In public schools, determining what is "inappropriate properly rests with the school board." Second, because the school paper was a "regular classroom activity, . . . school officials were entitled to regulate the contents of the *Spectrum* in any reasonable manner." Third, principal Reynolds acted reasonably in deleting the two articles because he wanted to "protect the privacy" of the "adolescents" who were cited in the stories.

While White methodically hammered in the nails, Brennan's dissent spun out a grand essay on public education, the "thought police," and the freedom of young minds. Though nearing his eighty-second birthday, Brennan could still get aroused by censorship of free speech. It was, of course, a lost cause. The majority was not interested in "student rights." Nonetheless, as long as he was there, Brennan was going to make sure they heard how wrong they were.

"The mere fact of school sponsorship does not, as the Court suggests, license such thought control in the high school," Brennan wrote. He mocked the principal's comment that an article on teenage pregnancies was "too sensitive for 'our immature audience of readers.'" The Hazelwood principal had displayed an "unthinking contempt," Brennan said, for the intelligence of his students. "The young men and women of Hazelwood East expected a civics lesson," he concluded, "but not the one the Court teaches them today." Marshall and Blackmun joined him.

The dissent did its job. In the news accounts of the decision, White was quoted as stating the ruling: Principals had the authority to regulate school newspapers. However, the more memorable lines were Brennan's. His message was heard, too: School officials who turn to clumsy censorship are going to be on the receiving end of lots of unfriendly free speech.

6

Mr. Clean

B y early October, it was clear to everyone—except perhaps
Bork and his family—that his nomination was headed to
defeat. At the Justice Department, Meese and Reynolds were
in a fighting mood. No one had better qualifications to serve
on the Supreme Court than Robert Bork, they asserted, yet he
had been tarred and feathered because he shared the conservative views of a president who won the votes of 49 of the 50
states. In their view, the liberals were still seeking to set an
agenda for America that had been hugely rejected at the ballot
box. They certainly were not ready to recommend a Supreme
Court nominee who would please Ralph Neas and the other
civil rights activists who beat Bork.

On Capitol Hill, the Republicans fumed also. The Republican Senate leader, Bob Dole of Kansas, adopting Reagan's
line, said he saw a "lynch mob" at work. Republican senator
Alan Simpson of Wyoming, one of Bork's staunchest defenders,
seethed at the press and the liberal lobbying groups, saying he
saw "an element of tyranny" in their treatment of Bork. Reagan
sounded the same note before a cheering crowd in New Jersey
by promising to send up to the Senate a new nominee who the
Democrats will "object to just as much as the last one."

Whom could they choose? Bork had been the heavyweight
who had topped the list of potential Reagan Supreme Court
nominees for so long that no other candidates had been seriously considered. The Justice Department attorneys had a list
with many names, but no list with *the* name as the successor
to Bork. Nonetheless, Reynolds and Meese certainly knew what

they did not want—a compromise candidate to please the Democrats.

At the White House, Howard Baker saw it differently. He had wanted to avoid a political bloodletting in the first instance. Now, he was convinced more than ever that the president must nominate someone who could be confirmed in the Senate.

"We were traditional Republicans: conservative, but not 'true believers,' " said White House counsel A. B. Culvahouse, a Baker aide. From the beginning, Baker and Culvahouse had been dubious about the Bork nomination. They knew it would set off a ferocious political battle, and they had been right. They did not want to make the same mistake twice.

When the "true believers" were mentioned, Culvahouse and others were referring in particular to Brad Reynolds, Meese's top deputy. His fervor during the Reagan administration had surprised even long-time friends. Having grown up wealthy, a graduate of Yale and the Vanderbilt Law School, Reynolds served in the Nixon Justice Department and was seen then as an establishment Republican. In the Reagan administration, however, he sounded like a different man. In 1981, he took a hot-seat job, as the civil rights chief in an Administration that had quite distinctive ideas about civil rights. No longer would the office be the special protector of blacks and other minorities. Reynolds wanted to protect individuals who were victims of what he considered reverse discrimination, including white males who lost out because of "affirmative action." When Meese took over as attorney general in 1985, he and Reynolds became nearly inseparable. Indeed, civil rights activist Ralph Neas referred to the two with one adjective, as in "the Meese–Reynolds strategy to undermine civil rights."

To formalize their relationship, Meese gave Reynolds the authority to act as his deputy. The attorney general needed the help, too. He was then under investigation because of possible conflict of interest growing out of the Wedtech scandal in New York. He was also under scrutiny on Capitol Hill because of his bungled preliminary investigation of the Iran–Contra affair. By mid-1987, "Brad Reynolds was really running the [Justice] Department," said Terry Eastland, the department's chief spokesperson. Reynolds wanted to hear no talk about finding a nominee who could be easily confirmed in the Senate. To him, that sounded like selling out principle for the sake of political survival.

Choosing Supreme Court nominees "was almost a sacred process pre-Baker," Reynolds said. "It was a White House nomination pure and simple. Baker felt Congress should be involved in offering advice. He wanted to know who could be confirmed easily. That was their agenda. They didn't want to go through the damned debate; they wanted a preemptive strike."

The Justice Department had come up with a dozen names as potential nominees to follow Bork, but no favorite. Starting with that list, Culvahouse and his staff did a little research of their own. They ran the names through NEXIS, a computerized file of news clippings. They were surprised at what turned up. One midwestern judge had been quoted as saying that "insider trading" should not be against the law. He was scratched off the list. A second had caused ripples during the 1970s as a U.S. ambassador. Several others had made controversial speeches. Still others had written a troublesome line or two. Judge Patrick Higginbotham of Texas had written an opinion in an abortion case that included a footnote that could be read as endorsing the *Roe* v. *Wade* ruling. The right-to-lifers would not tolerate that, and he was crossed off the list.

"It was a process of elimination," Culvahouse said.

The judge with the fewest problems of all was Anthony M. Kennedy of Sacramento. He had conservative credentials, experience on the bench, and a squeaky-clean personal life. That added up to "confirmable."

Kennedy had grown up in small-town Sacramento as the son of "Bud" Kennedy, one of the state capital's most prominent lobbyists. In the Sacramento of the 1940s and 1950s, lobbyists often wrote the law, and Bud Kennedy was one of the best. A broad man who chewed on unlit cigars, he protected the interests of the liquor industry in the state capital, and over poker games with lawmakers, he drank up his share of the industry's bounty. Though a Catholic by religion and a Republican by party affiliation, Bud Kennedy was remembered mostly as a man who liked everyone he met and who knew everyone who counted.

Bud Kennedy gave his three children a comfortable, secure life in Sacramento. His son, Anthony M. Kennedy, was born July 23, 1936. He grew up thin, shy, and bookish, a Boy Scout during the week, an altar boy on weekends. Young Tony met legislators and governors at his father's backyard parties.

At age 11 years, he became a page in the state senate chamber. He spent his summers swimming at the Del Paso Country Club. Later, as a lawyer and a federal judge, he would continue his membership there, as well as at the Olympic Club in San Francisco, even though blacks and women were excluded as members in both places. Kennedy's mother, Gladys, was a dynamo in Sacramento society, a volunteer for all manner of civic causes.

By several accounts, Bud Kennedy seemed perplexed by the straight-arrow son he had raised. He once offered to give his son $100 if he was ever called down to the police station to pick him up. He never had to pay. When friends from young Anthony's 1954 high school class tried to recall the worst thing he had ever done, they pointed to a school trip to Washington, D.C., where young Tony had dropped a piece of chewing gum off the top of the Washington Monument. In 1957, when young Kennedy and another prelaw student were setting off on a summer trip across Europe, his father packed away for him a bottle of his best, 100-proof whiskey. John Hamlyn, his traveling companion, cheered when young Kennedy opened his suitcase, but his cheer was short-lived. "It's strictly for medicinal purposes," Kennedy said: At the first onset of a sore throat, the whiskey came out; after a swish around his mouth and a swift gargling, he spit it down the sink.

Young Kennedy had always been a star student. After graduating as the valedictorian of his high school class, Tony went off to Stanford University in Palo Alto. Not yet established at the top of the nation's academic elite, Stanford was then better known as the private school for the children of California's elite. Predictably, young Kennedy flourished. Earnest, bespectacled, and hardworking, he studied long hours and stayed away from the hell-raising of his college peers. Before graduating, he spent a year at the London School of Economics. Then he was off to Harvard Law School in Cambridge, Massachusetts, where he graduated in 1961, near the top of his class.

Anthony Kennedy chose San Francisco, a two-hour drive from the family home, when he set up his law practice. His plans and his life changed suddenly in 1963, though, when his father died of a heart attack; the senior Kennedy had left his financial affairs and lobbying practice in something of a shambles. Dutifully, Tony Kennedy returned to Sacramento, first to straighten out the business and eventually to take it over.

The younger Kennedy was not cut out to be a lobbyist, however, at least not one from the backslapping, whiskey-chugging school of lobbying his father had known. Former legislators recalled the younger Kennedy as bashful and reserved; he was no Sacramento power like his father. Uncomfortable twisting arms or even asking for a vote, young Kennedy devoted more of his time to legal work and less and less to lobbying. In contrast to his difficulties with lobbying, Kennedy's smarts and orderly mind stood out when it came to drafting a piece of legislation. He was a "Rolls Royce in an used car lot," one lawmaker recalled. In the two years after returning to Sacramento, Kennedy came upon the two true loves of his life: Mary Davis and constitutional law. He married Miss Davis and the same year began teaching law during the evenings at the McGeorge Law School. Both relationships were happy and long-lasting.

In 1966, California politics were hit by an earthquake. The voters swept out of office the entrenched Democratic governor Edmund "Pat" Brown in favor of a Hollywood actor-turned-politician, Ronald Reagan. Pat Brown, like Lyndon Johnson in Washington, D.C., had championed the liberal approach to government: more money for public education and the huge network of state universities; more money for freeways and other public works; better prisons, and an understanding approach to crime and its causes. In the early 1960s, California was the Great Society.

Beginning in 1964, however, the Berkeley campus of the University of California had been torn apart by protests and demonstrations. The first protests concerned free speech and complaints about how the university was governed. Later, they centered on the Vietnam War, and then it was everything. Eventually, the Berkeley students seemed to condemn all that was America, except its ideals. The affluent society that had given so much to its youth found itself confronted by riots, hate, and disaffection.

Ronald Reagan gave voice to the political reaction in the state. He was fed up with long-haired, rebellious youth and with university officials who could not control them. He was angered by street crime and by judges who seemed more concerned with fairness for criminals than with the lives and dignity of crime victims. He was upset by politicians who thought that the best solution to every problem was shelling out more of the taxpayers' money. Two years before Richard Nixon and

George Wallace took this message nationwide in the 1968 presidential race, Reagan proved that it worked in his campaign for the governorship.

Reagan attracted to Sacramento a series of young, conservative-minded activists who wanted to leave their stamp on state government. Thirty-year-old Tony Kennedy, a lawyer–lobbyist with a small reputation, was no political activist, but he had donated money to the Reagan campaign. Through lawyer friends, he met some of Reagan's intimates, including a former Oakland prosecutor named Edwin Meese III. During Reagan's second term, the governor and his aides had occasion to call on Kennedy. They had grown frustrated with their ability to hold down state spending. The only way to stop the legislature from spending more money, they concluded, was to amend the state constitution and put a cap on state spending. Meese enlisted Kennedy to draft a proposed amendment to the state constitution. Proposition 1, as it became known, failed with the voters in 1973, although it paved the way for the big property-tax-cutting measure known as Proposition 13, which succeeded five years later. Proposition 1 helped Tony Kennedy's career enormously; when a judgeship vacancy came up in 1975 for the U.S. Ninth Circuit Court of Appeals, Meese and Reagan recommended Kennedy to President Gerald Ford. At age 39, the mild-mannered Anthony M. Kennedy became the nation's youngest federal appeals court judge.

A seat on a federal appeals court can be a ticket to dignified obscurity. The judges do not try big cases, they do not send criminals to prison, their pictures do not appear on TV, and their names rarely show up in the newspapers. Veteran appellate judges complain that their neighbors and friends wonder what they do for a living, and even explaining the job does not always end the doubts.

The huge U.S. Ninth Circuit Court of Appeals could be especially confusing. It heard federal appeals from nine western U.S. states, extending from Arizona to Alaska and out into the Pacific Ocean as far Guam and Samoa. All together, 28 judges made up the circuit. In groups of 3, they heard cases, usually in San Francisco, but also in Pasadena, Portland, and Seattle. Anyone who loses a case in a federal court has a right to appeal to the appellate court. The job of the appellate court is to make sure that the case was handled correctly and in line with the law as laid down by the Supreme Court.

Besides the dignified black robes that the judges wear and the not-ungenerous salary (currently $135,000 a year), an appellate judgeship has one other undeniable benefit: You can live wherever you want to. If a federal building can be found nearby, you can make it your office. Kennedy stayed home in Sacramento and found himself an office with a grand view overlooking the state capitol. His life changed remarkably little. He dropped all the lobbying work he disdained, but he kept teaching his law classes at McGeorge. When required to hear arguments, he drove down to San Francisco, perhaps staying a night or two at the Olympic Club, but he did the bulk of his work—reading briefs and writing opinions—close to home. When his mother died in 1981, he moved his family into his parents' white colonial home.

Kennedy's legal work did not go entirely unnoticed. In 1985, during his tenth year on the bench, he wrote the first appeals court opinion rejecting the notion of "comparable worth." Women employees of the Washington state government had contended they were paid less because their jobs were seen as women's work. For example, librarians or nurses with specialized training could be paid less than male clerks in a maintenance department. A federal judge ruled that these disparities violated the federal law banning gender discrimination in the workplace. Kennedy and his colleagues disagreed. The state did not intend to discriminate against the female employees, he commented, but rather simply paid the market rate for their services.

In a drug case, Kennedy authored an opinion that led to what later became known as the "good faith exception" to the exclusionary rule. Since 1961, the Supreme Court had said that if the police violate an individual's rights in the search for evidence, that evidence is excluded from his trial. Kennedy disagreed in part and ruled that if the police act correctly and their search warrant later turns out to be flawed, the evidence need not be excluded.

In a series of civil rights cases, he took a narrow, legalistic approach in order to reject claims. For example, in Los Angeles, a group of 100 black and white families had gotten together to test whether real estate brokers were using "racial steering" in violation of federal housing laws. Posing as home buyers, they found that brokers steered white families to white neighborhoods and blacks to mostly black areas. However, when they filed suit under the Fair Housing Act, Kennedy wrote an opinion throwing them out of court. Because these couples did not intend to buy a house, they had suffered no injury and therefore had no "standing" to sue, he wrote. The Supreme Court later rejected this interpretation. To civil rights attorneys in California, Kennedy seemed to be a judge who just did not understand discrimination.

In 1980, Kennedy was confronted with a lawsuit by gay navy personnel challenging the constitutionality of the Pentagon's regulation demanding the discharge of known homosexuals. Unlike Judge Robert Bork, who in a similar case grandly questioned whether anyone has a constitutional right to privacy, Kennedy wrote a hesitant opinion. "We recognize that to many persons the regulations may seem unwise," he said in his opening paragraph. The Supreme Court's past rulings "suggest that some kinds of government regulation of private consensual homosexual behavior may face substantial constitutional challenge," he said later. In a footnote, the opinion cited the constitutional law treatise authored by Harvard law professor Laurence H. Tribe.

After those preliminaries, however, Kennedy got down to business. This was a case about U.S. Navy personnel who work and live in the close quarters of a ship. In such a situation, he asserted, judges must make "unique accommodation" to the wishes of the military. Therefore, the lawsuits filed by the gay navy personnel were dismissed. Though he ruled for the Defense Department, Kennedy's few hesitant comments would almost cost him a seat on the Supreme Court.

As a scholarly young judge with a conservative reputation, Kennedy attracted as clerks some of the brightest young conservatives out of the nation's best law schools. In one year, he had a young Texan who came to California via the Harvard Law School and an extraordinary young Romanian who came to Los Angeles at age 12 and starred at UCLA's law school. The pair, Richard K. Willard and Alex Kozinski, were among the many young conservatives later drawn to Washington, D.C., by the Reagan administration. A third Kennedy clerk, Carolyn Kuhl, became the deputy solicitor general in the Justice Department.

In the early 1980s, when the Justice Department was drawing up lists of potential Supreme Court nominees, Willard, Kuhl, and Kozinski made sure Kennedy's name was included. Kennedy was a contender, but not a serious one, for the first nominations of Reagan's presidency. Nonetheless, he had what it took to stay near the top of the list: experience as a judge and conservative credentials. By the middle of October, as the Senate was readying to vote down Robert Bork, Kennedy had emerged as the favorite at the White House.

However, the more the White House talked up Kennedy, the more the Justice Department looked elsewhere. His opinions had a hesitant tone. Brad Reynolds did not like what he read. As those weeks passed by, the long shadows of Harry Blackmun and the late Abe Fortas hung over the participants. Their names were tossed about often, and both carried a lesson.

In 1970, Richard Nixon had had two of his Supreme Court nominees rejected by the Senate: Clement Haynsworth and G. Harrold Carswell. Having lost twice with southern nominees, he turned to a compromise choice, an obscure midwestern appeals court judge. Harry Blackmun was supposed to be a clone of conservative Warren Burger, his childhood friend. Instead, he became the author of the most controversial opinion of the decade: *Roe* v. *Wade*. He had joined with Brennan to uphold affirmative action and to block any form of school prayer. The lesson for Reagan's advisers: Beware of moderate Republicans whose judicial philosophy is not clear.

Then there was Lyndon Johnson and Abe Fortas. In 1968, LBJ tried to pull one more trick from a hat that had yielded countless surprises over the years. When Chief Justice Earl Warren announced his intention to retire, Johnson quickly nominated Justice Fortas as chief justice and Texan Homer Thornberry as his replacement. The Republicans balked, though, and so did the southern Democrats fed up with the left-leaning Court. With the presidential election approaching, they decided to freeze the nomination and let the next president fill the seat. For Reagan's advisers, this, too, was a cautionary tale: Don't wait too long to fill the Powell seat. If the vacancy carries over into 1988, the Democrats may stall in hopes of a presidential victory in November.

To some conservatives, Tony Kennedy smacked a little of Harry Blackmun. He was, after all, a little-known appeals court judge who wrote some moderate-sounding opinions. Also, there was that troublesome footnote in the gay sailor's case. Anyone who cited Larry Tribe as a constitutional authority became suspect in conservative circles. Plus, the opinion itself read as if its author could not decide. "No way, José," Senator Jesse Helms (R, North Carolina) responded famously when told about Kennedy and his opinion in the navy case. Senator Orrin Hatch (R, Utah) did not like the sounds coming out of the

"gutless wonders" who were running the show at the White
House, either.

If not Kennedy, though, who? Reynolds and Cooper came
up with an alternative candidate. He was "one of us," they
said, since he had earlier worked in the Reagan Justice Department. He was conservative, having studied at the University of Chicago, taught law at Harvard, had the strong backing
of Bork, and was young—only 41 years old.

The year before, the Reagan administration had put Douglas H. Ginsburg on the appeals court in Washington, D.C. He
had quickly lined up with the conservative faction led by Bork.
Unlike Bork, however, Ginsburg had written little, said little,
and done little. To Reynolds and Cooper, he was Bork without
a record. "Doug didn't have a long track record, but you don't
need it when you know someone," Cooper said. "We had talked
over all these issues. We knew where he stood. Or at least we
thought we did."

Ginsburg's specialty was economics and antitrust law. He
took a free-market approach. Like Bork, he could be described
as anti-antitrust laws: Get the government off the back of business. Reynolds also knew that Ginsburg could be trusted to
take the Administration's view on controversies such as abortion and affirmative action. "I knew it for a fact. Doug and I
were very good friends. We went back a long way. We had had
discussions," Reynolds said. When Bork also weighed in
strongly for Ginsburg, the Justice Department had itself a candidate.

The choice now came down to two: Kennedy or Ginsburg.
In Sacramento, Kennedy received a call from Reynolds, asking
him to take the next plane to Washington, D.C. There, he was
met by his former clerk, Richard Willard, who headed the Justice Department's civil division and lobbied everyone he knew
on behalf of his former boss. After a quick stop at Willard's
home in Falls Church, Virginia, Kennedy was whisked downtown to the Justice Department for a showdown meeting.
Meese and Reynolds from the Justice Department were there,
along with Baker, his deputy Kenneth Duberstein, and Culvahouse from the White House. The candidates were questioned separately. Judge William W. Wilkins, Jr., of South Carolina, a protégé of Senator Strom Thurmond, was invited too,
but no one was pushing for him. The talk was general and
philosophical; the specific controversies were clearly off-limits,
but the evening meeting only sharpened the dispute. Baker

and Culvahouse favored Kennedy—he could be confirmed easily in the Senate. Reynolds and Meese wanted their nominee, not someone who would be welcomed by the Senate Democrats.

Reynolds had no doubt that, if put on the Court, Kennedy "would come out the right way 99 out of 100 times. We had three of the most conservative people I know—Richard Willard, Alex Kozinski, and Carolyn Kuhl—swearing up and down that Kennedy was reliable. They gave us absolute assurances that we could trust him," Reynolds said. On the abortion issue, Kennedy would vote to overturn *Roe* v. *Wade*, Reynolds said. "We knew it for a fact. His clerks had talked to him about it. He is Catholic, too. I can be emphatic about it because we were certain," he said.

Even if Kennedy voted the right way, though, he would not cut a wide wake through the law, Reynolds added. "Bork would have written expansively. He had a flair to write phrases that would be remembered and would be useful in the future. So did Scalia. Ginsburg had some of that. Kennedy didn't. He wrote narrowly, within the four corners of the case. Kennedy was mechanically competent, but not much else," Reynolds said.

Kennedy did not get the backing of his fellow Californians, either. Though a long-time friend from the Sacramento days, Meese backed Ginsburg, as did former U.S. Attorney General William French Smith, who put in a call to Reagan touting Ginsburg. "Maybe it's the old line that 'familiarity breeds contempt,' but they seemed to think of him as a nice guy who didn't quite measure up," said one participant, describing the views of the Californians.

Baker, however, stood firm behind the judge from Sacramento. Kennedy had experience, and he would not set off sparks on Capitol Hill.

On the drive back to the Virginia suburbs that evening, Kennedy's former clerk thought Kennedy's prospects looked good. The judge did not. Kennedy recalled, "Richard said, 'You've got it.' I didn't think so. I could tell by the looks on their faces. Brad in particular."

Now, it was time to wait. For any lawyer or judge, a nomination to the Supreme Court hits like a lightning bolt. There is no predicting it, no preparing for it, and nothing is the same after it strikes. Kennedy paced the house. He walked around the suburban neighborhood with worries large and small. He

recalled, for example, that he didn't have another clean shirt—
what if he had to appear on television standing next to the
president? Unable to sleep, he wandered downstairs and found
a copy of William Manchester's biography of Winston Churchill. The second volume, *Alone*, portrayed Churchill's lonely
years out of power. It fit Kennedy's mood. He sat up half the
night reading.

The next day, Thursday, October 29, was decision day.
The Senate had finished off Bork six days earlier, and the Reagan White House needed a nominee quickly if the Supreme
Court seat was to be filled in 1987. Because his aides were
divided, Reagan would have to make the decision himself.

The president, Baker, and Meese met alone for 20 minutes
without their staffs. Baker spoke up for Kennedy. Meese
pressed for the 41-year-old Ginsburg. He was one of us. He
worked in the Administration. He shared our philosophy. Of
course, the Democrats on the Hill won't like him, but why
should we give them what they want? Ginsburg's youth impressed Reagan. Supreme Court justices often serve into their
80s. Forty years after the Reagan administration passed into
history, a Reagan appointee could still be making decisions on
the Supreme Court. On that note, Ginsburg got the nod.

The announcement would be made at 2 P.M., this time
before a cheering group of Reagan aides in the East Room. The
White House did not want to repeat that stiff scene in the press
room where a solemn Robert Bork stood mute next to the president. This nomination was going to go off on the right foot.

Kennedy had expected to hear something by 9 A.M., then
10, then 11. Finally, at 1:20, the phone rang, it was a call from
Ed Meese. The nomination was going to Doug Ginsburg. It was
for "a lot of complicated reasons," he said. There would be
more time to explain later, Meese commented.

Suddenly, for Kennedy, after the sleepless night and the
hours of pacing, it was over. The news reports had said that
he was the front-runner for the job. Instead, he had been passed
over for a man ten years younger who had no legal record. He
gathered together his few things and headed to the airport for
the first flight back to Sacramento.

Those who saw him upon his return to California were
struck by Kennedy's remarkable good grace in the face of a
crushing setback. "Mary, we dodged a bullet," he told his wife
of 24 years. He told reporters he was honored to have been
considered for the nomination and happy to be back home in

Sacramento. The judge had little time to wallow in regrets. He was scheduled to sit in on a case in Samoa. "First prize was a lifetime in Washington, D.C. Second prize is a week in Samoa," he told his friends. So, he packed his bags and was off again. There, he could unwind and get away from the news, including the latest from the nation's capital.

By the end of the week, Meese, Reynolds, and their aides might have wished to be in Samoa. "Every day it was a new disaster," Cooper said in describing the week-long Ginsburg nomination. The revelations might only have nicked a strong nominee, but Ginsburg was not that. He was barely known on Capitol Hill, including by the Republicans who were supposed to carry the fight for him. Each day's press reports seemed to raise a new problem. First, reporters learned he had run a computerized dating service as a college student. Then, it was discovered that his second wife, Hallee Morgan, a doctor, had performed abortions. A congressional committee suggested that Ginsburg, as head of a White House office overseeing new federal regulations, had sidetracked rules designed to clean up cancer-causing asbestos. At the Justice Department, Ginsburg had drafted a brief arguing that cable television, like the press, is entitled to First Amendment protections, while, unbeknownst to his superiors, he owned $140,000 in stock in a Toronto-based cable company. All that was known by Thursday of the first week—and the worst was yet to come.

Washington Post reporter Al Kamen and National Public Radio's Nina Totenberg had spent several days in Cambridge talking to Ginsburg's friends on the Harvard law faculty. Both were preparing profiles of the little-known Supreme Court nominee. In conversations, however, they turned up an interesting tidbit about his past. On occasion during the 1970s, Ginsburg had smoked marijuana at parties with friends.

Was this big news? Ginsburg's friends didn't think so. Back then, smoking marijuana was as common for many students as was drinking a few beers. Kamen's first instinct was to put the marijuana revelation in the middle of a long profile of Ginsburg. However, one fact transformed a little smoke into a major firestorm: Nancy Reagan's "Just Say No" approach to the drug problem. Spurred by the president's wife, intolerance had become a virtue within the Administration. Top officials lined up to see who could be hardest on drug use, whether casual use of marijuana or addiction to cocaine. Just six weeks earlier, Meese had initiated a mandatory urinalysis to test thousands

of white-collar Justice Department employees. By Thursday
evening, after Totenberg broadcast her story on Ginsburg, Administration officials had swung around 180 degrees, explaining
that a little marijuana use by a Supreme Court nominee was
no big deal.

Jokes about Ginsburg materialized overnight and quickly
made the rounds of Capitol Hill. "So that's why they call it the
high court!" In response to reporters' questions, Justice Department spokesperson Terry Eastland commented that Justice
Ginsburg would not have to recuse himself from drug cases
because his drug use was entirely in the past. By Friday evening, even Brad Reynolds had heard enough. He called Ginsburg at home and told him he must withdraw.

On Friday evening, after Kennedy's return to Sacramento
from his Samoan trip, his wife had arranged a full evening: a
dinner with friends and then a Sacramento Kings basketball
game. After all the travel, the judge would have preferred to
get into bed early, but instead, he got home after midnight. At
4 A.M., the phone rang.

"Tony. This is it!" It was Ed Meese. "Sometimes the Lord
works in mysterious ways," he said.

Sometimes Meese worked in mysterious ways, too. An
early riser, the attorney general was calling to tell Kennedy he
had an Air Force plane waiting at McClellan Air Base to fly
him back to Washington. Ginsburg was going to withdraw Saturday morning. Now the nomination would be Kennedy's, barring any last-minute hitch. Kennedy's one request was that the
plane wait until eight o'clock.

This time, Kennedy was put up in the Army–Navy Club,
a few blocks from the White House, and prepared to have his
life examined in minute detail. Ginsburg did not suffer from
Bork's fatal flaw—a long paper trail. Now, White House aides
were going to make sure Kennedy did not suffer from Ginsburg's flaw—a personal lapse that could prove embarrassing.
Before, nominees were asked general questions. Have you had
any problem with alcohol or other drug abuse? Is there anything in your past which, if revealed, could pose a problem?
Now, the interrogators were going to get specific. Culvahouse
had his young staffers sit down and write down every possible
human flaw or foible that could come to mind. The list, when
boiled down into question form, ran for 21 pages.

"I had to ask him questions Geraldo would have been
embarrassed to ask," said Culvahouse.

There were questions about massage parlors, pornography, group sex, and about marijuana, acid, hashish, and other drugs Kennedy had never heard of. Was your wife pregnant when you got married? (This was soon to be known as "the Pat Robertson question.") Also, of course, there was the "Gary Hart question."

"You're in for a dull afternoon," Kennedy said at the start, and he proved to be right. Kennedy responded to the questions with the dull, repetitive "no's" that the White House aides longed to hear.

Kennedy's Sacramento friends swore that he would not even walk across a quiet street against a red light. "He is the original Mr. Clean," said Willard, his former law clerk. The FBI, embarrassed, too, over the Ginsburg fiasco, had doubled its efforts to track down and question anyone who knew Kennedy. They went through tax documents, deeds, business records, anything they could get their hands on.

By Monday, they finally found something. Kennedy was visiting the White House when Culvahouse stopped him in his tracks with the news that a problem had turned up. Your daughter has an unpaid parking ticket, he reported.

This time, everything worked as planned for the Administration. On Monday evening, Kennedy went by to see Reagan in the family quarters of the White House, and they reminisced about Sacramento. Kennedy was pleased that Reagan sounded enthusiastic about the nomination rather than bitter about what had come before. "Tony, it took us a long time to get here, but I'm delighted we finally made it," Reagan told him. When it was time for Kennedy to leave, Howard Baker asked for a moment alone with the president. As Baker talked, Reagan shook his head. No, we won't announce the nomination tomorrow. Let's wait till Wednesday, Reagan commented, so Kennedy's family can fly east to be here.

First impressions count heavily in Washington, D.C., and in the White House pressroom, the first impressions Kennedy made when his nomination was announced were all good. The mood was entirely different this time. As Reagan spoke, Kennedy stood beaming, his wife and three children nearby. Asked by reporters to comment on the two failed nominations, Kennedy smiled broadly and said, "I'm delighted with this nomination."

By the time of the December hearings in the Senate Judiciary Committee, even the Democrats had joined in the effort to build up the judge from Sacramento. After all, if Kennedy was not an improvement, what good was it to have defeated Robert Bork? Professor Tribe, an official adviser to the committee, gave Kennedy his stamp of approval as a thoughtful judge. Committee chair Joseph Biden wondered aloud whether Kennedy might not be cut from the mold of Lewis Powell. At least the Democrats wanted to believe that. They had beaten a judge committed to rolling back the Warren Court of the 1960s. Robert Bork, the angry intellectual, viewed that era as illegitimate, an aberration. Beating Bork, in effect, affirmed the Senate's commitment to civil rights and civil liberties. Kennedy had to be better, the Democrats reasoned.

Kennedy "seems to possess the truly judicious qualities that Justice Lewis Powell embodied," they said in the committee report on the nomination. "Open-minded, fair and independent [he] will assure continuity on the Supreme Court at this moment of historical transition," they said.

Rehnquist knew better. Tony Kennedy was not "another Lewis Powell." For years, Rehnquist had read the opinions of lower-court judges with a keen eye. As part of his duties as a young justice, he oversaw appeals from the U.S. Ninth Circuit Court of Appeals in California, where Kennedy sat. Each year, he traveled out west to sit in on the annual meeting of all the circuit judges. Over breakfast, he and Tony Kennedy compared notes and exchanged gossip on other judges and their leanings.

On February 18, 1988, the chief justice stood on the steps posing with the newest addition to the Court. Anthony M. Kennedy did not exactly resemble a Supreme Court justice, at least not one of the pale, graying old men who look as if they have spent too long indoors squinting over law books. He was tall and lean, with a fresh face and thinning sandy hair. Certainly there would be lots of time to answer the question, Who is Anthony Kennedy? (Like Scalia, Kennedy would celebrate his eightieth birthday in the year 2016.) Rehnquist already knew the answer, though. As he stood next to the new justice, he had good reason to smile broadly, for Rehnquist knew that he was standing next to his fifth vote.

7

And Now There Were Five

K ennedy did not have much time to get ready for the first round of arguments. On Monday, February 22, 1987, four days after his swearing in, the Court would hear four cases. That would be followed by four each on Tuesday and Wednesday. Even for a seasoned judge, it made for a hectic start. At midterm, the other justices were busy writing opinions on cases already decided. Several months earlier, they had studied up on the cases that were now coming up for argument, and their clerks had eight months of experience researching cases and writing opinions. Kennedy, however, with little time to prepare and no help, had no choice but to plunge in headfirst.

He needed law clerks quickly. With appeal petitions coming in at a rate of 100 per week, no justice can keep up without help. On the other side of First Street, the senior members of the Senate have as many as 70 staff aides in their offices and committees. By contrast, a justice of the Supreme Court has two secretaries and up to four clerks. In Washington, D.C., the justices are held in high esteem, Louis Brandeis once observed, because "we do our own work." Brandeis's statement is not as true today as it was when he said it, but to an unusual degree among top government officials, the justices delve into the details of the hundreds of decisions they make every year. The clerks help to filter what the justices read and to research the precedents that give the justices' opinions legal weight. Kennedy turned to contacts in the Reagan White House and the Justice Department to find clerks who could be trusted as competent and conservative.

On February 29, the justices were scheduled to hear a
civil rights case that could test the temperature of the new
conservative Court. It concerned a century-old civil rights law
that had been revived during the Earl Warren era. Rehnquist
thought the law should be put back on the shelf again to gather
dust, but any dramatic change in the law would require the
vote of the newest justice.

At first glance, the case did not appear to have a broad
sweep. A disgruntled black woman, Brenda Patterson, had sued
her employer for race discrimination. Patterson, a college graduate, spent ten years doing clerical work for the McLean Credit
Union in Winston-Salem, North Carolina.

"Blacks are known to work slower than whites by nature,"
her supervisor Robert Stevenson told her when she asked about
a promotion, according to Patterson's allegations. He also hov-
ered over her desk, criticized her work, and promoted others
over her, she alleged further. Stevenson, denying these accusations, said Patterson was judged on her performance rather
than her race.

Patterson, however, believing she was the victim of racial
discrimination, quit her job and filed a suit seeking money damages. A federal judge short-circuited her claim, however, ruling
that federal law does not give an employee the right to seek
damages for racial harassment on the job. On appeal, the Fourth
Circuit Court of Appeals in Richmond, Virginia, affirmed this
conclusion. The law forbids discrimination in hiring, but not
on-the-job harassment, it ruled. On the first Monday of October, the day before the Senate committee voted on Robert
Bork, the Court had announced it would hear her appeal in
the case of *Patterson* v. *McLean Credit.* As with Sergeant Stanley
and his suit against the U.S. Army, the Court would not decide
whether Stevenson indeed harassed Patterson, but whether she
would have a chance to present her case to a jury.

To answer that question, however, required the justices
to look back more than 120 years. If Brenda Patterson had a
right to sue the credit union for damages, that right was established in the Civil Rights Act of 1866, the nation's first civil
rights measure.

A few months after the Civil War ended, President Andrew Johnson dispatched Major General Carl Schurz to tour
the defeated South. The new U.S. president, a Tennessee Democrat, hoped to welcome the southern states back into the

Union, but what Schurz found proved explosive. White planters had not renounced slavery, he reported, but rather were using violence and intimidation to preserve the old system. In many areas, whites refused to lease or sell land to the freed blacks. From Alabama and South Carolina came reports that blacks were shot on the roads because they did not have letters from their ex-masters giving them permission to leave. In towns, blacks were "publicly beaten and whipped" for alleged "insubordination" to whites. In Mississippi, an organization known as the "black cavalry" rounded up freedmen and forcibly returned them to work for their former masters. In Virginia, a black man was publicly hung by his thumbs because he refused to work for his former master. In Mississippi and Louisiana, the legislatures passed laws that restricted the legal rights of blacks and set harsh work penalties for crimes such as vagrancy. When the president refused to release the Schurz report, the Republican-controlled Senate voted to order its release. Some 10,000 copies were printed and shipped around the country. Congress and the northern public demanded action.

Seventeen days after the release of Schurz report, Senator Lyman Trumbull, chair of the Judiciary Committee, rose on the Senate floor to introduce a bill for the "protection of civil rights." A moderate Illinois Republican and highly respected, Trumbull had spent several recent evenings at the Freedman's Bureau in Washington, D.C., reading dispatches and reports from the South.

"Mr. President, I regard the bill to which the attention of the Senate is now called as the most important measure that has been under its consideration since the adoption of the Constitutional amendment abolishing slavery. That amendment declared that all persons in the United States should be free. This measure is intended to give effect to that declaration and [to] secure to all persons within the United States practical freedom," he told the Senate on January 29, 1866. He said his bill would "break down all discrimination between black men and white men." It would deal with the danger posed "by local legislation or a prevailing public sentiment in some of the states that persons of the African race should continue to be oppressed." His counterpart in the House, Representative James Wilson of Iowa, was more fiery, saying the bill was addressed to the "laws barbaric and treatment inhuman [being] meted out by our white enemies to our colored friends. We should put a stop to this at once and forever."

After several weeks of debate, the bill passed the Congress, but Johnson vetoed it, contending it put undue and unwise burdens on the defeated South. The veto was easily overridden, however, and on April 9, 1866, one year after Lee's surrender at Appomattox, the Civil Rights Act of 1866 became law.

The law contained three key sections. The first said that all Americans "shall have the same right . . . to make and enforce contracts, to sue, be parties, give evidence, to inherit, purchase, lease, sell, hold and convey real and personal property, and to full and equal benefit of all laws . . . as is enjoyed by white citizens." The second section set criminal penalties for "any person who, under color of any law, statute, ordinance, regulation, or custom," violates another person's rights under the law. The third section gave the federal courts jurisdiction over "all causes, civil and criminal, affecting persons who are denied . . . the rights secured by" the law. This provision allowed a person whose rights were denied to file a civil suit in a federal court, seeking damages.

Despite its grand send-off in Congress, the law had only a minor impact. The Supreme Court then gave all the civil rights laws a narrow reading. The Fourteenth Amendment, written a few months later, made it clear that the states could not enforce discriminatory laws. What about private acts of discrimination? The Supreme Court at the time implied—but did not rule explicitly so—that the 1866 law only covered discrimination by government, not by private persons.

Was it so limited, or did Congress also intend to allow damage suits against white planters or white merchants who refused to sell to blacks? In 1968, the Warren Court answered that question by ruling that the more than 100-year-old law was intended to "bar ALL racial discrimination, private as well as public, in the sale and rental of property." That year, the Court had been presented with a lawsuit filed by Joseph L. Jones, a black man, who had been denied the right to buy a home in an all-white suburban housing tract near St. Louis. He contended that the old federal law gave him "the same right" to buy property as "enjoyed by white citizens," but two lower courts dismissed his suit. The law prohibited discrimination only by public agencies, not by private developers, they ruled.

The Warren Court justices agreed to hear the appeal in *Jones* v. *Alfred Mayer Company*, and in doing so, reexamined the history of the post–Civil War law. Throughout the 1960s, the Warren Court had rediscovered and revived laws that had been passed by the Reconstruction Congress a century before, and on a 7–2 vote, they did so again with the Civil Rights Act of 1866. That law had been passed under the authority of the new Thirteenth Amendment, which ended slavery, noted Justice Potter Stewart. "Negro citizens . . . would be left with a mere paper guarantee if Congress were powerless to assure that a dollar in the hands of a Negro will purchase the same thing as in the hands of a white man," he wrote in *Jones* v. *Mayer*.

The dissenters were Byron White and John Marshall Harlan. They refused to believe that the Radical Republicans of 1866 had been so rash as to give blacks a right to sue whites for damages for practicing discrimination. They pointed out that Senator Trumbull had comforted his northern colleagues by saying the law would have "no operation in any state where the laws are equal." If so, Congress was seeking only equal treatment in law, not equal treatment by private sellers. In White's view, the old law gave blacks a legal right to buy real estate, but it did not mean that sellers were required to sell to them. After all, no white persons can sue developers who refuse to sell them a piece of property. If that is not a right "enjoyed by white citizens," how can it be said to be a right possessed by blacks? The majority countered, How many sellers refuse to sell to white persons who can afford to pay the price, simply because of their race?

Thereafter, the Court described the old law, now Sections 1981 and 1982 in the federal code, as "barring all racial discrimination." In 1976, the justices considered whether the law covered admission to private schools. In Arlington, Virginia, a child care center owned by Robert Runyon admitted only white children and refused to enroll a child of Sandra McCrary, who was black. Did Runyon's refusal to "make a contract" with McCrary violate the law? Yes, the Court had said on a 7–2 vote in the case of *Runyon* v. *McCrary*. This time, the dissenters were Byron White and William Rehnquist.

By the 1980s, the provisions of Sections 1981 and 1982 were important to civil rights lawyers for two reasons. The civil rights laws of the modern era forbid discrimination in employment and housing, for example, but they do not permit a victim to seek money damages. In flagrant cases of racial animus, the old law proved a powerful weapon. Second, the old law swept broadly and covered areas such as discrimination in private schools, which were not covered by the more recent civil rights measures.

Just how far the old law reached became apparent again during Rehnquist's first term as chief justice. Were Arabs and Jews covered by the law, just as blacks were? Could they, too, be considered victims of "racial discrimination"? A federal appeals court in Philadelphia had ruled that a professor of Arabic descent could sue a small private college for allegedly dismissing him because of his racial and ethnic background. However, the appeals court in Richmond ruled that Jews could not be victims of racial discrimination and therefore could not seek damages from persons who defaced a synagogue with anti-Semitic symbols. The justices took the cases to resolve the apparent conflict. Publicly, it appeared they had done so easily. In a pair of 9–0 rulings, the Court said in February 1987 that both Arabs and Jews were entitled to sue because they were perceived during the nineteenth century as having distinctive racial characteristics. Another victory for civil rights—and from a unanimous Court.

The vote, however, was deceiving. In conference, Rehnquist had argued that the earlier rulings in *Jones* v. *Mayer* and in *Runyon* v. *McCrary* were wrongly decided. In his view, the old civil rights act was limited to government discrimination, not discriminatory acts by private persons. White agreed wholeheartedly. So did Scalia. He read the old laws as giving blacks a legal right to make contracts and to buy real estate, not as protection against racist sellers. O'Connor, though less certain, thought the Court should reexamine the reach of the old law. The others, however, wanted no part of such a reexamination. Powell and Stevens had questioned the 1968 decision but said it was settled now. Congress had recently made it clear that it endorsed the broad view of the old law. Certainly the public agreed that racial discrimination was wrong and illegal. It was not wise to reopen the issue, they said. So, the Court agreed to the unanimous ruling on Arabs and Jews. There the matter stood on February 29, when Brenda Patterson's case came before the Court. At that time, Anthony Kennedy was beginning his second week on the Court.

Attorneys for the NAACP Legal Defense Fund (LDF) had taken Brenda Patterson's case to the Court and contended that the Civil Rights Act of 1866 barred on-the-job racial harassment, as well as bias in the making of a contract. Significantly, the Reagan administration joined the case on Patterson's side. Solicitor General Charles Fried said that as a matter of contract law, employees are entitled to "fair dealing." A campaign of "racially motivated" harassment—if true—violated the terms of Patterson's contract and therefore, her rights as protected by the law, he said. Usually, the Administration's legal views carried weight with the Court's conservatives. However, usually the Administration urged a conservative view.

Penda Hair, the LDF attorney, began her oral argument by telling the justices that if on-the-job harassment is legally permitted, an employer "can say to a [black] worker: 'We'll hire you but only if you submit to [being] humiliated and demeaned because of your race'. That type of condition is exactly the badge of inferiority that the Thirteenth Amendment [abolishing slavery] and Section 1981 were designed to prohibit." She soon ran into a buzz saw of questions from Rehnquist and White.

"Well, I don't think that's crystal clear, Ms. Hair, that the consequences like you're talking about, bad as they may be, necessarily implicate the right to make or enforce a contract," Rehnquist interrupted. "That certainly isn't an inclusive term."

The LDF attorney countered that it was. "I would submit that the right to make and enforce a contract has to include the right to perform that contract free of racial discrimination."

"Well, supposing, Ms. Hair, that an employer hires a black person for $50,000 and the black person later comes in and says, 'Well, if I'd been white, they would have paid me $55,000, so they violated [Section] 1981.' Do you think that if the black employee can prove that, that's a cause of action under 1981?"

"Yes, I do, Mr. Justice Rehnquist," she said. "It's intentional racial discrimination in pay."

The chief justice was unconvinced. "So [Section] 1981 really covers everything that Title VII [of the Civil Rights Act of 1964] does," he said. It made no sense, in Rehnquist's view, to think that Congress in 1964 would have passed a detailed anti–job discrimination law if such a law were already on the books.

When the justices left the bench, it looked to be a close vote. Brennan and Marshall certainly thought that racial harassment of an employee violated a black person's legal rights. The conservatives were convinced that the law had been stretched way beyond its bounds.

The conference on *Patterson* v. *McLean Credit* produced the major surprise of the 1987–1988 term. The question before the justices was, Does on-the-job racial harassment by a private employer violate Section 1981? However, the chief justice was determined to go further and rule that Section 1981 should not be applied to private employers at all. White agreed.

Scalia also agreed with Rehnquist and White. It griped him that civil rights measures had taken on a status as "special laws," not subject to the same rules as other laws. In his view, a law was a law. None carried more weight than another. He thought the language of the old law was clear: It gave blacks "the same right" to make contracts. Its second section punished officials who violated these rights. Obviously, then, the law addressed the legal right to make contracts, not discrimination by private contractors or sellers. It did not matter to him what the legislators were thinking as they wrote the law. It mattered only what the law said. Besides, "legislative history" was always political, Scalia believed. A judge could always find stray comments from a legislator that would endorse the judge's preferred view of what the law meant. O'Connor, though more cautious than Scalia, agreed that Section 1981 needed to be rethought. The Arabs and Jews case had convinced her that the law seemed to have no outer bounds.

The outcome depended on Kennedy. Rehnquist proposed that they reconsider the doctrine set down in the *Runyon* and the *Jones* cases. The justices had divided equally. Brennan, Marshall, Blackmun, and Stevens were aghast that the conservatives wanted to unsettle a well-settled precedent. If the law needed to be rewritten, let Congress do it, they said. However, Rehnquist had four votes to reconsider *Runyon*. The outcome depended on Kennedy, and when his turn came, he sounded uncertain. Nonetheless, he did indicate that there may be a need to reconsider the limits of Section 1981. The chief justice took Kennedy's comment as meaning that he agreed; there were five votes to reconsider *Runyon* v. *McCrary*, Rehnquist said.

The chief justice had wasted no time in using his new majority. A brief order was drafted to announce that the justices would not decide the *Patterson* case in the current term. Instead, a second round of arguments would be heard in the fall. This time, the attorneys were told to focus on whether *Runyon* v. *McCrary* should be overturned and the old civil rights act limited only to public agencies.

The four liberals were appalled. Stevens was especially incensed by what seemed to him this aggressive display of conservative activism. In the mid-1970s, he had questioned the correctness of the *Runyon* decision, but Congress let the ruling stand and, indeed, appeared to endorse it. In his view, that was the law now, and a justice, especially one who calls himself a "conservative," should not rewrite the law to suit his own preferences.

Just a few weeks before, Kennedy had won unanimous confirmation in the Senate, mostly because he was seen as a judge who would be conservative but not an aggressive reactionary. Robert Bork had been branded as just that—a justice who would roll back precedents in civil rights and would reopen old wounds. The Democrats had grilled Kennedy over his "sensitivity" to civil rights and came away satisfied that the California judge was, at minimum, not Bork. However, his first major vote suggested that the Democrats had been fooled—or had fooled themselves. Thanks to Kennedy's vote, the new five-member majority had taken the first step to sweep away two decades of legal precedent on racial discrimination. Robert Bork could not have done more.

Harry Blackmun fired off a short but sharp dissent. "I am at a loss to understand the motivation of five members of the Court to reconsider an interpretation of a civil rights statute that so clearly reflects our society's earnest commitment to ending racial discrimination, and in which Congress so evidently has acquiesced. I can find no justification for the bare majority's apparent eagerness to consider rewriting well-established law," he concluded.

John Paul Stevens, in a second dissent, panned his conservative colleagues for their unseemly judicial activism. The issue of overturning the Runyon decision had not even been raised by the attorneys in the case. Instead, the Court acted on its own, driven by its conservative agenda. "If the Court decides to cast itself adrift from the constraints imposed by the adversary process and to fashion its own agenda, the consequences for the Nation—and for the future of this Court as an institution—will be even more serious than any temporary encouragement of previously rejected forms of racial discrimination," Stevens said. "The Court has inflicted a serious—and unwise—wound upon itself today." Brennan and Marshall joined both dissents when they were released on April 25.

The brief order issued by the Court said the attorneys in Brenda Patterson's case should file new briefs and return in the fall to argue "whether or not the interpretation of 42 USC Sect. 1981 adopted by this Court in Runyon v. McCrary (1976) should be reconsidered?"

The five-member majority also published an unsigned message responding to the dissents. It set forth Scalia's view that Section 1981 should not be treated differently simply "because it benefitted civil rights plaintiffs. . . . We do not believe that the Court may recognize any such exception to the abiding rule that it treat all litigants equally. . . . We think this is what Congress meant when it required each Justice or judge of the United States to swear to 'administer justice without respect to persons and to do equal right to the poor and to the rich.' "

The brief order in the *Patterson* case sent a jolt through much of the legal community, not just civil rights lawyers. If the Court's order in the *Patterson* case were a portent of things to come, the stability of law was in danger. By the summer, the American Bar Association, the attorneys general in 47 of the 50 states, and two-thirds of the members of the U.S. Senate had filed briefs with the Court, urging it to let the *Runyon* decision stand.

Kennedy also made a mark in the final weeks of the spring session, with a case involving military contractors that had deadlocked the Court 4–4 in October. It was reargued in late April so that the new justice could break the tie.

On April 27, 1983, Marine Lieutenant David Boyle was at the controls of a helicopter during a training flight off Virginia Beach, Virginia. As the Sikorsky CH-53D helicopter banked right, it suddenly lurched and dove down into the water. Several members of the crew got out of the back of the submerged helicopter, but Boyle did not. The escape hatch nearest him opened only outward, against the pressure of the water. Trapped in his seat, he drowned.

His parents filed a suit against the United Technologies Corporation, the maker of the Sikorsky helicopter, contending that its escape hatch was defectively designed and had caused their son's death. After hearing the evidence, a jury agreed and awarded them $750,000 in damages. On appeal, United Technologies raised the question, Can a U.S. government contractor be sued under state law for a defectively designed product, just as the Ford Motor Company, for example, could be sued for a defectively designed Pinto automobile? Because the lower federal courts were split on the question, the justices had agreed to decide the case of *Boyle* v. *United Technologies.*

The potential stakes in the case were enormous. Lawyers for the military contractors dreaded the prospect of going before a jury in a case brought by the family of a young deceased serviceperson. The "Agent Orange" litigation also loomed over the *Boyle* case. Thousands of Vietnam-era soldiers had joined a lawsuit against Dow Chemical Company contending that it should have to pay damages for exposing them to a dangerous product. If the Boyles won in the Supreme Court, Dow could face a bankrupting series of damage verdicts. Why, the military contractors asked, should they be forced to pay damages for producing a product at the government's behest? On the other hand, if the Court ruled for United Technologies, the families of service personnel would be deprived of a right that all other Americans possess: the right to seek fair compensation if they are hurt by another. Moreover, companies would not be held accountable for making defective products that injured or killed service personnel.

In October 1987, Rehnquist, White, O'Connor, and Scalia voted to block damage suits against the military contractors. In their view, these companies were doing the government's work and deserved the same shield from liability. Brennan, Marshall, Blackmun, and Stevens sided with the Boyles. The Court, they said, had no authority to block these damages suits. The military contractors had urged Congress to write a law shielding them from lawsuits for defective products, but it had refused.

Nonetheless, in the spring 1988 session, thanks to Kennedy's vote, the Supreme Court wrote its own shield law for the military contractors. Writing for the 5–4 majority, Scalia said the "uniquely federal interests" served by government contractors justify shielding them from all liability for defective products. The previous year's rulings made it clear that service personnel may not sue the *government* for their death or injuries. The *Boyle* ruling said that they also may not sue the private company that supplied the serviceperson with a defective product. Further, Scalia's opinion did not limit itself to service personnel; he referred to all government contractors. For example, if the U.S. Postal Service contracted with the Ford Motor Company to purchase Pintos, and a mail carrier was killed in a rear-end collision, his family could *not* sue Ford over his death.

In dissent, Brennan used the conservative's own language against them. "The Court—unelected and unaccountable to the people—has unabashedly stepped into the breach to legislate," he wrote. Marshall, Blackmun, and Stevens agreed. Stevens, who sat next to Scalia on the bench, admired his young colleague's intelligence and spunk but thought the *Boyle* opinion was one of Scalia's poorest efforts. Scalia had heaped scorn on the liberals for supposedly making up laws or legal doctrines to rule for minorities or for the poor. Now, Scalia had made up a legal doctrine to protect huge military contractors.

That spring, Kennedy also cast the fifth vote to rule that the Constitution does not forbid states from charging the poor for the costs of public education. In North Dakota, the state had encouraged its rural schools to reorganize themselves into larger, more efficient districts. It had done so in part by charging parents in some rural communities for the cost of busing their children to school. Paula Kadrmas was required to pay $97 in 1985 to have her daughter bused to the Dickinson public schools. Because her husband was unemployed, she could not afford the cost and eventually filed a lawsuit against the school district. Because the busing charge discriminated against the poor, it violated the Fourteenth Amendment guarantee of the "equal protection of the laws," she maintained.

The Supreme Court disagreed on a 5–4 vote. Public education is not a "fundamental right," O'Connor said in *Kadrmas* v. *Dickinson Schools*. Moreover, discrimination against the poor is not "suspect," she said, unlike, for example, discrimination against blacks, Hispanics, or women. She was joined by Rehnquist, White, Scalia, and Kennedy. Brennan and Marshall, who began their law careers during the depths of the Great Depression, maintained that the Constitution did not permit government discrimination against the poor. Blackmun and Stevens dissented too, contending that the North Dakota law made no sense and should be struck down.

Overall, the 1987–1988 term had been rather quiet, thanks in part to the vacant ninth seat. The justices had taken on only a handful of major cases. Still, the term came to a close in late June on another surprising note.

Within official Washington, the case of *Morrison* v. *Olson* was easily the most important of the term. It represented a classic clash between the president and the Congress, with the Supreme Court acting as referee.

It began as a legacy of the Watergate affair. Richard Nixon's effort to contain and cover up the break-in at the Democratic campaign headquarters corrupted not just the White House but also the Justice Department, the FBI, and the CIA. The spreading scandal had raised an obvious legal question: How could the president's men in the Justice Department be trusted to vigorously investigate and prosecute crimes committed by the president or his top aides? In Watergate's wake, Congress passed the Ethics in Government Act of 1978, establishing a system of "independent counsels." In most instances, the U.S. attorney general would trigger the system. If given evidence of possible wrongdoing committed by an Administration executive, the attorney general would initially decide whether it warranted investigation. If so, the attorney general would ask for the appointment of an independent counsel to be chosen by a panel of three senior judges, who in turn were chosen by the Supreme Court's chief justice.

From the beginning, however, the top federal prosecutors—in the Carter administration as well as under Reagan—thought the scheme unconstitutional. In their view, the notion of an independent prosecutor was a contradiction in terms. U.S. attorneys worked in a hierarchical system. They had been officially appointed by the president and were obliged to follow the rules and guidelines of the Justice Department. How could the awesome power to investigate and prosecute be turned over to an independent operator? they wondered.

The case also concerned more than the power to prosecute: It concerned raw political power. Since 1980, clashes between the Republican White House and the Democratic Congress had grown in intensity. Who, after all, was going to run the country: the president and his Republican-run executive agencies, or the Congress and its Democratic-dominated committees and subcommittees? Both sides accused the other of poaching on their territory. The Democrats saw Reagan's executive appointees as seeking to make the law, rather than to execute the laws passed by Congress. Meanwhile, many conservatives portrayed the entrenched Democrats on Capitol Hill as systematically emasculating the powers of a strong, conservative president. The conservatives' complaints were featured regularly on the editorial pages of the *Wall Street Journal.*

They also found a voice on the U.S. court of appeals in
Washington, D.C., a court now dominated by Reagan appointees. In January 1988, that court, on a 2–1 vote, declared the
Ethics in Government Act unconstitutional. Judge Laurence H.
Silberman, a 1985 Reagan appointee, characterized the law as
a power grab by Congress. The independent counsel "may,
like a flicking left, confound the Executive Branch in dealing
with Congress. . . . Surely [it] saps the political vitality of the
Presidency and thereby renders the President a less effective
political force juxtaposed against Congress." He was joined by
Judge Stephen Williams, also a Reagan appointee, while Judge
Ruth Bader Ginsburg, a Carter appointee, dissented.

This ruling was good news for a number of top Reagan
confidants. Attorney General Meese, long-time Reagan aides
Michael Deaver and Lyn Nofziger, and Iran–Contra defendants
Oliver North and John Poindexter were under investigation by
independent counsels. If Silberman's opinion survived, those
investigations were dead.

What's more, that was just the beginning. If upheld by
the Supreme Court, Silberman's opinion had the potential to
reshape the federal government. Indeed, if its reasoning were
followed, it amounted to a power grab by the president. The
issue concerned the president's power to run the government.
The Constitution says little about the powers of the president,
except that "he shall take Care that the laws be faithfully executed." By contrast, the Constitution spells out in considerable detail the authority of Congress to shape the government.
For example, the U.S. Department of Justice, home to the defenders of presidential supremacy, was created by and paid for
by acts of Congress.

Silberman had spotlighted one sentence in the Constitution, known as the "Appointments clause," which says the president "shall nominate, and by and with the Advice and Consent
of the Senate, shall appoint Ambassadors, other public Minis-
ters and Consuls, Judges of the Supreme Court, and all other
Officers of the United States, . . . but Congress may by Law
vest the Appointment of such inferior Officers, as they think
proper, in the President alone, in the Courts of Law, or in the
Heads of Department." For the literalists, the independent
counsel case turned on this clause. Because the independent
counsel is an "Officer of the United States," that person must
be appointed by the president, Silberman asserted. However,

if the person were considered an "inferior Officer," the person could be appointed by the "Courts of Law."

Silberman's opinion also suggested that "Officers of the United States" must be under the president's control, just like cabinet officers. These officials serve "at the pleasure of the president," as the saying goes. Does the Constitution require such an arrangement for *all* "Officers of the United States"? Silberman suggested that it did. If so, a host of agencies were being run unconstitutionally, including the Federal Reserve Board, the Federal Trade Commission, the Federal Communications Commission, and the Equal Employment Opportunity Commission (EEOC). (Silberman's wife, incidentally, was a Reagan-appointed commissioner of the EEOC.) From the days of the New Deal in the 1930s, Congress had created scores of "independent agencies" with the power to enforce laws. Typically, the members of their governing boards are appointed, on a rotating basis, by the president, but they are then largely independent from the White House. If the independent counsels were unconstitutional, the "independent agencies" were in jeopardy, too.

Major constitutional cases do not always turn on the dry words of the old charter. Often, an appealing metaphor can speak louder. The conservatives favored the "separation of powers." That phrase does not appear in the Constitution, but former Chief Justice Burger, in his final years on the Court, and as head of the Constitution's bicentennial, stressed the separation of powers as the charter's overriding principle. Certainly, the eighteenth-century authors of the document believed in spreading power around. Freedom could not survive if a monarch could write the laws, enforce them according to personal preferences, and act as judge and jury for lawbreakers. However, did the "separation of powers" doctrine require that *all* executive power, including the power to prosecute, always be exercised by the president alone? Yes, said Judge Silberman.

Supporters of the law favored a different metaphor. The Constitution creates a system of "checks and balances," they said. The independent counsel law was simply a way to check corruption and lawbreaking in the upper reaches of the executive branch.

The case that reached the Court involved the least conspicuous Reagan administration official caught up in an independent counsel investigation. The facts of his case were ominous, too, for defenders of the system of independent counsels.

In 1981, Theodore B. Olson came to Washington with Reagan's first attorney general, William French Smith, and headed the Justice Department's Office of Legal Counsel. This was the same post held by Rehnquist in the Nixon administration. A year later, the Environmental Protection Agency (EPA) came under investigation in Congress on charges that it was directing federal cleanup funds for hazardous wastes in a way that benefited Republican candidates. A House subcommittee headed by Representative John Dingell, a Democratic power on Capitol Hill, demanded internal EPA documents. Olson told EPA officials to refuse the demand, citing "executive privilege" over "enforcement sensitive information."

To Dingell, this smacked of an Administration cover-up. Even after the EPA officials were removed and prosecuted, Dingell's House committee continued to insist that Olson's conduct be investigated. A lengthy House report suggested that in 1983, Olson may have deceived Congress by reporting that *all* the relevant EPA documents had been turned over. Dingell's investigators later found handwritten notes that they found relevant to their inquiry. On April 23, 1986, the special panel of judges appointed an independent counsel to look into the possibility that Olson violated criminal laws. The investigation came to be headed by Alexia Morrison.

To Olson and his many defenders, however, his case looked less like a criminal investigation than a political vendetta. After all, Olson had not enriched himself at the public's expense or committed some other apparent crime. Instead, he had vigorously defended the president's turf as an executive branch lawyer. Like most of the top Justice Department officials, he believed the independent counsel law to be unconstitutional and decided to challenge it. He refused to appear before a grand jury and contended instead that the independent counsel had no constitutional power to pursue him. Two Reagan appointees on the U.S. appeals court—Silberman and Williams—agreed and voted to quash the investigation. On April 26, 1988, the last day of oral arguments for the 1987–1988 term, the Supreme Court heard Morrison's appeal in *Morrison* v. *Olson.*

The political calculations were considerable. The Republican White House lined up on one side, the Democratic Congress on the other. By law, the solicitor general represents the federal government before the Court and defends the laws of Congress. Nonetheless, the solicitor is a Justice Department employee and an "Officer of the United States," serving at the pleasure of the president. To no one's surprise, the solicitor chose not to defend this act of Congress. Instead, Fried filed a brief endorsing Silberman's opinion. Lawyers for the House and Senate filed their own briefs with the Court, defending the law.

So, too, did the "independent" branch of the government—Alexia Morrison. She gladly characterized herself as an "inferior officer," with a limited mission of short duration. Morrison started with a handicap, however. Kennedy had announced, without explanation, that he would not participate in the case. Some justices, including O'Connor, White, and Rehnquist, will explain their reasons on the rare occasions they sit out a case. Perhaps a friend or family member has a tie to a law firm in the case, or perhaps they own stock in a company that will be affected by the ruling. Others, such as Scalia, refuse to explain why they choose to sit out a case. Kennedy followed Scalia's example. Despite his silence, however, one concern seemed apparent. A decision in the independent counsel case would affect his Sacramento friend Ed Meese, who was then under investigation himself. Kennedy's recusal created the possibility of a 4–4 tie. If that happened, Silberman's opinion would stand, the independent counsel law would be deemed unconstitutional, the Iran–Contra defendants could go free, and the Supreme Court would not have to say a word on the matter. For the conspiracy-minded, it seemed that the perfect solution had been found.

Almost everyone expected a close vote. Byron White believed firmly that Congress had broad power to shape the government. He would vote to uphold the independent counsel law. So, too, would Brennan, Marshall, and Blackmun. They saw little merit or wisdom in a rigid interpretation of the separation-of-powers doctrine. Stevens was more of a question mark. Then there were the Reagan appointees: O'Connor, Scalia, and Rehnquist. If they voted in tandem and were joined by Stevens, they would strike down the independent counsel law with a split decision.

No one was more predictable in his decisions than Rehnquist, or so lawyers and journalists often said. "He could mail in his votes at the beginning of the term," one prominent lawyer commented of the chief justice. Yet he had surprised most First Amendment lawyers with his decision in the *Hustler* case.

Now he had a surprise for the legal hierarchy of the Reagan administration.

Rehnquist led off the conference by stating his belief that the Ethics in Government Act was indeed constitutional. Laws of Congress are presumed to be constitutional, and Olson's attorneys had not convinced him that this was the exception. His vote essentially sealed the outcome, and the chief justice said that he wanted to speak for the Court in the case of *Morrison* v. *Olson*. His majority opinion firmly rejected the array of arguments used to challenge the law. The Constitution allows Congress to establish "inferior officers," which the independent counsel clearly was, he said. And the law does not "impermissibly undermine" the executive branch. O'Connor joined him, as did Stevens, White, Brennan, Marshall, and Blackmun. Only Scalia dissented—vigorously so, of course. The threat to the independent counsels had been extinguished; the criminal probe in the Iran–Contra case would continue.

Now, Rehnquist's friends in the Justice Department were amazed. How could he ignore the separation of powers and uphold such a law undercutting the president's power? For once, the conservatives were grumbling about Rehnquist. Speculation was rampant, though none of it made much sense. Was Rehnquist selling out? Was he moving toward the middle now that he was chief justice? Was he worried about the political fallout if the "Reagan Court" were to free a series of Reagan confidants?

Did he simply want to control the Court opinion, rather than dissenting with Scalia and leaving that power in Brennan's hands? If so, why did he write such a strong opinion? Besides, that strategy was not a Rehnquist one. Within the Court, everyone praised him for being a straight shooter. Burger had caused bad feelings by occasionally voting with the majority in a vital case even when he disagreed, so that he could keep control of the opinion. However, his maneuvers had prompted others to conspire behind his back to write an opinion that reflected the true majority sentiment. The back-and-forth maneuvering was well documented in Burger's least-favorite book, *The Brethren*, by Bob Woodward and Scott Armstrong. No one conspired behind Rehnquist's back. He stated his view directly and stuck to it.

In trying to second-guess Rehnquist, his conservative friends and young right-leaning clerks ignored an obvious explanation. Rehnquist nearly always upheld laws against constitutional challenges. As Chuck Cooper, his former clerk, often said, Rehnquist was a "hard sell on constitutional claims." If Olson had been an ordinary criminal defendant who claimed that prosecuting him violated his constitutional rights, Rehnquist would have been seen as a sure "no" vote. By this reckoning, the independent counsel case marked one of Rehnquist's finest hours as chief justice. He and the Court had been called upon to referee a dispute between the Republican White House and the Democratic Congress, but Rehnquist had decided the case just like any other. He upheld the law as written.

Scalia was livid at the outcome. He spent weekends working up a long, strongly worded dissent. His clerks often drafted a research memo for him as the basis for an opinion or dissent but not infrequently were amazed to see what the justice made of it. By their accounts, Scalia was Rumpelstiltskin at the computer: "He could take a piece of junk and turn it into gold," one clerk said of Scalia's opinions.

When the decision day came, he announced that he intended to read much of it from the bench. He did not pull any punches in deference to the chief justice: "This is not analysis," he said of Rehnquist's opinion. "It is ad hoc judgment." Scalia thought the Court should draw clear lines. Indeed that, he believed, was the purpose of the Constitution and of the Court—to draw sharp lines of law, not balanced judgments that depended on facts peculiar to a single case. What could be clearer than saying the president had the power to execute the laws and Congress to write the laws? Because prosecuting a crime involved executing the law, it was the president's task alone, Scalia complained. (It's worth noting that Scalia's view did not change based on who benefited and who got hurt. The following term, the Court would hear a challenge to the criminal sentencing laws set down by the U.S. Sentencing Commission, another independent agency created by Congress. The commission's stiff prison terms were challenged by several drug dealers as being the product of an unconstitutional system. Only Scalia would agree with them. In another lone dissent, he said the Constitution created only one lawmaking body— Congress—and it could not create on its own a "junior varsity" version in the Sentencing Commission.)

The clerks had noticed some tension between Rehnquist and Scalia. In general, they agreed on the law; Scalia cast his vote with the chief justice in about 85 percent of the cases. In addition, they still got together monthly for their poker game of long standing.

That alone might have suggested a unique after-hours friendship between Rehnquist and Scalia, because rarely did the justices see each other away from the Court. When others were asked about the feelings between the two justices, most described their colleagues as coworkers or office companions rather than as true friends. Their relationships were cordial but not warm.

Neither Rehnquist nor Scalia claimed a close relationship with the other. The younger Scalia was talkative, insistent, and supremely self-confident. He and his wife, Maureen, were a lively presence in Washington, D.C., social circles. If the justices of the Supreme Court were supposed to be stiff and somber, Nino Scalia broke the mold. He loved to sing, to play the piano, to dance across the ballroom, or—when the occasion called for it—to deliver lectures on the law. No wonder he was in constant demand.

One evening, several reporters spotted Scalia leaving the Court and took note of his natty black tuxedo. "Ah, yes. Esteemed jurist by day, man about town at night," he said, bouncing down the steps.

Scalia's energy and intellect made him, among lawyers at least, the most intriguing of the justices. He was the subject of dozens of law review articles and was the sole focus of a conference of law professors in New York. Having made the rounds of universities as a professor himself, he was referred to simply as "Nino" by many academics who knew him from years before.

On the other hand, Scalia's assertiveness also puts off some of his colleagues. To Rehnquist, Scalia seemed to believe each case had only one possible right answer—his. Rehnquist was more reserved and quite willing to accept the fact that others viewed matters differently. As chief justice, he ran an efficient operation. At the conferences, he ensured that each justice got a chance to state an opinion without interruption. Once the votes were tallied, he moved on to the next case. Just as in their poker games, Rehnquist cast a frown on anyone who talked too much.

The frowns were often directed at Scalia. The younger justice had suggested that the "conference" should be a true conference, not a vote-tallying session. He hadn't minded telling anyone who would listen that he found the intellectual tone of the Supreme Court to be supremely disappointing. He often was irked at Rehnquist's obsession with efficiency. Here they were, the nine justices of the highest court in the land, the keepers of the Constitution, yet they were not willing to take the time for a serious debate on matters of principle, Scalia had complained.

In his 1987 book on the Court, Rehnquist took on Scalia's complaints quite directly. "When I first went on the Court, I was both surprised and disappointed at how little interplay there was between the various justices," Rehnquist wrote. As the junior justice, "I thought it would be desirable to have more of a roundtable discussion" so the others could benefit more from his insights, he said. Over the years, however, Rehnquist came to realize that discussion changed few minds. Moreover, there was no formula, no method that would yield the right decision. Rather, the Court was made up of nine distinct individuals, each of whom had personal convictions. They studied the briefs and talked over cases with their law clerks, and they made decisions on their own.

"It is not as if we were trying to find a formula for squaring the circle, and all of those preceding the junior justice had bumblingly admitted their inability to find the formula; then suddenly the latter solves the riddle and the others cry 'Eureka! He has found it,' " Rehnquist wrote. His message, directed at Scalia, seemed to say, Yes, I was young, eager, and naïve once, too, but you'll get over it.

Of course, Scalia was not swayed or silenced. Rather, he used the Rehnquist book as a reason to air his complaints in public. "To call our discussion of a case a 'conference' is really something of a misnomer. It's much more a statement of the view of each of the nine justices, after which the totals are added," Scalia told a group of law students that spring. There was no back-and-forth debate, no discussion, no true conference, he suggested. "I don't like that. Maybe it's just because I'm new. Maybe it's because I'm an ex-academic. Maybe it's because I'm right," he said.

Scalia also had trouble containing his irritation with Sandra O'Connor. "She's a politician," he told friends. Though both were conservative and had a friendly relationship, Scalia and O'Connor approached the job differently. He wanted to set clear rules and follow rigid formulas. They were in the business of law, not politics.

However, she, like Lewis Powell, tried to carefully weigh the competing claims. She saw herself as a judge, not an academic who spun out theories. On the tough cases, including affirmative action and the death penalty, she had been torn. Where law for Scalia was an intellectual exercise, O'Connor worried about the impact of a decision on real people. He sought decisions that were intellectually consistent; she tried to be fair.

Throughout the spring, Scalia had been irked at O'Connor for taking months to decide whether to let a 15-year-old murderer be executed. In November, the Court had heard arguments on whether Oklahoma could carry out a death sentence against William Wayne Thompson who, at age 15, helped three others murder his brother-in-law, supposedly for abusing their sister. The Oklahoma courts upheld the conviction and the sentence.

Rehnquist, White, and Scalia voted to uphold the sentence. In Scalia's view, it was an easy case. Nothing in the Constitution prohibited such a sentence, so the Court should not interfere with it. Four others—Brennan, Marshall, Blackmun, and Stevens—voted to reverse it as "cruel and unusual punishment." The case of *Thompson* v. *Oklahoma* was heard before Kennedy arrived, so the decision rested with O'Connor. If she joined her fellow conservatives, a 4–4 vote would let the death sentence stand. If she joined the liberals, he would live.

"Sandra's tough. She's conservative. She's a state's righter. She wants to let states decide things like this," Blackmun told law students a few weeks after the term ended. "But here was a 15-year-old, and the soft spots in her armor . . . are children and women."

Week after week, O'Connor agonized and deferred a decision. Finally, with just a few weeks left in the term, she told the conference she would vote with the liberals to reverse the death sentence. However, she refused to join their draft opinion, which said that anyone under 18 should be exempted from capital punishment. Instead, O'Connor wrote an excruciatingly narrow, separate opinion, which decided only the 15-year-old's case and nothing more. Because Oklahoma lawmakers had failed to make clear that they intended juveniles as young as age 15 to face the death penalty, the death sentence given Thompson must be overturned, she said.

Scalia fumed. His dissent sought to demolish her rationale. In his view, the justices were there to sort out the logic of the law; individuals did not matter. If the logic was faulty, he attacked it. Why, he felt, should he spare O'Connor?

Death penalty laws do not say "15-year-olds can be executed," he said, but neither do they say "blind people can be executed," or "white-haired grandmothers can be executed." In his view, the law sets a punishment for a particular crime and then lets judges and juries decide whether a person committed that crime and deserves that punishment.

The day after the 5–3 ruling reversed the death sentence of the 15-year-old killer, the Court announced it would consider an appeal filed by a 16-year-old on Death Row. On that sour note, the spring term of 1988 came to an end.

PART FIVE
The
1988–1989 Term

8

A New Majority
Takes Control

J ust after 9 A.M., young Senate staffers hurried to work along First Street on Capitol Hill and took no notice of the gray-suited figure who strolled by. Nearly every morning, the chief justice went walking on the streets near the Court. Usually, he was alone, but occasionally a clerk accompanied him. Rehnquist's perennially sore back tightened up if he sat too long, and the walking helped.

It helped, too, with making decisions, he said. "I began to realize that some of my best insights came not during my enforced thinking periods in my chambers, but while I was shaving in the morning, driving to work, or just walking from one place to another," he wrote.

In his early years on the Court, Rehnquist wore long side-burns and was often casually attired in Hush Puppies and a sport coat. He drove to work in a well-worn Volkswagen. As chief justice, however, he began to trim the now-graying side-burns, to wear gray suits with fashionable green ties, and to arrive at the Court each morning in a long black limousine. On winter days, he donned a fedora and a dark overcoat for his morning walks. Still, in the hot days of the Washington, D.C., summer, when the Court was in recess, Rehnquist abandoned decorum. Strolling along the sidewalk in a white short-sleeved shirt and a broad-brimmed straw hat, he looked like a State Department official who had been assigned to Central America.

Rarely was he recognized on the street. On days when the Court was in session, hundreds of visitors would line up on the plaza, waiting their turn to walk up the long steps and to sit in the courtroom for 15 minutes. On occasion, before the 10 A.M. gavel sounded, Rehnquist would stroll past the lineup of visitors and not a head would turn. While most Washington politicians and government executives are drawn irresistibly to a bank of microphones or a TV camera, the justices prefer to be unseen, unheard, and unknown.

Sometimes, they succeed even beyond their own wishes. A few weeks after being sworn in, Anthony Kennedy was stopped on the Court steps by a young couple with a camera in hand. They asked the new justice to snap a photo of them standing before the edifice of the Supreme Court. He kindly complied and walked on, entirely unrecognized. John Paul Stevens, with his shock of white hair and bow ties, liked to walk out onto the Court steps in the afternoon to soak up some sun, but on one occasion he was perturbed to see tourists wave to him to move aside so he would not block their photos of the building.

Sometimes, their names are better known than their faces. During one summer break, Scalia and his wife piled their three youngest children into a van to drive cross-country to Los Angeles, where the justice was to teach law for several weeks. At the end of a long, hot day of driving, Scalia pulled into a motel and handed the desk clerk his credit card.

As she finished with his registration, she handed the card back and said, "Thank you, Mr. SKALLyuh."

"It's skuLEEuh," he corrected.

"Oh," she brightened, "like the Supreme Court justice."

"Yes," smiled Scalia.

The motel clerk aside, relatively few Americans can tick off the names of the justices. In the midst of the 1988 term, the *Washington Post* polled 1,005 persons to test their knowledge of courts and judges. Some 54 percent of those questioned were able to name the judge on TV's "The People's Court," Joseph Wapner. Asked to name the chief justice of the United States, only 9 percent named Rehnquist. Justice O'Connor was by far the best known, with a 23 percent recognition, while the others trailed Rehnquist with a single-digit response. As a college football star in the fall of 1937, the name of Byron "Whizzer" White was known nationwide. Now, after nearly three decades on the Court, only 3 percent of those surveyed could identify him.

Actually, Rehnquist and his colleagues are content to be virtually anonymous. While most Washington figures believe that power is linked to "visibility" and their "name recognition," the justices adhere to the opposite view. In their view, their rulings carry a special power because they are the pronouncements of nine somewhat mysterious black-robed figures.

In the fall of 1988, Rehnquist was especially pleased to have the Court and the justices stay out of the news. The term had ended in late June on a quiet note, and most of the justices quickly left the heat and glare of Washington for a summer of teaching and relaxation. Scalia took off for a teaching assignment in Greece; Kennedy went lecturing in England and Austria. Blackmun and Stevens returned to the Aspen Institute in Colorado, where each led a two-week seminar to further explore the large concepts of justice and equality. White was drawn to his native Colorado as well, where he enjoyed fly-fishing and golf. Rehnquist went to his Vermont vacation home to write, paint, and relax.

Throughout the summer, the chief justice, an avid fan of American politics, kept his eye on the developing race for the presidency. The next occupant of the White House would probably shape the direction of the Court through the early years of the twenty-first century, he knew. In July, Thurgood Marshall turned 80. He had already outlived all the predictions, but how much longer could he go on? In his chambers, Marshall joked often about his predicted demise. Should he die at his desk, he told his clerks, "Just prop me up and keep voting." He also offered his own prediction: "I expect to die at 110, shot by a jealous husband."

On November 12, four days after the election, Harry Blackmun, too, would turn 80. Along with the 82-year-old Brennan, the "three old goats," as Blackmun himself called the trio, formed the liberal core of the Court: the pro–civil rights, pro–abortion rights, and anti–death penalty bloc. The last Democratic appointee to the Court had come in 1967, with Lyndon Johnson's appointment of Marshall. Unless the Democrats won the White House in 1988, the Court, by the end of the century, figured to have nine conservative, Republican appointees.

In July 1988, however, the Republican hold on the White House looked to be in doubt. Massachusetts governor Michael Dukakis, Scalia's old Harvard law classmate, had won the Democratic presidential nomination and briefly united the squabbling factions of his party. He portrayed himself as smart and incorruptible—in sharp contrast to the current occupant of the White House, he suggested. It was not clear what Dukakis stood for, but it was clear who he was against—Ronald Reagan. He went into August with a double-digit lead in the polls.

Vice President George Bush, though Reagan's heir, decided not to ride Reagan's record of peace and prosperity. Instead, he and his advisers chose to play ideological hardball. Where Dukakis wanted to emphasize his managerial competence, Bush wanted to stress his opponent's philosophy. The Massachusetts governor was, he charged, a "liberal." That revelation appeared to unravel Dukakis and his campaign. Forced out of the closet, Dukakis looked uncomfortable; he did not want to defend the Democratic dogma on a host of social issues. On civil rights, for example, although the Democrats felt Reagan had a poor record, Dukakis downplayed the issue. Because civil rights had become a question of "affirmative action" for minorities, Democrat strategists knew it was no longer an issue that won votes for them.

Bush wanted to talk about crime, drugs, the death penalty, and the American flag. Ronald Reagan had indeed transformed the political landscape. Republican candidates proudly proclaimed their right-wing views, while the Democrats cringed at being called "liberals."

A spat over the Pledge of Allegiance symbolized Dukakis's troubles. In 1977, the Massachusetts governor vetoed a bill that would have required schoolteachers to begin the day by leading their pupils in the pledge to the flag. He based his decision on the Supreme Court's ruling in the 1943 case of *West Virginia* v. *Barnette*, one of the most inspiring and courageous opinions in the Court's long history. With America at war against three totalitarian regimes, the justices had been confronted with the question of whether all schoolchildren, including Jehovah's Witnesses, could be forced to salute the flag as a condition of attending the public schools. On a 6–3 vote, the Court said no.

"If there is any fixed star in our constitutional constellation, it is that no official, high or petty, can prescribe what shall be orthodox in politics, nationalism [or] religion . . . and force citizens to confess by word or act of faith therein," wrote Rehnquist's mentor, Justice Robert H. Jackson. The Court struck down the West Virginia flag-salute law, and the *Barnette* case has since stood for the principle that the government cannot demand from any citizen a ritualistic show of allegiance.

Defending that principle proved more difficult in peacetime 1988, however, than in wartime 1943. Bush, of course, had no interest in subtlety. He was wholeheartedly in favor of the flag, he said. "What is it about the Pledge of Allegiance that upsets him so much?" Bush asked of Dukakis at campaign rallies.

Within a few weeks in late August and early September, Bush and his advisers had turned the campaign around. Dukakis, knocked off balance, never recovered. Though the next president would shape the future of the Supreme Court, neither candidate had much to say about the subject.

That fall, Rehnquist had a chance to put his new majority to a test. Kennedy would be starting his first full term. If he joined with the chief justice and White, O'Connor, and Scalia, the conservatives would have control of the Court for the first time since the 1950s.

That prospect was a regular topic of conversation each morning as Brennan joined his clerks for coffee at 9 A.M. The justice liked to start the day with a casual talk, whether about the news of the day or a Court battle from three decades ago. For the clerks, it was clearly the highlight of their day. Brennan reminisced about cases from 30 years ago—and could recite passages from the opinions—or he vented his ire over an injustice he had read about that morning. If Brennan was older in his face and slower afoot, his mind remained sharp. He certainly had not lost his enthusiasm for the Court or for winning the big cases. For years, the conservative tide had been flowing against him; it had yet to wash over him. Still, Kennedy presented a concern. Though the new justice talked as if he were a moderate who shunned a rigid ideology, he had shown signs during the spring of casting reflexive votes for the conservative chief justice. If so, the Court term in 1988–1989 could prove momentous.

The docket brimmed with major cases. The justices had already agreed to reconsider the reach of federal job-discrimination laws, as well as to decide on the government's power to force employees to undergo drug testing. Thanks to O'Connor's agonized decision in June, the justices were set to decide whether a 16-year-old murderer could be put to death. In addition, as George Bush campaigned through flag factories in September, Texas state attorneys were preparing an appeal to the Court seeking a ruling on whether a flag burner could be sent to jail. The state attorneys in Missouri were at work on an appeal, too. A federal appeals court in St. Louis had struck down a state antiabortion law based on the *Roe* v. *Wade* ruling, but with Lewis Powell now gone, the Missouri attorneys wanted to see whether the Rehnquist Court was ready to reconsider its abortion ruling. Though each of these cases offered great potential import, the first major case of the term seemed to signal the many changes to come; it gave the Rehnquist Court an opportunity to call a halt to affirmative action by the government.

Richmond, the historic capital of the Confederacy and today the thriving capital of Virginia, has a population that is more than half black. In the five years prior to 1983, however, less than one percent of its $124 million in city contracts had gone to businesses run by minority entrepreneurs. The reason for this result was not clear. White businesspersons may have refused to hire or contract with blacks over the years, preventing the seeds of minority-owned businesses from ever sprouting. Perhaps blacks had not mustered the capital to begin businesses of their own. Perhaps, too, a white-controlled city government had ignored black businesses when handing out city work. Regardless of the reason, the Richmond city council, where blacks held five of the nine seats in 1983, determined to give minorities a more equal share of the city pie.

Three years earlier, the Court had given a green light to such plans. In the case of *Fullilove* v. *Klutznick*, the justices, on a 6–3 vote, upheld a public works law passed by Congress which required that at least ten percent of the funds be awarded to firms controlled by minorities—African-Americans, Hispanic-Americans, Asian-Americans, American Indians, or Eskimos. The ruling rebutted a challenge by white contractors, who said this "set aside" reserved for others denied them the equal protection of the laws. Only Rehnquist, Stevens, and Potter Stewart dissented from that decision.

"These dollars will be recycled back to minority businesses, in the interest of the entire community," Richmond councilperson Henry Richardson said in support of the new city council policy during an April 11, 1983, meeting. This plan "is based on good sound business practices that will help and assist the growth, the development, and the improvement . . . of all Richmonders."

The plan he referred to would require that at least 30 percent of city contract funds go to minority-owned firms. By the mid-1980s, hundreds of cities and counties, as well as state governments, had plans that benefited minority-owned businesses, either by giving them an advantage in competing for contracts or, like Richmond, demanding that they receive a certain share of the funds. Still, Richmond's 30-percent figure was unusually high. Typically, other cities or states reserved at most 15 percent of their contracts for minority-owned businesses.

Supporters lauded these plans for giving minorities a foot in the door, a chance for the excluded to join the mainstream. Detractors said these schemes inspired more fraud than new business. Often, white-owned businesses set up an offshoot company with a black or a Hispanic in charge. The government contracts were funneled through this offshoot firm, but the profits still went to the white owners. In other instances, the contracts flowed to genuine minority-owned businesses but succeeded only in enriching a few individuals, not a broader community. Because the low bidders could not always win contracts if they were white, these set-aside laws also raised the cost of city work.

Nonetheless, these criticisms questioned whether such plans were wise, not whether they were legal. The Supreme Court had to decide whether the constitutional rights of whites were violated by a decision of an elected city council on how to spend its own city funds. The notion that all citizens deserve equal treatment under the law is mentioned only once in the Constitution. The Fourteenth Amendment of 1868 says, "No State shall . . . deny to any person within its jurisdiction the equal protection of the laws." This amendment was intended to stop the southern states from discriminating *against* blacks. Because cities, counties, and school boards are legal creations of the state, the amendment applies to them, too. Was it intended to protect the legal rights of whites, too?

The Fourteenth Amendment could not be followed strictly and literally. If so, it could strike down nearly all laws. For example, a state law might say that only persons with a medical degree from an accredited school may practice medicine within the state. Persons who fancy themselves witch doctors with extraordinary healing powers may contend that such a law denies them the equal protection of the laws. So, too, might an ex-felon who is denied the right to own a gun by state law. Despite this possibility, a federal court would waste no time in tossing out a lawsuit filed by the witch doctor or the ex-felon. Because laws, by their nature, make distinctions and discriminations, a law cannot be declared unconstitutional simply because it makes a discrimination that favors one person and disfavors another.

For most of its history, the Fourteenth Amendment's equal protection guarantee had practically no significance. During the Earl Warren years, however, the Supreme Court constructed a scheme to give it some meaning—but not too much. Groups of persons who had been subjected to systematic legal discrimination were put into a special category deserving extra protection. Blacks were the obvious group. So, by extension, were other racial or ethnic groups, such as Asian- and Hispanic-Americans. In the 1970s, the Court split over whether women were protected from discrimination under the Fourteenth Amendment. Conservatives such as Rehnquist disputed giving women special protection because, they said, the Fourteenth Amendment was aimed at protecting blacks, not females. Brennan, however, put together a five-vote majority in the mid-1970s to rule that gender discrimination by the government violated the Fourteenth Amendment. Under the Court's method of analysis, any law that discriminated against a protected group was subjected to "strict" or "heightened scrutiny" by the justices. Unless the government could show it had a powerful and compelling reason for a discriminatory law, the Court would strike it down as unconstitutional.

All other laws—that is, those that did not discriminate against a protected group—fell into a second category. They would be upheld under a so-called rational basis test. If the law had a reason behind it—such as, "we don't think ex-felons should be walking the streets with guns"—it would be upheld. Law students were taught a simple formula: If "strict scrutiny" was applied, the government lost. If the "rational basis" formula was used, the government won. It was obviously of great importance, then, which groups were deemed worthy of special constitutional protection, and only the Supreme Court could decide which was which. Why not the poor, homosexuals, the elderly, or smokers? Because the Court deemed they had not suffered systematic legal discrimination.

Since the 1978 *University of California* v. *Bakke* case, the Supreme Court had danced around the question of whether whites were due special protection when the government discriminated in favor of the black minority. In the *Richmond* case, the Court's new majority would finally have a chance to answer that question.

In 1983, the J. A. Croson Company, an Ohio firm owned by whites, was the low bidder and won a Richmond city contract to install stainless steel plumbing in the city jail. The new city law demanded, however, that at least 30 percent of the work be subcontracted through a minority firm. Croson, in attempting to meet this requirement, was unable to find a minority firm to supply the plumbing fixtures, the cost of which made up about 75 percent of the contract's cost. The Ohio firm then asked for a waiver of the minority-business requirement. In response, the city ordered new bidders on the original contract. Croson filed suit against the city, contending that its rights to the equal protection of the laws had been violated.

The case split the U.S. Court of Appeals for the Fourth Circuit, based in Richmond. Initially, it upheld the city on a 2–1 vote, but after the Supreme Court sent the case back to be reconsidered under one of its muddled rulings on affirmative action, the appellate court struck down the law on a 2–1 vote. That decision was affirmed by the entire appeals court on a 6–5 vote. After Kennedy's arrival, the high court announced it would hear the case of *Richmond* v. *Croson.*

If you were unaware of the parties and the issue in this case, you would assume that the liberal justices would be on the side of the individual claiming to be a victim of government discrimination (Croson), while the conservatives would line up in defense of the city and its officials' exercise of their government powers. Such a guess would have been wrong in nearly every instance. No issue turned the tables as much as affirmative action. Brennan, Marshall, and Blackmun, who were usually quick to strike down laws that violated an individual's rights, suddenly proclaimed the wisdom of upholding the laws enacted by local officials when they endorsed preferential treatment for minorities. Meanwhile, Rehnquist and Scalia, who usually insist on deferring to local governments, staunchly defended the constitutional rights of the white males who were said to be victims of reverse discrimination. In the *Richmond* case, all of those five votes were certain. Brennan, Marshall, and Blackmun would vote to support the city ordinance; Rehnquist and Scalia would strike it down.

Byron White would probably join Rehnquist and Scalia. Almost alone among the justices, he could claim a record of consistency on the issue of racial discrimination. When confronted in the 1960s and 1970s with cases where blacks had suffered racial discrimination, White sided with them. This put him in the liberal camp, at least on civil rights. However, in the 1980s, when whites came to the Court with evidence that they had suffered racial discrimination, he sided with them, too. Because White was not much for explaining, his more recent votes were usually cited as evidence of his growing conservatism.

The outcome then depended on the justices in the middle: Stevens, O'Connor, and Kennedy. At times, Stevens had denounced affirmative action in the strongest term. In the 1980 case involving public works, he had raised eyebrows with a scorching dissent that suggested at one point that Congress's law smacked of Nazi-era racial codes. However, in more recent job-discrimination cases, including the *Santa Clara* case from two years before, he had endorsed affirmative action as a settled policy. To the attorneys—as well as to the other justices—he remained a mystery. Kennedy was too, but only because he had yet to cast a vote on the question of affirmative action.

On October 5, 1988, when the attorneys for the city of Richmond and for the J. A. Croson Company appeared before the Court for their hour-long argument, the most attention focused on Sandra Day O'Connor. Her vote would probably determine who won and lost. Like Lewis Powell, she had gone back and forth on the affirmative action issue. She had struck down plans that set a rigid "quota" but upheld others that gave a "plus" to the minorities or to women, such as in the *Santa Clara* case. She had upheld plans that were designed to make up for a blatant exclusion of minorities by a white employer, but not those designed to make up for 200 years of American history. As with Powell, her attempts to fashion a middle position on affirmative action had won plaudits outside the Court but were not always well received within it.

"If you read them closely, her decisions [in this area] don't make a lot of sense," said a conservative clerk. Often, O'Connor relied on hair-splitting distinctions between a "quota" and a "numerical goal" or between a plan that made up for blatant discrimination and one that made up for general "societal discrimination." In practice, her decisions seemed at times to ignore these distinctions. In the 1986 term, for example, she voted to strike down the hiring quota imposed on the Alabama state troopers, even though it was based on the state's blatant refusal to hire or promote blacks. However, she voted to uphold Santa Clara County's affirmative action plan, even though it had little to do with making up for blatant discrimination against female road workers. The clerks saw a simpler explanation: O'Connor was more sensitive to discrimination against women than to discrimination against black state troopers in Alabama.

As a former legislator, O'Connor was quite interested in the details of the legislation, and that posed a problem for the defenders of the Richmond city council, which, with little debate, had imposed its 30-percent quota for minority businesses. The argument had just begun when O'Connor, in a school-marmish tone, began to question the city's attorney on how the ordinance was put together.

"Is there any indication that the city considered any race-neutral alternatives before enacting a percentage set-aside requirement?" O'Connor asked attorney John Payton, representing Richmond. Why not give minority businesses help with preparing bids, she said, or waive some capital requirements rather than adopt a strict quota? In O'Connor's view, a good legislator should consider a variety of alternatives before adopting a last-resort plan that sets a fixed quota.

Also, why did the ordinance apply "in addition to blacks, to Orientals, Indians, and Aleut persons? Was there any evidence before the city that they had been subject to discrimination in the Richmond construction industry, do you know?" she asked.

"There is no evidence in the record with regard to that," Payton replied. To the Richmond attorneys, this seemed like nit-picking. There were no Eskimos in Richmond, but the city had simply adopted the federal government's standard definition of minority groups.

O'Connor considered the city to be guilty of sloppy lawmaking. Possibly a city could enact a legal system of preferences for new and developing businesses owned by minorities, she said, but this was not it. Rather, the Richmond council, by legislative fiat, had imposed a flat racial quota, and that violated the Fourteenth Amendment, O'Connor concluded.

Near the end of the argument, Kennedy raised a fasci-
nating question about the history of the Fourteenth Amendment: "If this ordinance had been enacted in 1870, would the
chances for its being sustained be any greater than now?" he
asked Croson's attorney. The new justice had spent part of the
summer reading the history of the Reconstruction era. The
Republicans in Congress not only wrote the Civil Rights Act
of 1866 and the Fourteenth Amendment to stop discrimination
against blacks but also created the Freedman's Bureau to give
blacks practical help in getting work, schooling, and housing.
It could have been described as the nations's first "affirmative
action" program.

Walter Ryland, Croson's attorney, sought to slip away
from the question. "I don't feel competent to answer that,
Justice Kennedy, because I don't know the context of the time
and what the courts would have done," he said.

Kennedy pressed ahead. "Well, we know about our history, we know about the context of the time, we know about
the necessity of the Fourteenth Amendment. We know about
the existence of slavery and of discrimination after slavery
ended," he continued.

Ryland noted that the Freedman's Bureau was providing
special aid to blacks throughout the South. "Nobody has suggested that that was unconstitutional or some sort of unlawful
preference," he conceded. Then he quickly returned to the
present. "Based on recent constitutional history," he said, the
Court should not approve "race-conscious legal remedies in
the absence of a shown violation." Because the Richmond city
government had not been convicted of discriminating against
blacks, it cannot now discriminate in their favor, he suggested.

Kennedy's point was dropped and never revisited, but his
question raised an interesting notion. The conservatives liked
to say that they, rather than the liberals, were guided by the
original intent of the Constitution. If so, then it was fair to ask:
Would the authors of the Fourteenth Amendment have been
troubled if a southern government, on its own accord, sought
to ensure that the black minority won a share of the city contracts? Chances are they would have been astonished and delighted.

Instead, the conservatives adopted a modern-day meaning
of the Fourteenth Amendment: It barred "racial discrimination" by government. The amendment speaks of "equal protection" for "any person," and if read literally, it certainly

includes white males as well as blacks. On the other hand, the conservatives did not read the amendment literally when it came to prohibiting the Pentagon from denying homosexuals equal treatment. Nor did Rehnquist in the 1970s think that women were due equal treatment because of the Fourteenth Amendment. Nonetheless, Rehnquist and Scalia had made up their minds. Rather than giving blacks special protection, the Fourteenth Amendment shielded everyone, including whites, from "racial discrimination" by government.

When the justices gathered on Friday morning, the chief justice moved to strike down the Richmond ordinance as violating the Fourteenth Amendment. White and Scalia agreed. Despite his musings about history, Kennedy voted with Rehnquist. Only Brennan, Marshall, and Blackmun voted to uphold the Richmond law.

Stevens had been troubled by set-aside laws that set a fixed quota based on race, and Richmond's seemed to be an especially clumsy one at that. He indicated that he would strike down the law as well. Stevens ensured Rehnquist a majority, but the chief justice did not assign him the opinion. Rehnquist didn't trust him to write a major opinion. Independent-minded and uncommitted, Stevens would write an opinion that suited him, not one that would mesh the views of four or five others. Rehnquist steered away from Scalia, too. His written opinions were too strong and too sweeping, enough so to scare away a wavering member of the majority. Faced with an uncertain majority, Rehnquist usually assigned the opinion to the least certain member of the majority, or he wrote it himself, to reflect the views of his wavering ally. Here, he chose the former course and assigned the Richmond opinion to O'Connor. Certainly, she thought the Richmond ordinance was unconstitutional, but why so? Was it because the government may never write a racial preference into law, or was it because Richmond had gone about it in a ham-handed way? Depending on how it was worded, O'Connor's opinion could spell the end of affirmative action or merely add another wrinkle to a decade's worth of law on the subject.

The next week, the Court heard the second round of arguments in *Patterson* v. *McLean Credit*. When the case had been first heard in February, it had drawn little attention and few legal briefs. However, Rehnquist's threat to strip blacks of the legal protection against private discrimination under the old

Civil Rights Act of 1866 had turned the case into a huge battle.
Now, the justices had before them a foot-thick file of briefs,
dozens of which came from legal and civil rights groups, urging
them to leave the law as it stands.

Since the Court's surprise announcement in the spring
that it would reconsider the prevailing interpretation of the
law, the conservatives had been accused of being right-wing
zealots, anxious to undercut civil rights. None of the criticism
seemed to faze Rehnquist, White, or Scalia. That's why they
had life tenure, Scalia said, so the justices could ignore such
ranting. He was unswayed, too, by the legal argument. The old
1866 law gave blacks the "same right" as whites to make contracts, and in his view, that meant the free slaves had a legal
right to enter into contracts, not a guarantee against racism in
private business dealings.

In Scalia's mind, the *Runyon* decision applying the law to
private schools was wrong when it was decided, but that alone
was not enough reason for the Court to overturn it now, he
knew. Scalia needed something more, some evidence that the
Court's mistake was wreaking havoc in the law and in the business world. He was troubled because the briefs for *McLean
Credit* failed to show the problems with the current Court rule.
For example, could a corporation be subjected to a huge damage suit because a supervisor or an executive made an off-the-
cuff racist comment? Could that alone amount to racial discrimination on the job? Because the business attorneys had not
made a convincing case for overturning the *Runyon* decision,
Scalia tried to coax it out of them during the oral argument on
October 12.

For the reargument, the NAACP LDF brought in its general counsel, Julius Chambers, while McLean Credit hired New
York attorney Roger S. Kaplan. When Kaplan devoted his opening minutes to arguing that the *Runyon* case had been wrongly
decided, Scalia grew impatient.

That much was understood, Scalia asserted, interrupting
him, but the Court had made other highly questionable inter-
pretations of the law before, and they were allowed to stand.
"Why is this case so special?" he asked.

Kaplan explained that Congress, in the Civil Rights Act
of 1964, had set up detailed procedures for handling job discrimination complaints. The EEOC (Equal Employment Opportunity Commission) must investigate those complaints and
try to work out settlements. Congress wanted to avoid lawsuits,

and even if the discrimination complaint cannot be resolved, employees cannot seek general damages against an employer under the more recent laws, Kaplan noted. What sense would it have made for Congress in 1964 to pass such a modest law, he said, if 100 years earlier employees had already been given a legal weapon to win damage verdicts from their employers?

Scalia rubbed his hair in frustration. Kaplan's explanation was not reason to overturn the *Runyon* decision now. He wanted evidence, examples, horror stories even. He leaned up to his microphone. "You keep telling us it's wrong. Let's concede it's wrong. So what?" Scalia asked.

Kaplan tried another explanation of how the *Runyon* ruling distorted the legal scheme set up by Congress. The Court's ruling "intrudes on the fundamental power of Congress," Kaplan said.

Scalia was irked. "If that's all you have, Mr. Kaplan, I'm afraid it's nothing," he said. Around the conference table, Scalia would need ammunition to fight for overturning the *Runyon* ruling, but the attorneys had not given him any.

Brennan, Marshall, and Blackmun rarely joined in the arguments. They usually sat silently and let the younger conservatives carry the debate. Even Stevens had little to say during the reargument. Like the liberals, he thought the Court had no business moving to upset a settled doctrine of law. Kaplan's failure to cite examples of how the current law caused problems only confirmed his view that it should not be tampered with now.

While Scalia tried to coax out a convincing argument for overturning the *Runyon* ruling, Kennedy at the opposite end of the bench sounded a different note. He didn't seem to agree with what Scalia and Kaplan assumed was obvious: that the *Runyon* ruling was wrong in the first place. "Mr. Kaplan, you don't deny that there's a great deal of legislative history that suggests that Congress was also concerned about private discrimination in the South?" Kennedy asked.

Kaplan demurred. He thought the Congress of 1866 was concerned only with legal rights for blacks.

Kennedy had read a brief submitted by historians of the Reconstruction era and had examined 1866 debates on the law. The Radical Republicans had spoken out against the pervasive discrimination against the newly freed slaves. Senator Lyman Trumbull, the primary sponsor of the law, said he wanted to attack not only "local laws" but also the "prevailing public sentiment" in the South that caused blacks "to be oppressed and in fact deprived of their freedom."

"Suppose in 1868 that the only grocery store in a small town refused to sell groceries to blacks. Was that covered by the statute?" Kennedy asked. Did such discrimination deprive blacks of the "same right" to make contracts as enjoyed by whites?

No, Kaplan responded.

"And you find no historical evidence that Congress was concerned about this?" he asked again.

The new justice disagreed. Kennedy's reading of the Reconstruction-era debates had convinced him that the members of Congress wanted to combat the systematic discrimination against blacks, both private and public. If so, the *Jones* v. *Mayer* and the *Runyon* v. *McCrary* rulings may have been right after all. Moreover, the Court usually stood by its own precedents unless confronted with a compelling reason for changing the law. In Kennedy's view, reasons here were far short of compelling. He was now convinced the Runyon ruling should stand.

When the justices convened on Friday morning, Brennan argued that the *Runyon* ruling should be upheld as a matter of history and precedent. Kennedy, who had cast a fifth vote with Rehnquist in February to reconsider the *Runyon* decision, now cast his vote with Brennan to ensure that it would stand after all.

Brennan held that according to the *Runyon* ruling, the law barred "all racial discrimination" in the making and enforcing of contracts, and on that basis, Brenda Patterson should win the case. She claimed she had been harassed on the job and denied a promotion because of her race. Brennan opined that if a jury believed her, she was entitled to damages. Kennedy agreed that Patterson had a strong claim if the law was to stand as is, but he remained uncertain on one point. How far did it extend? Was a single comment by an employer, such as "blacks are known be slower than whites," enough to trigger a lawsuit and a damage claim? An isolated racist comment did not seem to be the kind of systematic discrimination that had troubled the Reconstruction Congress, but where should the line be drawn? Brennan took on the opinion to try to draw a line that would satisfy Kennedy and the others. With Kennedy's vote, Brennan would have a five-vote majority. Once again, the aging liberal had pulled a rabbit from the hat.

After the first two weeks of hearing arguments, the Court took a two-week recess, a pattern that was followed throughout the year. The justices did not go on vacation during the recess. Rather, they went to work on opinions and on preparing for the next round of arguments in 12 cases. O'Connor had put her clerks to work on drafting an opinion in the Richmond case on affirmative action. Rehnquist had also assigned her an opinion that would sharply restrict the rights of Death Row inmates to file new appeals in federal courts. As a former state judge, O'Connor took umbrage at the thought that federal judges were often given a free hand to pluck criminal cases out of the state system and to transfer them to a federal court. She agreed entirely with Rehnquist; the appeal rights of prison inmates should be restricted.

O'Connor, however, was probably the most moderate of the five conservatives. Since Lewis Powell retired in 1987, she had become the pivotal justice; she held the balance on abortion, affirmative action, religion, and the death penalty. The Rehnquist Court would move as far right as Sandra O'Connor was willing to go. She still worked relentlessly, more certain than ever that the right outcome in each case depended on her.

On Friday, October 21, however, her legal responsibilities suddenly seemed beside the point. A routine test had found a small lump in her breast. With her surgery set for Friday morning at the Georgetown University Hospital, she nonetheless kept a commitment to speak Thursday evening at Washington and Lee University in Lexington, Virginia, a seven-hour drive from and to the nation's capital.

A few hours after her operation, she released an optimistic statement through the Court's press office. The cancer "was found to exist in a very early form and stage. The prognosis is for total recovery. I do not anticipate missing any oral arguments," the statement said. It was perhaps a bit too optimistic. A few days later, she learned there had been some spread of the cancer to her lymph nodes. She would have to undergo chemotherapy in hopes of preventing a recurrence.

O'Connor was 58, the third-youngest member of the Court. She had played tennis and golf with the same steely determination as she showed in her Court work. She exercised in the morning and skied during winter breaks; she had been in robust health. Suddenly, she faced her mortality. She later told friends that the two weeks after her cancer diagnosis were the worst, most frightening days of her life. It had been "the first major crisis of her life," her sister Ann said. O'Connor approached her disease with her usual resolve. "She took her cancer as a challenge," her sister added. She set out "learning everything she could about it, reading every book, talking with people and making the necessary decisions about her treatment and options." She talked with old friends—and made new ones—who had gone through the struggle of breast cancer. The doctors do not talk of cures for cancer or offer guarantees, only odds. Her odds were good, but they were just odds.

Despite her illness and her anxieties, O'Connor kept her pledge to return to work quickly. In March, she had undergone an emergency appendectomy during a two-week recess. Strong-willed and stoic, O'Connor returned to work in time for the next set of arguments, not having missed a day on the bench. With her cancer surgery, she did the same. When the oral arguments resumed on Monday, October 31, O'Connor was there. Before, she had worked hard out of a sense of duty. Now, she told friends, she was glad to have work that kept her mind off the cancer.

The chemotherapy clearly took its toll on her. Within a few weeks, O'Connor looked gray and tired and wore a wig, but on the bench, her energy never flagged. If an attorney loosely paraphrased the law to stretch its meaning, O'Connor could be counted on to correct him. "Well, now, it doesn't quite say that, does it?" she said, proceeding to read the exact language of the law. She resumed playing golf and tennis, too, unwilling to give in to her illness. One day, though, she admitted to her husband that she felt a bit tired. "Welcome to the human race," he replied.

With each month, too, her role as the pivotal justice grew in importance. On religion, she stood on the fault line between the liberal and conservative factions of the Court. In October, the justices announced that they would hear a case from Pittsburgh that would test that fault line again. In response to a suit by the American Civil Liberties Union (ACLU), a federal appeals court had ruled that city and county officials may not display a huge Christmas tree, a menorah, and a creche depicting Christ's birth at the city hall and county courthouse. The conservatives voted to hear the appeal in *Allegheny County v. ACLU.*

O'Connor also figured to hold the deciding vote on the two key death-penalty cases on the docket. In the fall, the justices said they would agree to rule on whether a mentally retarded murderer could be put to death. Earlier, the Court had agreed to consider whether a 16-year-old who commits murder can be executed.

In addition, the term's biggest case was yet to come. In September, Missouri's attorney general, William L. Webster, had filed an appeal asking the justices to revive a 1986 state law, which barred abortion in public hospitals. It also forbade the use of public funds for "encouraging or counseling a woman to have an abortion not necessary to save her life." Lawmakers wanted to get the state out of the abortion business entirely, but several doctors and patients challenged the law, contending it violated women's rights to abortion. They named Webster, the state's chief law enforcement officer, as the defendant. In response to the suit, the federal appeals court in St. Louis struck down the law as unconstitutional under the *Roe* v. *Wade* ruling, but Webster thought the state had done nothing more than refuse to subsidize abortion, which did not block a woman's right to choose abortion.

Any case that mentioned the word *abortion* was bound to attract attention, but the Reagan Justice Department made sure that Webster's appeal would become a landmark decision. In the summer, as Missouri's state attorneys prepared their appeal, Brad Reynolds called to urge that they challenge directly the *Roe* v. *Wade* ruling. Having played a key role in the nomination of Scalia and Kennedy, Reynolds knew with certainty what others only suspected: that the two new justices would vote to overturn the right to abortion. Along with Rehnquist and White, original dissenters from the 1973 ruling, that made four justices who would scrap *Roe* v. *Wade*. Moreover, O'Connor had sharply criticized both Harry Blackmun's opinion in the abortion case and the elaborate trimester system of regulations, though O'Connor had not said what she would replace it with, or whether she would vote to overturn the abortion right entirely. Why not put her to the test? Reynolds figured.

The Missouri officials, however, wanted to contest the lower-court ruling on narrow grounds. In their view, the law did not run afoul of *Roe* v. *Wade* because pregnant women were certainly permitted to seek abortions from doctors or in private clinics. They simply could not use public facilities. Reynolds, however, wanted them to raise a broader challenge to the right to abortion. "We damn near had to twist their arms," Reynolds said later. "[They] were afraid to take it on directly."

Unless the *Roe* issue were raised in the appeal petition, it would not become the focus of the Court's deliberations. Instead, the justices would concentrate on the narrow issue. Reynolds said he spoke to Webster and officials in the governor's office, as well as to attorneys who worked directly on the appeal.

State officials denied consulting with Reagan administration lawyers on their appeal. Webster specifically denied speaking with Reynolds and said it was "ludicrous" to think he would take advice from the Justice Department in Washington, D.C.

Reynolds agreed that "for political reasons," it would not look good to have the Administration working closely with the state to devise its appeal. Reynolds pressed ahead, nonetheless, confident that the Court was ready to change the law on abortion—if it were asked to do so. "We just wanted them to get it in the case, and we could take it from there," Reynolds said. "It was an eleventh hour deal, but we made it."

The state's appeal in *Webster* v. *Reproductive Health Services* raised six specific questions challenging the details of the ruling that struck down the state law. If the justices resolved those points in the state's favor—which was likely—the law would be revived, but on narrow grounds. In addition, Webster's appeal also contained a seventh and broader question. It asked "whether the *Roe* v. *Wade* trimester approach for selecting the test by which state regulation of abortion services is reviewed should be reconsidered and discarded."

Those few words asking whether *Roe* should be "reconsidered" transformed Webster's appeal into the biggest case yet faced by the Rehnquist Court.

In November, just days after George Bush had safely beaten Michael Dukakis, Reynolds and the Justice Department filed a brief with the Court urging that Webster's appeal be granted. "If the Court is prepared to reconsider *Roe* v. *Wade*, this case presents an appropriate opportunity for doing so," it concluded. Reynolds had turned up the pressure on Sandra O'Connor.

In early November, the Court took up one of the major new constitutional disputes of the 1980s. As part of its war on drugs, the Reagan administration had advocated routine drug tests for particular kinds of public employees and for workers in federally regulated industries, such as airlines and railroads. Such tests could be justified for safety reasons. Who would want to consider the possibility of flying with a drug-impaired pilot? In addition, the mass testing of employees also sent a broad message that drug use of any sort would not be tolerated.

In 1986, the hard-charging U.S. Customs Commissioner William Von Raab was first to the starting line with a new program that mandated testing for new customs agents in three kinds of jobs: those employees who (1) interdicted drugs, (2) carried firearms, or (3) handled sensitive information that could be useful to drug dealers. Von Raab did not expect to find many drug users. Rather, the testing would simply confirm, he said, that his frontline troops in the war on drugs were themselves "largely drug free." He was proven correct. By the time the issue reached the Court, drug tests had been administered to 3,600 customs employees, only 5 of whom tested positive for some illegal substance.

According to union lawyers, drug testing in the workplace raised questions about the privacy rights of innocent employees. Could they be forced to undergo what some called "a demeaning and humiliating" exercise simply to send out a message about drug intolerance? Also, what about their private lives? The urine tests were best at picking up substances such as marijuana, traces of which remained for up to two weeks. The result was that the tests would not detect just heavy drug users or impaired employees, but also the casual, weekend user of marijuana.

The stakes were high on both sides. If the Court struck down the U.S. Customs Service program and ruled that individual employees may not be drug tested unless they show signs of drug use, the government would have no reliable method of keeping drug abusers out of air traffic control towers or the engineer's cabins of high-speed locomotives. Thousands of lives could be put at risk to protect the privacy rights of these employees.

Just to make sure that the point regarding risk was not ignored, Rehnquist had also scheduled on the same day as the customs workers case a separate, hour-long argument on the rail union's challenge to the federal regulations that require alcohol and other drug testing of train employees after an accident. The year before, an Amtrak train speeding north from Baltimore had slammed into a Conrail locomotive that had ignored warning lights and crossed directly into its path. Sixteen passengers were killed. The Conrail engineer and the brakeman were found to have drugs in their systems. The vivid image of those crumpled train cars weighed heavily in the balance. Compared to the smashed locomotives and the crushed bodies, the idea of urinating in a bottle seemed at most a minor inconvenience.

The U.S. customs case, however, posed a much broader issue. These agents and other white-collar employees were not in control of speeding locomotives. Nor, unlike in the rail industry, was there any evidence that agents were prone to alcohol or other drug abuse. If they could be forced to undergo drug testing as a part of their job, so could hundreds of thousands of other employees, including police officers, firefighters, and equipment operators, and possibly teachers and health-care workers. The outcome of this case depended on what the nine justices considered "reasonable"—nothing more.

The Fourth Amendment says, "The right of the people to be secure in their persons, houses, papers and effects, against unreasonable searches and seizures, shall not be violated, and no Warrants shall issue, but upon probable cause, supported by Oath or affirmation, and particularly describing the place to be searched, and the persons or things to be seized." The amendment speaks in the spirit of American colonists fed up with British soldiers and their penchant for breaking down doors. In the eighteenth century as well as in the twentieth, the use of arbitrary and unchecked force made for a police state.

Throughout its long history, the Court had struggled to balance the "right of the people" to be free of unreasonable searches against the demands of government, especially law enforcement. Prior to the Warren Court, the amendment was read narrowly to apply only to homes, and then only to searches where officials entered a home. By that standard, wiretapping a telephone was not a search because the police did not need to enter a house.

During the Warren years, however, the Court broadened the scope of the Fourth Amendment to protect a person's "reasonable expectation of privacy." Wiretapping a person's telephone certainly violated the person's expectation of privacy. So would forced blood tests to check for alcohol or other drugs, the Court said. Before undertaking a wire tap or administering a blood test to an unwilling subject, the police would have to get a search warrant by convincing a magistrate they had "probable cause" for suspecting wrongdoing.

In addition, the liberal Court stressed that the government must have an "individualized suspicion" before undertaking a search. If, for example, an officer saw a person peering into a closed storefront, the officer would have reason to stop and question the person: so, too, in the case of an auto weaving in traffic. Spotting it, an officer could pull the driver off the road. However, the police could neither randomly detain and question all pedestrians on the sidewalk nor pull all drivers to the side of the road. That kind of unrestrained police conduct violated the Fourth Amendment, the Warren Court said.

By the time of the Rehnquist Court, however, the notion of individualized suspicion had been eroded. At the U.S. borders and at international airports, customs agents routinely searched the bags of all travelers, and that search did not violate the Fourth Amendment, the Court ruled; nor did fire inspectors when they checked business establishments for code violations. Those, too, were searches, but they were different, the Court determined. They were "regulatory searches," not criminal searches. Of course, if a customs agent found drugs in luggage, the owner would be subject to criminal charges, just as if the person had been stopped on the street. However, labeling the searches as "regulatory" seemed to take away some of the sting. When, in response to the wave of air hijackings, the nation's airports installed metal detectors at their gates and began searching the bags of all passengers, the Court did not even bother to hear a challenge to the practice. Who was going to insist that these searches were unconstitutional?

Increasingly, the law of the Fourth Amendment became a maze of rules and exceptions to those rules. Lacking an overriding principle or rule, the justices fell back on the key word in the Fourth Amendment: "unreasonable." Was it unreasonable to demand that thousands of U.S. customs agents undergo drug tests, even though none of them as individuals had shown signs of drug use? Each of the justices had to balance the public interest in a drug-free work force versus the privacy of the individual employees.

On November 2, Attorney General Dick Thornburgh made his first appearance before the justices to argue the railroad case, *Burnley* v. *Railway Labor Executives Association.* Though he stumbled over the details of the case, Thornburgh's argument had been made for him by the fatal Amtrak accident near Baltimore. The second hour was devoted to the customs workers' case, known as *National Treasury Employees Union* v. *Von Raab.*

When the justices convened to decide the outcome, Brennan and Marshall voted for the workers. They had insisted that the government not undertake a search without "probable cause" to suspect wrongdoing by an individual. What could be a more clear violation of the Fourth Amendment, they wondered, than a mass search of innocent persons? As Marshall put it, "dragnet blood and urine testing ensures that the first, and worst, casualty of the war on drugs will be the precious liberty of our citizens." Stevens agreed that the testing of the customs workers should be blocked because the government had no evidence of a problem among these white-collar workers. The railroads were another matter; unlike Marshall and Brennan, Stevens voted to uphold the testing after train accidents.

On the other side, Rehnquist, White, and O'Connor upheld the drug tests in both cases. In their view, the government's interest in a safe, drug-free workplace outweighed the relatively minor inconvenience for workers of submitting to drug tests.

The voting produced two surprises, though, one of which came from the Reagan administration's proudest addition to the Court. In general, Antonin Scalia strived for clear rules of law. In his view, the Court should lay down "bright line" rules so that the outcome of cases would be governed by the rules, not by the justices' personal opinions. He abhorred the thought of giving judges a free hand to balance the competing factors. That made the law too subjective, too uncertain, too dependent on the personal whims of unelected lawyers. In one sense, it would not even be *law* as he understood the term. He once entitled a law review article "The Rule of Law as the Law of Rules." Law was law because it established rules. For all that, however, the Fourth Amendment seemed to defy simple rules. It required him to do what he did not want to do: weigh the competing interests and come to a personal judgment. Nonetheless, because that is what was required, Scalia did it, and with fervor.

"In my view the Customs Service rules are a kind of immolation of privacy and human dignity in symbolic opposition to drug use," Scalia said. He agreed that the government could demand the testing of train crew members who had been involved in an accident. The reason for such testing was apparent. However, in the customs case, the government had failed to come up with a single convincing reason to justify its bodily search of innocent federal workers.

"Those who lose because of the lack of understanding that begot the present exercise in symbolism are not just the Customs Service employees, whose dignity is thus offended, but all of us—who suffer a coarsening of our national manners," Scalia wrote in a dissent joined by Stevens.

Scalia's dissent could have tipped the ruling in favor of the liberals. This time, however, Harry Blackmun was not with the liberals. On civil rights, free speech, and certainly abortion, Blackmun lined up regularly with Brennan and Marshall, but he was not so predictable on criminal cases. He also always had his own view if doctors or medicine were somehow involved. Blackmun fancied himself the Court's expert on medical matters. In 1950, he had resigned a law firm partnership to become the general counsel to the renowned Mayo Clinic in Rochester, Minnesota. In one interview, he said that if he had it to do all over again, he would have become a physician rather than a lawyer.

His first major opinion for the Supreme Court, in *Roe* v. *Wade*, read more like the work of a physician or a medical historian than a lawyer. He set forth the history of abortion from Greek and Roman times. In nineteenth-century America, abortions were forbidden, he pointed out, but not necessarily to protect the life of the fetus; rather, it was to protect the lives of women. Before antiseptics and anesthesia, an abortion was a dangerous procedure and often fatal. By 1973, however, abortion had became safe and simple, at least when performed by a qualified physician. With that understanding, a law forbidding abortions amounted to an arbitrary and irrational restriction on the freedom of women, Blackmun believed. Abortion should be a matter between a woman and her doctor. Almost as an aside, he concluded that the right to abortion was grounded in the Fourteenth Amendment's protection of liberty and the implied right to privacy.

After the *Roe* opinion, Blackmun appeared to undergo one of the great transformations in Supreme Court history. In 1970, Nixon had selected him as a midwestern Republican with a law-and-order reputation. Boyhood friends, he and Nixon's conservative chief justice, Warren Burger, were allies the press had dubbed "the Minnesota Twins." By the mid-1970s, however, Blackmun had broken with Burger and aligned himself with the Court's liberals. In private conversations he mocked

Burger, and in the conference room he voted with Brennan. He became a staunch advocate of equal rights for blacks, women, and homosexuals, and he ended up in "the chief's doghouse," as he put it.

Explanations abound for Blackmun's conversion. Liberal academics liked to say Blackmun "grew" during his years on the bench. Confronted with the duty to enforce the Constitution's great promises of freedom and equality, his vision expanded. Conservatives tended to scorn him as a "mistake," a weak and indecisive man who was captured by Brennan and the glow of his liberal ethos. Many of his law clerks maintained that Blackmun had changed less than the Court. He joined a Court that had just passed its liberal high-water mark and was beginning a long, slow retreat, while Blackmun stayed largely in place.

Still another possibility is that Nixon and the press had typecast him incorrectly in the first place. In fact, Blackmun was never a Nixon Republican and had little allegiance to the conservative dogma. He shunned doctrines and legal theories. During his brief confirmation hearings, Blackmun promised to be sensitive to the "little people" whose cases came before the Court. He said he had been struck by letters he had received since his nomination.

"What comes through most clearly is the utter respect which the little person has for the Supreme Court of the United States. The little person feels this is a real bastion for the protection of his rights," he said. If Blackmun was not a great legal theorist, he certainly lived up to his pledge to be a protector of the little people whose cases came before the Court.

Harry Andrew Blackmun had grown up in a serious and somber household, the silence of which was broken only by the sound of classical music from the Victrola. He was born November 12, 1908, in the southern Illinois village of Nashville, but he grew up in a working-class neighborhood of St. Paul, Minnesota. He once described his home as being on "the wrong side of the tracks." Blackmun's father, though he had had ambitions of becoming a lawyer, struggled as the owner of a grocery store. The store owner and his wife had met at a Methodist college in Missouri and remained active in the Methodist church. Their firstborn child, Harry, was quiet, bookish, and something of a perfectionist in his schoolwork. He had a variety of jobs in his school years, including delivering milk from a horse-drawn carriage. In one interview at the time of his nomination, he praised today's young people for taking time to "think about issues" but added quickly, "My generation was concerned with survival."

In 1925, the year fellow St. Paul native F. Scott Fitzgerald published *The Great Gatsby*, young Harry Blackmun won a scholarship to Harvard College. Rigorous and precise in his thinking, he majored in mathematics, to the dismay of his father, who feared math would not prepare his son to study law. He wrote of his concern to Harvard president A. Lawrence Lowell. The return letter reassured the Blackmuns; math teaches logical reasoning, Lowell maintained. The son, on the other hand, was concerned about a different conflict. He was interested in medicine and thought of becoming a physician, but he chose finally to enroll in the Harvard Law School, from which he graduated in 1932 with a good but not outstanding record.

Like Brennan and Marshall, he began his law practice in the depths of the Great Depression. He joined a prominent Minneapolis firm and specialized in what some lawyers saw as dry work: tax, wills, and estate planning. He also taught law in the evenings at the William Mitchell College of Law in St. Paul, where Burger earned his degree as a night law student. On a tennis court in 1937, he met a bright and vivacious young woman named Dorothy Clark. The methodical and cautious lawyer courted Miss Clark for four years before they finally married in 1941 and later raised three daughters together.

Blackmun never lost his interest in medical matters, and he leaped at the Mayo Clinic position when it was offered him in 1950. Over the next decade, his closest friends were cardiologists, psychiatrists, and other medical professionals, rather than lawyers. By day and on weekend social occasions, he heard and talked of the problems and frustrations of the medical profession. He left the Mayo Clinic in 1959, when Dwight Eisenhower appointed him to the U.S. Eighth Circuit Court of Appeals, the jurisdiction of which stretched from the Dakotas to Arkansas. The judges heard cases in St. Louis and St. Paul, and Blackmun was there in St. Louis on April 14, 1970, when the Nixon White House issued a statement announcing Blackmun's nomination to the high court. Senate Democrats had already rejected two Nixon nominees—Clement Haynsworth of South Carolina and G. Harrold Carswell of Florida. With a light touch of humor, Blackmun later bragged that he was a

member of the exclusive "number three club," later to be
joined by Anthony Kennedy. In the Senate, Blackmun's nomination was greeted with relief, and he won a quick, unanimous
confirmation.

At the Court, Blackmun soon developed a reputation as
a scholarly plodder. He was neither a quick thinker nor certain
of his views, but he was surely a worker. He put in prodigiously
long hours. Only his clerks worked harder. Year after year, they
have followed the same routine. The justice met with his clerks
in the cafeteria for breakfast at 8 A.M. They adjourned promptly
at 9 and headed upstairs to work. His clerks worked late into
the evening and throughout the weekends, too. In Blackmun's
chambers, the clerks have earned all of their $37,000-a-year
salary. One described her year as "12 to 14 hours a day, seven
days a week." The justice himself left at the dinner hour but
took home a briefcase full of briefs and memos. Though he was
past age 80, Blackmun could be seen wandering the dark halls
of the Court on a Sunday afternoon in search of a working
vending machine.

"Everything has to be on paper for him, and the more
paper the better," said one clerk. For Blackmun, no point was
too small to ponder. He wanted 30-page memos from the clerks
on the most trivial of the 150 or so cases the Court hears each
term. He also made it very clear that his clerks were not to
refer to the tax or bankruptcy cases as "dogs" around him.
They are very important cases, he would advise, especially to
the parties involved. He sought five- or six-page memos even
on the appeal petitions, which arrive at the Court at a rate of
100 per week. When assigned an opinion for the Court, he
labored for months over a draft.

"He would even check the citations in the footnotes," one
of his clerks said. His opinions were thoroughly researched,
informative, and long—often too long, he conceded. All they
lacked, his critics said, was legal reasoning.

In the years since the *Roe* v. *Wade* decision, he had been
lionized by women's rights advocates and vilified by the right-
to-life movement. In person, however, he hardly looked like a
legendary figure, either lion or villain. He was short and soft-
spoken, usually attired in a pale cardigan sweater. Once, as
antiabortion marchers paraded in front of the Court, he stood
watching on the plaza, alone and unnoticed. The comedian
Garrison Keillor once dubbed his fellow Minnesotan "the shy
person's justice."

Around the Court, he could be grumpy and sullen, especially at the end of a wearying Court term. "He's a sour little old man," said a clerk from another chamber, voicing a not-uncommon view. While Rehnquist and Brennan would quickly learn the names of new clerks and greet them in the hall, Blackmun would walk by, head down. "He always has on what I would call a 'Do Not Disturb' expression," one clerk said.

Old friends and acquaintances were often struck by the odd pairing of Dorothy and Harry Blackmun. She was a dynamo—talkative, energetic, and enthusiastic—while he had the personality of a shy accountant. Women's rights advocates often speculated that Blackmun's wife, who one friend described as a "real feminist," had a strong influence on the justice's view of women's rights issues.

As the Court moved to the right under Rehnquist, Blackmun spoke ominously of the future. *Roe* "will go down the drain," he said, the Court will be in the "grip" of conservatives for decades to come.

At times, Blackmun felt personally under siege. In 1984, he had received death threats from an antiabortion group called the "Army of God"; federal marshals were assigned to provide protection for him. One evening in March 1985, as Blackmun and his wife were sitting in the living room of their third-floor riverfront apartment in Arlington, Virginia, a bullet crashed through the window and embedded in a chair. The bullet tore a hole "the size of an orange" in the window and sprayed glass around the room, but neither of the Blackmuns was injured. No individual or group took credit for the shot, and FBI investigators were puzzled. The bullet came from a handgun, not a rifle, yet its trajectory indicated it was fired from the other side of the Potomac River. From that distance, however, a handgun could not be aimed accurately. The investigators said the bullet appeared to be a random shot, a conclusion that Blackmun, understandably, never accepted.

When called on to speak to a law group, the aging justice often read from venomous letters he had received. He had been called the "Butcher of Dachau, Pontius Pilate, King Herod, a child murderer—you name it," he said. Another typewritten letter promised "to blow the justice's brains out" and "to laugh at his funeral." At Christmas one year, he received this message of good cheer: "Dear Justice Blackmun, I pray that this Christmas will be your last one." No wonder the justice has a gloomy demeanor, a friend said.

Away from the Court and his legal work, however, Blackmun could be relaxed, charming, and cheerful. Each summer, he made new friends through the Aspen Seminars. Far from considering him a forbidding figure, they found Blackmun to be warm and personable. He always inquired about husbands and wives and children. He delighted in talking of his own three daughters.

One woman friend said that he wanted to know all about her new boyfriend. "I think he is something of a romantic," she said. Another friend said she was amused to see Blackmun and his wife together. "They teased each other and had fun like two teenagers," she said.

Blackmun also remained an avid baseball fan, especially of his hometown Minnesota Twins. When he had a chance, he loved to take in a ball game, although while the others enjoyed the beer and hot dogs, he carefully charted the hits, runs, and outs.

On the bench, Blackmun usually sat silently. He rarely asked a question and never engaged the attorneys in a back-and-forth debate. If a medical fact was introduced, however, his interest would be alerted.

In the drug-testing case, the attorneys for the U.S. customs employees built their case around the right to privacy and the demeaning nature of the urine tests. It made no sense to Blackmun. "Do you think any urine collection is demeaning? Surely you have had a physical examination," he commented to attorney Lois Williams, representing the customs workers. Noting his "relationship with the medical profession, . . . I wonder a little bit about this super sensitivity about blood tests and urine collection," Blackmun said.

As usual, Blackmun looked at the issue through a doctor's eyes. Every patient has undergone urine tests or had a sample of blood taken. Patients do not react with alarm, nor do they feel they have been humiliated or that their privacy has been violated. The government certainly had a strong interest in detecting drug abusers, and these tests seemed at most a minimal intrusion on the employee's privacy. Blackmun cast his vote to uphold them.

With Blackmun's vote, Rehnquist had four. The outcome then depended on Kennedy. Scalia had given the forced drug tests a fiery denunciation, but Kennedy cast his vote with the chief justice. He agreed that the government's interest in stopping drug abuse outweighed the privacy rights of the individuals. A grateful chief justice assigned him the opinions in the two drug-testing cases, which figured to be among the three or four major rulings of the term. It marked Kennedy's first chance to speak for the Court in a major case. It also showed that the chief had not lost any confidence in him, even if he joined Brennan in the *Patterson* case.

Brennan's attempt to fashion a majority opinion in the Patterson case hit a setback in December. The 82-year-old justice, suffering a high fever and chills, was taken by ambulance to Bethesda Naval Hospital. The doctors treated him with antibiotics, believing he had come down with pneumonia. On Monday, December 13, however, the doctors changed course and removed his diseased gall bladder. Brennan stayed another week in the hospital and spent the holiday period recovering at home. Despite his condition, he kept up a steady stream of phone calls to Kennedy, hoping to find a formula that would ensure a fifth vote in the *Patterson* case.

On Friday, January 20, the justices joined the members of Congress and the executive branch at the west front of the Capitol for the presidential inaugural ceremony. The new vice president, Dan Quayle, had asked O'Connor to administer his oath of office. Moments later, as Ronald Reagan looked on, Rehnquist read the oath to George Bush.

When the justices reconvened on Monday, they released an opinion that symbolized how much Reagan had transformed the Court. For more than 30 years, the Court had prodded government to do more to aid racial minorities and to bring about true equality in America. Now, the new conservative majority intended to put a brake on efforts that aided minorities at the expense of white males. O'Connor and her clerks had spent several months drafting and reworking a majority opinion in the *Richmond* case involving affirmative action. Her opinion dismayed the liberals—Brennan, Marshall, and Blackmun—but irked Scalia, too. In Scalia's view, O'Connor had waffled and failed to make clear that "affirmative" racial preferences by the government were *always* unconstitutional. He refused to sign her opinion.

Nonetheless, the ruling in *Richmond* v. *Croson* signaled the beginning of a new chapter on affirmative action. The Rehnquist Court, unlike the Burger Court, would not look upon affirmative action by local and state governments as a "benign" effort to bring about equality. Rather, it would be considered racial discrimination and treated as such.

O'Connor read much of her opinion from the bench; she began on a strong note. "The standard of review under the Equal Protection Clause is not dependent on the race of those burdened or benefited by a particular classification," she said. That conclusion, though stated in legal language, had the potential to transform state governments, universities, school systems, police departments, and all manner of public agencies. Since the 1978 *Bakke* case, public officials had been told they may "take race into account" when hiring and promoting employees, enrolling students, or giving out public contracts. Because blacks, Latinos, and women had been discriminated against before, these officials could discriminate in their favor, the Burger Court had said.

O'Connor's opinion set a new rule. Discrimination against whites violated the Constitution just the same as discrimination against blacks. From now on, government discrimination against whites will be subjected to "strict scrutiny" and presumed to be unconstitutional, she said. Certainly members of the Court had voiced this view before, but O'Connor's opinion in *Richmond* v. *Croson* marked the first time that a five-member majority agreed. Rehnquist, White, Scalia, and Kennedy agreed with this aspect of O'Connor's opinion.

Because the Constitution restricts only the government— not private employers—the *Richmond* case would have no impact on corporations or private colleges that gave preferences to minorities or women. These private entities would still be governed by the lenient rules Brennan had set in the *Santa Clara* case. When these employers wanted to remedy a "manifest imbalance" in their work force, they could give preferences to women, blacks, or other minorities.

However, O'Connor's opinion appeared to set a far more stringent rule for agencies of the government. Indeed, had she stopped after the first section of her opinion, it would have hit like a thunderclap in state colleges and in municipal governments. *Any* preference for minorities could have been deemed unconstitutional.

Instead, however, O'Connor went on to criticize the details of Richmond's 30-percent quota for city contracts. For example, the city council enacted its 30-percent quota before holding hearings to determine why so few minorities received city contracts. The council had failed to consider alternatives such as a "race-neutral" program designed to encourage new businesses, she emphasized. Her focus on the facts in *Richmond* suggested that a better-designed affirmative action program would be legal. She implied that a "remedial program" that favored blacks would be constitutional if the city could prove it was making up for actual discrimination in the past. "In the extreme case, some form of narrowly tailored racial preference might be necessary to break down patterns of racial exclusion," she said at one point.

The second half of O'Connor's opinion muddied the water. Were racial preferences unconstitutional, or were city councils and state universities merely being told to hold more hearings and compile more reports before announcing a racial preference program? Not surprisingly, many city and state officials took the latter view after examining O'Connor's opinion with their lawyers. They could still give preferences in hiring and contracts to minorities, they asserted, so long as they could show they were making up for past discrimination. For example, if the local building trades unions had excluded blacks in the 1950s and 1960s, that would justify giving minority firms a guaranteed percentage of new construction contracts in the 1990s, they maintained. O'Connor had fashioned a moderate-conservative position on affirmative action; racial preferences could be used only as a last resort, she insisted.

Reagan's two youngest appointees, Kennedy and Scalia, were upset. They thought she left the door open for government agencies to find new reasons for using racial preferences. Both wrote concurring opinions to take a stronger stand on affirmative action. "The moral imperative of racial neutrality is the driving force of the Equal Protection Clause" in the Fourteenth Amendment, Kennedy wrote. Though he joined most of O'Connor's opinion, he said he would have preferred a simple "rule of automatic invalidity for preferences in almost every case."

Scalia had argued for just that and was angered that O'Connor failed to write a clear, simple opinion outlawing racial preferences by the government. He agreed only with her opening statement that discrimination against whites should be subjected to the "strict scrutiny" test and presumed to be unconstitutional.

"It is plainly true that in our society blacks have suffered discrimination immeasurably greater than any directed at other racial groups," Scalia wrote. "But those who believe that racial preferences can help to 'even the score' display, and reinforce, a manner of thinking by race that was the source of the injustice and that will, if it is endorsed within our society, be the source of more injustice still." To Scalia, the Constitution demands that no one be treated better or worse because of race. "When we depart from this American principle, we play with fire," he said.

Where O'Connor seemed to say of racial preferences they may be used "rarely," Kennedy said "almost never." Scalia saw no exceptions: never.

Marshall, Brennan, and Blackmun saw the *Richmond* ruling as a fateful step. For the first time, a solid majority of the Court had concluded that the Fourteenth Amendment, which was designed to ensure equality for blacks, forbids local and state agencies from taking affirmative action to benefit blacks. By ruling that a "remedial" program should be viewed the same as "the most brute and repugnant forms of state-sponsored racism, a majority of this Court signals that it regards racial discrimination as largely a phenomenon of the past," Marshall said. He derided the conservatives for a "cynical . . . second guessing" of the Richmond city council and for adopting a perverted interpretation of the Fourteenth Amendment. Congress passed the Reconstruction amendments because it feared "the States would not adequately respond to racial violence or discrimination against the newly freed slaves. To interpret these Amendments as proscribing state remedial responses to these very problems turns the Amendments on their heads," he said.

Blackmun added a brief note of dissent and dismay. "I never thought that I would live to see the day when the city of Richmond, Virginia, the cradle of the old Confederacy, sought on its own, and within a narrow confine, to lessen the stark impact of persistent discrimination. But Richmond, to its great credit, acted. Yet this Court, the supposed bastion of equality, strikes down Richmond's efforts as though discrimination never existed or was not demonstrated in this particular litigation," he wrote.

The *Richmond* decision demonstrated what the reargument order in the *Patterson* case had first hinted at. On the issue of civil rights, the Court had a new majority, one that now questioned whether blacks still suffered discrimination and that was more willing to believe that the new victims of discrimination were white males. For the civil rights advocates, the ruling in the *Richmond* case marked the beginning of a dreadful year.

When the Court revisited the death penalty in January, Sandra O'Connor was put on the spot again. In the cases to be heard, the crimes were brutal and horrifying, and there was no question that the defendants were guilty. These were not Perry Mason cases—these murderers were properly convicted and would never leave prison, regardless of whether they won their appeals at the Supreme Court. In these cases, the justices had to decide whether a killer who was mentally retarded or age 16 deserved the ultimate punishment.

On the morning of October 25, 1979, Johnny Paul Penry, then 22, delivered appliances to the home of Pamela Carpenter in Livingston, Texas. He carried a switchblade knife and attacked the young woman, raping her and stabbing her repeatedly with a pair of scissors. She died a few hours later at a hospital but gave a detailed description of her assailant. Police quickly arrested Penry, who had been paroled only seven months earlier on two other rape counts involving knife attacks on women. He confessed to Carpenter's murder.

Before his trial, a hearing was held to judge Penry's competency. He had an IQ between 50 and 63, which indicates mild retardation, a clinical psychologist testified. He "has the ability to learn and the learning or the knowledge of the average six-and-a-half-year-old kid," he said. Penry's social maturity, or ability to function in the world, was that of a nine- or ten-year-old, he added. A psychiatrist testified that Penry suffered organic brain damage, probably at birth, which resulted in an inability to control himself or learn from his mistakes. He was also beaten often as a child and was locked in his room. He never finished first grade.

Penry himself seemed alert and aware. He was able to testify about his life and told the jury he had held a job as a busboy for $2.50 an hour. After hearing the evidence, the jury concluded that Penry was not insane, did understand right from wrong, and was therefore competent to stand trial. He was found guilty of murder. Under Texas law, the jury must impose a death sentence if it concludes the murder was "committed deliberately" and that the defendant was "a continuing threat to society." Based on those instructions, the jury sent Penry to Death Row.

In his appeal to the Supreme Court, his attorneys contended that his sentence violated the Eighth Amendment. It reads, "Excessive bail shall not be required, nor excessive fines imposed, nor cruel and unusual punishments inflicted." Because the Bill of Rights begins with the words, "Congress shall make no law," the Court for most of its history believed that words such as "cruel and unusual punishment" limited only Congress and the federal government, not the states, where 95 percent of crime cases are prosecuted. Until 1962, state lawmakers and judges decided the severity of each state's criminal punishments without interference by the Supreme Court. In that year, however, the Warren Court said for the first time that the justices would reject state laws or prosecutions that they deemed "cruel and unusual." Punishments must be judged by the "evolving standards of decency that mark the progress of a maturing society," Earl Warren had said. This sounds like the kind of progressive formula that appealed to the Warren-era liberals but riled the conservatives of the Rehnquist Court. The conservatives had pledged to abide by the "original intent" of the Constitution's words, not a modern-day meaning of those words. They wanted no part of an "evolving" Constitution. However, even Antonin Scalia agreed that the Court had to consider contemporary "standards of decency" and not just rely on the accepted practices of 200 years ago. As he noted during his confirmation hearings, public whippings and torture may have been used in 1787, but they would certainly be considered "cruel and unusual punishment" today.

The American Association on Mental Retardation, the American Psychological Association, and a host of the groups representing the mental health professionals and the retarded filed a friend-of-the-court brief urging that the death penalty be outlawed for the mildly retarded. Already, as a matter of common law, those who suffered severe mental illness were considered incompetent to stand trial. The brief argued that the mildly retarded also have difficulty controlling their behavior and cannot be held fully responsible for their acts. In 1986, Georgia had put to death Jerome Bowden, who had an IQ of 65. The execution drew attention to the issue of mental retardation on Death Row. In response, the Georgia legislature became the first to specifically exempt the retarded from capital punishment. Even where the death penalty was popular, few wanted to see it applied to the retarded. For example, a poll of Texans found that 86 percent supported the death penalty, but 73 percent opposed its use against retarded persons.

When Penry's case was argued before the Supreme Court on January 11, his lawyer, Curtis Mason, described his client as having "the mind of a six- or seven-year -old."

The chief justice leaned forward, his hand on his chin. "Isn't there more apt to be debate or disagreement, though, about one's mental age than about one's chronological age?" Rehnquist asked. The IQ tests were not precise, and they measured only one aspect of a person's development. Throughout the argument, Rehnquist turned in his chair and chatted with White. Both sounded skeptical of using IQ measurements for making constitutional distinctions among types of murderers.

Rehnquist leaned forward again at another point in the argument. "You don't want us to consider Penry a nine-year-old, do you?" he asked.

The state's attorney had a ready reply to that query. "Children of that age do not commit these sorts of acts," Charles Palmer, an assistant attorney general, told the justices. Despite what the psychologists may say, Penry was no child, he said. In his two earlier rapes, Penry had lured women outside their homes by shutting off an outdoor light. Then, he attacked them with a switchblade knife. "Regardless of whether [Penry] fits within the clinical definition of mentally retarded," Palmer said, "he knew what he was doing."

The other case concerned the death penalty for juveniles. Heath Wilkins had grown up in a chaotic house, where he was beaten by his mother and her boyfriend. An uncle started him using drugs when he was six years old, and he began robbing houses and setting fires in his neighborhood. On one occasion, he tried to kill his mother by putting rat poison in a Tylenol capsule. Wilkins was sent away to several homes for boys by the time he was ten and tried to commit suicide. On July 27, 1985, Wilkins, then 16, and a friend decided to rob a convenience store in Avondale, Missouri. Working behind the counter was Nancy Allen, a 26-year-old mother of two. They threatened her with a knife and demanded the store's cash. After she helped them open the cash register, Wilkins stabbed her in the chest and neck until she fell to the floor and bled to death. The pair helped themselves to liquor, cigarettes, and $450 in cash, and fled, but Wilkins was soon arrested and confessed to the murder and robbery. Because he was a juvenile, a hearing was held to decide whether he should be tried as an adult. His

crime was vicious and violent, and he showed little hope for
juvenile rehabilitation. As a result, he was turned over to the
adult criminal justice system. Wilkins then pled guilty and
asked for the death penalty. His wish was granted. Later, however, as he sat on Death Row, he changed his mind and signed
an appeal to the Supreme Court.

In March 1989, the justices heard arguments in Wilkins's
case and the companion case of Kevin Stanford, who at age 17
committed a murder that put him on Kentucky's Death Row.
Quite often, the friend-of-the-court briefs filed in a case supply
the justices with more useful information—and more powerful
arguments—than are supplied by the two competing lawyers
who appear in the Court. In the *Wilkins* and *Stanford* cases,
briefs filed by religious and international human rights groups
dramatized just how unusual it was to execute a juvenile. Capital punishment had been abolished in Western Europe, and
nowhere in the industrialized world were teenagers put to
death.

"Since 1979, out of thousands of executions recorded by
Amnesty International, only eight were reported to have been
executions of juvenile offenders," one brief reported. These
executions took place in Bangladesh, Barbados, Pakistan (two),
Rwanda, and the United States (three). There were also two
unconfirmed reports of juvenile executions in Iraq, the brief
added. Of the more than 2,200 inmates then under a death
sentence nationwide, 28 had committed their crimes when they
were under age 18. Five of them, including Wilkins, had been
16, and 23 were 17 years old at the time of their crimes.

Lawyers for Wilkins and Stanford argued that the states
had already drawn a legal line between youth and adulthood.
Under Missouri law, Wilkins was too young to serve on a jury,
too young to get medical care without his parents' permission,
too young to vote, too young to control his own finances, and
"too young and impressionable" even to witness an execution.

Those laws give "strong support to the notion that there
is a national consensus against executing the young," said attorney Nancy McDerrow. "When we draw a line between
childhood and adulthood, we usually choose 18," she said.

Rehnquist and Scalia quickly challenged that statement.
How can there be "a national consensus" against the death
penalty for juveniles, Rehnquist asked, when 18 states permit
it? Scalia wondered why there need be a line based on age
when juries can consider each individual's case, including the

Warren Burger (center), William H. Rehnquist (right), and Antonin Scalia, upon Burger's retirement from the Court, and Rehnquist's appointment as Chief Justice, September 26, 1986. (Courtesy Frank Johnston, *The Washington Post*)

The Supreme Court of the United States. (Courtesy Ralph D. Jones, Supreme Court Historical Society)

The Burger Court, posing with President Reagan at the White House. From left to right: John Paul Stevens, Lewis Powell, Harry Blackmun, Byron White, Warren Burger, President Reagan, William Brennan, Thurgood Marshall, Sandra Day O'Connor, William Rehnquist, and retired justice Potter Stewart. (White House photo)

William Rehnquist, standing beside his wife, Natalie, taking the oath as Chief Justice. (White House photo)

Byron White in his chambers. (Collection of Supreme Court)

Sandra Day O'Connor. (Collection of Supreme Court)

The third time is the charm: Anthony Kennedy giving the thumbs-up sign moments after being sworn in as a new justice of the Supreme Court. Reagan's two previous nominees had failed to win confirmation. From left to right: Mary Kennedy, Rehnquist, President Reagan, and the new justice. (White House photo)

Harry Blackmun. (Collection of Supreme Court)

John Paul Stevens. (Courtesy Robert S. Oakes, *National Geographic*, Collection of Supreme Court)

The aging liberals, Brennan and Marshall, in a rare lighter moment together during their last days on the court. (Coutesy of Ray Lustig, *The Washington Post*)

President Bush talking with David Souter hours before he named Souter as his Supreme Court nominee to replace William Brennan. (Courtesy David Valdez, The White House)

The new Rehnquist Court, 1990–1991 term. Top left: Kennedy, O'Connor, Scalia, and David Souter. Bottom left: Blackmun, White, Rehnquist, Marshall, and Stevens. (Courtesy Supreme Court Historical Society)

The best man for the job. President Bush introducing Clarence Thomas to the press as his nominee to replace Thurgood Marshall. Behind Bush, at his Kennebunkport home, are John Sununu, press secretary Marlin Fitzwater, counsel Boyden Gray, Attorney General Dick Thornburgh, and Andrew Card. (Courtesy David Valdez, The White House)

Clarence Thomas with his key Senate supporters, Senator John Danforth (left) and Senator Strom Thurmond, at the hearing before the Senate Judiciary Committee. (U.S. Senate)

Chief Justice Rehnquist, with fellow conservative Kennedy, now firmly in command of the court. (Courtesy Dane A. Penland, *Smithsonian*, Collection of Supreme Court)

person's age. "If we could do that in voting, I'd be willing to have a voting age of 13," Scalia said. "I can think of some 15-year-olds I'd like to have vote and maybe some 30-year-olds I wouldn't."

The clerks had prepared memos for the justices on how the various states treated capital punishment for a 16-year-old. Among the 50 states, 36 have laws that now authorized the death penalty, while 14 forbid it entirely, regardless of the age of the defendant. Of the states that allow the death penalty, 15 of them set a minimum age at 18 or 17, meaning that a 16-year-old such as Heath Wilkins could not be sent to Death Row. Three states—Kentucky, Indiana, and Nevada—set a minimum age of 16, and 18 other states have capital punishment and set no age limits.

Not surprisingly, the liberals and conservatives on the Court read the statistics differently. Brennan added the 14 states that prohibit capital punishment and the 15 that would not allow someone as young as Wilkins to be executed, which made a total of 29 states. On the other side, three states had considered the age issue and would allow the execution of a 16-year-old. That ratio—29 to 3—strongly suggests that a death sentence for a 16-year-old is unacceptable to most state lawmakers, he said. Moreover, throughout the civilized world, such a punishment has been deemed barbaric; even Americans who favor the death penalty in opinion surveys oppose it for juveniles, Brennan noted. All that evidence gives "a strong grounding to the view that it is not constitutionally tolerable" for the state to undertake "execution of adolescent offenders," Brennan said. Marshall, Blackmun, and Stevens agreed with him.

Scalia and Rehnquist thought the state data rebutted the notion that a death sentence for a juvenile was cruel and unusual. By their reckoning, 21 of the 36 states that permit capital punishment would allow the execution of a 16-year-old. The evidence suggests "neither a historical nor a modern societal consensus forbidding the imposition of capital punishment on any person who murders at 16 or 17 years of age," Scalia said. The liberals may think the death penalty is immoral, but the justices are not "a committee of philosopher kings," Scalia said, with the power to write their moral notions into law.

Once again, the outcome in the death penalty cases depended on O'Connor and Kennedy. The ninth justice had said during confirmation hearings that he believed capital punishment in general was constitutional, but he had not been called upon to rule whether a murderer who is retarded or under age 18 deserved the ultimate punishment. During the last term, O'Connor had agonized for months over the fate of a 15-year-old. Now, she would have to consider the issue all over again.

In February, the justices considered the creche case from Pittsburgh. For centuries, disputes over religion had ignited wars, destruction, and division, but in the United States, thanks in large measure to the understood separation of church and state, religious disputes had been muted. Nonetheless, few issues could splinter the Court as religion could.

The First Amendment forbids government actions "respecting an establishment of religion." Since the early 1960s, Brennan had insisted this clause demanded a strict separation of church and state. A Roman Catholic, Brennan believed in God and the church but saw religion as a private matter only. In his view, religion had no place in the public schools, in public squares, or in government-funded programs. In 1963, he had written a long opinion in the case of *Abington* v. *Schempp* explaining why he believed the Constitution prohibited daily Bible readings in the public schools.

"It is implicit in the history and character of American public education that the [public] schools serve a uniquely PUBLIC function: the training of American citizens in an atmosphere free of parochial, divisive or separatist influences of any sort—an atmosphere in which children may assimilate a heritage common to all American groups and religions," Brennan wrote. "This is a heritage neither theistic nor atheistic, but simply civic and patriotic."

Brennan not only insisted that religion be kept out of public schools, but he also pressed to keep public money out of parochial schools. In 1985, he wrote an opinion for a 5–4 majority disallowing the 20-year-old practice of using federal aid to send public school tutors into inner-city private and parochial schools. Despite the government's laudable goal of helping poor children, public money may not be used to puncture the wall of separation between church and state, Brennan said. Marshall, Blackmun, and Stevens agreed with Brennan on the strict separation of church and state.

However, Rehnquist disputed every one of these decisions that removed religion from public life. In his view, the First Amendment prevented the government from creating a national church or using tax money to fund churches, but it did not demand that religion be expunged from public schools, public buildings, or public aid programs that benefited parochial schools.

In the early 1980s, Lewis Powell usually decided the religion cases. He joined with Brennan in the school cases but sided with the conservatives in several cases involving religion in ceremonies or public displays. In 1983, the Court upheld the Nebraska legislature's practice of beginning each session with a prayer delivered by a state-appointed chaplain. Prayers such as these are "traditional and time-honored," Burger said in an opinion for the Court. The following year, the Court in a 5–4 decision upheld a city's construction and display of a life-sized nativity scene in a park. Again, Burger insisted that because Christmas celebrations were time-honored and traditional in this nation, they were not strictly religious and did not violate the First Amendment. He noted that the display in the Pawtucket, Rhode Island, city park included Santa Claus, reindeer, and a Christmas tree, which suggests celebration of a "winter holiday" rather a Christian religious ceremony. The dissenters, led by Brennan, said that Burger had not only misinterpreted the First Amendment but also cheapened religion in the process by suggesting that Christmas was mostly a winter holiday.

The Pittsburgh case renewed the battle. Each year, in late November, the Holy Name Society, a local Roman Catholic group, erected the creche on the grand staircase inside the Allegheny Courthouse. It depicted the manger in Bethlehem after the birth of Jesus, as described in the Gospels of Matthew and Luke. Included in the display were the figures of Jesus, Mary, Joseph, farm animals, shepherds, and the wise men. Above the manger was an angel bearing a banner that read: "Gloria in Excelsis Deo!" The display did not include the other, more secular holiday decorations such as a Santa Claus, reindeer, or colored lights. Outside, city employees erected a 45-foot Christmas tree in front of the city–county building. It was decorated with lights and ornaments and included a message proclaiming a "Salute to Liberty." It said, "During this holiday season, the City of Pittsburgh salutes liberty. Let these festive lights remind us that we are the keepers of the flame of liberty and our legacy of freedom." Finally, city workers erected an 18-foot Chanukah menorah next to the Christmas tree. Chanukah commemorates the rededication and relighting of the

Temple of Jerusalem but—like Christmas—it has become cultural event as well as a religious holiday.

The Pittsburgh chapter of the ACLU sued, contending these displays amounted to government promotion of religion in violation of the First Amendment, but a federal judge refused to stop the displays. His ruling relied on Burger's opinion in the 1984 Pawtucket, Rhode Island, case. A federal appeals court, however, said that the displays in Pittsburgh were different. They were prominently located at key public buildings, were solely religious in character, and did not include the more secular decorations such as a Santa Claus. Therefore, on a 2–1 vote, the court ruled that the displays must be removed because they appeared to put the government's stamp of approval on religion.

During the February 22 argument, attorneys for the city and county argued that they simply sought to "accommodate" the various religions in the city, rather than promoting one. After all, because a menorah was prominently featured, the city could not be accused of endorsing Christianity through its holiday displays. ACLU lawyers countered that others, such as Muslims or atheists, would have reason to think the local government was indeed promoting religion.

When the justices voted, they split into three factions. First, four conservatives—Rehnquist, White, Scalia, and Kennedy—voted to allow all the religious displays, believing they did not amount to an establishment of religion. For years, many conservatives had privately viewed the Court's bans on prayer and Bible reading in the public schools as evidence of an antireligious bias among the liberals. Kennedy appeared to share that view. He complained about the Court's "hostility toward religion," an accusation that angered the liberals.

Brennan, Marshall, and Stevens voted to affirm the appeals court. They insisted that all the displays in Pittsburgh be removed because they were religious in nature.

Blackmun and O'Connor took a third position. They said the creche inside the County Courthouse was purely religious and, therefore, must be removed. However, the Christmas tree and the menorah on the street near city hall were secular as well as religious and, therefore, could remain standing, they said. Given the lack of consensus, Kennedy, Stevens, and Blackmun each began writing opinions to explain why his view of the case was correct, in hopes of swaying his fellow jurists.

On the morning of March 21, Kennedy announced the second major opinion of the term. On the 5–4 vote in the customs workers case, the Rehnquist Court cleared the way for the government to require drug tests of employees whose jobs involved safety or security. "The Government's compelling interests in preventing the promotion of drug users" to key positions "outweighs the privacy interests of those who seek promotion," Kennedy said.

His opinion emphasized the duties of a particular job, whether it was running a train, collecting information on drug smugglers, or carrying a gun to apprehend drug dealers. For lawyers representing city and county governments or federal agencies, the ruling was good news. They could require drug tests of any employee whose job involved public safety or sensitive information. For thousands of police officers, firefighters, bus and truck drivers, and white-collar workers who were involved in public safety or who handled sensitive information, the Court's ruling carried a different message. Their rights to privacy were, as Kennedy put it, "minimal" when matched against the enormity of the drug scourge.

That afternoon, the justices heard arguments on an issue that the Warren Court had ducked: Does the First Amendment's guarantee of free expression protect a protester who burns an American flag? In the fall, as George Bush campaigned in flag factories, the Texas attorney general had filed an appeal of a state court ruling that had freed a radical protester from Dallas. On a 5–4 vote, the Texas Court of Criminal Appeals said that the First Amendment prohibited the prosecution of a flag burner. The majority relied on Justice Jackson's opinion in the 1943 case of *West Virginia* v. *Barnette* concerning the daily flag salutes in the schools, the same ruling that had gotten Michael Dukakis in so much trouble.

"Recognizing that the right to differ is the centerpiece of our First Amendment freedoms," the Texas court said, "government cannot carve out a symbol of unity and prescribe a set of approved messages to be associated with that symbol." When the Supreme Court announced it would hear the state's appeal, it put a spotlight on a young radical who seemed more suited to the late 1960s than to the Reagan–Bush era.

Gregory "Joey" Johnson belonged to the Revolutionary Communist Youth Brigade and was proud of it. While the Communist world was busy abandoning Communism, the self-described "Maoist" and full-time protester carried on the fight for revolution in the streets of America. He proclaimed the United States "a sick and dying empire" and its flag "a symbol of international plunder and murder." During the Vietnam War era, his splenetic attacks on "Amerika" might have drawn a crowd, but no one was paying him much attention during the Reagan era. So, Joey Johnson carried his protest campaign to the flag-draped, flag-waving Republican National Convention of 1984, where Reagan was to be nominated for a second term.

While the Republicans met at a nearby Dallas convention hall, Johnson and several dozen demonstrators marched in the street to denounce the "Rambo-mania mentality" of the Reagan administration. As they neared the Dallas city hall, a demonstrator pulled down a flag from a bank building and gave it to Johnson. While the protesters chanted, "America, the red, white, and blue, we spit on you," Johnson covered the flag with kerosene and lit it on fire. A few onlookers stood by and watched.

When police arrived, Johnson was arrested and charged with violating a Texas law covering the "desecration of a venerated object." Forty-six other states had laws against flag desecration, as did the federal government. The Texas law made it a crime, punishable with up to a year in jail and a $2,000 fine, to "deface, damage or otherwise physically mistreat . . . a state or national flag . . . in a way that the actor knows will seriously offend one or more persons likely to observe or discover his action." Johnson was not charged with stealing the bank's flag or receiving stolen property. He was, however, found guilty of flag desecration and sentenced to a year in prison and a $2,000 fine.

The later ruling in his favor by the Texas Court of Criminal Appeals prompted the Supreme Court justices to hear the case of *Texas* v. *Johnson*. It raised directly the question of whether burning a flag can be a form of free speech protected by the First Amendment. Implicitly, too, the case raised the broader question of whether the more conservative Rehnquist Court would protect radical dissent in the United States.

For most Americans, it is commonplace to say that the First Amendment protects the right to protest and to dissent. As a matter of constitutional law, however, that principle has a relatively brief lineage. In 1919, for example, the Court upheld a prison term for a Socialist party official named Charles T. Schenck for having printed a pamphlet urging other military

recruits to challenge the draft. "Write to your Congress-
man. . . . You have a right to demand the repeal of any law.
Exercise your rights of free speech, peaceful assemblage and
petitioning the government for redress of grievances. . . . Help
[us] wipe out this stain upon the Constitution," the pamphlet
said. Schenck had a much higher regard for the principles of
the Constitution, evidently, than did the Supreme Court. Without a single dissent, the Court affirmed his sentence for violating the Espionage Act. A week later, the Court unanimously
upheld a ten-year prison term for Eugene Debs, the Socialist
presidential candidate, for having criticized the draft during a
speech.

In constitutional law, the *Schenck* case is recalled because
Justice Oliver Wendell Holmes wrote, in a seemingly casual
aside, that the test for protected free speech is whether it poses
a "clear and present danger" to incite lawbreaking. Holmes
simply assumed that Schenck's pamphlet might inspire recruits
to resist the draft. A year after Holmes's comment, however,
both Holmes and Justice Louis Brandeis dissented when the
Court upheld the conviction of Jacob Abrams, a Russian émigré
living in New York City. Abrams had published a pamphlet
calling U.S. officials "shameful" and "cowardly" for sending
troops to put down the Bolsheviks. He was convicted under
the Espionage Act of 1918 for having printed "disloyal, scur-
rilous and abusive language about the form of Government of
the United States."

In dissent, Holmes wondered how "the surreptitious pub-
lishing of a silly leaflet by an unknown man" could "present
any immediate danger" to the government of the United States.
"The theory of our Constitution," Holmes wrote, is "that the
ultimate good desired is better reached by a free trade in
ideas." Unless shown evidence of a "clear and present danger"
to incite disruption, the Court should be "eternally vigilant
against attempts to check the expression of opinions that we
loathe." Added Brandeis in a subsequent opinion, "Those who
won our independence by revolution were not cowards. They
did not fear political change. They did not exalt order at the
cost of liberty. Only an emergency can justify repression" of
free speech. While those words helped win Holmes and Brandeis a place in the pantheon of Supreme Court justices, they
spoke only in dissent. The seven-member majority dismissed
Abrams's free-speech challenge in two sentences and upheld
his 20-year prison term.

By the 1930s and 1940s, the Court often cited the "clear and present danger" test for free speech but rarely used it to strike down a criminal conviction. In 1969, during the final days of the Warren Court, the justices wrote the test into law in the case of *Brandenburg* v. *Ohio*. A Ku Klux Klan leader, Clarence Brandenburg had been arrested for his part in a rally that took place on a farm outside Cincinnati. The hapless ranting of the white-hooded knights would have gone unnoticed, but for the fact that a TV news crew filmed the event. Brandenburg was shown saying that "if our president, our Congress, our Supreme Court, continues to suppress the white, Caucasian race, it's possible that there might have to be some revengance [*sic*] taken." Ohio prosecutors then took some "revengance" and charged him with violating an old state law that prohibited "advocating . . . crime, sabotage or violence." In a brief, unanimous opinion, the Court overturned Brandenburg's conviction and said that "mere advocacy" of violence is protected as free speech. The line is crossed, the Court said, only when there is "incitement to imminent lawless action."

While the *Brandenburg* rule was considered settled law, some conservatives, such as Robert Bork, disagreed with it. Bork said he saw no reason why the Constitution should protect persons who despise the United States and advocate the overthrow of its government—persons, perhaps, such as Gregory Johnson.

Even the liberal justices of the Warren Court refused to say that the First Amendment protected flag burning. During the Vietnam War, they avoided ruling directly on the issue. In the 1969 case of *Street* v. *New York*, they considered the flag-burning conviction of a black man who, upon hearing of the shooting of civil rights leader James Meredith, rushed into a Brooklyn street and burned a flag. "If they let that happen to Meredith," Sidney Street told police, "we don't need no damn flag." In a 5–4 ruling, the Court sidestepped the flag issue and overturned his conviction on the grounds that his incendiary comments may have caused his arrest and conviction. The dissenters included liberals Hugo Black, Abe Fortas, and Earl Warren, as well as Byron White. Warren wrote in dissent, "I believe that the States and the Federal Government do have the power to protect the flag from acts of desecration and disgrace."

In 1974, the Court, in narrowly worded rulings, refused to allow the convictions of a Washington state college student for having sewn a peace symbol onto a flag that flew in his apartment and a Massachusetts man for wearing a small flag sewn into the seat of his pants. Rehnquist, White, and Blackmun had dissented against the majority opinion. The right to free speech "is not absolute," Rehnquist wrote, and it is outweighed by the government's interest in "preserving the flag as an important symbol of nationhood and unity."

Now, Rehnquist had a solid conservative majority behind him, and it was not even clear that a literalist such as Scalia would see flag burning as deserving of any First Amendment protection. The words of the amendment forbid laws "abridging the freedom of speech or of the press." Burning a flag was conduct, but was it "speech"?

Certainly one way to sharply restrict the reach of the First Amendment would be to say it only covers words, spoken or written. To do so would overturn decades of precedent, of course. Marches, protest rallies, and sit-ins were considered acts of free speech. So was the wearing of black armbands during the Vietnam War. That was described by the Court as "symbolic speech." However, it could be argued that those were acts, not speech, and therefore need not be shielded by the First Amendment. On second glance, however, such a constricted view had real problems. What if Congress passed a law requiring that citizens salute the president and each member of the House and Senate as they pass on the street? No one need speak a word, simply perform the act of saluting. Violators would be given a year in jail and a $2,000 fine. Would that law be constitutional? If not, why not?

If that example seems too extreme, what about a law that made it a crime to make "an offensive gesture or facial expression" in the direction of the president or any federal official? Certainly, you may mutter that the president is a "buffoon" as he walks by, the law's sponsor might say, but you may not make any gesture that shows disdain. Would that be constitutional under the First Amendment? Would a T-shirt that portrayed George Bush and Dan Quayle as a pair of clowns be protected under the Constitution?

Scalia loved to argue with his law clerks. His was a "no-holds-barred chambers," one clerk said. Where Kennedy had relaxed, gentlemanly conversations with his clerks and Blackmun exchanged memos with them, Scalia relished a true argument. For hours on end, he and his clerks could go back and forth on a difficult issue. Short and stocky, with a cigarette in his hand, Scalia would pace the room and jab at the air with his cigarette. They were unforgettable times for some of the young clerks, simply because the justice was open to being challenged. Some of the issues were still new for Scalia. He had not firmed up a position, and he wanted to argue it through.

No one, however, accused Scalia of being indecisive. In the end, when he had heard all sides and argued it through, he would come to a conclusion, his mind made up. Also, once he had decided, Scalia was virtually unshakable. He had gone back and forth on the meaning of the First Amendment but was now convinced that "freedom of speech" meant something more than the freedom to utter words. He was a literalist but also a believer in tradition. From the beginning, the First Amendment was intended to protect something broader—*communication* was probably the best word—and in particular, communication about political ideas. The medium did not matter, nor did the message. It was all part of free speech.

The flag-burning case reminded observers of a 1960s revival with regard to the legal issue being revisited, and sure enough, radical attorney William Kuntsler was there to represent Gregory Johnson. Throughout the Vietnam era, when dissenters and protesters were on trial, Kuntsler was nearly always there to represent them. When the so-called "Chicago Seven" were on trial for disrupting the 1968 Democratic convention, Kuntsler turned their defense into an attack on the Chicago police and city officials. His unkempt hair was grayer now, but he still had a grand, bombastic style that was rarely seen among the buttoned-down lawyers who appeared before the Supreme Court.

Kathi Alyce Drew, an assistant district attorney from Dallas, had the lectern for the first half hour, representing the state of Texas. Rarely could she put two sentences together in her argument before she was stopped by a question from one of the justices. The rapid-fire exchanges would have made the case ideal for television.

Drew began by arguing that the state has a strong interest in the "preservation of the flag as a symbol of nationhood and national unity." That was the argument Rehnquist made in 1974, and she intended to mimic it.

"Why did the defendant's actions here destroy the symbol?" Scalia interjected. "His action does not make it any less a symbol." Johnson had burned *a* flag, but he did not destroy *the* flag, Scalia suggested.

Drew responded, "Your Honor, we believe that if a symbol over a period of time is ignored or abused that it can, in fact, lose its symbolic value."

"I think not at all," Scalia answered. "It seems to me you're running a different argument, not that he's destroying its symbolic character, but that he is showing disrespect for it . . . You don't want just a symbol, but you want a venerated symbol."

"Your Honor, I'm forced to disagree with you," Drew countered, "because I believe that every desecration of the flag carried out in the manner that he did here—and certainly I don't think there can be any question that Mr. Johnson is a hard-core violator of this statute . . . "

"They desecrate the flag indeed," Scalia interjected again, "but do they destroy the symbol? We may not have a respected national symbol, but that's a different argument."

Drew answered, "Texas is not suggesting that we can insist on respect. We are suggesting that the right to preserve the physical integrity of the flag . . . because its symbolic effect is diluted by certain public acts of flag desecration."

The chief justice leaned up to his microphone. "Well, in a sense you're arguing a minimal form of respect for the flag, aren't you? Not that you have to take your hat off or salute when it goes by," Rehnquist said. The *West Virginia* v. *Barnette* case made clear the government cannot force citizens to salute the flag, but this was different, the chief justice suggested.

Rehnquist was concerned about Scalia's barrage of questions. The Texas attorney had been backed into a corner; the chief justice sought to rescue her.

"Now, the state can't require [a salute to the flag], but at least can't it insist that you not destroy it?" Rehnquist asked.

"Yes, Your Honor," Drew replied. "To the extent we are asking for any respect for the flag, we are asking for respect for its physical integrity. Certainly we do not demand that any individual view it with any discernible emotion whatsoever, only that its physical integrity be respected."

Now, Kennedy joined in. "Over the years, over the centuries, the cross has been respected. I recognize [that] one's a religious symbol, the other's a national one, but there's no legislation that has appeared necessary to protect, say, the cross."

"That's true, Your Honor," Drew responded.

"So, it may be that you can protect symbols by public respect and by measures other than the imposition of criminal law," Kennedy continued.

A few moments later, Drew conceded in response to Kennedy's questions that burning the flag was a kind of symbolic speech. If so, Kennedy asked, what rule was she suggesting that the Court adopt "in order to say we can punish this kind of speech? Just an exception for flags? Is there just a flag exception to the First Amendment?"

"To a certain extent, we have made that argument in the brief," Drew answered. "We believe there are compelling state interests that will . . . override this individual's symbolic speech rights, and preserving the flag as a symbol . . . is one of those."

Drew noted that the Texas legislature had made the bluebonnet the state flower but had not made it a crime to destroy one.

"Well, how do you pick out what to protect?" Scalia asked. "I mean, you know, if I had to pick between the Constitution and the flag, I might well go with the Constitution. I don't know."

Drew tried to return to her basic argument that the government can protect the "physical integrity" of the flag without infringing on freedom of speech, but Kennedy and Scalia countered that the state was insisting on only one message: The flag can be used as a symbol to honor the nation but not to denigrate it.

No, Drew said, "what we are arguing is that you may not publicly desecrate a flag regardless of the motivation of your action."

"Well you give me an example where somebody desecrates the flag in order to show that he agrees with the policies of the United States," Scalia replied, to laughter in the courtroom.

O'Connor asked, "Do you suppose Patrick Henry and any of the founding fathers ever showed disrespect to the Union Jack?"

"Quite possibly, Your Honor," Drew replied.

"You think they had in mind when drafting the First Amendment that it should be a prosecutable offense?" asked O'Connor, sounding as skeptical of the state's argument as Kennedy and Scalia.

As her half hour neared an end, Drew tried to argue that the flag was a "national property," which is owned by the people but which government can protect, like a national monument. "I think the flag is this nation's cherished property [and] that every individual has a certain interest in it," she said.

Then Scalia got in the last rejoinder. "If we say so, it becomes so. But that certainly isn't self-evident. I never thought the flag I owned is your flag," he said.

As Kuntsler rose, it looked as though he had his case won. Rehnquist's usual conservative allies did not appear ready to buy the argument that the First Amendment permitted the government to create a symbol and then prosecute someone who uses it for the wrong message, but Rehnquist and White took turns trying to undercut Kuntsler's case.

Kuntsler quoted from Justice Jackson's opinion in the flag salute case, *West Virginia* v. *Barnette*. "No official, high or petty, can prescribe what shall be orthodox in politics, nationalism, religion or other matters of opinion," Jackson had written.

Rehnquist looked up. "Well, the facts of *West Virginia* v. *Barnette* were quite different from this. There, the students were required to salute the flag."

Kuntsler said, "And here, Chief Justice, people are required not to do something."

"Yes," Rehnquist replied.

"And I think that's a comparable situation," Kuntsler argued. "We can't order you to salute the flag. We can't order you to do all these obeisances with relation to the flag."

Rehnquist responded, "Well, to me they're quite different. . . . It seems to me one could quite easily say you can't do one but you can do the other."

Kuntsler then moved on to a series of other cases, arguing that the Court had in effect already said that an act such as burning a flag is protected free speech. Rehnquist challenged each one.

Kuntsler stopped at one point and looked up at the bench. "I don't know if I have convinced you."

Rehnquist grinned. "Well, you may have convinced the others," he said.

As usual, Brennan had sat silently through the oral argument, but he was never silent at the conference of the justices. The First Amendment protected free speech, he said, and the real test of the Court was its willingness to protect, as Holmes had put it, "the expression of opinions we loathe." Flag burning was certainly loathsome, but a nonviolent political protest must be protected, he argued. Marshall and Blackmun, his usual allies, agreed entirely.

Stevens, however, angrily disagreed. He had served as a World War II naval intelligence officer in the South Pacific. If Americans could give their lives to erect the flag on tiny, rocky islands in the Pacific, why can't the government protect the flag at home? he wondered. As Rehnquist had argued, Joey Johnson is entirely free to denounce the flag in the most vitriolic terms, he noted. No one questions his right to free speech, but the government need not tolerate "the spray painting of the Lincoln Memorial," nor need it stand by idly as the flag is torched, Stevens remarked.

The chief justice, White, Stevens, and O'Connor voted to uphold the Texas law and send Johnson to prison, but Reagan's two youngest appointees, Scalia and Kennedy, joined with Brennan to strike down the law and free the protester.

In the 1980s, conservative intellectuals had adopted the right to free speech as one of their own. They were convinced that the "free trade in ideas," just like the free marketplace for goods, made for a thriving democracy. In China, young students were challenging the Communist government with symbols of American democracy, including the Statue of Liberty. In Eastern Europe, protesters were waving flags in which the Soviet hammer and sickle had been cut out. How could an American cheer these protesters abroad while insisting that Americans at home could be imprisoned for desecrating the U.S. flag?

Unlike White, Stevens, and Rehnquist, Scalia and Kennedy were not World War II veterans. They were only boys during the war. They were also part of the younger generation of conservatives who put a high value on the clash of ideas. Scalia made clear he had nothing but contempt for the flag burners, but his duty, he said, was to enforce the First Amendment as it was written. By that standard, the Texas law was unconstitutional, and Johnson must be freed. Kennedy cast the decisive fifth vote, agreeing with Brennan and Scalia. The Constitution spoke louder than the parties involved in this particular case, he said, and it demanded that right to free expression prevail. With a five-member majority, Brennan said he would write the opinion himself. The chief justice said he would author a dissent.

In April 1989, the justices turned their attention to abortion. No issue divided the nation as abortion did. Not just one right was at stake, but two. There was, first, a woman's right to control her body and her life. If she found herself accidentally and unhappily pregnant, prochoice advocates said, she should have the right to end the pregnancy before the fetus grew. Could the state have the power to, in effect, commandeer a woman's body and force her to carry a pregnancy to term against her will? Maybe in the Romania of Nicolae Ceauśescu, but not in America, they said.

The prolife advocates said that they spoke for the rights of the fetus, the unborn child. What could be more innocent and more in need of protection, they said, than a fetus in the earliest stages of life? They described widespread use of abortion as a "holocaust," a mass and thoughtless killing of millions to which the civilized world had turned a blind eye. Because both the Declaration of Independence and the Constitution spoke of a right to "life," abortion is not only morally wrong but legally so also, they maintained.

Those were the polar positions as abortion was debated and disputed around the nation. It was a moral issue and an emotional one. It was also a religious and scientific issue involving the question of when life begins. Neither perspective, however, was how abortion was discussed at the Court, and the phrase *unborn child* was rarely used. Nor were there discussions about when human life begins, as most of the justices seemed to approach that issue as agnostics. They could not decide when life begins, and they need not. From the beginning, Rehnquist had opposed the right to abortion created in *Roe* v. *Wade*, but he appeared equally uninterested in the rights of the unborn child. In his view, the Constitution neither gave women a right to choose abortion nor guaranteed the fetus a right to life. Because neither was decided by the Constitution, the states and their elected officials could decide for themselves.

This was no surprise to Court observers. Rehnquist took the same view in nearly every case involving the Constitution. As he wrote in the flag-burning case, "Surely one of the high purposes of a democratic society is to legislate against conduct that is regarded as evil and profoundly offensive to the majority of people—whether it be murder, embezzlement, pollution or flag burning." He might have added "abortion" to the list.

In its fight to preserve legalized abortion, NARAL, the National Abortion Rights Action League, had adopted the slogan "Who Decides?"—a woman or a group of politicians? The

Court's conservatives might have adopted the same slogan:
Who decides—judges or the people? When in doubt, they said,
the majority should decide a divisive public issue, not a committee of unelected judges.

Rehnquist and White filed dissents in the original *Roe* case,
and they still stood alone on the abortion issue in 1981, when
Ronald Reagan took office. The Republican platform called for
appointing justices who would respect "the sanctity of innocent
human life." Reagan's first choice, Sandra O'Connor, proved
to be a sharp critic of the *Roe* ruling in dissents issued in 1983
and 1986, but her true position on the abortion right remained
a mystery. Scalia and Kennedy had not yet voted on an abortion
case, but no one considered their views a mystery. Both were
not only personally opposed to abortion but also considered
the *Roe* ruling legally unjustified. The Missouri case would be
the first real test of Reagan's legacy on the abortion issue.

In the original *Roe* opinion, Blackmun devised a system
of permitted regulations based on the trimesters of a woman's
pregnancy, just as a doctor might have. During the first trimester, or about the first 12 weeks, the abortion decision would
be hers alone. During the second trimester, the state could
enact regulations to protect the health of the mother but not
the fetus. During the third trimester, or after 24 weeks, the
fetus becomes viable, or able to live outside its mother's womb.
At that point, the state can ban abortion to protect the fetus,
Blackmun said.

He based this regulatory system on "present medical
knowledge," not on a principle found in the Constitution. As
a matter of common sense and medical understanding, his opinion was appealing. All but the absolutists on both sides agreed
that the woman's rights were strongest, and the government's
the weakest, in the first weeks of a pregnancy, when an embryo's physiological systems are undifferentiated, immature,
and smaller than a golf ball. Months later, however, when the
fetus had become a recognizable baby, abortion was a gruesome undertaking. Late-term abortions are rare and mostly un-
dertaken because of evidence that the fetus has severe defects.
About 91 percent of abortions take place during the first
trimester.

If Blackmun's opinion made medical sense, however, it
did not succeed as well in making convincing legal sense. He
based the abortion right on the Fourteenth Amendment of
1868, which said that a state may not "deprive any person of

life, liberty or property without due process of law." For the literalist, these words could have been said to create a "right to life" with as much ease as Blackmun said they create a right to abortion. History did not help much either, because in 1868, 36 states had laws against abortion. Certainly the states that ratified the Fourteenth Amendment did not think they were making their abortion laws unconstitutional.

Still, the abortion right was grounded in the nation's legal tradition that personal matters are private and off-limits to the government. When in doubt, the liberals said, give individuals the right to make personal decisions about their lives, rather than let the government make those decisions. Americans have an understood right to marry and to have children. The government cannot interfere in these matters, they said, even though the Constitution says nothing about a "right to marry" or a "right to have children."

At first, the Court seemed a bit tentative about the strength of the right to abortion. In his *Roe* v. *Wade* opinion, Blackmun described it as a "qualified" right, not absolute or unquestioned. Burger, in a concurring opinion, said that the Court had not legalized abortion "on demand."

In the years following the decision, however, antiabortion majorities in several state legislatures, notably Missouri, Illinois, Pennsylvania, and Massachusetts, tested just how "qualified" this right was. They enacted regulations designed to dissuade women from having abortions. For example, a pregnant woman who came to a doctor seeking an abortion was told she must get her spouse's consent, or wait 48 hours, before going ahead. Doctors were told they must inform women of the "risks" of abortion and tell them of other choices, such as adoption. The Court, however, rejected nearly all these regulations because they intruded into the first two trimesters of the woman's pregnancy. Blackmun said that the right to choose abortion was a "fundamental" right, upon which the state could not infringe.

The antiabortion forces won on only one major issue. In 1977 and 1980 decisions, the Court ruled that the government may refuse to pay for abortion, even if it pays for other medical care for poor women. Lewis Powell provided the key vote. He believed that women had the right to abortion, but the government need not subsidize this right.

Otherwise, however, the Court followed a steady path of striking down increasingly petty regulations that infringed on the right to abortion. The high-water mark was reached on June 11, 1986, when the Court struck down a series of Pennsylvania regulations in the case of *Richard Thornburgh* v. *American College of Obstetricians and Gynecologists.* (The doctors had filed suit against the then-Pennsylvania governor who was later to lead the Reagan and Bush administration's fight against the Roe ruling as the U.S. attorney general.) The Pennsylvania law would have required, among other things, that doctors give women a pamphlet with "objective, nonjudgmental . . . and accurate scientific information" on a fetus. Blackmun viewed these regulations as a meddlesome interference with the doctor–patient relationship. Certainly, doctors can give women accurate information without an unwanted assist from the state. The state's only purpose was to "deter" patients from seeking abortion, he said, so the regulations were declared invalid prior to a trial on the issue. The once "qualified" right to abortion had become nearly absolute. By this time, however, it had the support of only five justices: Brennan, Marshall, Blackmun, Stevens, and Powell.

Byron White was furious at the decision. Blackmun and the liberals had first invented the right to abortion and now they were using it to strike down any law that might even "deter" abortions. Thanks to Blackmun's opinion, the Court had become the nation's "ex officio medical board," White complained. He and Rehnquist said Roe should be flatly overruled. Six days after the Pennsylvania ruling was handed down, Reagan announced that he had nominated Rehnquist to be the new chief justice.

The most intriguing opinion in the Thornburgh case was written by Sandra O'Connor. She refused to join White in calling for *Roe* to be overturned, but she nonetheless dissented, believing the Court had erred by striking down Pennsylvania's regulations.

"The Court is not suited to the expansive role it has claimed for itself in the series of cases that began with *Roe* v. *Wade*," she said. In her view, the justices should not perch themselves on the shoulders of state legislators and reject regulations that they deem meddlesome or silly. Where Blackmun saw the matter through a doctor's eyes, O'Connor saw it from the vantage point of a former state legislator. She had earlier described Blackmun's trimester system as "completely unworkable." Why can't the state require that a pregnant woman in her first or second trimester hear of the risks of abortion or alternatives such as adoption? That sort of regulation may violate the trimester scheme created by the Court, but it certainly did not violate the woman's right to choose abortion, O'Connor believed.

O'Connor also had the distinction of being the one member of the Court who had experienced the kick of an unborn child. Beginning in the late 1950s, she had given birth to three boys—Scott, Brian, and Jay—and had spent several years at home raising her family. While O'Connor later said she found abortion to be repugnant, other friends said she viewed it as a "necessary evil." Her pregnancies caused her to question the Court's trimester system, however. By the fourth or fifth month of a pregnancy, a mother begins feeling a baby's kick. Yet, under the trimester framework, the Court acted as though the fetus did not come into being until the seventh month of pregnancy, the start of the third trimester.

O'Connor's dissenting opinion in the *Thornburgh* case left unanswered the larger question: What about a law that actually forbids a woman from getting an abortion? "I do remain of the view [that] the state has compelling interests in ensuring maternal health and in protecting potential human life . . . throughout pregnancy." Nonetheless, the Court should examine "with heightened scrutiny," she added, those instances "in which the state has imposed an undue burden on the abortion decision," she wrote. "An undue burden will generally be found in situations involving absolute obstacles or severe limitations on the abortion decision, not wherever a state regulation may inhibit abortions to some degree."

On affirmative action and religion, O'Connor had fashioned a middle-of-the-road position, a compromise between the liberal and conservative factions. Her dissent in the *Thornburgh* case looked like an attempt to do the same for abortion. Undoubtedly, she would uphold the states' abortion regulations, such as Pennsylvania's required pamphlets on fetuses. However, she did not appear ready to uphold laws that would set up "absolute obstacles or severe limitations" on women seeking abortions.

The Reagan administration, which had come to Washington promising to get the government "off the backs" of the people, preached a different message on abortion. While health and safety regulations of business were derided as wasteful and unnecessary, regulation of abortion was steadfastly defended by the Justice Department. In their final months in office, Brad

Reynolds and the other Reagan attorneys stage-managed the *Webster* case to put Sandra O'Connor on the spot. Their brief to the Court in the *Webster* case called for scrapping Blackmun's opinion and nullifying the right to abortion, and it did so using O'Connor's own words. The trimester system was "completely unworkable," the Justice Department said, citing a 1983 O'Connor dissent. Also, the state should be allowed to protect "potential human life . . . throughout pregnancy," the brief said, quoting O'Connor's dissent in the Pennsylvania case.

The Justice Department was not interested in O'Connor's attempts to fashion a compromise on abortion. The brief gently but firmly rejected her "undue burden" standard for judging abortion regulations. Such an approach would require the Court to engage in "arbitrary line drawing" to decide which laws go too far, the brief said. "If a political resolution of the abortion controversy is ever to become a reality," it added, "the Court must unequivocally announce its intention to allow the states to act free from the suffocating power of the federal judge." Women need not fear a return to the era of back-alley abortions, the Administration said. Rather, it predicted that the state legislatures would "arrive at humane solutions," which took into account the "competing interests involved in the abortion controversy."

Women's rights advocates did not need the Administration's legal brief to tell them the right to abortion was in great danger. The simple arithmetic of the Court did that. When Justice Powell retired, there were no longer five votes to affirm *Roe* v. *Wade*. For too long, supporters of the right to abortion had been the new silent majority. With the *Webster* case approaching, the prochoice forces raised their voices. Each year on January 22, the anniversary of the Roe ruling, the right-to-life movement marched in Washington to condemn the decision. In January 1989, 65,000 right-to-lifers turned out to march. Three months later, the abortion rights movement determined to do even better to show it had broad political support. On April 9th, police estimated that 300,000 persons marched in the abortion rights rally, while the march organizers put the figure at closer to 600,000.

The huge throng of marching women only accented the pressure on Sandra O'Connor. A woman's right to obtain an abortion would probably be determined by her, the lone woman on the Court—a woman whose own life had been put into jeopardy by cancer; a woman who was a conservative Republican, a mother of three children, and an appointee of Ronald Reagan; and a woman who had personally experienced gender discrimination. A hero and a role model to some young women, her decision could affect the lives of millions. Each day during the spring, Court employees brought bags full of mail into her chambers, nearly all wanting to advise Justice O'Connor on the abortion case.

Her clerks and others who saw her were impressed with how O'Connor handled the pressure. The abortion case was a difficult one, but so were the cases involving the death penalty for juveniles, flag burning, and job discrimination. She was closemouthed about her own views, especially on abortion. Even justices who had sat around the table with her for years had no idea whether she would vote to overturn *Roe* v. *Wade*.

Over her years at the Court, O'Connor had developed a routine for herself. Because there were no easy cases, she approached them all in the same lawyerly way. She read as much as she could, looked back at old opinions, talked with her clerks, and reserved her decision. What we do in these chambers may determine the Court's decision, she told her clerks, so we need to do our work well. She was in no hurry to make a snap decision.

The April 26 argument turned into an event. Hundreds of persons, many of them activists in the abortion struggle and others just curious, wanted to see arguments in the *Webster* case. Dozens of them stood in line all night to get 1 of about 100 visitors' seats in the courtroom. As the argument began inside, hundreds of demonstrators, separated by police, battled each other from a distance, waving signs and hurling invective.

Inside, the argument began sedately. Webster took the first 20 minutes to explain and defend Missouri's law. The justices asked about details. For example, how could the state ensure that no public funds were used for "encouraging" abortion? Would a physician be fined or sent to jail for saying the wrong words? Webster said the law had no enforcement provisions except that the state could cut off future funding to a hospital that ignored the law.

By agreement, the final ten minutes of Webster's half hour would be used by the U.S. Justice Department to attack *Roe* directly. Charles Fried, the solicitor general during the Reagan administration, had returned to the Harvard Law School in January 1989 to teach, but because his successor had not yet been sworn in, Fried returned for a cameo appearance. Tall and angular, a native of Czechoslovakia, Fried spoke in a grand, formal manner, which, at times, reduced the justices' questions to the level of petty distractions. Once, one of the justices was asked privately whether Fried was an effective advocate before the Court. Yes, despite "his supercilious manner," he replied.

Fried had had a difficult tenure in the Justice Department, torn between law and politics. He served as the chief courtroom attorney during Reagan's second term, and some conservatives accused him of being fainthearted in advocating the Administration's views. Others accused him of bowing to politics and pushing the Reagan ideology too fervently. It was hard to keep all the factions happy as solicitor general, but no one could charge Fried with being fainthearted on the abortion issue. He had challenged *Roe* directly in the 1986 Pennsylvania case and rose to the lectern in the Missouri case to do so again.

"Today the United States [*sic*] asks this Court to reconsider and overrule its decision in *Roe* v. *Wade*. At the outset, I would like to make quite clear how limited that submission is," Fried began. It was a startling opening, and distinctly Friedian. Only he would urge the Court to reverse its best known and most sweeping ruling of the past two decades and say in the very next sentence that this was a "limited . . . submission."

Fried had a distinctive strategy. He wanted to separate the *Roe* v. *Wade* ruling from the 1965 decision on contraceptives, *Griswold* v. *Connecticut,* in which the Court announced the "right to privacy." Robert Bork had maintained that this decision was wrong because the Constitution says nothing of a "right to privacy," but Bork failed to convince the Senate on this point and was defeated. Regardless of the precise wording of the Constitution, most Americans—and most members of the Senate—were convinced that they have a right to privacy, including the right to buy contraceptives. Attacking *Griswold* was a losing strategy, and Fried was not about to repeat it.

"First, we are not asking the Court to unravel the fabric of unenumerated and privacy rights which this Court has woven" in past rulings, Fried said. "Rather, we are asking the Court to pull this one thread. . . . Abortion is different. It involves the purposeful termination, as the Court said, of potential life."

Kennedy looked puzzled. "Your position, Mr. Fried, then is that *Griswold* v. *Connecticut* [the contraceptive case] is correct and should be retained."

"Exactly, your honor," Fried replied.

"Is that because there is a fundamental right involved in that case?" Kennedy asked.

Yes, Fried replied, but it was a "quite concrete" right, "not an abstraction such as the right to control one's body [or] the right to be let alone."

In the *Griswold* opinion, William O. Douglas had said that highly personal matters, such as contraceptives, are within a "zone of privacy" that is off-limits to government regulation. What did this zone of privacy protect? Kennedy wondered. "Does the case stand for the proposition that there is a right to determine whether to procreate?" he asked.

Fried sounded appalled by the thought. "*Griswold* surely does not stand for that proposition!" he replied.

While Fried had a dramatic manner, Kennedy spoke in a slow monotone, his voice rarely rising. At times, he sounded like a professor patiently waiting for a student to offer the correct answer. "What is the right involved in *Griswold*?" he asked.

Fried opined that the *Griswold* case established "the right not to have the state intrude, in a very violent way, into the details of marital intimacy." It is not clear what was "violent" about the state's ban on selling contraceptives, but Fried was determined to define the case narrowly.

From the beginning, everyone in the courtroom knew that O'Connor's vote would probably decide the case. As Fried tried to reduce the "right to privacy" set forth in the *Griswold* case into something smaller and more manageable, O'Connor leaned up to her microphone.

"Do you say there is no fundamental right to decide whether to have a child or not?" she asked Fried.

As he began to respond, she interrupted. "A right to procreate? Do you deny that the Constitution protects that right?"

It was a simple but powerful question. If there was indeed a constitutional "right to procreate," it would take only a small leap to reach a "right to abortion." However, if Fried answered "no," could he defend the proposition that Americans have no constitutional right to have children?

Fried avoided a "yes" or "no" answer and instead talked around the question. "I would hesitate to formulate the right in such abstract terms, and I think the Court prior to *Roe* v. *Wade* quite prudently also avoided such sweeping generalities. That was the wisdom of *Griswold*," Fried said.

O'Connor was not finished. "Do you think that the state has the right to, if in a future century we had a serious over-population problem, has a right to require women to have abortions after so many children?" she asked. If the Constitution does not protect an individual's "right to procreate," why couldn't the government here, as in the People's Republic of China, force women to have abortions?

"I surely do not. That would be quite a different matter," Fried replied.

"What do you rest that on?" O'Connor asked. How is it that the Constitution, on the one hand, says nothing about abortion, yet it would violate the Constitution to force women to have abortions?

"Because unlike abortion, which involves the purposeful termination of future life, that would involve not preventing an operation, but violently taking hands on, laying hands on a woman and submitting her to an operation," Fried said.

Fried's ten minutes were gone quickly. He had made his argument for overturning the abortion right, but O'Connor certainly sounded skeptical.

Frank Susman, a St. Louis attorney representing the Missouri abortion clinics, had first gone to court to challenge the state's law against abortions in public facilities by contending it infringed on women's rights. Because he had won in the federal courts in St. Louis, he now found himself before the Supreme Court defending *Roe* v. *Wade* itself and the basic right to abortion.

About 30 percent of pregnancies end in abortion, he said, about 1.5 million of them per year nationwide. "Abortion today is the most common surgical procedure in the United States," he said. "It is . . . 17 times safer than childbirth, 100 times safer than appendectomy," the operation O'Connor had undergone the year before.

"I suggest that there can be no 'ordered liberty' for women without control over their education, their employment, their health, their childbearing, and their personal aspirations," Susman said. He added, there is "a deeply rooted tradition that the government steer clear of decisions affecting the bedroom, child bearing, and doctor–patient relationships."

Scalia interrupted. "I don't see that tradition," if abortion were included, he said. Through most of American history, abortion was forbidden in most states, he noted. How could it be a deeply rooted tradition? At one point, Scalia said he agreed with Susman that there was much doubt and disagreement over whether a fetus was a human life.

"But what conclusion does that lead to?" Scalia asked. "That there must be a fundamental right to destroy this thing . . . or rather, isn't it a matter that you vote on? Since we don't know the answer, people have to make up their minds the best way they can."

Susman disagreed. "The conclusion to which it leads . . . is that you have an issue that is so divisive and so emotional and so personal and so intimate, it must be left as a fundamental right to the individual to make that choice," he said.

The argument had aired the issues but not changed any minds. On Friday, the justices gathered to vote. The appeals court in St. Louis had struck down the Missouri law, so the first question before the justices was, Should the lower court ruling be upheld or reversed? Would Missouri's law preventing abortions in public facilities be struck down, as the appeals court said, or reinstated?

The chief justice came to the conference confident he had five votes. Besides his own vote, he could count on four other votes to rule for Missouri: White, Scalia, Kennedy, and O'Connor. From the beginning, O'Connor had said she thought the states could regulate abortion, and even under the prevailing rulings, the states were not required to subsidize or encourage abortion. Certainly Missouri's law did not put "an undue burden" on a woman's right to choose abortion, because private doctors and private clinics were unaffected. Only four percent of the state's physicians were considered public employees, and only 19 of 160 hospitals and clinics in Missouri were state facilities. Despite the state's restrictions, the right to abortion would still exist in Missouri. As Rehnquist expected, O'Connor voted to uphold the Missouri law, giving the chief justice a majority. Brennan, Marshall, Blackmun, and Stevens dissented.

For Rehnquist and his majority, the second question was how to write the opinion. The *Webster* case had drawn enormous attention not because of the significance of the Missouri law, but because it could allow the Court to overturn *Roe* v. *Wade*. Rehnquist knew that O'Connor would not go that far. In her view, the issues in the Missouri case did not touch directly on the basic right to abortion. Because the case did not require the Court to rule directly on the right to abortion, the justices should not do so, O'Connor held.

Nonetheless, she had often criticized Blackmun's *Roe* opinion with its trimester framework and the declaration that abortion was a "fundamental right." As Rehnquist saw it, he could write an opinion that would knock down the legal superstructure built up around the right to abortion. That way, the states would be free again to regulate abortion, as states such as Missouri, Pennsylvania, and Illinois had sought to do. His opinion would not go as far as to overturn the basic right to choose abortion; states could not make all abortions a crime again. That issue, if it arose, could be considered in a later case. Nonetheless, the *Webster* case offered an opportunity to remove the strict limits on the state's power to regulate abortion. With that understanding, Rehnquist announced that he would write the opinion in *Webster* v. *Reproductive Health Services.*

Blackmun had spent months in law and medical libraries in 1972 working on his *Roe* opinion. Because the term had only two months left until the summer recess, Rehnquist could not take much time on his *Webster* opinion. He wanted a clear majority ruling that spoke for five justices, not a collection of separate opinions. He determined to write his draft opinion within two weeks and circulate it around the building.

In June, as the term began its final month, decisions were still pending in 55 cases, more than a third of the year's total. Throughout the spring, the Court had heard arguments in half a dozen cases involving the federal antidiscrimination laws. Though none of the cases had drawn wide public attention, civil rights attorneys were worried. In the 1960s, Congress had passed broadly worded laws outlawing discrimination in the workplace, in housing, and in schools. Based on this skeletal structure, the Supreme Court had built a body of law that gave life to these laws, but the same process could work in reverse. If Kennedy sided with Rehnquist in each of the pending cases, the civil rights lawyers could find themselves holding just a skeleton—no flesh.

On June 5, their worst fears began to come true. On a 5–4 vote in the case of *Wards Cove Packing Company* v. *Atonio,* the Rehnquist Court announced it had rewritten the rules for handling some kinds of class-action job discrimination suits. For years, business attorneys and some conservatives in the Justice Department had complained that the Burger Court had tilted the law so that minorities and women could use statistics—

rather than proof of actual discrimination—to win lawsuits. Their complaints had some validity.

In the 1971 case of *Griggs* v. *Duke Power*, the Court, in a unanimous opinion written by Burger, ruled that federal law banned not only "overt discrimination" in the workplace, but also "practices that are fair in form but discriminatory in practice." Prior to the Civil Rights Act of 1964, the Duke Power Company had refused to hire blacks. Afterward, the company adopted a requirement that employees, including janitors, have a high school diploma. While this job requirement was not discriminatory in itself, the Court said, it had a discriminatory "impact" on local blacks, who were less likely to have high school diplomas. If an employment standard has a discriminatory impact on minorities or women, Burger said, the company must show that it is a "business necessity." Otherwise, it will be considered illegal discrimination in violation of federal law, the Court said.

The opinion in *Griggs* v. *Duke Power* stood as a landmark in civil rights law. Thereafter, attorneys for civil rights plaintiffs did not have to prove in all cases that an employer, public or private, intended to discriminate against employees. Instead, they could show that a company's hiring or promotion standards had a discriminatory "impact." Armed with these *Griggs* rules, lawyers challenged height and weight rules that had tended to keep women out of police and firefighting jobs. They challenged tests that kept blacks and Hispanics from being promoted into white-collar positions. Unless a company or public agency could "show" that its tests or hiring standards were "essential" to performing the job, they were illegal, the Court said in follow-up cases.

In the 1980s, the stakes were raised higher. Lower courts began to apply the *Griggs* rules to cases involving "subjective" job standards, such as interviews and job evaluations. Suppose, for example, that a bank had 100 employees, about half of whom were women and about one-fourth of whom were racial minorities. However, the supervisors, who were chosen based on interviews, were nearly all white males. If the bank were sued by female and minority employees who contended that the promotion standards were discriminatory, the management would bear the burden of proving that its job interviews were fair and "essential" in selecting supervisors. Corporate lawyers worried that they could not "prove" to a jury that their interviews and job evaluations were fair and essential. Civil rights lawyers had the opposite fear. If companies did not have to explain and defend all their hiring and promotion standards, an unspoken bias could ensure that white males would still dominate the upper hierarchy of American business.

In the Reagan administration, the complaints from business officials won a hearing. Why is it discriminatory or illegal, the corporate lawyers asked, to set high standards that select the best applicants rather than simply those who are minimally capable of doing a job? Under the *Griggs* rule, employers who set such high standards had to "prove" their innocence, they complained. Besides, they thought companies should be permitted to set job standards that were good for business, even when these standards had a harsh impact on women or minorities. The airlines, for example, wanted to require that female flight attendants not weigh more than 150 pounds. Such a standard was good for business, they said. However, if sued under the *Griggs* rules, the airline managers surely could not prove it was "essential" to the job for a flight attendant to weigh less than 150 pounds.

At the Justice Department, Brad Reynolds and Charles Fried agreed that the *Griggs* case had perverted the meaning of the federal job-discrimination laws. The new conservatives on the Court agreed with them, too. Scalia and Kennedy pointed to the language of the 1964 law. It said employers are guilty of discrimination if they refuse to hire persons "because of" their race or gender. Those words mean, they said, that persons who claim to have lost a job or promotion must prove it was because of illegal discrimination and not some other reason. With a new majority in control, the conservatives sought a change in the law. The Reagan administration lawyers also found a code word that echoed long after the Court had ruled. The strict rules set by the *Griggs* case force employers to resort to "quotas" to avoid lawsuits, they said.

"Our opportunity to tame Griggs came in *Wards Cove Packing Company* v. *Atonio*," Fried wrote in his account of his years as solicitor general *(Order & Law: Arguing the Reagan Revolution*, Simon & Schuster, 1991). The case looked "terrible" at first, Fried said, because it involved a peculiar situation. Thirteen years before, lawyers representing the mostly Philippine work force at an Alaskan salmon cannery had filed a class-action job discrimination suit in which they contended that nonwhites were excluded from better-paying, skilled jobs, such as technician, accountant, electrician, and manager. The

federal judge who tried the case ruled that the Wards Cove
Packing Company had not intentionally discriminated against
the Philippine cannery workers. However, a federal appeals
court in San Francisco revived the lawsuit under the *Griggs*
rules. Because the Philippine workers had statistics showing
that the minorities were concentrated in low-paying jobs, the
company must "prove" that its various hiring and promotion
standards were necessary and essential.

The company's appeal to the Court arrived soon after Kennedy took his seat. The justices had split 4–4 on an earlier case
involving the *Griggs* rule. With Kennedy on board, the chief
justice moved to take up the appeal in the *Wards Cove* case.

On June 5, Byron White announced the result. As usual,
White's opinion reflected none of the intellectual and political
debate that had swirled around the *Griggs* rules. Among the
justices and the clerks, White said little and revealed nothing;
he disdained long debates. Nonetheless, Rehnquist trusted him
with major opinions. White would not write a long opinion that
grappled with the competing ideas, nor would he seek to explain the Court's reasons for changing its view of the law. Instead, he would write a brief opinion announcing the conclusions, but not much else. Like their author, White's opinions
were terse and tough.

Unlike the other justices, White refused to read a portion
of his opinion from the bench. "It's a waste of time," he said.
Instead, he simply announced that the appeals court ruling had
been reversed. His opinion, released that morning, made three
crucial changes in the law.

First, he said, civil rights lawyers may not rely just on
statistics to suggest a pattern of discrimination. Instead, they
must show that a particular hiring or promotion standard
caused the statistical disparity. This sounds like a reasonable
rule, although job-discrimination lawyers say it is often difficult
to isolate which of a company's practices—recruiting, adver-
tisements, interviews, tests, recommendations, or whatever—
result in a work force that is strikingly unbalanced by race or
gender.

Second, White said, employers may defend themselves by
showing their job standards further "legitimate employment
goals." For employers—such as the airline managers confront-
ing the flight attendants—this is a much easier standard to meet
than the *Griggs* rules. Rather than showing that a weight re-

quirement or test is "essential" to the job, the company must show only that it furthers a legitimate goal.

Third, White said, the workers, not the employer, have the ultimate burden of proving that discrimination took place. A statistical pattern of discrimination does not require that the employer prove the fairness of the hiring and promotion standards. White announced the final change in law with a surprisingly brief, almost casual comment. In earlier rulings, the Court had said that once the workers show a statistical pattern of unfairness, the employers had the burden of proving that their standards were necessary and fair. White dismissed these statements as if they were typographical errors.

"To the extent that those cases speak of an employer's 'burden of proof' . . . they should have been understood to mean an employer's production—but not persuasion—burden," he wrote. Employers who are sued must produce some evidence to explain their hiring and promotion standards, he said, but "the persuasion burden here must remain with the plaintiff." White's opinion was signed by Rehnquist, O'Connor, Scalia, and Kennedy.

The issues raised by the *Wards Cove* case were complicated. They involved the rules for deciding huge discrimination cases that often extended for years. Unquestionably, however, the ruling would make it far harder to win such cases in the future. The decision sounded a death knell for class-action lawsuits, one civil rights attorney proclaimed.

Brennan, Marshall, Blackmun, and Stevens dissented in the *Wards Cove* case. Stevens faulted the conservatives for "this latest sojourn in judicial activism." It is "a mystery to me," he said, why the Court would want to shield from liability an Alaskan cannery that "resembles a plantation economy." Blackmun added a brief, pointed dissent. "One wonders whether the majority still believes that race discrimination—or, more accurately, race discrimination against nonwhites—is a problem in our society, or even remembers that it ever was."

A week later, the Court handed down two more reversals for civil rights lawyers. The first of the decisions had the potential to unravel affirmative action plans for hiring city and county workers, while the second made it harder for women to challenge seniority systems that protected the jobs of men.

During the 1970s, many cities and counties were sued for having excluded blacks from their police and fire departments. Rather than fight those suits—or having fought and lost during a trial—the local officials agreed to settlements. Typically, the police or fire departments promised, in a "consent decree" signed by a federal judge, to recruit, hire, and promote more minorities so that their employees more closely reflected the population of the city. What was not addressed was the potential impact on white firefighters or police officers who could lose a promotion to a black with less seniority or lower qualifications. Could they challenge this consent decree years later if it hurt their chances for promotion? Most lower courts said no. Usually, persons who have a stake in a court settlement must come forward when the settlement is being negotiated and before the judge signs off on the final decree.

Soon after Kennedy arrived on the bench, however, the Court announced that it would hear the case of *Martin* v. *Wilks,* in which white firefighters from Birmingham, Alabama, sought belatedly to challenge the city's affirmative action plan. They said they were victims of reverse discrimination. In their defense, city officials said they agreed to the consent decree to end the litigation; they should not have to refight the issue repeatedly, their attorneys argued. Usually, the conservatives sided with city officials and sought to keep new cases out of the federal courts, but not in this instance.

On June 12, the chief justice announced the 5–4 ruling in favor of the white firefighters. Because of "our deep-rooted historic tradition that everyone should have his own day in court," Rehnquist said, white employees who suffer because of a court's affirmative action order deserve a chance to challenge the plan in federal court. White, O'Connor, Kennedy, and Scalia joined the chief's opinion in *Martin* v. *Wilks.* The ruling sent the case back to a trial judge in Birmingham, with instructions to hear the claims of the white firefighters. Brennan, Marshall, Blackmun, and Stevens dissented.

The same morning, Scalia announced the Court's decision in a case in which women workers were seeking their day in court to challenge what they said was a biased seniority system. It had begun in 1979, when Patricia Lorance was an hourly wage worker at an AT&T (American Telephone and Telegraph) plant in Illinois. None of the women in the plant held skilled jobs such as "testers," although the company was under pressure to promote females into these better-paying jobs.

That year, the company and its male-dominated union negotiated a change in the seniority rules. Before, an employee's seniority was based on his or her time at the plant. Afterward, seniority for skilled workers would depend on how long they held that particular job. However, after five years in a skilled job, these employees would regain their plantwide seniority.

Under these new rules, Lorance and several other women won promotions to skilled jobs. During the 1982 recession, however, AT&T announced cutbacks, and workers were laid off based on their seniority. Thanks to the new seniority rule, the women who had just won their promotions were among the first to lose their jobs. In April 1983, they filed suit, charging the company with gender discrimination in violation of the Civil Rights Act of 1964. Lawyers for Lorance and the other women workers charged the company and its union with having "conspired to change the seniority rules in order to protect incumbent male testers" and to discourage women from seeking the skilled jobs.

A federal judge dismissed their lawsuit without a trial because it was filed too late. The 1964 law says that workers must file suits within 300 days of when "the alleged unlawful employment practice occurred." In Lorance's case, the judge ruled that the unlawful practice occurred in 1979 when the rules were changed, not in 1982 when the new rules caused Lorance and her female coworkers to lose their jobs. Because the lower federal courts were divided on this issue, the justices agreed to hear *Lorance* v. *AT&T* in March.

As with the case of the Birmingham firefighters, the justices would decide only whether Lorance and her female coworkers would get their day in court. The case marked a rare alliance of the NAACP LDF, which represented the women, and the Reagan and Bush administrations, which filed briefs supporting the women's position.

Despite the Administration's briefs, on June 12, the Court ruled that Lorance's lawsuit was properly dismissed without a trial. Scalia, Rehnquist, White, and Kennedy concluded that such a lawsuit comes too late if it is filed more than 300 days after the company announces a change in its seniority rules. O'Connor had disqualified herself from the case, perhaps because she owned AT&T stock. Stevens cast the decisive fifth vote. He said he did not actually agree with Scalia's opinion because it was based on an incorrect interpretation of the 1964 law. Nonetheless, the Court in earlier decisions had restricted the allowable time period for filing suits, he said. Based on those precedents, Stevens agreed that the women's suit must be dismissed.

The three dissenters—Marshall, Brennan, and Blackmun—accused the majority of reading the law in a way that creates a nonsensical result. Some of the women in this case did not go to work at AT&T until 1981. Under the court's decision, they should have filed a lawsuit in 1979 to challenge work rules that would not affect them until 1982. "Today's decision is the latest example of how this Court [is] flouting the intent of Congress," Marshall said in his dissent.

Brennan was angry at the conservatives but sad, too. They simply did not understand discrimination, he maintained. "You know as well as I do that we still have racial discrimination in this country," he said. Yes, the nation had made great progress, and yes, discrimination was not as blatant as before—but it was still there. Look at the facts in these cases! White males hold all the preferred jobs, while minorities and women take the back seat. The *Griggs* rules were crucial for rooting out the subtle, perhaps unconscious discrimination, he remarked. In his chambers, Brennan sunk back in his chair and reminisced about all the justices who had come and gone during the past three decades. The eight justices who were on the Court when he arrived in 1956 were now long dead. He also liked to talk of the glory days of the Warren Court when "we" had the majority. Of the current crop of justices, Brennan had only fond words. "I've never had a cross word with any of them," he said. But on matters of discrimination, they disappointed him. They just did not seem to understand it, Brennan noted.

In the view of the younger, more conservative clerks, Brennan, Marshall, and Blackmun did not get it either. They were still living in the America of the 1930s and 1940s, when racial bias was still rife, the clerks commented. Having spent decades now in the confined quarters of their marble palace, the old liberals were fighting the fights of long ago, or so said the young conservatives. "They're in a time warp," said one former clerk of the octogenarian liberals.

Kennedy and Scalia were part of the new generation of conservatives. Both entered law school after the *Brown* decision, after the worst of official racism had been wiped off the law books. By the 1980s, they saw the civil rights "movement" as being more concerned with pushing group interests than with upholding the principle of equal treatment. The two new justices came along at the same time, Scalia said, and tended to see things alike. However, they had little in common with the liberals who were nearly 30 years older. The generation gap was apparent to the justices and their clerks. Rarely did Scalia and Kennedy, for example, even speak to their liberal colleagues except at the conference table. Though Brennan had once been fabled for walking the halls and talking with the other justices to resolve hard cases, he rarely left his chambers in his later years. Scalia said he never spoke to Brennan about a pending case—but then, neither did the rest of the others converse much. They exchanged memos, to be sure; they worked out their problems on paper, not in person.

One clerk said he spent much of his year carrying memos back and forth to the different chambers yet never saw two justices together in the same office. Finally, on one afternoon, he came upon three justices, all gathered in Byron White's chambers. They were searching for a golf ball. White had constructed a putt-putt range in his chambers, where he and his clerks took turns putting a golf ball around an obstacle course of desks and chairs. Occasionally, the other justices would take a turn. On this afternoon, Sandra O'Connor and John Paul Stevens were searching for an errant shot that had gone into hiding under a desk.

Though Brennan did not leave his chambers often, he kept up a steady stream of memos when he was working on an opinion. All through the fall and winter, despite his gallbladder operation, he tried to find a formula that would persuade Kennedy to join him on the *Patterson* case. After the October reargument, Kennedy had agreed that because of history and precedent, the old Civil Rights Act of 1866 should be applied to private as well as government discrimination. At first, that seemed to be the major issue in the case. The Rehnquist Court would not, after all, scrap the precedents that applied the law to private schools and private businesses. That alone, however, did not resolve the case of Brenda Patterson and her claim of "racial harassment" on the job. Kennedy said he had been uncertain how to draw a line. Surely the Congress of 1866 did not intend that one uncouth comment by a supervisor would be enough to subject a company to a large damage suit, but where could a line be drawn?

Brennan had drafted an opinion that would allow victims of on-the-job racial harassment to sue their employers if the harassment was "severe or pervasive." A black person's right to "make and enforce contracts" free of racial discrimination surely means that a white employer may not mistreat black employees once they have been hired, he insisted. Indeed, the

Reagan administration's Justice Department had taken a similar view when the *Patterson* case was first heard. (After much internal bickering, the Administration had taken no position in October 1988, when the case was reargued.)

Kennedy remained unconvinced, nonetheless. In his view, Brennan was trying to stretch the law beyond its words. The more he struggled with the issue, the more Kennedy was persuaded that the Court should stick to a strict, literal reading of the law. If a black person was refused a job because of his or her race, that employee was denied the "same right" as whites "to make and enforce a contract." However, racial harassment on the job, while repugnant, did not deny that person the same right to make and enforce a contract, or so Kennedy concluded.

The clerks in Brennan's chambers blamed their counterparts in Kennedy's office for his stiff approach to Patterson's case. The new justice had surrounded himself with young conservative clerks, they said. He was also close to Scalia. In their view, Kennedy could not bring himself to break with the conservatives and join Brennan in a major civil rights case.

Because the outcome hung on Kennedy's vote, the opinion was turned over to him in the spring. As a result, Brenda Patterson lost her case after all.

On June 15, Kennedy read from the bench what sounded to be a compromise decision in *Patterson* v. *McLean Credit*. First, he said that the Court would uphold its past rulings which extended the 1866 law to racial discrimination by private employers. This doctrine "is entirely consistent with our society's deep commitment to the eradication of discrimination based on a person's race or the color of his or her skin," Kennedy said. All nine justices ended up agreeing on this point.

However, Kennedy continued, the five conservatives would not agree to extend the law to cover racial harassment on the job. Brenda Patterson's supervisor had called blacks "slower" than whites and looked over her shoulder constantly, she had claimed. If true, "this type of conduct [is] reprehensible," Kennedy said, but it does not violate the terms of the 1866 law. Patterson was not denied the right to "make and enforce a contract" because of her race, so she cannot claim her rights were violated under this law. Parenthetically, he noted that the 1964 Civil Rights Act would prohibit an employer from engaging in racial harassment on the job, but that newer law does not give employees the right to seek damages from the company. Under the 1964 law, Brenda Patterson could have gone before a federal judge and won a court order telling her supervisor to stop harassing her—hardly a powerful remedy or deterrent, according to the civil rights lawyers.

Kennedy concluded with words of reassurance. "Discrimination based on the color of one's skin is a profound wrong of tragic dimension," Kennedy said. "Neither our words nor our decisions should be interpreted as signaling one inch of retreat" from the nation's commitment to eradicating racial bias, he said.

Brennan said he was chagrined and puzzled by Kennedy. How could he say the Court had not retreated "one inch" on ending racial discrimination, while refusing to go along with an opinion making illegal racial harassment that was "severe and pervasive"? The senior liberal filed a dissent that was joined by Marshall, Blackmun, and Stevens.

Was the *Patterson* ruling a victory or a defeat for the civil rights advocates? After all, the Court upheld the *Runyon* ruling that extended the old law to private conduct. However, it also refused to extend it to on-the-job racial harassment.

The civil rights lawyers in Washington wasted no time in pondering that question. Within hours after the opinion was released, they branded the outcome another devastating defeat for civil rights. The Rehnquist Court had dealt another blow to fairness in the workplace, they said. Penda Hair, the NAACP LDF lawyer who represented Patterson, called Kennedy's opinion an "underhanded way to erode a settled civil rights law. We're left with a shell of a law," she said. Ralph Neas, the executive director of the Leadership Conference on Civil Rights, pointed to the string of recent reversals. "We've lost more in two-and-a-half weeks than we had in the previous two-and-a-half decades," he said.

In the Senate, Edward Kennedy denounced the Court for "its fourth decision in 11 days," which dealt a "significant setback to civil rights law." He referred to the decisions in *Wards Cove* v. *Atonio*, *Martin* v. *Wilks*, and *Lorance* v. *AT&T*, in addition to the *Patterson* case. Because the rulings interpreted federal law, Congress could reverse the decisions by rewriting the law. Now that the Court had spoken, the battle over civil rights and job discrimination moved across First Street to the Capitol. "Congress must not let these decisions stand," Kennedy said.

During first two weeks of June, the drumbeat of civil rights rulings drew attention to the new, more conservative Supreme Court, but the Court shared the spotlight with news of events in China. On June 4, 1989, the Chinese Army had been sent into Beijing's Tiananmen Square and had crushed the democracy movement with its tanks. A new wave of repression gripped China as protest leaders were rounded up. On June 21, three young men in Shanghai were publicly executed, the first state killings since the crackdown in Beijing.

That same day, the Court announced that the U.S. Constitution protected the right of a protester to publicly burn an American flag. In a weak, gravelly voice, the Court's 83-year-old liberal leader spoke for a 5–4 majority. The opinion was vintage Brennan.

"If there is a bedrock principle underlying the First Amendment, it is that the Government may not prohibit the expression of an idea simply because society finds the idea offensive or disagreeable," he said. "To paraphrase Justice Holmes, we submit that nobody can suppose that this gesture of an unknown man will change our nation's attitude toward the flag. We are tempted to say, in fact, that the flag's deservedly cherished place in our community will be strengthened, not weakened by our holding today. Our decision is reaffirmation of the principles of freedom and inclusiveness that the flag best reflects, and of the conviction that our toleration of criticism such as Johnson's is a sign and source of our strength. It is the nation's resilience, not its rigidity, that Texas sees reflected in the flag—and it is that resilience that we reassert today."

As Brennan read on, Rehnquist sat back in his chair and glared at him in silence. In his written dissent, the chief justice skewered Brennan for what he called a "regrettably patronizing civics lesson," though much of Rehnquist's dissent also read like a schoolboy's history lesson. He quoted Ralph Waldo Emerson's "Concord Hymn" and reprinted Francis Scott Key's "Star Spangled Banner" and John Greenleaf Whittier's Civil War poem "Barbara Frietchie." He told the history of the U.S. flag and its many alterations over the years, its role in war and peace, in literature and song, in death and life.

"The flag is not simply another 'idea' or 'point of view' competing for recognition in the marketplace of ideas," Rehnquist wrote. "Millions and millions regard it with an almost mystical reverence regardless of what social, political or philosophical beliefs they may have," he wrote. Rehnquist obviously put himself among those "millions and millions." In his view, the flag stood outside—or perhaps, above—the clash of free speech in a democracy. White and O'Connor joined Rehnquist's dissent.

Stevens shared Rehnquist's view but read a separate, emotional dissent from the bench. He spoke of the Marines on Iwo Jima and Omaha Beach who fought and died to protect the flag. He spoke with force and conviction, although his legal analysis sounded curious at some points. The First Amendment does not protect an individual's right to "paint graffiti on the Lincoln Memorial," Stevens argued. This was unquestionably correct; no one had a right to deface government property. However, suppose that a person built a clay model of the Lincoln Memorial and then destroyed it. Could that person be jailed for destroying "a national monument"? If persons could be jailed for burning their own flags, they could, by the same logic, be jailed for destroying their own replicas of the Lincoln Memorial.

Scalia and Kennedy had supplied the crucial votes. While Kennedy joined Brennan's opinion, he added a brief concurring statement. "The hard fact is that sometimes we must make decisions that we do not like," he said. "We make them because they are right, right in the sense that the law and the Constitution, as we see them, compel the result. . . . It is poignant but fundamental that the flag protects those who hold it in contempt." Scalia conveyed an eloquent message of his own—by saying nothing. He simply signed on to Brennan's opinion, along with Marshall and Blackmun.

The final decision in *Texas* v. *Johnson* set off political fireworks, which caught Brennan and the other justices by surprise. After thinking it over a few days, President Bush announced that the decision had struck him viscerally. He proposed an amendment to the Constitution to protect the flag. Congress was in an uproar, too. Those members who were not already angry at the Court for its civil rights rulings were now upset over the flag-burning ruling.

Still, the ruling showed that the First Amendment and the principle of freedom of speech retained its special luster at the Court. The flag itself was a symbol, and the Court's ruling stood as a symbol of its willingness to protect radical, nonviolent dissent.

On the same day as the flag ruling, on a 6–3 vote, the justices also reversed a $100,000 judgment against a Jacksonville, Florida, weekly newspaper, which had mistakenly printed a rape victim's name, in violation of state law. A police officer had given out the woman's name by mistake to a newspaper intern, who in turn put it into print in violation of the paper's policy. Nonetheless, in *Florida Star* v. *B.J.F.*, the Court ruled that the First Amendment's protection of the free press forbids punishing a newspaper for printing "truthful information" that was "lawfully obtained." Brennan, Marshall, Blackmun, Stevens, Scalia, and Kennedy formed the majority; White, Rehnquist, and O'Connor dissented.

Two days after the flag ruling, the Court unanimously struck down part of a 1988 federal law that forbade telephone companies from carrying sexually explicit messages. The so-called dial-a-porn business boomed in the early 1980s, much to the irritation of millions of parents who were shocked when they received their phone bills. In response, Congress passed a law ordering telephone companies to stop carrying messages that were "indecent." The Justice Department defended the law on the grounds that it would protect children.

In the interim, however, the telephone companies had devised new techniques to allow households to block the dialing of these for-pay messages. When the test case of *Sable Communications* v. *Federal Communications Commission* reached the Court, the justices concluded that the issue involved whether the government could regulate the phone conversations of two consenting adults. On that basis, the Court struck down the law as a violation of the First Amendment.

The death penalty cases that had been heard during the winter were finally ready to be released on June 26. The outcome figured to depend on Kennedy and O'Connor. With the exception of the flag case, Kennedy had proven to be reliably conservative, and he joined the chief justice in voting to allow the execution of killers who were mentally retarded or juveniles. For most conservatives, the death penalty did not raise a difficult issue. In their view, the Constitution as written clearly permitted capital punishment. Therefore, the decision to impose the death penalty rested with state lawmakers, state judges, and juries, they said.

For O'Connor, however, the cases involving juveniles and the retarded were difficult ones. They raised questions of jus-

tice and fairness. While the Constitution allowed capital punishment, it also prohibited punishments that were "cruel and
unusual." The Court's decision as to whether 16-year-olds or
mentally retarded killers could be executed rested entirely
with her. The year before, she had agonized for months over
whether to permit the execution of a 15-year-old murderer
from Oklahoma. When she finally refused to do so, Scalia fired
off a dissent aimed directly at her. He lambasted her opinion
as illogical and confused.

On matters of crime and punishment, O'Connor was no
soft-hearted liberal. As a trial judge, she handed out stiff sentences to convicted criminals. As a justice, she also sought to
defer to the judgment of state lawmakers. In her view, the
liberal-dominated Court had been cavalier in deciding matters
that should have been left to state legislators. Brennan and
Marshall carried little weight among the other justices on the
death penalty. They opposed all death sentences all the time.

Moreover, in O'Connor's view, the liberals tried to have
it both ways when the death penalty was debated. During the
1970s, they struck down laws that imposed a mandatory death
sentence for crimes such as murdering a police officer. They
said juries must be permitted to weigh the evidence in each
case and impose a punishment appropriate for that individual.
Now, they wanted to turn that argument around and say that
juries may not be permitted to decide whether some individuals, such as a juvenile murderer, may be sent to death. A jury
in Texas had considered the evidence in Johnny Penry's case
and had sentenced him to death. A jury in Missouri had done
the same in the case of 16-year-old Heath Wilkins, yet the
liberals were now insisting that these decisions should be taken
out of a jury's hands.

After long deliberation, O'Connor would not go along
with the liberals. Presumably, most juries would not impose
the ultimate punishment on a 16-year-old killer, but O'Connor
did not believe that the Constitution absolutely prohibited such
a sentence in all instances. She voted with Rehnquist and the
conservatives to uphold the death sentences for 16-year-old
Heath Wilkins and 17-year-old Kevin Stanford.

The notion of executing a juvenile might cause some
judges, such as Justice O'Connor, to flinch, or at least to show
some discomfort, but not Scalia. With undisguised zeal, he
wrote the 5–4 opinion upholding the two death sentences.
"The punishment is either 'cruel AND unusual' or it is not,"

he said. According to a recent study, 126 persons under age 17 had been put to death in American history, which suggests, he said, that such punishment is not unusual, even though some may consider it cruel.

He also dismissed what he labeled the "socioscientific and ethicoscientific evidence" that had been furnished by human rights groups. So what if learned societies find the death penalty abominable or European governments oppose it? State lawmakers, reflecting the popular will, wrote the death penalty into law. He continued, "The audience for these arguments [against the death penalty] is not this Court, but the citizenry of the United States. It is they, not we, who must be persuaded," Scalia said.

Ronald Reagan had promised his justices would practice "judicial restraint." No better example could be found than Scalia's opinion in *Stanford* v. *Kentucky*. If state officials wanted to execute juvenile criminals, neither the Constitution nor the Supreme Court would stand in their way, Scalia asserted. In dissent, of course, were Brennan, Marshall, Blackmun, and Stevens.

While O'Connor signed on with the conservatives in the two juveniles' cases, she refused to go along entirely in the case of Johnny Penry, the mentally retarded murderer from Texas. Indeed, she voted with the liberals to overturn his death sentence because the jury instructions were unfair. Her opinion for the Court typified O'Connor's work: It was a long, careful dissection of all the issues, and it came to a middle-ground conclusion. Brennan, Marshall, Blackmun, and Stevens agreed with some passages. Rehnquist, White, Scalia, and Kennedy agreed with others.

She set forth two main conclusions. First, a person's "mental age" is not reason to take away the person's legal rights or responsibilities, whether to marry or to be punished for a crime. "Mental retardation is a factor that may well lessen a defendant's culpability for a capital offense. But we cannot conclude that the Eighth Amendment precludes the execution of any mentally retarded person of Penry's ability . . . simply by virtue of his mental retardation alone," she said. The conservatives signed on to this conclusion, allowing capital punishment for the retarded.

Second, however, a state must ensure that jurors carefully consider the evidence of a murderer's retardation. This "mitigating evidence" might cause them to sentence him to life in prison rather than death, and the Texas jurors did not have that opportunity, she said. They were told to send Penry to death if he posed a danger to society, which he surely did. O'Connor concluded that Penry deserved a new sentencing hearing, for jurors to consider whether his retardation "may diminish his culpability." Brennan, Marshall, Blackmun, and Stevens agreed with this result.

Scalia's opinion in *Stanford* v. *Kentucky* and O'Connor's in *Penry* v. *Texas* were read back to back on June 26. By a one-vote margin, the Rehnquist Court had upheld the death penalty for murderers who were under age 18 and for those who suffered mental retardation. Such punishments were not automatically "cruel and unusual," the Court said.

Since late May, rumors had gone back and forth on the abortion case. According to one story, the five conservatives planned to overturn *Roe* v. *Wade* so that they would be done with the issue. Better to do it now so that the impact on George Bush and the Republicans would be muted before the 1992 election, said the explanation that went along with this story. Others had "heard" nearly the opposite. Kennedy planned to stick with the abortion precedent and uphold the right to choose, it was said, even though he disagreed with the original ruling. Others said, with equal conviction, that they had been "told" that Sandra O'Connor was gravely ill with cancer, and nearly every week, the lawyers in the case heard rumors that the opinion would be released *this* week. O'Connor, who, during the spring, had kept up her round of speeches and meetings with visitors, assured everyone she was in good health. She also sounded like the one person unaffected by the rumors and the hype surrounding the *Webster* case. Without being indiscreet, she made it clear to visitors that the right to choose abortion would survive the case of *Webster* v. *Reproductive Health Services*.

The remaining question was, How would abortion rights survive? Would abortion remain a woman's "fundamental right" with legal power behind it, or would *Roe* survive only as a weak and dying precedent whose days were numbered? That decision still rested in O'Connor's hands.

The chief justice had drafted an opinion designed to appeal to her. It cited her earlier dissents criticizing Blackmun's trimester framework. Rehnquist's draft said it left "undisturbed" the "holding of *Roe*," which was that a state may not make all abortions a crime. Nonetheless, as the previous 16 years had shown, antiabortion lawmakers can devise many regulations that make it difficult for a woman to get an abortion. Under Rehnquist's draft, those regulations would now be upheld.

The bulk of Rehnquist's opinion dealt with the Missouri law. The justices had been asked to consider four provisions of that law, and Rehnquist disposed of the first three in an uncontroversial way. First, the law's preamble said that the Missouri legislature believes that "the life of each human being begins at conception" and that "unborn children have protectable interests in life, health and well-being." At first, this statement looked to be a key test of the Court's views. After a second look, however, the justices concluded that the preamble was legally meaningless. It was merely philosophy, not law. Because it had no legal effect, "We therefore need not pass on the constitutionality of the Act's preamble," Rehnquist said.

Second, the statute made it "unlawful for any public facility [such as a public hospital] to be used for the purpose of performing or assisting an abortion not necessary to save the life of the mother." The Court had already said the states need not subsidize or assist abortion, so this provision is constitutional, he concluded. A third provision of the law said neither "public funds" nor "public employees" may be involved in "encouraging or assisting" in abortion. This too figured at first to provoke a major dispute because it seemed to limit the free-speech rights of physicians who receive public funds. However, during the argument in April, Attorney General Webster said the law was directed at state officials who distribute money, not at physicians. By this interpretation, the law prohibited state officials from giving funds to doctors who are "encouraging or assisting" abortions, but it set no penalty for physicians who encouraged abortion. If that is all the law means, Rehnquist said, it is constitutional because the state need not subsidize abortion.

The fourth provision looked to be insignificant. It said, "Before a physician performs an abortion on a woman he has reason to believe is carrying an unborn child of 20 or more weeks gestational age, the physician shall first determine if the unborn child is viable by using and exercising that degree of care, skill and proficiency commonly exercised by the ordinarily skillful, careful and prudent physician. . . . In making this determination of viability, the physician shall perform or cause to be performed such medical examination and tests as are necessary to make a finding of the gestational age, weight and lung maturity of the unborn child."

Missouri lawmakers had wanted to make sure that no "viable" fetus suffered abortion. The *Roe* ruling itself permitted the state to forbid abortions of fetuses that were "viable," or capable of living outside their mother's womb, which occurs after the twenty-fourth week of a pregnancy. The Missouri legislature wanted to prevent any mistakes. Often, women are not certain when they became pregnant. A woman with a viable fetus of 24 weeks may think she is only 20 weeks pregnant. The 1986 law put doctors on notice to be cautious.

What exactly did this provision demand of physicians? Did it simply require that they should use their medical judgment in deciding whether the fetus was viable, or did the law also require that they perform tests of the fetus's age, weight, and lung maturity, in order to be sure? The appeals court in St. Louis took the latter view. It said that the law meant that physicians "must perform" these tests, which cost up to $250 and can pose a health risk to both the woman and the fetus. Because this regulation imposes a severe burden on a woman during her second trimester, it is unconstitutional under *Roe* v. *Wade*, the appeals court said.

Rehnquist, however, read the two-line provision differently. He insisted that it requires a doctor only to perform tests that are "necessary" in his best judgment, and that requirement is reasonable and certainly constitutional, he concluded. The chief justice could have stopped right there. The appeals court ruling would have been reversed, the state law upheld, and the case finished. If he had done so, however, the *Webster* case would have accomplished nothing. Rehnquist and White wanted to scrap Blackmun's trimester scheme, and this was their chance to do so.

"We think that the doubt cast upon the Missouri statute" because its regulation touched upon the second trimester "is not so much a flaw in the statute as it is a reflection of the fact that the rigid trimester analysis . . . enunciated in *Roe* has resulted . . . in making constitutional law in this area a virtual Procrustean bed," Rehnquist said. The Court had not hesitated to overrule "a prior construction of the Constitution that has proved to be unsound in principle and unworkable in practice.

We think the *Roe* trimester framework falls in that category,"
Rehnquist wrote.

Rehnquist made it clear that he was overturning Blackmun's opinion in the *Roe* case, not the Court's ruling that struck
down a Texas law making all abortions a crime. The basic right
to choose abortion would remain "undisturbed," he said.

"There is no doubt that our holding today will allow some
governmental regulation of abortion that would have been prohibited under the language of [earlier] cases. But the goal of
constitutional adjudication is surely not to remove inexorably
'political divisive' issues from the ambit of the legislative process, whereby the people through their elected representatives
deal with matters of concern to them," he wrote.

The Rehnquist draft did just what O'Connor had suggested before. It would allow states to regulate abortion.
Antiabortion lawmakers would see it as an opening to enact
new regulations that would make abortion more difficult and
more unpleasant for women, but the draft did not overturn
Roe entirely or allow abortion to be made a crime. The chief
justice sent his opinion to O'Connor, confident she would sign
on to it.

All spring long, O'Connor had heard from thousands of
women who feared that the *Roe* decision would be overturned
and that pregnant women would suffer indignity, discomfort,
and even death from self-administered abortions. There were
many mere "regulations" that could prove oppressive. For example, some had suggested that a medical board might be given
the authority to approve abortions. Before deciding, its members could interrogate women to learn their reasons for seeking
abortions. It was the kind of regulation that could strip women
of their dignity as well as of the control of their lives. In meetings with women and conversations with friends, O'Connor
assured them that the *Webster* case was not the end of the right
to abortion. It posed relatively minor issues, really, she said,
ones that could be resolved without a great change in the law.

Rehnquist's draft, however, would make for a great
change in the law. It would invite the states to try out new
regulations designed to protect "potential human life," as he
said at one point, and none of that was necessary to resolve the
Missouri case. Why unsettle the law, and millions of American
women, if there were no need to do so? After considering the
draft for several weeks, O'Connor surprised the chief justice

by telling him that she would not sign on to his opinion. Instead, she said she would write a separate concurring opinion.

In a cautious, lawyerly way, she agreed that each of the provisions in Missouri's law should be upheld. They did not pose "an undue burden" on pregnant women. She agreed with Rehnquist that the provision calling for prudent tests to see whether a fetus was viable can be upheld under earlier decisions—and that should be the end of the matter. "There is no necessity to accept the state's invitation to reexamine the constitutional validity of *Roe v. Wade*" and its trimester framework, she wrote. If the Missouri law is constitutional under earlier rulings, why go back and revise those earlier rulings?

"When the constitutional invalidity of a state's abortion statute actually turns on the constitutional validity of *Roe* v. *Wade*," O'Connor wrote, "there will be time enough to reexamine *Roe*. And do so carefully," she added. That was all she would say about *Roe* in the *Webster* case.

Because of O'Connor's defection, Rehnquist was without a majority for the key portion of his opinion. Without her, his was a plurality opinion that did not have the full force of law. As a legal matter, Rehnquist's opinion decided very little. The majority on the Court—made up of Rehnquist, White, Scalia, Kennedy, and O'Connor—had simply agreed that states may refuse to offer routine abortions in their public hospitals, hardly a surprise.

Scalia was furious. O'Connor had done it again. Just like the year before with the 15-year-old murderer, she had delayed and delayed, tested the political wind, and then refused to decide. Where O'Connor thought she was being prudent, Scalia thought she was being political. Her nondecision just prolonged this abortion business, he complained. She had turned the *Webster* case into a trivial one. Not only would the right to abortion stand, but so would Blackmun's opinion. Scalia considered the original decision an abomination, as bad as the *Weber* decision allowing affirmative action. Like Bork, he believed that *Roe v. Wade* was an unconstitutional decision, a political rewriting of the nation's laws, not an interpretation of the Constitution. He wanted it overturned as soon as possible, but Scalia had been willing to go along with Rehnquist's halfway opinion because at least it would have swept away Blackmun's trimester scheme. The chief's opinion called the basic abortion right into question, too, speeding the day when it would be overturned entirely; but now, Rehnquist's opinion was legally meaningless.

White and Kennedy signed on to Rehnquist's opinion, but Scalia refused. Instead, he sat down at his computer and vented his anger. He called O'Connor's refusal to decide the broader issues "perverse" and "irrational" and said her reasons for sticking to a narrow decision "cannot be taken seriously."

"The outcome of today's case will doubtless be heralded as a triumph of judicial statesmanship," Scalia wrote. "It is not that, unless it is statesmanlike to prolong this Court's self-awarded sovereignty over a field where it has little proper business. . . . We can now look forward to at least another Term with carts full of mail from the public, and streets full of demonstrators, urging us—their unelected and life-tenured judges who have been awarded those extraordinary, undemocratic characteristics precisely in order that we might follow the law despite the popular will—to follow the popular will." The fact that millions of Americans believed that the Constitution did indeed protect the right to abortion was evidence to Scalia that the issue was political, not legal. He concluded, "It thus appears that the mansion of constitutionalized abortion-law, constructed overnight in *Roe* v. *Wade*, must be disassembled doorjamb by doorjamb, and never entirely brought down, no matter how wrong it may be."

Though he vehemently denounced the "right to abortion," Scalia did not advocate in its place a "right to life," nor did he despair of the "unborn child." Many attributed Scalia's fierce denunciation of *Roe* to a Catholic's animus toward abortion. While that may be so, Scalia did not propose to make abortion illegal. Like Rehnquist, he wanted the decision left to state lawmakers. Even if Roe were overturned, many states would permit abortion. Also, if Catholicism explained Scalia's views, his record was spotty that spring. The Catholic bishops had also urged the Court to end the death penalty for juveniles, but Scalia was nearly as vehement in upholding the states' power to impose capital punishment as he was insistent that the states retain the power to ban abortion. In both cases, he was joined by fellow Catholic Anthony Kennedy.

Harry Blackmun had been gloomy all year, and Rehnquist's draft opinion confirmed his worst fears. The conservatives, without saying so directly, intended to overturn *Roe* v. *Wade*. As much as he tried to deny it, *Roe* was the essence of his career on the Court, the high point of his working life. It would be his epitaph and the first line of his obituary. When he interviewed new clerks, he would mention in an offhand way that he had written the *Roe* v. *Wade* opinion several years back. Some saw it as a shy man's way of bringing up the subject of abortion and his strongly held convictions. Others saw it as evidence he was a bit odd. What law graduate in America did not know that Harry Blackmun wrote the *Roe* opinion? Rehnquist's draft did not say directly that it was overruling *Roe* v. *Wade*, but that was its intent, Blackmun believed, and he meant to sound the alarm: "I fear for the future. I fear for the liberty and equality of millions of women who have lived and come of age in the 16 years since *Roe* was decided," he wrote. "I fear for the integrity of, and public esteem for, this Court."

Blackmun had drafted his dissent in response to Rehnquist's draft, but O'Connor's decision surprised him, just as it had Scalia and Rehnquist. He found himself with a dissent that attacked an opinion that no longer spoke for a true majority.

Rehnquist had planned to have the *Webster* decision out by the last days of June so that the Court could recess for the summer. However, first Scalia and then Blackmun said they needed more time at the computer: Scalia to denounce the Court for doing nothing, and Blackmun to denounce it for doing far too much. Blackmun faced something of a dilemma. In legal terms, the Court had done little. But it was clear *Roe* v. *Wade* no longer had the support of five justices. The right to abortion now hung by only a thread. The next case could finish it off, and certainly the addition of another conservative vote would do so: "Although the Court extricates itself from this case without making a single, even incremental, change in the law of abortion," Blackmun wrote in his revised dissent, "a plurality of this Court implicitly invites every state legislature to enact more and more restrictive regulations."

Day after day through late June, there were rumors that the *Webster* decision was ready to come down. The Court announces in advance only that the justices will be on the bench on certain days of the week. What decisions will be released is kept secret. Finally, on the last Friday of June, Blackmun's revised dissent was complete. He told the chief justice he wanted to read a portion of it from the bench. The *Webster* decision and the dissent would be released on Monday, July 3.

Rehnquist and Blackmun were not the only ones who were preparing their lines, however. Nor were theirs the lines that would be best remembered. For weeks, the interest groups on both sides of the national abortion battle had been formulating their reaction. Unlike the members of the Court, they were in the business of politics and public relations.

Throughout June, civil rights advocates had reacted quickly and ferociously to each of the Court's job-discrimination rulings. Their powerful denunciations often carried more weight than the words used by the justices in their opinions. While the Bush administration tried to say that the job-discrimination rulings were mere technical revisions in the law, the civil rights lobby shouted out the message that fairness and equal rights had been dealt a punishing blow—and that message stuck.

The prochoice and right-to-life groups were determined to do the same with the *Webster* case. Their reaction to the ruling would be heard more clearly than the words spoken by the Court. "Spin control" had come to the Court as well as to national politics.

Though the two sides in the abortion fight usually agreed on nothing, they had a similar message to convey from the *Webster* case. NARAL and its executive director, Kate Michelman, had become convinced that the abortion battle must be won in the political arena. The Rehnquist Court would not protect the right to abortion. *Roe* v. *Wade* may not be overturned in the *Webster* case, but it would go eventually unless the political momentum was changed. Without prochoice majorities in the state legislatures and a prochoice president in the White House, the right to abortion would soon be gone, she said. For weeks prior to the release of the *Webster* decision, Michelman knew what her message would be. Unless, she said, the justices strongly reaffirmed *Roe*—which no one expected—Michelman would say directly into the TV cameras that the abortion battle has moved from the courts into the political arena.

For years, right-to-life advocates had been pushing state legislators to regulate and restrict abortion, but many lawmakers responded that the Court had tied their hands. The National Right to Life Committee wanted to get out the message that the *Webster* decision had untied their hands. Without the tight restrictions of Blackmun's *Roe* opinion, abortion could be restricted by law. Abortion would move into the political arena again, the right-to-lifers said.

On the morning of July 3, the justices announced that they would release their final two decisions of the 1988–1989 term. The mood in the courtroom was tense and subdued, in contrast to the circus atmosphere outside, where scores of cameras and microphones were there to record the clashes—physical as well as verbal—between the opposing groups of abortion activists.

Rehnquist said first that Blackmun would deliver the opinion in *Allegheny County* v. *ACLU,* the creche case. The decision sounded like a mockery of the Court's rulings on religion. Asked to decide a straightforward question, the justices came up with a splintered ruling that seemed to make no sense. A menorah could stand tall in front of the city–county building, but a creche could not stand on the steps inside. "You need a scorecard" to figure out how the justices vote, Blackmun joked.

From the bench, he sought to explain the decision. The creche in the city hall was a solely religious display. "The government may acknowledge Christmas as a cultural phenomenon, but under the First Amendment it may not observe it as a Christian holy day by suggesting that people praise God for the birth of Jesus," said Blackmun, who was active in the Methodist church. By contrast, the Christmas tree is not strictly religious and symbolizes the winter holiday. Therefore, Pittsburgh's tree in front of its government buildings does not unconstitutionally promote religion, he said. He described the menorah as a "closer constitutional question" because it had both religious and cultural significance. Because city officials displayed the Christmas tree and the menorah together, "it would be a form of religious discrimination against Jews to allow Pittsburgh to celebrate Christmas as a cultural tradition while simultaneously disallowing the city's acknowledgement of Chanukah," Blackmun said. The creche must come down, but the tree and the menorah can stand, he concluded.

A close reading of the many opinions in the case showed that O'Connor still held the balance on the role of religion in public life. Brennan, Marshall, and Stevens insisted on a strict separation of church and state; they would have disallowed even the Christmas tree. Rehnquist and the conservatives would have permitted a purely religious display in the city hall. O'Connor's middle position prevailed. If a government action appeared to "endorse" religion, it was unconstitutional, she said.

Among First Amendment lawyers and Justice Department officials, the most significant words in the Pittsburgh case were written in dissent by Anthony Kennedy. In a sharp, angry opin-

ion joined by Rehnquist, White, and Scalia, he accused the
majority of "an unjustified hostility toward religion." Kennedy
also proposed a radically new approach. In his view, the government may "aid" or show "support for religion" so long as
it does "not coerce anyone" to give money or force them to
participate in religious activities. It was not clear how far Kennedy would go, but his dissent suggested he would allow government aid to parochial schools and organized prayer in the
public schools.

Through his first full year on the Court, Kennedy had
made his mark by quietly voting with Rehnquist. His only significant split from the chief justice came in the flag-burning
case, where he joined Scalia in the majority. Kennedy had not
written majority or dissenting opinions showing that he had
strong, distinctive views on the law, or at least not ones that
differed much from the status quo. Religion, as it turned out,
was another matter. Around the conference table, Kennedy had
complained about the Court's hostility toward religion and
irked several of his colleagues in the process. For years, many
conservatives had viewed the Court's ban on school prayer and
Bible reading as evidence of an antireligious bias among the
liberals. Kennedy appeared to share that view. Blackmun, in
his majority opinion, shot back at Kennedy, labeling his accusations "as offensive as they are absurd."

Still, in his dissent in the creche case, Kennedy had staked
out a powerful new position on religion. With one more conservative vote, it could become the law. If so, the "wall of
separation between church and state" would be knocked down
and replaced with what Kennedy called "government policies
of accommodation, acknowledgement and support for religion."

With the creche case disposed of, Rehnquist announced
he would deliver the opinion in *Webster* v. *Reproductive Health
Services*. Blackmun was set to follow him with a scathing denunciation of the Court, and Rehnquist was not happy with the
tone of Blackmun's dissent. He was playing to the crowd again.
In Rehnquist's view, Blackmun's was a political message, not
a legal dissent. In a partial response, the chief justice added a
final paragraph to his opinion, responding to Blackmun's suggestion that the days of back-alley abortions may return.

The notion "that legislative bodies, in a Nation where
more than half of our population is women, will treat our decision today as an invitation to enact abortion regulation rem-

iniscent of the dark ages not only misreads our views but does scant justice to those who serve in such bodies and the people who elect them," Rehnquist said from the bench.

When the chief justice finished, he nodded toward Blackmun. Speaking in a deep, almost disembodied voice, Blackmun sounded as ominous as his message. He accused Rehnquist of having written a "deceptive" opinion, which claims to do little but in fact "is filled with winks and nods and knowing glances to those who would do away with *Roe* explicitly." He concluded, "For today, the women of this nation still retain the liberty to control their destinies. But the signs are evident and very ominous, and a chill wind blows."

On that note, the marshal banged his gavel, and the justices recessed for the summer.

Outside on the Court steps, before the justices had finished reading the final words of the opinion, the abortion activists began telling the cameras what the Court decided and what it meant.

"We are at war," said Molly Yard, then-president of NOW (National Organization for Women). NARAL's Michelman said, "We have awakened the sleeping giant, and today we begin mobilizing that giant for the battles that lie ahead." Right-to-life activists said lawmakers in the states will be put on the spot and pressed to restrict abortion. "They're not going to be able to hide," said Burke Balch, state legislator coordinator for the National Right to Life Committee. By the end of the day, their message was heard clearly. The states can now regulate abortion. The battle has moved to the political arena.

It had been a historic term, a watershed year for the Court. Long-time observers of the Court could not recall a term when the justices had so clearly changed direction on so many vital areas of law. On affirmative action, civil rights, abortion, and the death penalty, the conservatives had taken charge. On religion, Rehnquist needed only one more vote to scrap the "separation of church and state" doctrine. Another vote would also be enough to finally overturn *Roe* v. *Wade*.

It had taken 20 years, from Richard Nixon's election in 1968 to Anthony Kennedy's ascension in 1988, but the conservatives had finally succeeded in capturing control of the high court. The fierce battle over Robert Bork's confirmation two years earlier showed that both sides knew what was at stake in the struggle over the ninth seat. The generation that grew up after World War II had never known a truly conservative high court. The liberal activists who fought Bork realized that Lewis Powell's replacement could tip the Court sharply to the right. They won the battle over Bork, but it now appeared they had lost the war. So far, the mild-mannered Anthony Kennedy proved to be just what the conservatives needed. He had proven to be a steady, reliable ally of the right.

With rare exceptions, Kennedy did not rage at the liberals as Bork would have. Indeed, Kennedy saw himself as something of a middle-of-the-road justice, certainly not an ideologue. "It's easier to be a Rehnquist or a Scalia than a Kennedy," he once commented. In conversation with his clerks, he often sounded receptive to the liberal argument in a particular case, but at the conference table, he was no middle-of-the-roader. Week after week, on major cases and minor ones, he cast his votes with those on the right. Because of Kennedy, the right side was now the winning side. In his first full term, Kennedy voted with the chief justice in 92 percent of the 143 cases decided by written opinions. Only O'Connor was more consistent, siding with Rehnquist 93 percent of the time, but this statistic was misleading in her case. For example, in the *Webster* case, she voted with Rehnquist to uphold the state law but disagreed with his opinion. Kennedy rarely carved out a different position from the chief justice. Combined with White (who voted 88 percent of the time with Rehnquist) and Scalia (82 percent), the chief justice usually had at least a five-vote majority.

On the left, Brennan could no longer always count on even four votes. He could rely on Marshall (who joined him in 94 percent of the cases during the 1988–1989 term), but Blackmun (78 percent) and Stevens (72 percent) were not faithful liberals in crime cases. In the close cases, it was now Rehnquist who could "count to five." Of the 33 cases that year where the Court split 5–4, the chief justice won 27.

While the new justice had been a pleasant surprise to the Justice Department and to Rehnquist, he was not viewed so favorably by some at the court, especially the clerks who worked for the more liberal justices. They portrayed him as a mediocre figure without clear views or a strong backbone. Rather than think through his positions, he simply followed Rehnquist and Scalia, they said. "He's clerk-driven," said one clerk, an accusation that was considered a stinging rebuke. According to this assessment, the conservative young law clerks who surrounded him had pushed him along a straight and narrow path on the right. Even some of the justices appeared to give Kennedy low marks. When asked about Kennedy, one replied, "I understand he gives very good speeches." Still, many of those who voiced the sharpest criticisms of the new justice would probably have spoken well of him had he thoughtlessly joined Brennan and Marshall on occasion.

It was also dangerous to make a firm early assessment of any new member of the Court. Even experienced judges who ascended to the high court said it took them three to five years to get on top of the work. Harry Blackmun spent his first years on the Court acting as a clone of his old friend Warren Burger. In her first years, Sandra O'Connor said she had a hard time just keeping up with the work, let alone making a new or original contribution to the development of the law. In both instances, an in-depth assessment of justices Blackmun and O'Connor would have come to far different conclusions after their tenth year of service, as compared to their second year.

Despite his detractors' remarks, no one could doubt Kennedy had made a mark. Because of him, the chief justice had a working majority. Rehnquist now loomed large over the law. With Kennedy's vote, he had taken firm control of the Court. He was unquestionably its dominant member and probably the most powerful figure in American law since Earl Warren retired in 1969. Rehnquist himself would be the last to acknowledge his influence. In conversation and in speeches, he played down the power of the chief justice. The other justices are not his subordinates, he insisted. They need not follow his lead, and the chief has only one vote, his own.

Rehnquist's description of the chief justiceship aptly described the tenure of Warren Burger, his predecessor. Burger had one vote and little influence over his eight warring colleagues. Unlike Burger, however, Rehnquist had sketched out in his early years on the Court a distinct approach to constitutional law, one that he had followed faithfully over the years. The Bill of Rights does indeed protect individual liberties, he said, but it does not replace democratic government. Judges should not make the major decisions in America; that job is left to those who are elected by the people. The justices do not have "a roving commission to second-guess Congress, state legislatures, and state and federal administrative officers concerning what is best for the country," he said in a 1976 speech. Whether the issue was the drug testing of government employees, the execution of juvenile murderers, or a state's attempt to restrict abortion, Rehnquist could always be counted upon to furnish the same answer. He would vote to uphold the law and reject an individual's claim that his or her constitutional rights had been violated.

Rehnquist's views were not novel or original, but they were well defined. His ideological consistency shaped the new emerging conservative Court just as surely as Brennan's firm faith in the rights of individuals helped shape the Warren Court. In large measure, the ideology of the Rehnquist Court was the ideology of William Rehnquist.

There was one glaring exception to Rehnquist's usual hands-off approach of upholding laws and supporting the government—affirmative action. Repeatedly over the years, and without exception, he had voted to strike down laws—city, state, or federal—that gave preferences to blacks, Latinos, or women. In *Richmond* v. *Croson*, where the city council sought to set aside 30 percent of its new contracts for minorities, Rehnquist voted to strike down the law. Among the constitutional cases during the 1988–1989 term where the justices were divided, it marked the only time that Rehnquist voted against a government body.

The case of Birmingham firefighters had a similar result, although Rehnquist based his opinion on the federal rules of civil procedure rather than the Constitution. Those who claim their rights were violated usually had little success in the Rehnquist Court, but in the Richmond and Birmingham cases, white males claimed their rights were being denied—and they won. While Rehnquist's view of affirmative action was not odd in itself—many legal scholars and most Americans think that the Constitution forbids any distinctions based on race or gender—it is somewhat peculiar for a justice who normally upholds the government. Under Rehnquist's view of the Constitution, state officials may execute juveniles for murder, may arrest gays for engaging in homosexual acts in their own homes, and may prohibit women from getting abortions, but they may *not* give a preference to black students seeking admission to a state university.

On the other side of First Street, the Democrats in Congress were certainly convinced that right-wing politics drove the Rehnquist Court. While the Court's conservatives liked to say they faithfully interpreted the laws as written, those who wrote the laws did not agree. According to the Democrats, the Rehnquist Court got it wrong nearly every time in the civil rights cases. Nearly two-thirds of the members of the House and Senate were ready to overturn a half dozen of the Court's recent decisions on job discrimination. The lawmakers in Washington, and around the country, were probably pleased to see the Court go on a recess. What with the rulings on flag burning, civil rights, and abortion, the lawmakers had a busy summer ahead, thanks to the justices.

On the Thursday evening before the term ended, Rehnquist arranged a going-away party for the clerks, complete with beer, snack food, and printed songbooks. At the annual Christmas party, Rehnquist also led the singing of Christmas carols. One Court employee said her child, having attended several parties at the Court, was convinced that William Rehnquist was its musical director.

"He's an American original," one of his admiring clerks said of the chief justice. Rehnquist loved popular Broadway show tunes and patriotic songs and thought everyone should join in and sing along. It had been a tense and testy spring around the Court, and Rehnquist wanted to end it on a happy note. Most of the other justices made at least a brief appearance and circulated in the room. The beer helped break the tension, and so did the singing. The chief justice himself was in a jovial mood, and with good reason. He had never had a better term. He held no grudges either, as he led the chorus of "It's a Grand Old Flag."

PART SIX

The
1989–1990 Term

9

The Liberals' Last Surprise

O ctober is the time for Rehnquist to go searching for wa- gers. The chief justice likes to make small bets—$5 or so—on practically any contest, and October is the best time of the year for that. College and professional football are in mid- season, while the World Series brings out the betting instinct in nearly every sports fans. Rehnquist stops in the halls to place bets with Court employees, reporters, or fellow justices. In October of 1987, he pressed and cajoled a reluctant Harry Blackmun into wagering $5 on his hometown Minnesota Twins in the series—a bet that earned Blackmun $5.

Rehnquist was such an ordinary guy, Court employees said, such a welcome change from Burger. He would stop by to talk to the police officers on duty around the building, to chat about sports or to pay off a $5 bet from a weekend football game. When Burger had come walking by, employees said that they had ducked into their offices. "When he quit, it was, 'Ding dong, the Wicked Witch is dead,' " one said of Burger.

By contrast, Rehnquist does not seem to take himself too seriously. Nor does he limit his interests to the law and the Court. He reads widely in history, literature, and the law; he was at work on a biography of Samuel Chase, an early justice who was nearly impeached in 1805 for partisan politicking. Rehnquist said he found Chase to be an amusingly cantankerous character. A moment later, the chief justice might speak with amused curiosity about the latest Madonna video.

He likes to challenge his law clerks in trivia contests: Ge- ography, history, weather, and sports are his best subjects.

What state recorded the all-time lowest high temperature?
(Rhode Island.) Name the college with a fight song that begins
with the following sentences. Rehnquist might then jot down
five opening lines and stump the recent college graduates.
Name four professional sports teams with names that do not
end in "s." (Example: Utah Jazz.)

Rehnquist's betting interests explain an unusual photo that
appeared in the *Washington Post* on January 23, 1987. The day
before, antiabortion activists held their annual march to the
Court in heavy snow, and the *Post* photographer snapped Rehnquist and several clerks standing on the plaza as the marchers
went by. Was the conservative chief justice assessing the size
of the antiabortion demonstration? Hardly. When the snow had
begun the day before, Rehnquist, a World War II meteorologist,
had taken $5 bets among the justices on the depth of the ac-
cumulation by 10 A.M. With rulers in hand, several clerks and
the chief justice were there to settle the matter. "I sent my
law clerk out, too," Lewis Powell reported later, just to make
sure the measurements were honest.

In the photo, the chief and his clerks are also holding
tennis rackets. There is a simple explanation for that too. It
was Thursday. Every Thursday morning, Rehnquist and his
three law clerks piled into an old car and headed for the courts
in Potomac Park. All the justices are entitled to four law clerks,
but Rehnquist picks only three each year: just enough to fill a
doubles team. It had become a joke among the other chambers
that in hiring law clerks, Rehnquist looked for tennis players.
He could put up with a clerk who did not go to the finest law
school, whose academic record was short of superb, even one
whose political views were liberal, but the clerk had to be at
least competitive on the tennis court.

In his early years on the Court, Rehnquist and White often
joined the clerks to play basketball in the Court gym on the
fourth floor, which was known by all as the "highest court in
the land." However, once Rehnquist reached his mid-60s, he
confined his exercise to swimming and playing doubles in tennis. He had no speed on the baseline, clerks said, but he patrolled the net effectively. At six feet two inches, he used his
long reach to smash returns.

Rehnquist was a competitor and liked to win but did not
quite match Scalia on that score. The younger justice was absolutely relentless. He did not look like a tennis player; since
he quit jogging, he had gained weight in the middle. He made

up for it, however, with sheer competitiveness. Clerks who took him on often came away surprised. One clerk who fancied himself a first-rate tennis player had set up a singles match with Scalia but came back to the building stunned. "I can't believe I got beat by a 55-year-old fat Italian," he told his coclerks.

Rehnquist and Scalia were competitive at the Court too; neither liked to lose, as they had done so often during the 1986–1987 term. Since Powell's departure, however, the two conservatives rarely found themselves outvoted. Rehnquist in particular held a commanding position to reshape the law. As the fall term of 1989 got underway, the justices had before them a half dozen major cases covering abortion, affirmative action, criminal searches, and religion, as well as a new area for the justices: the "right to die."

The flag-burning case was coming back to the Court, too. In July, President Bush had sought a constitutional amendment to prohibit flag burning, but the Democratic Congress instead passed a revised federal law. The move deflected temporarily the outrage over the Court's decision. It would also give the majority justices a chance to reconsider their decision, knowing that the Constitution might be amended if they held fast.

The *Webster* case, decided in July, had made it clear that five justices were willing to uphold more state regulation of abortion. In November, the justices planned to consider the most common state regulatory law: a restriction on the rights of pregnant teenagers who sought abortions. About one million teenagers became pregnant each year, and studies estimated that 42 percent of those pregnancies end in abortion. In six cases over the previous 14 years, the justices had examined state laws that restricted the abortion rights of unmarried minors. Those decisions did not yield clear majority opinions, however, sowing confusion rather than clarity. Two principles, however, had been enunciated:

1. Parents had a legitimate interest in being involved in all matters affecting their daughter's life and welfare. In medical matters, this principle was especially well established. Doctors could not operate on any minor without the parents' permission.
2. No one, including a parent, can block a young woman's choice to end her pregnancy. The right to choose abortion established in *Roe* v. *Wade* left that final decision with the pregnant woman.

3. Obviously, these two principles can conflict. Ideally, the pregnant teenager and her parents could talk it over and decide what would be best, but if they disagree, whose rights should prevail: the girl's or her parents?

The Court's splintered rulings had been read to mean that states could not absolutely require a parent's "consent" before a teenager under the age of 18 had an abortion. What if the parents were drunks or child abusers, or if the pregnancy were the result of incest? For the same reasons, a law that absolutely required doctors to "notify" the parents of their daughter's plight was also deemed unconstitutional. Lewis Powell had suggested a compromise: States could require parents to be notified or to consent if they also gave the pregnant girl the option of going to a judge to get a waiver of this requirement. That way, the young girl from a miserable home could get an abortion in private. The judge should grant the waiver, Powell said, if the young woman appears "sufficiently mature" to make the decision on her own or if the judge concludes an abortion would be "in her best interests"

On paper, this so-called judicial bypass may have looked to be an appealing solution, but no one liked it in practice. Pregnant teenagers, parents, abortion counselors, and right-to-life advocates all criticized it. A pregnant teenager with alcoholic or abusive parents had enough problems without being required to explain herself in a courtroom. Nonetheless, 31 states had laws covering teenage abortions with the obligatory judicial bypass provision, though most went unused because of legal challenges. The ACLU (American Civil Liberties Union) had succeeded in blocking many of them before they went into effect by pointing out procedural flaws.

In Minnesota, however, the ACLU tried a different tactic: It stood back and let the law operate for five years. Its lawyers wanted to be able eventually to confront federal judges not with legal abstractions, but with the real-life stories. They were convinced that some of them—especially Justice Sandra O'Connor—might be moved by the reality of the law.

In 1981, Minnesota lawmakers decreed that a doctor who sees an unmarried minor under age 18 seeking an abortion must notify "both parents" and then wait at least 48 hours before performing the procedure. The statute had been drawn up by the state's leading antiabortion group, but what lawmaker could vote against a bill that required parents to be told of their daughter's problem? Over the next five years, about 7,000 teenage girls sought abortions, and half of them went to court seeking a waiver of the requirement that they notify "both parents"—meaning both biological parents. This included a man who had never married the mother or lived with her and her daughter as a family. A mother's consent alone was not sufficient to waive the requirement. Even if the mother and daughter had not seen the father in years, the law still required that he be told the news that his daughter is pregnant. The purpose of this requirement? The "fostering of parent–child relationships" and "promoting counsel to a child in a difficult and traumatic choice," state officials said.

Quite often, a young girl showed up at court with an angry mother to explain to a judge why they could not and would not notify a father who had not seen his daughter in years. After hearing their stories, judges routinely waived the notice requirement, but mothers and daughters still fumed at having to go through such a silly ordeal. The ACLU filed a suit against the law on behalf of Dr. Jane Hodgson, who had run an abortion clinic, and dozens of young women who had gone through the judicial bypass, many of whom testified during the trial or submitted affidavits to the court.

Heather P. had been 14 years old and pregnant when she and her mother were told they must go before a Hennepin County judge before Heather could have an abortion. Her memories of her father were dim, distant, and unpleasant. "They were divorced when I was five. He was an alcoholic and I remember him hitting my mother," she said in an interview. As she saw it, the law required her to tell "a strange man" about her pregnancy, but it gave her a choice of whom to tell: either her distant father or a black-robed judge. Her mother went along to appear before the judge. "She was mad," Heather recounted. "She thought the whole thing was stupid. It was my body and my decision. We didn't see why we needed this man's approval."

Heather at least had the advantage of living in the Minneapolis area. From all around the rural state, young pregnant girls traveled by car and bus to the Hennepin County courthouse to get permission to have an abortion. They refused to go to local judges, knowing the word would soon get around the community and back to their families. Moreover, abortions were hard to come by outside of the large cities. For these young pregnant teenagers hundreds of miles from the Twin

Cities, the law was more than a nuisance. For some, it made an abortion an impossibility.

Other young women recounted their stories with a simmering anger. Amy S., a University of Minnesota student at the time of the trial, had grown up in an upper-middle-class community and became pregnant during her senior year of high school. She thought the trip to the abortion clinic would be scary, but she was more frightened by what they told her there. If she wanted to keep the news from her mother and her ailing father, the 17-year-old would have to go downtown to explain her predicament to a judge. "It was the worst, most degrading thing I've ever gone through," she said. "To stand there in front of a judge, answering very personal questions. Everyone staring at you like you're some kind of criminal. It was awful."

During a five-week trial in 1986, U.S. District Judge Donald D. Alsop, a Nixon appointee, heard testimony from those who opposed the law, including counselors, psychologists, juvenile court judges, state attorneys, and dozens of young women. Allen Oleisky, a Hennepin County juvenile judge, had heard more than 1,000 waiver requests from teenagers and had become convinced that the law was a waste of everyone's time. The hallway outside his courtroom regularly held nervous teenage girls, some wearing cheerleader's outfits or band uniforms.

"You could see this was very stressful for the kids," he said. "They had to play all sorts of games. They lied to their parents and their friends to come down here. I can't see [that the law] did any good for anyone." In 99 of 100 cases, the judge simply approved the request. The only exceptions came when the teenager blurted out that she did not want an abortion, but her boyfriend or parent had insisted.

After hearing the evidence, Judge Alsop struck down the law as unconstitutional. It had "no beneficial effect" and served only as "traumatic distraction" for the pregnant teenagers, he said. In those families where mother, father, and daughter could discuss sensitive matters, they would, but the law applies to all families, and some do not fit the "Father Knows Best" image. Fewer than half of Minnesota's teenagers lived with both of their biological parents, he noted. "Notification of an abusive or even disinterested absent parent may reintroduce that parent's disruptive or unhelpful participation into the family at a time of acute stress," he wrote. His decision was affirmed by a three-judge panel of the U.S. Eighth Circuit Court of Appeals, Harry Blackmun's old court.

The full appeals court had changed since Blackmun's day, however. Ronald Reagan appointees now dominated, and they ordered a rehearing of the Minnesota case. With six Reagan judges making up the majority, the full appeals court reinstated the law. Parents have "significant interests . . . in the rearing and welfare of their children," the majority said, and "these interests are [not] contingent upon the parents having custody of the child." So long as the judicial bypass is available, the entire law is constitutional, the court said.

In the spring, when the *Webster* case was pending, the Supreme Court agreed to hear the case of *Hodgson v. Minnesota*. The argument was set for November 29. The case posed this question: Can a state require that "both parents" be notified of their daughter's pending abortion? Yes, noted the state, because parents have a right to know. No, asserted the ACLU, because the young woman's right to privacy sometimes outweighs the parent's right.

In their legal briefs, the state's attorneys contended that Minnesota should be permitted to require doctors to notify parents in all instances and without the option of getting a waiver from a judge. The ACLU attorneys said the Minnesota case showed that forcing teenagers to go to court had not worked to anyone's benefit. They wanted the law struck down entirely.

On the bench, only O'Connor seemed interested in the facts of the case. Her eight colleagues had already made up their minds. From the start, O'Connor honed in on the requirement that "both parents" be notified in all instances, a standard that was unique to Minnesota. The law "just doesn't provide for any exceptions," O'Connor complained. How could it be "in the best interest of the child," she asked, to force a young pregnant girl to talk with a father who had abused her or who had been absent for years?

John Tunheim, a deputy state attorney general, gamely defended the law, arguing that parents, even if separated or divorced, can "be very helpful to minors in a time of trauma." About 50 percent of the state's teenagers lived at home with both of their parents, he noted.

"Put another way, 50 percent do not," O'Connor interjected.

Scalia moved in to rescue the state attorney. "Mr. Tunheim, I had assumed the purpose of this provision was not just to assist the child, but that . . . the biological parents were presumed to have the right to provide advice on this matter if they wanted to."

"That's correct, Justice Scalia," Tunheim replied.

"I mean there's a parental interest involved as well as a filial interest, isn't that so?" Scalia asked.

Tunheim nodded in agreement. "Both parents have those rights and responsibilities," he said. "Minors are [peculiarly] vulnerable and . . . parents in most cases act in the best interest of their minor children."

O'Connor listened until Scalia finished and then resumed her questioning. "Well, that might be true in general, but probably you would concede that there are some circumstances in which it would not be in the best interests of the child to tell one of the two parents of her problem and intention." Though O'Connor seemed skeptical of the Minnesota law, the ACLU attorneys were not confident she would vote to strike it down. In her years on the Court, she had yet to vote to strike down any abortion regulation.

Meanwhile, Janet Benshoof, the ACLU attorney from New York and the architect of its national strategy to defend the right to abortion, tried—but with little success—to convince the other conservatives that the Minnesota law had been shown to be a failure. "It tries to force a parental role where one may never have existed," she said. "It undermined families that do exist and drove minors from timely, critical medical care." The two-parent rule, she added, "is out of step with the reality of family life."

After listening quietly for a while, the chief justice, his chin on his hand, leaned forward to his microphone. He had no interest in the evidence produced during the trial. Rather, he wanted to know why a judge had "second-guessed" the state legislature by gathering the evidence in the first place.

"Is that an ordinary thing you would expect a district court to do, to hold a factual trial on whether a statute 'achieves' the goals that the legislature set out to achieve?" Rehnquist asked.

Benshoof looked astonished. For years, the Court's conservatives had criticized the ACLU and other legal groups for challenging laws before they went into effect. Typically, the lawsuits alleged that the laws would create problems. For example, in this case, the ACLU might have alleged that the Minnesota law would cause heartache and trauma for families rather than encouraging closer family relationships. The conservatives had always responded the same way: Where's the evidence? Laws should not be struck down based on trumped-up fears of what could happen, they insisted. Now that the ACLU lawyers had gathered the evidence of how the Minnesota law worked in practice over five years, the chief justice contended that it was irrelevant.

In the *Hodgson* v. *Minnesota* case, on the other hand, Benshoof had no hopes of getting Rehnquist's vote anyway. The chief would not be persuaded to strike down a state law based on any evidence. As the argument ended, it was clear once again that the Court's decision would be Sandra O'Connor's decision.

While the Minnesota case gave the justices another chance to resolve an old issue, the case of Nancy Beth Cruzan gave them a first chance to consider a new one. Each year now, about two million Americans die, and 80 percent of those deaths take place in a hospital or nursing home. This marked a decided change from earlier generations. Until the late 1940s, most persons died at home, having spent their final hours of life in the care of their families. Now, as a result of advances in medical technology and the growth of institutional care, death was no longer a private, family affair. Doctors, nurses, and hospital administrators played a part as well.

In nearly every contemporary death, a crucial decision was made on whether to start, stop, or continue a potentially life-prolonging course of medical treatment. This leads to the question, Who is empowered to make those life-and-death decisions for a comatose person: the family, the health-care professionals, or the state? The case of Nancy Beth Cruzan gave the justices their first chance to rule directly on that issue.

Cruzan was 25 years old when she lost control of her car on an icy road on January 11, 1983. When a Missouri state trooper found her, she was lying about 35 feet from her overturned auto. She had no pulse and was not breathing. For all practical purposes, Nancy Cruzan was dead. A few minutes later, however, a team of county paramedics arrived; they inserted a breathing tube down her throat and restarted her heart. Her brain had been without oxygen for 12 to 14 minutes, but Nancy Cruzan was alive again. Over the next three weeks, she remained in a coma but made slight progress. Her parents agreed to have a feeding tube surgically inserted into her stomach. But by October, nine months after her accident, her condition had not improved further, and she was transferred to a state hospital for long-term care. From that point on, the state paid a reported $130,000 a year to keep her alive in what doctors called a "persistent vegetative state." She could not speak, move, or recognize her family, and her brain damage was irreversible.

By 1987, her parents had lost all hope. They did not want to see their daughter vegetate for another 30 years in a hospital bed. If Nancy could speak for herself, they said, she would wish to die, but the hospital officials refused to halt her food and water without a court order. In their view, Nancy Cruzan was alive if not well. She was neither terminally ill nor receiving extraordinary care. If she were to die, it would occur because she had been starved, they said.

In response to the Cruzans' petition, Judge Charles E. Teel, Jr., heard three days of testimony on Nancy Cruzan's case. A former roommate testified that a year before, in a conversation prompted by the sudden death of a relative, Nancy had said quite emphatically she would not want to continue living if she were to "just lay in a bed" and exist "as a vegetable." Her mother and sister testified that they were certain Nancy "would not want to be like she is now." The family members said in all their visits to the hospital, they had seen no signs of recognition from Nancy. The nursing staff and doctors told a different story. They said Nancy often looked toward whomever was speaking and once cried when a Valentine's Day card was read to her.

The judge sided with the Cruzan family. He concluded that Nancy was oblivious to her environment except for reflex actions and had no hope for recovery. Because she could not eat or drink on her own, the hospital's use of the feeding and hydration tube amounted to "medical treatment," he said. Moreover, the testimony of her family and friends provided "clear and convincing evidence" that Nancy would wish to die if she could speak for herself. He granted the Cruzans' petition and ordered the hospital to stop their daughter's food and water.

Once again, Nancy's death was near, but for the intervention of the state. Attorney General William Webster appealed on behalf of the state health director, and the Missouri Supreme Court agreed to hear the case. On a 4–3 vote, it reversed Judge Teel and ordered Nancy to be kept alive.

The ruling marked a clear break with 12 years of state law precedents. Since 1976, when a New Jersey Court ruled that the family of Karen Ann Quinlan could halt the breathing machine that kept alive their brain-damaged daughter, the state courts around the nation had consistently said that patients who were terminally ill or perpetually comatose had a right to die. Further, this right could be exercised by their families, the courts added. Because the state rulings followed a uniform pattern, the Supreme Court did not intervene.

By 1989, however, these state decisions had come under criticism from both a philosophical and practical perspective. As a matter of philosophy, some critics disputed the idea of allowing persons to die for reasons of life-style or quality of life. Who will be put to death next, they wondered: the disabled, the profoundly retarded, or the aged?

Actually, it was the practical problem that worried prosecutors. For example, if a husband comes into a hospital with his wife in a coma and says he wants no extraordinary treatment for her, the hospital officials will probably follow his wishes. A few weeks later, he may tell the hospital staff he wants them to "pull the plug" because, he says, his wife would not want to live as a vegetable. However, hospital officers and the state have a duty to protect life, too. What if the wife's sudden illness was caused by her husband, or what if he would benefit financially if her life were ended? Is he then the best and most reliable person to speak for her interests? Because of these concerns, hospitals and the state courts could not say that a family member had the sole and unquestioned right to speak for a comatose relative. Instead, they insisted on careful procedures to determine what was in the best interest of the patient.

This practical concern did not figure in the *Cruzan* case. The state supreme court had agreed that Lester and Joyce Cruzan were loving parents who kept their daughter's best interests foremost. The Missouri decision turned on philosophy. The state court majority relied heavily on the state's antiabortion law and its asserted belief in the right to life, the preamble that Rehnquist had pronounced legally meaningless.

"This state has expressed a strong policy favoring life. We believe this policy dictates that we err on the side of preserving life," the state supreme court said. "The state's interest is not in quality of life. . . . The argument made here, that Nancy will not recover, is but a thinly veiled statement that her life in its present form is not worth living. Yet a diminished quality of life does not support a decision to cause death." The evidence from her family and friends that Nancy would wish to die "is inherently unreliable and thus insufficient" to outweigh the state's interest in life. The state court concluded, "This interest [in life] outweighs any rights invoked on Nancy's behalf to terminate treatment."

Her parents appealed to the U.S. Supreme Court, and on December 6, the justices heard arguments in the case of *Cruzan* v. *Missouri*, a week after the Minnesota abortion case. For the first time, the justices were confronted with the question of whether the Constitution gives individuals "a right to die," and if so, who can exercise that right for a comatose person?

The Reagan administration and the conservative movement often voiced support for "profamily" policies. During the teenage abortion case, Scalia seemed especially sympathetic to the state's argument that parents had "the right" to be involved in their daughter's decision whether to abort. In the *Cruzan* case, the parents were seeking the right to carry out their daughter's wish, as they saw it, to end her life, but this time, the state was on the opposite side, and so were the conservatives.

William H. Colby, a Kansas City attorney representing the Cruzans, relied on two deeply rooted American traditions: (1) that each person has a right to be free of "unwanted medical treatment," and (2) that a family member is called upon in the first instance to act in the best interests of a gravely ill relative. Though he could have stressed that these ideas are incorporated in the constitutional "right to privacy," Colby steered away from that danger zone because of *Roe* v. *Wade*.

The justices said that the difficulty of the case was in determining whether a comatose individual wants to die. "Can't we view this case as being one in which the state simply is saying that there must be a mechanism where the state can make a clear determination of what the wishes were one way or other?" Kennedy asked. "If that determination cannot be made, the state simply opts for life."

Colby agreed that the state "has an important interest in protecting life," but the state supreme court had translated this notion into "an unqualified interest in life that is going to win in every case."

"No, it's not in all situations," Kennedy countered. "It's where the wishes of the person cannot be determined with accuracy."

For a comatose person, at least one who had not left written instructions, it was always hard to discern her wishes with certainty, Colby said. That argued for turning to the patient's family, he said.

The justices were quick to disagree. The state had adopted a "right to life" philosophy, and its courts believed that a patient should be kept alive unless there was "clear and convincing evidence" she wished to die. What's wrong with that? they wondered.

"I mean, some people think living is better than not living, no matter how terrible the life may be," Scalia said. "And other people think, no, if the quality of life is not good, let's end it. That's a philosophical debate. . . . But why can't the state take a position, 'We don't deal in philosophy. We deal in physics, and life is preserved'?"

The answer was obvious, but it was not a winning argument in the Rehnquist Court. The Constitution and the American legal tradition puts such personal and private decisions in the hands of the individual and her family, not the state, Colby maintained.

The Bush administration's solicitor general Kenneth W. Starr, in a brief appearance, urged the Court to uphold Missouri and keep Nancy Cruzan alive. He noted that this case involved the "delicate issue" of cutting off a patient's food and water, not pulling the plug on a respirator. He recommended the same basic approach that the Administration had urged in the abortion case. Because the Constitution does not give patients or their families an absolute right to die, the Court should give states "wide latitude" to set their own rules.

Roughly one-third of the appeals sent to the Court arise from criminal cases. During the Earl Warren era, the liberal majority often agreed to hear appeals from convicted criminals and used their cases to rewrite the standards of criminal procedures. The party that is appealing the lower-court decision is named first in Supreme Court cases, so the major rulings of the Warren Court had names such as *Miranda* v. *Arizona, Mapp* v. *Ohio,* or *Gideon* v. *Wainwright* (a Florida prison director). In the Rehnquist Court, the process worked in reverse. The conservative majority rarely agreed to hear an appeal from a criminal whose conviction was upheld by a state or federal court. However, when prosecutors lost a case in the lower courts, the Rehnquist Court could be counted on to hear the appeal filed by a state or the Justice Department. As a result, criminal cases now had names such as *Florida* v. *Riley, California* v. *Brown,* and *Maryland* v. *Buie.* Where the Warren Court gave a second chance to convicted criminals, the Rehnquist Court gave prosecutors a second chance to affirm convictions.

The justices heard a dozen criminal cases filed by state or federal prosecutors during the 1989–1990 term, and two yielded especially significant rulings.

To fight the war on drugs, the Reagan and Bush administrations sent federal agents into countries from which narcotics were shipped to the United States. This aggressive pursuit of the drug trade raised a broad legal question: Does the U.S. Constitution restrict U.S. agents when they operate abroad? In January 1986, Mexican police, at the request of U.S. marshals, apprehended Rene Martin Verdugo-Urquidez, the reputed leader of a large and violent Mexican drug smuggling gang. He was also a suspect in the kidnapping and murder of U.S. Drug Enforcement Administration (DEA) agent Enrique Camarena-Salazar. Mexican police turned over Verdugo-Urquidez to U.S. marshals at the border crossing near San Diego. With the suspect safely in custody, DEA agents sought to build their case against him. After consulting Mexican police again, they crossed the border and searched the suspect's homes in Mexicali and San Felipe, in Baja California, Mexico. They seized documents, among them a tally sheet that was said to record shipments of marijuana.

However, lawyers for Verdugo-Urquidez filed a motion to suppress this evidence, contending it had been illegally seized without a search warrant. A federal judge in San Diego agreed, ruling that the Fourth Amendment demands that U.S. agents obtain a search warrant before undertaking such a mission. The government appealed, but the U.S. Ninth Circuit Court of Appeals upheld the decision on a 2–1 vote. This ruling did not affect the arrest of Verdugo-Urquidez—surprisingly, the Constitution put few limits on the government's power to bring a suspect before a judge—but the ruling meant that the tally sheets could not be used during a trial.

The Justice Department filed an appeal, and to no one's surprise, the Court announced it would hear the case of *U.S.* v. *Verdugo-Urquidez.* With a solid majority behind him, Rehnquist took on the opinion, not only to rule against Verdugo-Urquidez but also to make clear that the U.S. Constitution does not protect aliens from unreasonable searches abroad by U.S. officials, even when those aliens are then brought here for trial. "The purpose of the Fourth Amendment was to protect the people of the United States against arbitrary action by their own Government," the chief justice announced on February 28. "It was never suggested that the provision was intended to restrain the actions of the federal government against aliens outside of the United States territory." His opinion in *U.S.* v. *Verdugo-Urquidez* was joined by White, O'Connor, Scalia, and Kennedy.

Brennan, Marshall, and Blackmun dissented, while Stevens filed a narrow concurring opinion. Stevens saw Rehnquist as a knee-jerk conservative. He would nearly always rule for the government in a criminal case, regardless of the facts. On the other hand, he considered Brennan and Marshall to be knee-jerk liberals. Regardless of the facts—and ignoring the Court's precedents—they always ruled in favor of Death Row inmates, he noted, and in most criminal cases, Brennan and Marshall sided with the defendant. Stevens went his own way. In criminal cases, he wrote separate concurring opinions rather than join the conservatives in upholding convictions or separate dissents rather than sign on to the knee-jerk liberal opinions of Brennan and Marshall. He also went his own way whenever the justices were not meeting in conference. For example, one Monday each month, the justices made a largely ceremonial appearance on the bench to hand down a list of orders in pending cases before beginning a ten-day recess. Often, Stevens was missing. He and his wife had taken off for Fort Lauderdale, where they had a condominium. There, the justice could work on opinions and play tennis with the other 70-year-olds, some of whom had no idea he was a sitting justice of the Supreme Court.

In the Mexican drug-search case, Stevens sharply disputed Rehnquist's opinion that gave U.S. agents the unlimited authority to ignore the rights of all "the people" who are not Americans. However, in this case, Mexican police had been consulted and approved the search of Verdugo-Urquidez's two homes in Mexico. In that instance, the search was "not unreasonable" and did not violate the Fourth Amendment, Stevens wrote. His narrow solution resolved the case but appealed to neither the liberal nor the conservative members of the Court.

Brennan may not have been pleased by Stevens's opinion, but he was outraged by Rehnquist's broad opinion. It gave U.S.

agents a free hand to treat foreigners with contempt. In dissent, he concurred with the observation that America's three biggest exports in the 1980s were "rock music, blue jeans and United States law." If the U.S. agents are going to travel abroad, the U.S. Constitution should go along, he said. The ruling prompted from Brennan a grand essay on the law and the Constitution, the kind which was rarely seen from Rehnquist or White, the now dominant voices of the Court.

"If we seek respect for law and order, we must observe these principles ourselves. Lawlessness breeds lawlessness. When U.S. agents conduct unreasonable searches and seizures, whether at home or abroad, they disregard our nation's values. For over 200 years, our country has considered itself the world's foremost protector of liberties. The privacy and sanctity of the home have been primary tenets of our moral, philosophical and judicial beliefs. . . . We take pride in our commitment to a government that cannot, on mere whim, break down doors and invade the most personal of places. We exhort other nations to follow our example. How can we explain to others—and to ourselves—that these long-cherished ideals are suddenly of no consequence when the door being broken down belongs to a foreigner?" Brennan wrote.

The passage gives a hint as to why Brennan held sway so long. Many had credited his success in creating majority opinions to his sunny personality or his gentle arm-twisting, but the justices who knew him said the reasons were less personal. He could tap a deep sense of idealism toward the Constitution, an idealism that could draw toward him justices who had been labeled moderates or conservatives. Unfortunately for him, the young Reagan appointees were not easily or often touched. Only Marshall and Blackmun, his fellow octogenarians, joined the dissent.

The day before Rehnquist announced the ruling in the case involving cross-border searches, the justices heard arguments on whether the police could routinely stop motorists on American roadways to check their sobriety. During the 1980s, sobriety checkpoints on the highways were used with increasing frequency, especially during the holiday periods, when more inebriated drivers took to the roads. Police officials admitted these checkpoints were most effective in warning the public about drunk driving. Typically, officers would stop each motorist for 30 seconds and ask a few questions. Unless the

officer detected some sign of intoxication, the driver would be
sent on. Though statistics varied considerably, several studies
found that roughly one to two percent of the motorists were
found to be impaired.

In 1988, the Michigan courts ruled that such mass
searches violate the Fourth Amendment. According to these
state judges, the Constitution did not allow the police to stop
hundreds of innocent motorists on the likelihood that they
would find one or two impaired drivers. When state prosecutors appealed, the Court agreed to hear the case of *Michigan
State Police* v. *Sitz* and reversed the ruling. Rehnquist cited as
a precedent the recent decision in the drug-testing cases.
Drunken driving, like drug abuse, is a social scourge, while the
invasion of the individual's privacy—the required stop at the
roadblock—is minimal, the chief justice said. White, O'Connor,
Scalia, and Kennedy joined the opinion. Blackmun, noting the
"slaughter on our highways," concurred in a separate opinion.

Brennan and Marshall dissented, arguing again that the
Fourth Amendment demands that government agents have an
individualized suspicion before they stop anyone. Stevens
wrote a separate dissent, contending that sobriety checkpoints,
like drug testing, are more "symbolic" than effective in combatting drunk driving. "Unfortunately, the Court is transfixed
by the wrong symbol—the illusory prospect of punishing countless intoxicated motorists—when it should keep its eyes on the
road plainly marked by the Constitution," he wrote.

In one sense, these criminal rulings could have been predicted, given the new makeup of the Court. It was a rare day
when the Rehnquist Court agreed to restrict the police or voted
to overturn a criminal conviction, but the most sweeping
change in the law during the term came from a case that had
drawn little attention. The case involved two Native Americans
who were fired from their jobs as drug counselors because they
had ingested the drug peyote.

The First Amendment includes two clauses concerning
religion. One forbids laws "respecting an establishment of religion." The second forbids laws "prohibiting the free exercise" of religion. Jefferson, in his "separation of church and
state" letter, mentioned both clauses. The government may
neither promote an official religion nor interfere with an individual's freedom of worship, he said. Religion is a private
matter, off-limits to the government.

The Court had little trouble enforcing the freedom of religious beliefs and conscience, but problems arose when religious practices clashed with the practices and beliefs of the majority. What about polygamy among Mormons, Christian Scientists who refuse medical care for their gravely ill child, Amish parents who refuse to send their children to school in defiance of the compulsory schooling laws, Jewish soldiers who want to wear skullcaps with their military uniforms, or Seventh Day Adventists who seek state unemployment benefits but refuse to work on Saturdays? How is the Court to decide when an individual's claim to the "free exercise" of religion conflicts with a general law or government policy?

In the early 1960s, the Warren Court and Justice Brennan had worked out an approach to these cases that protected out-of-the-mainstream religions. Because the right to practice religion is fundamental, the government may not infringe on a religious practice unless it has a "compelling interest." This legal test gave the benefit of the doubt to those religious practices that conflicted with the majority. It also required exceptions to accommodate the minority. For example, the Court ordered Wisconsin to waive its compulsory schooling laws for the Amish children. The government did not always lose either, though. The gravely ill child of the Christian Scientists could be administered medical care despite the religious wishes of her parents, because the government's interest was compelling in that instance.

Over the years, the Court's religious liberty rulings had become hard to reconcile. They were almost as confusing as the rulings on Christmas trees, creches, and the "establishment of religion." Could the Jewish serviceperson wear a skullcap? No, the Court said. No exceptions to the standard military uniform. Could a Muslim prisoner be exempted from a midday work detail to attend worship services? No. No exceptions. Could a Seventh Day Adventist receive unemployment benefits despite a refusal to work Saturdays? Yes. The government cannot force a person to ignore the practice of her or his religion.

For his part, Rehnquist had been consistent. He ruled for the government in all these cases and dissented alone when the Court had upheld the unemployment benefits for the Seventh Day Adventist. When Scalia joined the Court, he thought the religion cases made no sense. He wanted clear and firm rules, but the religion cases seemed to turn on the whim of one or two justices. They would weigh the importance of the religious practice on one hand and its significance to the government on the other hand. The Amish who won the right to keep their children out of school lost later when they asked for a religious exemption to paying Social Security taxes. Staying away from school was one thing, but not paying your taxes was quite another, the majority said. Scalia abhorred these so-called balancing tests. He favored a clear rule that would sweep aside all these cases. In the peyote case, he got his chance.

Alfred Smith, a Klamath Indian, and Galen Black, a non-Indian who had recently converted to the Native American church, worked as county drug counselors in Cascadia, Oregon. Both were recovered alcoholics and had agreed as a condition of their employment to refrain from using alcohol or other drugs. In 1983, however, both admitted to ingesting peyote during a Native American church ceremony. Peyote is a bitter-tasting cactus containing mescaline, an illegal substance that produces hallucinations, similar to LSD. Both the federal government and at least a dozen states make an exception for Native Americans who use it during worship services.

Oregon was not one of those states, however. Smith and Black were fired from their jobs, and the state later denied them unemployment benefits because they had been dismissed for "misconduct." They sued, claiming their rights to the "free exercise" of religion had been violated, and they won. The use of peyote is illegal in the state, the Oregon Supreme Court said, but the First Amendment demands that the Native Americans be exempted from the law. The state appealed, and the justices agreed to decide the case of *Oregon* v. *Smith and Black.*

It appeared to raise another vexing but narrow question. Did the state have a "compelling interest" in forbidding drug counselors from using peyote, an illegal drug, or did the First Amendment entitle Native Americans to an exemption for a drug regularly used during their religious ceremonies? However the Court ruled, the decision figured to add only another small wrinkle to the law. This narrow view proved overly limited. When the votes were counted, Rehnquist had six who sided with the state, and he decided to have Scalia write the opinion. Given an opportunity, Scalia promptly rewrote First Amendment law on the "free exercise" of religion.

The government no longer need show it has a "compelling interest" to win in a case where it was challenged on religious grounds, Scalia asserted. Rather, a "valid and neutral law" which does not single out a religion, will be upheld, he insisted,

even if it stifles the practice of a religion. "Any society . . .
would be courting anarchy," Scalia said, if it tried to shield all
religious practices and determined to "coerce or suppress none
of them. . . . We cannot afford the luxury," he added, of carving
out "constitutionally required religious exemptions" for every
minority religion. Of course, the states may do so, as some have
done with peyote, but the Constitution does not *require* that
they do so, he concluded.

Scalia conceded that under his approach, prominent and
mainstream religions would be protected because of their political clout, while minority religions could suffer. He described
that fact as an "unavoidable consequence" of democracy. "It
may fairly be said that leaving accommodation to the political
process will place at a relative disadvantage those religious
practices that are not widely engaged in," Scalia wrote. "But
that unavoidable consequence of democratic government must
be preferred to a system . . . in which each conscience is a law
unto itself and in which judges weigh the social importance of
all laws against the centrality of all religious beliefs."

The year before, the four conservatives in Anthony Kennedy's dissent accused the liberals of "an unjustified hostility
toward religion." That was so because the majority had concluded that a Christian manger scene may not be displayed
inside a county courthouse. Now, the same four—Rehnquist,
White, Scalia, and Kennedy—combined to rule that those with
out-of-the-mainstream religious practices are not shielded from
stifling government policies. The conservatives did not seem
worried about a perceived "hostility to religion" when the
rights of only minority religions were at stake.

Stevens had cast the key fifth vote. He agreed that the
two Native Americans could be fired, and he signed on to Scalia's opinion. Stevens consistently opposed religious claims,
whether they came from prominent or fringe religious groups.
He voted to forbid the use of the creche and the Christmas
tree in Pittsburgh and also voted to deny the religious exemption to the peyote users in Oregon.

The peyote case had provoked another sharp clash between Scalia, the professor, and O'Connor, the politician.
Scalia had written a sweeping opinion that rigidly rejected religious claims. He sought an intellectual consistency in the law.
O'Connor wanted the Court to be fair to both sides and to
make careful, balanced judgments. Yes, she emphasized, Oregon could fire the two drug counselors, because the state

indeed had a "compelling interest" in enforcing its drug laws, but Scalia's opinion virtually removed the religious liberty clause from the Constitution, she contended.

"In my view, today's holding dramatically departs from well-settled First Amendment jurisprudence . . . and is incompatible with our nation's fundamental commitment to individual religious liberty," O'Connor wrote in dissent. She, too, quoted Justice Jackson from *West Virginia* v. *Barnette,* the flag salute case involving the Jehovah's Witness children. "The very purpose of a Bill of Rights was to withdraw certain subjects from the vicissitudes of political controversy, to place them beyond the reach of majorities and officials and to establish them as legal principles to be applied by the courts," Jackson had written in 1943. The rights to free speech, a free press, and freedom of worship do not depend on the wishes of legislature, he declared, and "they depend on the outcome of no elections."

O'Connor said the Court had devised the "compelling interest" test to "preserve religious liberty to the fullest extent possible in a pluralistic society. For the Court [that is, Scalia] to deem this command a 'luxury' is to denigrate the very purpose of a Bill of Rights," she said. Her dissent was joined by Brennan, Marshall, and Blackmun.

The religion rulings sharply illustrated the change from a liberal to a conservative Court. When Brennan and the liberals were in charge, they restricted the government from promoting religion—through school prayer or Bible readings—while protecting the rights of minority religions, such as the Jehovah's Witnesses and Seventh Day Adventists. Rehnquist reversed the equation. With five votes, he would allow the government to promote the mainstream religion, while refusing to shield the minority religions.

The Scalia opinion in the peyote case stunned attorneys who represented the nation's churches and religious organizations. The American Jewish Congress, the Baptist Joint Committee on Public Affairs, the Presbyterian Church U.S.A., and the Lutheran Church, Missouri Synod, quickly petitioned the Court and urged the justices to rehear the case. No one had even raised the possibility of throwing out the "compelling interest" test, they complained. The rehearing petition was dismissed by the Court just as quickly.

Privately, the attorneys asked, Is Scalia serious? Does the Court mean it? What would happen if a zealous prosecutor charged the Catholic church with violating state alcohol laws protecting minors by giving communal wine to children and violating the gender discrimination laws by refusing to hire female priests? Would the Court conclude that the church was entitled to no exemption from these laws in order to practice the "free exercise" of its religion? Of course, the Court need not answer hypothetical questions, and the mainstream religions need not worry unduly. What prosecutor would directly challenge the Catholic and Protestant churches?

Still, the peyote opinion was distinctively Scalia's. He had taken a small case and used it to sweep aside nearly 30 years of precedent. "He's the only one [of the nine] who would have done that," one clerk noted. While the other justices reflexively decided cases by juggling the existing precedents, Scalia would gladly brush them aside to set forth a clear principle. In this case, the principle was that general laws that apply to all must prevail over individuals seeking a special exemption.

Scalia had also pushed Rehnquist aside as the hero for the younger generation of conservative lawyers at the Court and at the Justice Department. "The real battle is between law and politics, and Nino is the one who is fighting it up there," said an attorney who had clerked at the Court and worked in the Bush administration. Scalia grappled with the big ideas and principles and sought to apply them in a neutral manner. That was law, they said. The rest was just politics.

Rehnquist had slipped a notch or two in their estimation. He was commonly described as the flip side of Brennan, a politically oriented conservative. "I was surprised to see how political he was," said one conservative clerk after a year at the Court. "He doesn't put a lot of effort into his opinions," he said. Rehnquist cared about getting the right result, where Scalia cared about getting the reasoning right, they said.

The chief justice could be counted on to back the government and to rule against individuals claiming their constitutional rights were violated. Usually, Scalia agreed with him, but sometimes the Constitution set forth an entirely clear principle of individual rights, a principle that Scalia would defend with the same zeal he had shown in attacking what he saw as phony constitutional rights such as abortion.

One of those principles was the First Amendment's protection of free speech in political affairs.

In March, the Bush administration urged the Court to uphold the new Flag Protection Act, Congress's response to the flag-burning decision in *Texas* v. *Johnson*. The new law said it was a crime to "knowingly mutilate, deface, physically defile, burn, maintain on the floor or ground, or trample upon any flag of the United States." Solicitor General Starr gamely argued that the new law differed from the unconstitutional Texas law because it prohibited *all* desecrations of the flag, not just acts that "seriously offend" onlookers, as in the Texas case.

No one bought the argument. The new law certainly read as though it were aimed at one type of message. During the argument, Scalia repeated the words of the statute: "mutilate, deface, defile, trample." Those words do not describe a value-free law intended simply to protect flags, he said. Rather, they describe a law that was intended to punish those who viewed the flag with contempt. He noted that the law did not make it a crime to leave the flag outside on the pole so that it could be worn or damaged by the weather.

It had been quite a year for flags since the first decision. Throughout Eastern Europe, protesters for democracy had defaced the flags of their Communist regimes, while Americans cheered this symbolic show of freedom triumphant over government tyranny. When faced again with the question of whether the Constitution would allow Americans to be sent to prison for the same act at home, five justices said no. Scalia and Kennedy joined the liberals, Brennan, Marshall, and Blackmun, to strike down the new law in the test case *U.S.* v. *Eichman*.

This time, the decision was met with silence from the Bush administration and Congress, and the flag-burning issue quickly faded. The chief justice, who had dissented fiercely the year before, doubted the flag decision would have much impact. "Surely there are not many people who burn flags in this country," Rehnquist commented to a lawyers' group, "and I suspect, now that it . . . has finally been established it is legal, there were will be far fewer."

Though Scalia and Kennedy had stood up for the principle of free speech in the flag case, the liberals did not always stand with them on First Amendment matters. In March, the Court upheld a Michigan law that made it a crime for a corporation to take out a newspaper advertisement endorsing a candidate. Rehnquist and White, predictably, voted to uphold the law, and they were joined by Brennan, Marshall, Blackmun, and Stevens. The dissenters were Scalia, Kennedy, and O'Connor.

The case had begun in 1985, during a special election to fill a seat in the Michigan state house. The Michigan Chamber of Commerce, a nonprofit group that was supported by 8,000 companies, wanted to take out an ad in the Grand Rapids newspapers endorsing one candidate. "Michigan Needs Richard Bandstra to Help Us Be Job Competitive Again," its headline read. However, a state law forbade the use of corporate funds for "independent expenditures" in its electoral campaigns, such as sponsoring ads or flyers. Because most of the state's labor unions were not incorporated, they could take out ads endorsing candidates. The chamber filed suit, contending that the law violated its First Amendment rights to free speech, and a federal appeals court agreed.

The Court reversed this ruling, however, and upheld the state law. Since the Watergate era, both Congress and the Court had agreed that money can corrupt the electoral process. With huge campaign contributions, wealthy donors and big businesses could sway elections in their favor. When Congress put strict limits on campaign contributions, the Court upheld them as constitutional. According to the majority, the Michigan case added only a small new wrinkle to well-established rules of law. Marshall's perfunctory opinion for the Court in *Austin* v. *Michigan Chamber of Commerce* said that the state law was justified in "preventing corruption or the appearance of corruption" in elections.

Scalia was furious at the ruling, as was Kennedy. In their view, the liberal members of the Court fiercely protected a constitutional right that was not in the Constitution—abortion—but refused to protect a right that was included—free speech—simply because it benefited big business. In a sharp dissent, Kennedy accused the majority of "censorship" that is "repugnant to the First Amendment and contradicts its central guarantee, the freedom to speak in the electoral process."

Rarely was a dissent read from the bench, and the chief justice had an informal rule that allowed only one such dissent per term per justice. Scalia used his opportunity in the Michigan elections case. "Attention all citizens," he began. "To assure the fairness of elections by preventing disproportionate expression of the views of any single powerful group, your Government has decided that the following association of persons shall be prohibited from speaking or writing in support of any candidate: . . ." The Court's ruling, he said, "endorses the principle that too much speech is an evil that the democratic majority can proscribe." If the flag burner's protest was worth protecting, so was the speech of the Michigan Chamber of Commerce, he proclaimed.

Scalia's zealous defense of free speech clearly distinguished him from Rehnquist. The chief justice read the First Amendment just as narrowly as the other parts of the Bill of Rights. It did not matter to Rehnquist that big business opposed the Michigan law; he voted to uphold it. The First Amendment was not the only point of disagreement between the two justices. Scalia was, if anything, even more zealous in defending the constitutional rights of those alleged to have committed the most damnable of crimes—the sexual abuse of children.

One of the most publicized phenomena of the mid-1980s, along with junk bonds and the homeless, were reports of the mass sexual abuse of small children, especially by child care workers. The allegations exploded first at the McMartin Preschool in Manhattan Beach, California, where seven employees were accused of conspiring to molest children. Soon, similar cases arose across the nation. Some child care workers and prosecutors insisted that new laws were needed to cope with these crimes. They suggested that because these young, frightened children were the only witnesses to the crimes, the courts would have to make special accommodations to gain their testimony. By 1990, 37 states had enacted laws allowing child witnesses to testify via videotape or closed-circuit television so they would not have to sit in the presence of their abuser—or alleged abuser. Other states relaxed rules on "hearsay testimony" so that child care workers, psychologists, and pediatricians could testify on behalf of children they had interviewed.

The number of skeptics had grown, too, though. Some of the most publicized charges of child molestation, including the McMartin case, seemed to unravel at trial. Critics saw a modern-day version of the witchcraft trials. Rumors became accusations, and the web of conspiracy spread. Child therapists and psychologists were called in to confirm the suspicions. More incidents were "disclosed" and more adults were accused, sometimes dozens in all. How could the truth be determined when the young witnesses had only hazy memories of the events?

Also, what about the rights of the accused molesters? That question was not much on the minds of state legislators who rushed to enact the new laws, but Scalia had already staked out a position for himself. The Sixth Amendment says that "in

all criminal prosecutions, the accused shall enjoy the right . . .
to be confronted with the witnesses against him." This ancient
right to confront your accusers means, he insisted, that defendants have an absolute right to "a face-to-face confrontation" in the courtroom. The witnesses here may well be small,
frightened children, but the Sixth Amendment says "all criminal prosecutions." No exceptions, declared Antonin Scalia, devout Catholic and father of nine children.

On the last day of the term in June 1988, Scalia had written an opinion for the Court reversing the conviction of an
Iowa man who had sat behind a screen during his trial so his
young accusers could not see him. "It is always more difficult
to tell a lie about a person to his face than behind his back,"
he wrote in *Coy* v. *Iowa.* "That face-to-face presence may,
unfortunately, upset the truthful rape victim or abused child,
but by the same token it may confound and undo the false
accuser, or reveal the child coached by a malevolent adult."
Only Brennan, Marshall, and Stevens agreed in full with Scalia's
opinion. O'Connor and White agreed only that the Iowa man
deserved a new trial. Rehnquist and Blackmun dissented.

In the spring of 1990, the issue was back before the Court
in two cases. A Maryland case raised the question of whether
the Sixth Amendment permits child witnesses to testify via
closed-circuit TV. In a case from Idaho, the justices considered
whether a pediatrician can testify based on what a child told
him in his office.

Sandra Ann Craig, the operator of a preschool center in
Howard County, Maryland, was accused in 1986 of having sexually abused several children in her care. Under a new Maryland law, the child witnesses were permitted to testify via television so that they did not have to face Craig. A child therapist
who had worked with the children said they would have "considerable difficulty" testifying in Craig's presence. If forced to
do so, they would "probably stop talking, . . . withdraw and
curl up," she said. Better to get their testimony before the jury
than abandon the case, the judge concluded. They testified via
television, and Craig was convicted, but Maryland's appeals
court overturned the conviction on the basis of Scalia's opinion
in *Coy* v. *Iowa.*

In April, the justices heard arguments in *Maryland* v.
Craig, along with the Idaho case on a pediatrician's testimony.
Maryland attorney general J. Joseph Curran, Jr., said the state

was justified in shielding the young children from the emotional trauma of appearing before Craig, who frightened them. Besides, he said, the closed-circuit TV allows the jury to see them as well as hear their testimony. "If we're looking for truth," he said, "we've got to get the evidence in."

Scalia attacked from the beginning: "But isn't the best way [to have the jury] look at the witness and look at the witness's reaction to the questions, the expression of the questioners, and to see the way the [witness] interacts with the defendant who is supposed to have done this harm to the witness?" Scalia asked. "Isn't that the most effective way to determine the truth?"

Scalia was especially skeptical of testimony from a social worker who said the child cannot testify and will "curl up in a ball." "You want to put away somebody for 15 years based on that prediction? . . . What if the child comes into the courtroom and says, "Hi! Mommy,'?" he asked, referring to a case of a mother accused of abuse.

While Scalia hammered away at the major premise of the state law, Sandra O'Connor questioned the Maryland attorney about its details. Once again, she held the key vote. In the earlier case from Iowa, Brennan, Marshall, and Stevens had signed on to Scalia's opinion that insisted on a "face-to-face confrontation" in all criminal cases. Like them, O'Connor was concerned that the defendants get a fair trial. If she joined them, the 37 state laws allowing closed-circuit TV or video-taped testimony would be deemed unconstitutional.

However, O'Connor worried, too, about the rights and the welfare of the child witnesses. Scalia's view was too rigid, too absolutist for her. O'Connor could not ignore the reality that some abused children were in fact terrified of being in the presence of an adult molester. Better that they testify on TV than not all, she said. However, O'Connor could not dismiss Scalia's argument entirely. The Sixth Amendment gives defendants a right to confront their accusers where possible, and surely a right to challenge their accusers' statements. Rehnquist thought Scalia's view was typical of him: There was only one possible right answer, and of course, it was his; only he spoke the true faith.

When the votes were counted, O'Connor cast the deciding vote in both cases and was assigned both opinions. In the Maryland case, she upheld the use of testimony via closed-circuit TV because jurors were able to see the children testify. When a defense lawyer cross-examined the children, the jurors could listen to their responses and observe their demeanor. The Sixth Amendment does not "guarantee criminal defendants the absolute right to a face-to-face meeting with the witnesses against them at trial," she wrote in *Maryland* v. *Craig.* Her opinion was joined by Rehnquist, White, Kennedy, and Blackmun.

In criminal cases, Blackmun was no doctrinaire liberal. He considered the gravity of the crime as well as the significance of the right involved. In the sobriety checkpoints case, Blackmun said the "slaughter" on the highways outweighed the brief invasion of a motorist's privacy. In the drug-testing cases, he had concluded that combatting drug abuse outweighed the minor inconvenience of urine tests. In the child-abuse case, he believed that the use of closed-circuit TV testimony posed only minor infringement on a defendant's rights, especially when weighed against the horror of child abuse.

While O'Connor's vote created a conservative majority in the Maryland case, she voted in the Idaho case to reverse the abuse conviction of Laura Lee Wright, the mother of two young girls. During her trial, a pediatrician testified on what he said Wright's two-and-a-half-year-old daughter said during an office visit. However, the doctor did not take detailed notes or tape-record the conversation. A defense lawyer contended that the child had responded to leading questions so that the pediatrician's testimony amounted to unreliable "hearsay." O'Connor agreed and said such conversations may not be used at trial without clear evidence that the statements are "trustworthy." This time, in *Idaho* v. *Wright*, she was joined by Brennan, Marshall, Stevens, and Scalia.

Both written opinions were typically O'Connor. She had carefully balanced the interests on both sides and arrived at a middle-ground position. In the Maryland case, she made it clear that the TV testimony can be used only if it is "necessary to protect the welfare of the particular child." Her Idaho opinion was qualified, too. Sometimes, doctors could testify if their observations were recorded.

Her carefully balanced opinions irritated Scalia. It was not the Court's job, he said, to balance constitutional rights against the state's interest. When the rights were clearly stated, the Court should enforce them, and with no exceptions. At times, Scalia sounded like Hugo Black, a literalist as well as a liberal, who in the 1950s and 1960s wanted to strike down all laws limiting free speech, including the antiobscenity statutes.

Why? Because the First Amendment says the government shall make "no laws . . . abridging the freedom of speech," and no laws means no laws, Black liked to say.

"Seldom has the Court failed so conspicuously to sustain a categorical guarantee of the Constitution against the tide of prevailing current opinion," Scalia wrote in dissent in the Maryland child abuse case. Thanks to the ruling, "the following scene can be played out in an American courtroom for the first time in two centuries: A father whose young daughter has been given over to the exclusive custody of his estranged wife, or a mother whose young son has been taken into custody by the State's child welfare department, is sentenced to prison for sexual abuse on the basis of testimony by a child the parents had not seen or spoken to for many months; and the guilty verdict is rendered without giving the parent so much as the opportunity to sit in the presence of the child, and to ask, personally or through counsel, 'is it really not true, is it, that I—your father [or mother] who you see before you—did these terrible things?' Perhaps that is a procedure today's society desires; perhaps [though I doubt it] it is even a fair procedure; but it is assuredly not a procedure permitted by the Constitution," Scalia wrote. "For good or bad, the Sixth Amendment requires confrontation, and we are not at liberty to ignore it."

In the spring, the Court revisited affirmative action. The year before, in the *Richmond* case, five justices agreed for the first time that the Fourteenth Amendment demanded equal treatment for white males as well as blacks, women, and minorities. That conclusion was a breakthrough for the conservatives. O'Connor's opinion, though hazy in parts, nonetheless said that the state and local governments may not use racial preferences, except in the "extreme" instances where they were making up for blatant past discrimination. If she really meant it, the Rehnquist Court was set to outlaw affirmative action by the government.

The Richmond ruling did not cover the federal government, however. The Fourteenth Amendment was written by Congress after the Civil War to put restrictions on the states, especially the southern states. It did not limit the powers of Congress or the federal government. The Fourteenth Amendment has the only words in the Constitution that require government—in this instance, state and local government—to treat citizens equally. Nowhere is there a clause in the Constitution that specifically requires the federal government to do the same.

The Warren Court finessed that problem, though, in the aftermath of the *Brown* v. *Board of Education* ruling. The Washington, D.C., schools were racially segregated, but they were then controlled by Congress, not a state. The Fourteenth Amendment could not be used to end school segregation in the nation's capital, so Warren decreed that the Fifth Amendment also requires the federal government to give each person the "equal protection of the laws." The Fifth Amendment does not contain those words, but it does say no person may be "deprived of life, liberty or property, without due process of law" by the federal government, and racial discrimination by the federal government denies black children their right to liberty without due process of law, Warren had said in *Bolling* v. *Sharpe.*

That kind of creative lawmaking by Warren had infuriated conservatives such as Robert Bork. In his 1987 Senate confirmation hearing, Bork insisted that he still found no justification for saying the "equal protection" clause in the Fourteenth Amendment also applied to the federal government. Now, however, the conservatives did not want to replay that fight. Thanks to Warren's creativity, they could now outlaw affirmative action by Congress and the federal agencies. After all, if affirmative action discriminates against white males, and the Fifth Amendment forbids racial discrimination by the federal government, then affirmative action by the federal government must be unconstitutional, too.

Once the *Richmond* case was settled, the Court looked for an affirmative action case involving the federal government, and it found one in a long-running dispute over broadcast licenses issued by the Federal Communications Commission (FCC). Since the late 1970s, the FCC had given an edge to minority-controlled companies in the competition for new broadcast licenses. Though blacks, Hispanics, and Asians then made up 20 percent of the U.S. population, they controlled "fewer than 1 percent of the 8,500 commercial radio and televisions stations" operating in 1978, the FCC said. Giving a "plus-factor" to bids from minority-controlled companies will foster "diversity," the FCC said, both in the ownership of stations and the programming on the nation's airwaves. Like the minority-contract guarantees in Richmond, the FCC program had been much criticized for encouraging sham companies with a black or Hispanic nominally in charge.

The Reagan administration opposed these preferences for other reasons. This kind of official racial and ethnic preference violated its "color-blind" approach. Under its new Reagan-appointed commissioners, the FCC sought to revoke its minority-preference policies, but Congress stepped in and passed an appropriation bill forbidding the Administration from using money "to repeal" the FCC's minority-preference policies. There the matter stood until the federal courts got involved.

In 1983, the FCC asked for bids on a new ultra-high-frequency (UHF) television station in Orlando, Florida. Metro Broadcasting Company, a Florida firm that was owned by nine men, one of whom was black, filed a bid. So did Rainbow Broadcasting Company, consisting of two women and one man, all of whom were Hispanic. Based on its local ownership and its plans for the station, an administrative law judge recommended the license go to Metro Broadcasting, but an FCC review board noted that Rainbow's owners had more broadcasting experience, and they were all minorities. It recommended that the license go to Rainbow instead. The dispute got caught in the back-and-forth battle between the Reagan administration and the Congress, but finally, in 1988, the FCC awarded the license to Rainbow. Metro then filed suit, contending that its owners had suffered unconstitutional reverse discrimination.

A few months after the *Richmond* ruling, the case of *Metro Broadcasting* v. *FCC* appeared on the Court's appeal docket. It raised a simple question: Can the federal government give preferences to minorities because of their race or ethnic background? Does such a policy deny whites the equal protection of the laws? The justices announced they would hear the arguments in late March.

Gregory Guillot, a lawyer for Metro Broadcasting, began his argument by attacking the FCC's policies as discriminatory and unconstitutional.

"One thing is certain," he said. "That is, the commission's policies impose race, gender, and ethnic-based classifications, and those classifications, we feel, are presumptively invalid."

Scalia quickly interrupted. "Excuse me, Mr. Guillot. Is it clear that the gender-based issue is necessarily before us here?

"It is absolutely clear," Guillot replied, noting that the policy certainly covers women, too.

That was not the answer Scalia wanted. He tried again. "You wouldn't win if we just found the racial preferences invalid. Is that what you are saying?" asked Scalia.

"It's a close call, Your Honor," the attorney continued, explaining further the FCC policy. Guillot would not take the bait.

Now the chief justice leaned forward. "You mean it's clear that the Commission would have reached the same result had it not given your opponent the racial preference. Is that clear?"

"That is not clear, Your Honor," he replied.

"Then, we can't affirm the Commission's decision if we invalidate the racial preference. Isn't that right?" Rehnquist asked.

After a few more queries, Guillot finally seemed to agree. Yes, the Court could look at this as a case involving race and ethnic preferences, not gender preferences for women. The visitor in the courtroom might have wondered why Scalia and Rehnquist were so insistent on narrowing the case and removing women from it, but then, they were trying to nail down a fifth vote: O'Connor's. It would be harder to get O'Connor's vote, they figured, if it meant revoking an affirmative action policy that benefited women.

After Guillot finished, an FCC attorney and lawyers for the minority-controlled firms took to the lectern to defend the minority-preference policies. In short order, they were roasted by Scalia, Rehnquist, and Kennedy.

The FCC policy is intended to foster "diversity of expression over the airways" by increasing the number of minority station owners, said Daniel Armstrong of the FCC.

Why are those two necessarily linked, the chief justice wondered. Why do you assume "that if there are more minority owners, there will be more diversity in the airwaves?" he asked.

Because Congress and the agency made the "defensible, predictive judgement" that black and Hispanic station owners would present a different kind of programming, he said.

"Let me understand this," Scalia said. "You mean . . . that white people think and express themselves one way and Aleutians another way and Asians another way. I thought this was what we were trying to get away from. . . . So you're saying that if you have black owners you will have black programming, whatever that means," he asked.

"What I'm saying is that . . . we each are a product of our backgrounds," replied Margaret Polivy, representing Rainbow Broadcasting. "Now that is not just the color of our skins, but it is a fact that we all come from different places. . . . That leads to a panoply of views and voices."

Scalia took over again. "A black who gets a minority preference here could have been born and raised in Scarsdale. Isn't that right?"

Polivy: "Certainly."

Scalia: "You're saying our background, where we come from. It has to do with nothing here except blood. Isn't that right? Isn't blood what counts?"

Polivy: "I would say yes. . . . Whether you are born in Scarsdale or you were born in Harlem, the fact of who you are is what contributes to your perspective."

"And who you are is your race?" Kennedy snapped.

Polivy noted that minorities still have a small stake in broadcasting. An estimated 3.5 percent of broadcast outlets are owned by minorities, she noted.

Scalia wondered aloud what it would mean for the government to say it is legitimate to "make a prediction about a person's action on the basis of his or her blood." Hispanics are likely to do certain things and favor certain programs, while blacks will do something else.

"The truth is, that while the Constitution may be color-blind, race is still with us," answered attorney J. Roger Wollenberg, representing another minority broadcaster.

"Tell me how it's going to help to announce that 'Yes, indeed, race does make a difference,' " Scalia countered, "that you can indeed predict how people will act on the basis of their blood. How is that going to help the situation of racism that you're concerned about?"

"I think only with respect to sensitivity," Wollenberg said. "The people who own a newspaper or own a station are obviously going to be affected by their background and environment."

Scalia pounced again. "Blood, Mr. Wollenberg. Blood." His voice cut through the courtroom. "Not background and environment. Isn't that right? It doesn't matter where the person of that race was raised, in the most privileged family in the most exclusive residential community. Blood!"

The hour-long argument had turned into a harsh, prolonged diatribe dominated by the Court's conservatives. All

the while, the three octogenarian liberals sat silently. None
had raised a voice as the younger conservatives picked apart
the attorneys defending the affirmative action policy, but Scalia's last comment seemed to arouse Marshall.

"You are constantly talking about blood," he said in a thick
voice to Wollenberg. "What statistic . . . or what do you have
that there's a difference in people's blood?"

Wollenberg said that he was not talking of blood.

Marshall seemed not to hear the response. "Sir?"

"I said I'm not talking about blood, your Honor. I am not
suggesting a difference in blood." Marshall sat back in his chair,
frustrated but silent again.

It was a fitting end to a thoroughly lopsided argument.
The brain power, the energy, even the anger, all seemed concentrated on the ideological right. Each month, the pattern
seemed to grow more pronounced. The conservatives, especially Scalia, Kennedy, and Rehnquist, controlled the arguments. Lawyers defending civil rights, Death Row inmates,
criminal defendants, or abortion rights advocates could count
on rough treatment. The conservatives were sharp and relentless. They rarely let these attorneys make a point unchallenged.
Meanwhile, if their opponents stumbled, they would get a helping hand from the same justices. The arguments seemed entirely unbalanced, even unfair, but in the *Metro Broadcasting*
case, it did not matter much after all. The vote proved to be
the major surprise of the 1989–1990 term. Byron White fooled
everyone again.

For most of his career, White had been considered something of an enigma. He shunned ideology, liberal or conservative. After 1980, however, he had regularly voted against affirmative action issues and became a reliable member of
Rehnquist's conservative majority. "That great Democrat!"
Marshall groused once after White had cast a key vote for the
conservatives.

Nonetheless, White, the old Kennedy Democrat, did differ in important ways from the conservatives of the Rehnquist
Court. Unlike Rehnquist or O'Connor, White was not enrap-
tured with the notion of "states' rights." In 1961, Bobby Kennedy had sent him to Alabama to lead a contingent of federal
marshals. His mission was to save the "Freedom Riders" from
the citizens from Alabama and the Alabama state police, who
seemed unable or unwilling to defend the young activists. Not
surprisingly, White never voiced a naïve enthusiasm for states'

rights, having seen it at close range, and when old-fashioned racial discrimination arose, White was still with the liberals. In criminal law, he took a hard-line stand but nonetheless stuck with precedents, even liberal ones that he had originally disputed.

Most important of all, White could be counted on to uphold the acts of the Democratic Congress. Over the years, he had been the most consistent member of the Court on that point: The Constitution gave enormous power to Congress, he maintained. Nothing in the document could be read to say Congress cannot give an edge to minorities in seeking broadcast licenses.

As a general matter, the conservatives prided themselves on upholding Congress and federal agencies against challenges based on constitutional rights. In the *Metro Broadcasting* case, a company controlled by white males contended its rights had been violated by the FCC. Normally, the conservatives sided with the government. If so, then only White voted true to form. Scalia, Rehnquist, and Kennedy voted to strike down the government program, but they were stunned when White deserted them. They had thought they needed only O'Connor to form a majority. They never anticipated losing White.

Stevens fooled everyone, too, although that alone was no shock. Stevens was predictably unpredictable. Ten years before, he had compared a minority-preference program for federal construction contracts to a Nazi-era law. In the *Metro* case, however, he voted to uphold the FCC's minority-preference program. Suddenly Brennan, who had sat silently through the FCC argument while the conservatives jabbed away, had a five-vote majority. Federal affirmative action would survive for another day.

As the term came to a close in the last week in June, three major rulings were still pending. The right-to-die case from Missouri and the teenage abortion case from Minnesota had been argued just after Thanksgiving, but the justices had spent more than six months drafting opinions. Now, they were ready for release, as was the affirmative action decision.

On June 25, the chief justice announced that he would speak for the Court in the case of *Cruzan* v. *Missouri*. From his center chair, Rehnquist directly addressed the large crowd that had filled the courtroom. He always recounted the cases and explained the rulings so that a first-time visitor to the Court could understand what had transpired. If a legalistic word or phrase came up, Rehnquist stopped and explained it in ordinary English. He described Nancy Cruzan's accident, her present condition, and the rulings of the state courts.

"This is the first case in which we have been squarely presented with the issue of whether the United States Constitution grants what is in common parlance referred to as a 'right to die,' " Rehnquist said. The Fourteenth Amendment says that no state shall "deprive any person of life, liberty or property, without due process of law," he noted. "The principle that a competent person has a constitutionally protected liberty interest in refusing unwanted medical treatment may be inferred from our prior decisions," he said. He also referred to this "liberty interest" as a "right to refuse medical treatment." Though persons who are terminally ill or kept alive through medical technology would have a right to insist that their treatment end, the chief justice made clear he was not announcing an absolute right to die. "We do not think a state is required to remain neutral in the face of an informed and voluntary decision by a physically-able adult to starve to death," Rehnquist said at one point, adding that states may make it crime to assist in a suicide.

"For the purposes of this case, we assume that the U.S. Constitution would grant a competent person a constitutionally protected right to refuse lifesaving hydration and nutrition," he said. However, "the difficulty with the [Cruzans'] claim is that in a sense it begs the question: an incompetent person is not able to make an informed and voluntary choice to exercise a hypothetical right to refuse treatment. Such a 'right' must be exercised for her, if at all, by some sort of surrogate."

He then turned to the state's interest. "We think a state may properly decline to make a judgment about the 'quality of life' . . . and simply assert an unqualified interest in the preservation of human life," he said. The state may also "establish a procedural safeguard" to ensure that the decision to withdraw the patient's food and water reflects her wishes.

"Missouri requires that the evidence of the incompetent's wishes as to the withdrawal of treatment be proved by clear and convincing evidence. The question, then, is whether the U.S. Constitution forbids the establishment of this procedural requirement by the State. We hold that it does not," Rehnquist said.

He ended with a note about the Cruzans. They are surely "loving and caring parents," he said, and if the Constitution created "a right of substituted judgement," they would be properly given the power to make decisions for their comatose daughter.

"But we do not think the Due Process Clause [of the Fourteenth Amendment] requires the state to repose judgement on these matters with anyone but the patient herself. Close family members may have a strong feeling—a feeling not at all ignoble or unworthy, but not entirely disinterested, either—that they do not wish to witness the continuation of the life of a loved one which they regard as hopeless, meaningless and even degrading. But there is no automatic assurance that the view of close family members will necessarily be the same as the patient's would have been. [That] leads us to conclude that the State may choose to defer only to those wishes, rather than confide the decision to close family members."

The Cruzans had lost, the state had won, and their daughter would live on in a "persistent vegetative state." White, O'Connor, Scalia, and Kennedy had cast their votes with the chief justice.

The opinion was classic Rehnquist. He had what could be called a modest view of the Constitution. For him, it decided little and left most of the decisions to others: state legislatures and state courts in this instance. Repeatedly, he said the Constitution "does not require" or does "not forbid" the state from setting its own rules. The states "may" follow the approach adopted by Missouri. He did not say they *must* do so. Indeed, most do not. Had Nancy Cruzan suffered her near-fatal accident in any state but Missouri and perhaps New York, she would have been allowed to die at her parents' request. However, according to the chief justice, the Constitution does not demand that Missouri follow the lead of the other states. His opinion ensured that the rules for these life-and-death decisions—or the death-in-life decisions—be made elsewhere. He invited state legislatures to devise clearer rules. The ruling also invited persons to make "living wills." Had Nancy Cruzan's wishes been in writing, even Missouri officials would have waived their "unqualified interest in life" and would have permitted her to die.

Sandra O'Connor had pondered the issue for quite a while before finally agreeing to join Rehnquist's opinion in full. In a concurring statement, she urged state lawmakers to devise their own rules and procedures for handling "this difficult and sensitive problem."

Scalia signed on, too, although he would have preferred a shorter, stronger opinion saying simply "that the Constitution has nothing to say about the subject" of a right to die. In a concurring statement, he conceded there are "difficult, indeed agonizing questions . . . presented by the constantly increasing power of science to keep the human body alive for longer than any reasonable person would want to inhabit it." The answers to those questions, however, "are neither set forth in the Constitution nor known to the nine justices of this Court any better than they are known to nine people picked at random from the Kansas City telephone directory."

The four dissenters—Brennan, Marshall, Blackmun, and Stevens—found much more in the Constitution than their conservative colleagues. They said the Constitution prevents the state from intruding into a family's personal tragedy. Nancy Cruzan has "dwelt in a twilight zone for six years," said Brennan, even though she had made it clear that she would not want to exist that way. "Yet the Missouri Supreme Court has determined that an irreversibly vegetative patient will remain a passive prisoner of medical technology—for Nancy, perhaps for the next 30 years." He lambasted the Missouri judges for showing "disdain" for Nancy's wishes, and he faulted the Court majority for deferring to the state's abstract interest in life. Brennan concluded, "No state interest could outweigh the rights of an individual in Nancy Cruzan's position."

Despite the Court's ruling, Nancy Cruzan did not "remain a passive prisoner of medical technology." Rehnquist's opinion had spotlighted the notion that Nancy could be allowed to die if her parents had "clear and convincing evidence" of her wishes. In a subsequent hearing before the probate judge, they and her lawyers were able to bring forth more witnesses who made a convincing case that Nancy would wish to die if she could speak for herself. When the probate judge again granted the family's petition, the state supreme court affirmed the decision, and on December 26, 1990, Nancy Cruzan died.

The Minnesota abortion case came down the same day as the "right-to-die" ruling. O'Connor had cast the deciding vote, but she made her decision as narrow as possible. Minnesota may not demand that both parents of a pregnant minor be notified in all instances. That is unreasonable, she said, because of absent or abusive fathers. However, the state may demand

that the young girl explain this to a judge, who in turn can waive the notification requirement.

The case had split the Court into three groups. The ACLU wanted the state law struck down entirely so that the pregnant young women could decide for themselves or consult with their parents. Brennan, Marshall, and Blackmun supported this position. The state of Minnesota wanted to require that both of her parents be notified, with no exceptions. A judge could not waive the requirement. Four justices backed that position: Kennedy, Rehnquist, White, and Scalia. In the middle stood O'Connor and Stevens. They said that the state has a valid interest in demanding that doctors notify the girl's parents and wait 48 hours before performing the abortion. However, they also agreed that the state must allow a judge to waive this requirement, especially the demand that absent fathers be notified. The bottom line was that the state law would stand as it was before the court case began. A pregnant teenager in Minnesota who will not or cannot tell both her parents would have to go to the courthouse, sometimes with her mother at her side, to explain her predicament to a judge.

In a companion case released the same day, the Court upheld an Ohio law that required a pregnant minor to prove to a judge through "clear and convincing evidence" that she was mature enough to decide for herself on an abortion without notifying a parent. This was a high standard of proof, the same high standard the Court had just approved in the Cruzan case—but with one glaring difference. The parents lost in the Missouri case, but the parents' interests were upheld in the Ohio case.

Because of Ohio's abortion law and its high standard of proof, the parent's right to be notified of the pending abortion would almost always prevail over their daughter's wish to make her decision alone. The parents' wishes, which the conservatives had dismissed in the Missouri case, now took on primary importance for them in the teenage abortion cases. Without blinking an eye, they launched into a tribute to the family and its fundamental role in personal affairs.

These state abortion restrictions for teenagers "rest upon a tradition of a parental role in the care and upbringing of children that is as old as civilization itself," Anthony Kennedy wrote, dissenting from the waiver of the two-parent notice requirement in *Hodgson* v. *Minnesota*. In his view, even absent fathers had a right to be notified of their daughters' pregnancies. The government may surely "recognize and promote the primacy of the family tie," he wrote in the Minnesota case.

While O'Connor's vote created a liberal majority to slightly limit the Minnesota law, she voted to uphold the Ohio law and thereby created a conservative majority. Rehnquist assigned the opinion in *Ohio* v. *Akron Center for Reproductive Health* to Kennedy, who seemed to endorse the right-to-life view.

"A fair and enlightened society may decide that each of its members should attain a clearer, more tolerant understanding of the profound philosophical choices confronted by a woman who is considering whether to seek an abortion. Her decision will embrace her own destiny and personal dignity, and the origins of the other human life that lie within the embryo. The state is entitled to assume that, for most of its people, the beginnings of that understanding will be within the family, society's most intimate association," Kennedy said. "It would deny all dignity to the family to say that the State cannot take this reasonable step . . . to ensure that, in most cases, a young woman will receive guidance and understanding from a parent." Rehnquist, White, and Scalia joined Kennedy's opinions in both cases. It marked the first time the Court had spoken of protecting the "human life . . . within the embryo."

The two decisions cleared the way for at least 31 states to enforce laws restricting the abortion rights of teenagers. The prophecy of the *Webster* case had proven accurate: The Rehnquist Court would permit regulation and restriction of abortion, while the ultimate fate of the abortion right depended on new cases and new justices.

It was left for the three octogenarians to point out that today's families do not always match the ideal of long ago. Brennan, Blackmun, and Marshall took the side of the teenager in trouble. The trial record, they said, brimmed with examples of parents who were drunk and abusive and who beat and intimidated their children. Some teenagers even got pregnant in hopes of escaping an unhappy home. Certainly these were the exceptions, they said, but the law covered all teenagers, not just most of them, and no law was needed for the families where daughters and parents communicated on good terms. Blackmun said he found it "bewildering" that the conservatives showed a "selective blindness to this stark social reality." Marshall said these state laws "force a young woman in an already dire situation to choose between two fundamentally unacceptable alternatives: notifying a possibly dictatorial or even abusive parent or justifying her profoundly personal decision in an intimidating judicial proceeding to a black-robed stranger."

Still, the liberals were not entirely consistent regarding teenagers, either. The year before, they had said teenagers were immature and not fully responsible for themselves when they deliberately committed murder, but when abortion was the issue, they were convinced that teenage girls were mature and capable of exercising responsibility on their own. In any event, the views of Brennan, Marshall, and Blackmun no longer mattered much on either the death penalty or abortion. They had been pushed aside to a large extent by the dominant conservatives.

The clerks for Brennan and Marshall knew they were witnessing the final years, perhaps the final days, of two legends of the law. Marshall moved in a painful waddle. He gasped for breath after walking a few steps. His eyesight had deteriorated, too. He could only read greatly enlarged type, but Marshall joked about his sad condition and persevered, determined to "serve out my term," as he put it. His clerks joked, too, that they had been given the best opportunity in the building to goof off on the job without being detected because "we can hear the boss's wheezing from 50 feet away."

Brennan looked weakened and shrunken since his gallbladder operation. The always sociable justice and his wife, Mary, still liked to go to dinners and receptions. She told friends she was not as liberal as her husband and considered voting for a Republican now and then, "and I would defend her First Amendment right to do so," Brennan joked.

Still, the 84-year-old justice looked all of his age. He shuffled as he walked, and he tired easily. At receptions, he could stand unassisted for only a few minutes. In the hallways at the Court, an aide propped him up as he walked among the offices. On the bench, Rehnquist noticed Brennan dozing off to sleep during the oral arguments. When called upon to read an opinion, his weak, raspy words sometimes never fully rose from the gravel of his throat.

Each morning, Brennan still gathered with his clerks at 9 A.M. to share a cup of coffee and the news of the day. He could reminisce about old cases or get his Irish dander up about an injustice he had read about in that morning's paper. He had not lost his energy for fighting for the liberal causes, but lawyers and friends who had known him for years saw that he could no longer persuasively argue and reason his way through a difficult case. He simply repeated words and formulations from long ago. On the death penalty, for example, Brennan insisted that the Constitution was intended to protect "human dignity," and capital punishment was therefore inhumane and unconstitutional. End of discussion.

Still, within the conference room, he remained a formidable presence. He stated his liberal positions clearly and without qualifications. During the spring, he had prevailed in half a dozen cases, mostly when Byron White sided with him. On June 21, he read a 5–4 ruling declaring that low-level public employees may not be penalized because they do not belong to the political party in power. In Brennan's view, the First Amendment protection of free speech shielded public employees, such as a state rehabilitation counselor and a cafeteria manager, from losing their jobs or promotions because of their political views.

The biggest surprise, however, came on June 27, the last day of the term. The courtroom was filled because the final few decisions were to be announced. Marshall's wife, Cecilia, entered the room and sat in the guests section near the bench. Why was she there? Marshall's wife came only for major rulings or—perhaps!—for the announcement that her husband was retiring.

The answer came soon enough. Rehnquist announced that the Court's opinion in *Metro Broadcasting* v. *FCC* would be read by Brennan. From the front rows, only the top of Brennan's head could be seen if he sat back in his chair. Now, he leaned forward so his face nearly touched his microphone. In a faint, scratchy voice, he recited the facts of the case. Rainbow Broadcasting had been chosen over Metro to receive a new TV license in part because it was controlled by minorities. This was in line with an FCC policy to increase "diversity" in the broadcast industry by giving some preference to blacks, Hispanics, and other minorities. Metro challenged this policy as unconstitutional.

As he came to the heart of the ruling, his energy revived and his voice rose higher. "We hold today," he said, his words crackling through the courtroom, "that benign race-conscious measures mandated by Congress—even if those measures are not 'remedial' in the sense of being designed to compensate victims of past governmental or societal discrimination—are constitutionally permissible!"

He referred more than once to a "benign racial classification." It was a jarring phrase, but a proper one according to Brennan and Marshall. For years, they had argued that the Constitution forbids discrimination that stigmatizes blacks or other groups because of their race or ethnic background. However, they said, it does not prevent "benign" discrimination designed to aid minority groups. As a historical matter, the Fourteenth Amendment was intended to further equality for blacks, they contended, not to protect the rights of white males. However, the two old liberals had never succeeded in writing this view into the law. Who would have guessed that such a ruling would emerge from the solidly conservative Rehnquist Court?

The ruling had potentially profound consequences. The Republican White House for a decade had worked incessantly to stamp out preferential policies for blacks and other minorities. Thanks to White's backing, though, Brennan had now written an opinion that gave the Democratic-controlled Congress a free hand to mandate affirmative action throughout the federal government.

The conservatives were astonished and angry. For weeks, Scalia had fumed about the decision. It put a blot on the entire term for him. In a dissent, O'Connor recited a series of recent opinions—including hers in the *Richmond* case—where the Court had said the Constitution required equal treatment for all. With five votes, Brennan simply ignored those decisions, she said.

Kennedy turned out a second, eloquent dissent, which accused the majority of returning to the thinking of *Plessy* v. *Ferguson* nearly 100 years before. Then, the justices thought the separation of the races was benign and helpful to both, he said. "Perhaps the Court can succeed in its assumed role of case-by-case arbiter of when it is desirable and benign for the Government to disfavor some citizens and favor others based on the color of skin," Kennedy wrote. "But history suggests much peril in this enterprise, and so the Constitution forbids it. I regret that after a century of judicial opinions we interpret the Constitution to do no more than move us from 'separate but equal' to 'unequal but benign.'"

The affirmative action opinion ended the term on a sour note for the chief justice and the three Reagan appointees, but Rehnquist figured he would have a chance in the future to overturn the ruling. As he told a judges' conference a week later, "The ball game is never over in our Court."

What Rehnquist and others did not know was that the *Metro Broadcasting* opinion would be Brennan's last. The justice and his wife booked a Norwegian cruise in early July, hoping the relaxation and the sea air would help Brennan regain his strength, but the vacation had problems from the start. In the Newark Airport, the justice blacked out, fell, and struck his head, but a few minutes later he felt better and was wheeled onto the plane to continue with his trip. Throughout the voyage, though, he had periods of being disoriented. When he returned to Washington, his doctor confirmed his fears. He had suffered a stroke. His memory faded in and out. At times, he could talk lucidly, but there were moments of confusion, too. He had no choice, he concluded, but to retire from his life's work on the Court.

He had served nearly 34 years, longer than all but four justices in the Court's 200-year history. He had written enough opinions to fill several thick volumes of the *U.S. Reports.* In the 1960s, he had breathed new life into the Bill of Rights as a member of the dominant liberal wing on the Court. During the 1970s and 1980s, he had held back the conservative tide, but now, the end had come.

On Friday, July 20th, the Court building was quiet. Most of the justices were gone from hot and steamy Washington when Brennan came by the Court to compose a retirement letter.

The main news that day had come from the U.S. Court of Appeals a few blocks away. Judge Laurence H. Silberman, the Reagan appointee who had declared unconstitutional the independent counsel law in 1988, had joined with a second Reagan appointee to void the criminal convictions of Lieutenant Colonel Oliver North, the key figure in the Iran–Contra affair. Two years before, Rehnquist had thrown out Silberman's first opinion and thereby allowed Independent Counsel Lawrence Walsh to continue his probe of North, which resulted in a jury convicting the former Reagan aide on three counts. Silberman overturned these convictions, not because North's Congressional testimony had been used against him, but because Walsh failed to prove that none of the witnesses in the case were influenced by what North said in that testimony.

In his chambers, Brennan wrote out a two-line letter.

"My dear Mr. President,

"The strenuous demand of court work and its related duties required or expected of a justice appear at this time to be incompatible with my advancing age and medical condition.

"I therefore retire effective immediately as an associate justice of the Supreme Court of the United States."

Brennan planned to meet Monday morning with his four new clerks to tell them first of the news. Only then would he send the letter to the president and make his announcement public. Brennan also placed calls to a few friends, including Thurgood Marshall, to tell them of his plans. The word soon spread around Capitol Hill, where Marshall's son worked for Senator Edward Kennedy. The Massachusetts Senator put aides to work drafting a tribute to Brennan. He "ranks with [John] Marshall, Holmes, and Brandeis as one of the greatest justices the country has ever had," said Kennedy's statement. "No justice has more faithfully reflected our country's defining ideal of commitment to the Bill of Rights and equal justice under law."

By late afternoon, calls were coming into Brennan's chambers asking whether the rumors were true. Brennan decided his announcement could not wait. His clerks were hurriedly dispatched to deliver his letter to the White House, where it was then sent electronically to President Bush aboard *Air Force One*. At 7 P.M., the Court announced the news.

The Court career of William J. Brennan, Jr., one of the truly great justices of the twentieth century, was over.

10

From Weare to the White House

Boyden Gray, the tall, lanky lawyer for the president of the United States, was enjoying an afternoon away from the office. With George Bush traveling out west, the White House had slowed in late July to its summer vacation pace. Gray had left early to play tennis with friends and planned to join them for a relaxed dinner.

Like George Bush, Gray had a patrician background. He was the son of a wealthy and prominent North Carolina family and had grown up in the white-columned home of the university president in Chapel Hill. At Harvard and at the University of North Carolina law school, Gray had excelled as an intense, hardworking student with a minimal social life. Though he joined a prominent Democrat-dominated Washington law firm in the 1970s, Gray grew dismayed at the failures of Democratic liberalism and drifted toward the Republican party. In 1981, he met the newly elected vice president George Bush. They soon discovered that the Bush and Gray families had known each other for years, and their fathers had played golf together. Bush offered Gray the position of counsel to the vice president, and Gray cemented their relationship over eight years with smart, discreet, and loyal service.

When Bush became president, he selected as his first appointment C. Boyden Gray as the White House counsel. An heir to the R. J. Reynolds tobacco fortune who motors to work in an old, ethanol-powered Chevy Citation, Gray was often portrayed as a shy eccentric, but no one questioned that he was a behind-the-scenes power in the Bush administration. Unlike the volatile chief of staff John Sununu, Gray shunned the spotlight and maintained a deliberate, unruffled manner. Nonetheless, his words carried weight with the president, who delegated to him the task of selecting potential candidates for the Supreme Court.

On his way home from the tennis court, Gray received a call from *Air Force One*. Justice Brennan was retiring, and the president wanted to meet in the Oval Office at 8 A.M. Saturday to go over the possible replacements. Bush liked to move quickly, as evidenced by how he played golf at a near sprint. The president would want to weed out names and be ready to make a nomination in a day or two. Gray needed to move quickly, too. He showered, skipped dinner, and headed back downtown to the White House to get the briefing files together on a dozen potential nominees.

According to Gray, he had inherited "the files and the institutional memory" of the Reagan administration. Many of the top candidates on his list were carryovers from the Reagan years: judges with a conservative track record. Bush also wanted Hispanic candidates, and several judges from Texas and California had been added to the list, but the president already had a favorite in mind.

Clarence Thomas had a big handshake and a hearty laugh. He had grown up poor in Pin Point, Georgia, had made it through the Yale Law School with brains and drive, and had come to Washington with Senator John Danforth (R, Missouri). Conservatives of all stripes fared well in the Reagan years, but Thomas stood out as special. He was a black conservative, a forceful and articulate advocate for a new Republicanism that could draw in minorities. George Bush was mightily impressed. "He's always impressed by the underdog who makes it against the odds," Gray said.

Under Reagan, Thomas—at age 34—became chair of the U.S. Equal Employment Opportunity Commission, the agency charged with enforcing the federal laws against job discrimination. Upon taking office, Bush nominated Thomas to the U.S. court of appeals in Washington, D.C., where, like Scalia, Bork, and Ginsburg before him, he could get some judicial seasoning and await nomination to the Supreme Court.

After the first Saturday morning meeting, the list of candidates had been whittled to five: Thomas; Judge Laurence H. Silberman, who sat on the same court with Thomas; Judge Edith Jones, of Houston; Judge David H. Souter, a New Hampshire Supreme Court judge who only weeks before had joined the U.S. appeals court in Boston; and Solicitor General Kenneth Starr.

Gray and Attorney General Dick Thornburgh urged that Thomas be removed from the list of finalists. He had been on the appeals court for only a few months; he had not gotten his feet wet yet, Gray argued. He had not written any opinions yet and may not even like being a judge. It would be unfair to him to elevate him to the Supreme Court so soon. Reluctantly, Bush agreed. Starr was doing a fine job as solicitor general but had already put his name to briefs urging that Roe v. Wade be overturned. Bush and Sununu wanted to avoid a summer-long battle on abortion. Starr was highly capable, well-liked, and young. Better to leave him where he was for now.

Silberman was the next to go. A veteran of past Republican administrations, the 54-year-old Silberman had won admirers for his intelligence and drive but had made an equal number of enemies with his explosive temper. Fortunately for him, his admirers were concentrated in the upper reaches of the Justice Department and the White House. As a judge, he had fought to defend the powers of the president. For example, in his opinion striking down the independent counsel law, Silberman worried that the president's powers could be impaired if his top aides could be investigated at the behest of Congress. Still, Gray acknowledged it "could pose a problem" to select him now for the Supreme Court, just days after he had freed Oliver North from criminal charges. His name was struck from the list.

Edith Jones had become the favorite among Washington conservatives. She had come from the same Houston law firm as Secretary of State James Baker and had been active in the Texas Republican Party. After becoming a judge on the U.S. Fifth Circuit Court of Appeals, she wrote several bluntly conservative opinions and made the rounds of conservative legal meetings, such as the Federalist Society. She had won influential advocates, but neither Bush nor Gray had met her yet.

By chance, Gray had had a lunch a few months before with Souter when he was in Washington, for his Senate confirmation hearing as an appeals court judge. In the final years of the Reagan administration, Souter had vaulted to the top of the Justice Department list of Supreme Court candidates. His legal opinions were well-crafted and conservative, but unlike the work of Judge Jones, they lacked a sharp edge. He had refused to promote himself, but Senator Warren Rudman of New Hampshire and ex-New Hampshire governor John Sununu undertook that task with relish.

The low-key White House counsel and the reclusive New Hampshire judge hit it off immediately. "I remember thinking to myself, 'This guy is Supreme Court material,'" Gray recalled.

Souter had a decided New England accent and spoke in measured tones. Short and grayish in pallor, the 50-year-old judge had a scholar's demeanor coupled with a dry sense of humor. Thornburgh had met him and, like Gray, was thoroughly impressed. They were struck by the sense that Souter seemed a man of an earlier century. One long-time friend said a conversation with Souter reminded him of a talk "with one of our Founding Fathers."

He lived for books, hiking, and shopping for antiques. He had little use for television and airplanes, and none for computers and "word processing." He wrote his legal opinions with pen and paper. He lived alone in an unkempt farmhouse near Weare, New Hampshire, in which books were stacked everywhere. Inside, it looked as though "someone was moving a bookstore and stopped," Souter joked. His favorites included

Dickens, Proust, Shakespeare, and Oliver Wendell Holmes, the legendary Bostonian who served 30 years on the high court and was the subject of Souter's senior thesis at Harvard College. His most recent purchase had been a first edition of the letters of Charles Francis Adams, the Boston-born son of John Quincy Adams.

On Sundays, Souter took his 82-year-old mother to services at the local Episcopal church, but Saturdays were reserved for working in his chambers. On this Saturday, before driving to Concord, he stopped his well-worn Volkswagen at the Weare post office.

A postal clerk asked him, What do you think about "Judge Brennan quitting?" Souter was briefly taken aback. He knew Arthur Brennan to be a prominent attorney and adviser to the governor but had not heard that he had even been appointed as a judge. How could he be quitting?

On television and radio Friday night, the retirement of Justice Brennan, the liberal leader of the Supreme Court, had been the number-one news story around the nation. It also led the newspapers on Saturday morning. So far, however, the news had not reached David Hackett Souter.

"He sure was there a long time," the clerk added. Finally, Souter realized he was speaking of "Justice Brennan" of the Supreme Court. In a few earlier news stories, Souter had seen his name mentioned as a possible Supreme Court nominee. Certainly, Senator Rudman, a moderate Republican who hired Souter when he was the state attorney general, had talked up his name in Washington.

Souter thought he was at best a long shot, though, for several reasons. First, he told friends, he came from a small, politically insignificant state. George Bush did not share that view, however, because New Hampshire's Republicans rescued his flagging candidacy in the 1988 primary election. Souter also pointed out that he did not know Bush and that he had not written provocative articles or given speeches. Moreover, he had served only a few weeks on the U.S. appeals court. Having gone through a Senate confirmation in Washington and having moved into new offices in Boston, he was looking forward to a quiet summer. He told friends he had been "running on empty" for a few months.

By Saturday evening at the White House, however, Souter and Jones had emerged as the two finalists. At midday on Sunday, Gray was dispatched to call Jones and Souter to ask them to fly immediately to Washington to meet with him and with the president. Reaching Souter proved a bit difficult. Gray reached Souter's mother by phone and asked how he could reach Judge Souter. She was dubious and thought the call might be a prank. Why would someone need to reach the judge on a Sunday? Finally, Gray convinced her he was indeed the White House counsel and very much needed to reach her son as soon as possible. The rest was easy. Souter was at work in his chambers in Concord, New Hampshire.

Rudman already had been busy on his friend's behalf. At Sununu's suggestion, the senator had faxed to Bush a long detailed letter describing Souter's virtues. A few minutes after Gray's call, Souter called Rudman. He sounded perplexed.

Why would they want me? he wondered. There must be plenty of judges more qualified than he was, and some of them must know the president personally, he told the senator. On the other hand, Mr. Gray has asked me to come to Washington, so I suppose I should go, he added.

Rudman and Souter had worked well together in the New Hampshire attorney general's office. Some said Rudman watched over Souter like an older brother. The senator had a broad bulldog's face. Where the younger Souter was thoughtful and reserved, Rudman was direct and decisive.

"What do mean 'suppose?' " Rudman replied. "You pack a suitcase, and I'll pick you up." In Washington, Michael Luttig, a Justice Department official, met Souter at the airport and hid him away overnight at Luttig's house. At dinner, Luttig broke out the only bottle of wine in the house, a cabernet sauvignon, which included the inscription, "Best Wishes, Chief Justice Burger," a souvenir of Luttig's year as a Burger law clerk.

In a TV interview Sunday, Republican Senate leader Bob Dole said he feared a summer-long "blood bath" in Washington if the president chose a Court nominee who had spoken out on the abortion issue. In comments to reporters, senior White House officials seemed to agree, saying that the president preferred someone with a "fuzzed-up view" on abortion, a good, conservative judge who has not voiced an opinion on *Roe* v. *Wade.*

On Sunday evening, Bush met with his small circle of advisers and divided them into two groups to argue for Jones and for Souter. Vice President Dan Quayle and Sununu made the case for Jones as an unabashedly conservative nominee, "a strong 'in your face' political appointment," as one described it later. Because Jones was a woman, it would be hard for the Democrats to "hang the abortion issue around her neck," Sununu said.

Souter's team of Gray and Thornburgh said an appointment of a staunch conservative should wait until later. It was better to pick someone now who could be confirmed without a major fight, a judge who would get high marks for legal acumen. Souter had not written any articles or made speeches on controversial topics, and his New Hampshire court opinions dealt mostly with dry issues of state law. "About the only thing you can tell by reading New Hampshire Supreme Court opinions," one law professor observed, "is that you wouldn't want to be a New Hampshire Supreme Court judge."

On Monday morning, Gray visited with both Jones and Souter at the homes where they were staying and assured himself they had "no skeletons" in their closets. Then, the two nominees were snuck into the White House to meet with the president. Bush spent 30 minutes talking with Jones in the family quarters of the White House and then went to the Oval Office for a scheduled meeting with the visiting president of Ecuador. Then, he walked back to the residential part of the mansion, where, for 45 minutes, he and the New Hampshire judge sat alone and talked. Bush found Souter to be humble, quiet, and studious, a man who has made the law his life. Justice Department aides believed the conservatively inclined jurist would frown on an expansive Supreme Court ruling such as *Roe* v. *Wade*, but neither they nor the president broached the subject with Souter.

Bush then called his advisers together for one more "freewheeling discussion" on the two nominees. Souter was perceived as the more "brilliant" of the two. He was scholarly and nonpolitical, but he could be criticized as a reclusive bachelor. Jones had a husband and young children, but she would be seen as more political and ideological. For the president, it was decision time. It was 3 P.M., and he intended to announce his choice in time for the national evening news broadcasts.

Bush returned to the residence one more time to think over his decision in private. Throughout the earlier discussions, he had jotted notes on the pros and cons of each nominee. Now, he sat alone and scratched down more notes, comparing the candidates' strengths and weaknesses. By 4 P.M., he had filled up six pages and made his decision. He would nominate Souter. Press Secretary Marlin Fitzwater was told to get together the biographical information on Souter. The president and his nominee would appear in the pressroom in a few minutes to make the announcement.

The nominee had not caught up as yet with the whirlwind. Just the day before, the taciturn judge had awakened in his Weare farmhouse looking forward to a few quiet days of work in his chambers. Now, his life was about to be turned upside-down, his face and name put before tens of millions of Americans. All day, he had felt in a "daze." When Bush told him the news, his condition appeared to grow worse. "It looked like all the blood had drained out of him," said Gray, who was dispatched to inform Jones that the choice had been close, but she came in second.

"I'm most pleased to announce that I will nominate as an associate justice of the U.S. Supreme Court a remarkable judge of keen intellect and the highest ability, one whose scholarly commitment to the law and whose wealth of experience mark him of first rank—Judge David Souter of the U.S. Court of Appeals for the First Circuit," Bush said. He said that he had not "used any litmus test" or relied on "politics or special interests" in making the selection. "Judge Souter is committed to interpreting the law, not making it," he said. As Bush spoke, Souter gazed down at the floor. A few feet away, out of the camera's range, Gray stood watching it all. He was happy with the outcome. Souter did not appeal to any political faction or interest group; he had won the job on merit, Gray believed.

The TV networks had cut into their scheduled broadcasts to show the announcement. Thurgood Marshall was watching at his home in the Virginia suburbs, Rehnquist at his summer home in Vermont. Scalia had just come in from playing tennis in Malibu, California, where he was teaching a summer class. Their reaction mirrored that of nearly everyone else: Who is David Souter?

A few nights later, Marshall appeared on TV for an interview with ABC network's Sam Donaldson. "Never heard of him!" he replied when asked about Souter. "The first thing, I called my wife and said, 'Have I ever heard of this man?' She said, 'No.' " The 82-year-old justice said he gave the interview to speak of Brennan's retirement, but it convinced many viewers it was time for Marshall to retire, too. Within days, some young conservatives in Washington had T-shirts printed up that said, "Honey, have I ever heard of this man?"

Souter's profile became a bit clearer within days. He had been born September 17, 1939, the only child of Joseph and Helen Hackett Souter. His father was a loan officer at a Concord, New Hampshire, bank. Their friends recalled David as a churchgoing, bookish, and unathletic boy who always carried a leather briefcase. His worst offense, they recalled, was loitering after hours in the New Hampshire Historical Society. David's friends, however, did not dismiss him as a shy bookworm. In his 1957 high school class, he was voted "most literary," "most sophisticated," and "most likely to succeed." At Harvard College in 1961, some friends also put together for him a scrapbook of imaginary news stories of the future. One was headlined, "David Souter Nominated to the Supreme Court." He won a Rhodes scholarship to study at Oxford University and then returned to the Harvard Law School. Friends recalled him as a serious student and a witty storyteller. In his law school class of 1966, he did well but was no standout. One classmate remembered him as "just a quiet brain sitting there."

He went to work for a law firm in Concord, New Hampshire, but was bored. In 1968, Rudman offered him a job in the state attorney general's office, and Souter soon became Rudman's top deputy. When Rudman resigned eight years later, he persuaded the arch-conservative New Hampshire governor Meldrim Thomson, Jr., to name Souter as attorney general. In that job, Souter defended in court the governor's order to fly the state flags at half-mast on Good Friday. He also fought all the way to the Supreme Court seeking to prosecute a motorist who, for religious reasons, covered up the state's motto on his license plate. The motto says, "Live Free or Die." He aggressively prosecuted those who fought the building of the Seabrook nuclear plant, at one point personally urging a judge to impose a sentence of 15 days at hard labor for nine protesters who had occupied the plant.

Still, lawyers and long-time friends said Souter was no political ideologue. Indeed, many said they had no idea of his political convictions, even though they had known him for years. In 1978, he was appointed to be a trial judge. Five years later, Governor Sununu named him to the five-member New Hampshire Supreme Court. His colleagues joked about his drab wardrobe—that it was enlivened by the addition of the black robes—and his Yankee frugality.

"When his electric bill got over $30 a month, we all heard about that," said U.S. Representative Charles Douglas, a former justice. "Some of us were shocked he even had electricity." Souter worked long hours; his regular lunch consisted of an apple and yogurt. Though he had dated in high school and college, he never married, and he now appeared to be a confirmed bachelor.

An editorial in his hometown *Concord Monitor* summed up a concern voiced around the nation. "He has lived a cloistered life, devoted exclusively to the law, in one of the nation's most homogeneous states. Has his narrow life experience limited his grasp of the human complexities?" the paper asked. "Does he have empathy for groups of people with whom he has had little or no contact?" His hero, Oliver Wendell Holmes, had made a similar point in one of his many epigrams: "The life of the law has not been logic but experience," he had said. Souter had a logical mind, but did he have the life experience to make a great justice?

No one could answer that question. The Senate Judiciary Committee and Washington's liberal activists spent the rest of the summer trying to answer a different question: What was Souter's view of abortion and of *Roe* v. *Wade?* They did not find an answer to that one either.

After three days of hearings in mid-September, during which Souter adeptly discussed U.S. constitutional law, the Judiciary Committee approved his nomination on a 13–1 vote. Only Massachusetts Senator Edward Kennedy voted "no." The full Senate took up the nomination on October 2, and on a 90–9 vote, it confirmed Souter as the 105th justice of the Supreme Court.

PART SEVEN

The
1990–1991 Term

11

The Rush to the Right

O n Monday, October 1, the day Rehnquist marked his sixty-sixth birthday, the Court began its 1990–1991 term. The next day, the Senate was set to confirm David Souter as the ninth justice. Before thinking about the new justice, however, the chief justice paused to note the passing of an era on the Court's opening day. For the first time since the fall of 1956, the Court opened a term without William J. Brennan on the bench.

Moments before the marshal banged the gavel, Brennan entered the courtroom, walking slowly with the aid of a cane. He looked somber as he took a seat near the front. When "Oyez! Oyez! Oyez!" had sounded and the justices were seated, Rehnquist looked down toward Brennan and addressed him directly. He noted his 34 years of service and his "profound influence upon American constitutional law" but then turned to a more personal note. "We, who have been your colleagues, have had the benefit of knowing you in a way that scholars viewing your place in history cannot. The personal warmth which you radiate has enriched all of our lives and has inspired all of us to maintain the cordial relations so necessary among those who may find themselves in disagreement," he said.

Certainly Rehnquist and Brennan had found themselves in disagreement, almost without fail, for nearly 20 years. Through it all, however, they had remained friends. Like two football players who butt heads all afternoon, they could still walk off the field as comrades. The closeness between the two often surprised new clerks. By the end of the term, many were convinced that Rehnquist was Brennan's closest friend on the Court. "I liked him the first day I met him, and we have been friends ever since," Brennan said simply of his relationship with Rehnquist. A decade before, when Brennan's wife was dying of cancer, Rehnquist always offered words of kindness and support, Brennan recalled. Now, Rehnquist was suffering the same agony as the health of his wife, Nan, declined. On bad days, Rehnquist acted testily toward lawyers in the courtroom, but Brennan noted that these ill-tempered outbursts usually coincided with a change in his wife's medical condition.

Where Brennan had a notoriously sunny disposition, Rehnquist's personality had many sides. His writings were often curt and sarcastic. He had never rhapsodized about our common humanity with criminals. Where Brennan saw the best in the lowest of human beings, Rehnquist saw murderers, thieves, and thugs. He could be snappish with lawyers, yet with acquaintances, Court employees, and especially his law clerks, Rehnquist was unfailingly pleasant and considerate.

Clerks never got over their first meeting with him. They expected to be intimidated. After all, these young people just a year or two out of law school were entering the chambers of the chief justice of the United States. Instead, Rehnquist went out of his way to put the nervous young applicants at ease. He asked about their home towns, looked them up on a map, talked about their colleges, their hobbies, or their families. He was friendly, funny, and down-to-earth, and he remained that way throughout the year. No wonder then that Rehnquist, like Brennan, inspired an extraordinary loyalty among his clerks.

With his fellow justices, he was much the same. He joked with Marshall and Blackmun, visited Brennan when he was hospitalized, and told his colleagues that he still wanted to be known as "Bill." They did not comply; to them, he was "the chief." Nonetheless, as always, he remained considerate, genial, and unpretentious. He did not let disagreements on the law poison his personal relations. Earl Warren had once compared the life on the Court to a marriage, a forced marriage to be sure, but nonetheless a close, day-to-day relationship that lasted for years. At times, the marriage had failed miserably. Holmes once referred to the justices as "nine scorpions in a bottle." Later, in the 1940s and early 1950s, the Court was again torn by personal feuds. Robert H. Jackson, Rehnquist's mentor, had come to despise several of his colleagues, and his bitterness corroded his last years on the Court; he died at age 62, just a year after Rehnquist left his employ.

Certainly, lawyers would argue and disagree among themselves. They are professionals at arguing, and no distinction is too small to prompt a dispute. However, during his tenure as chief justice, Rehnquist has been determined that cordiality will prevail. He does not badger his colleagues to vote with him, nor does he hold a grudge against those who do not. Usually, he shows no reaction at all when a vote goes against him. "It strikes me as a bizarre notion," he commented once when the majority sided with Brennan, "but it's all yours, Bill."

Rehnquist's relaxed manner and dry wit had not only tempered disputes among the justices but also inspired loyalty to the chief. During the Burger era, the justices often mocked the chief's pomposity and scoffed at his legal ability. Rehnquist is not disparaged behind his back. In private conversations, the justices repeatedly emphasize the general good feeling among the nine members of the Court, regardless of their legal disputes. Yes, we disagree, they say, but we remain friends, or at least friendly colleagues.

Scalia liked to visit law schools and speak with students, but increasingly he met with hostile demonstrations on campus. His sharply written opinions on abortion and affirmative action made him a target for leftist students. At the University of Iowa in September, demonstrators shouted slogans through bullhorns and pounded on the walls as Scalia prepared to speak in the law school auditorium. For a time, university security officials feared for the justice's safety, and they recommended that he skip a planned reception after the speech. A group called the "New Wave" at the Iowa campus charged Scalia with taking "racist stands on affirmative action" and said he opposed "reproductive rights and gay and lesbian rights." Law professors who were in the auditorium had said that the demonstration was unnerving. "They were so close and banging so loud, it was a bit scary," one said. Scalia looked briefly irritated but otherwise unaffected, they reported. "He was charming to the faculty. He's an impressive character," another professor said.

Scalia had fared better at Pepperdine University in August, at least with the students. The Malibu, California, campus draws a more conservative student body, and Scalia mixed easily with faculty and students. He did not fare as well at the

beach house where he was staying. On his first evening, the
justice tried surf casting, and in short order, he reeled in several
large fish. Pleased with his success, he went to a nearby bait
house to get more rigs and bait. When he reported his catch,
he was asked whether he had a state license to fish in the surf.
Scalia was astonished at the question. A license to fish in "God's
ocean"! The state of California does not own the ocean, he
exclaimed. Perhaps not, but it does require fishers to have a
license, he was told, and there are stiff fines for violators. Scalia
could imagine the headline: "Supreme Court Justice Arrested
for Fishing Without a License. Claims He Was Ignorant of the
Law." Licenses were sold by the day, but Scalia planned to be
there for several weeks. The yearly rate for an out-of-state
resident was $60! Muttering to himself, Scalia paid for his an-
nual fishing license and then spent the next two weeks trying,
in vain, to hook another fish.

In the first week of the term, before Souter took his seat,
the Court heard two major cases. One case would show that
the Court had a conservative majority even without Brennan's
replacement. The other was to show that it was not the kind
of conservative Court that some conservatives had wished for.

For about 25 years, from 1955 to 1980, the Court had
devoted much energy to desegregating the public schools. In
several opinions written by Brennan, the justices had insisted
that formerly segregated school districts had "an affirmative
duty" to "eliminate the vestiges" of segregation, even if it
meant busing students across town. It was a policy that Rehnquist—as a parent in Phoenix, an official of the Nixon administration, and a justice of the Supreme Court—steadfastly opposed. However, a liberal majority of the Court had pressed
ahead with forced busing, despite widespread public opposition. Still, the justices had not specifically said whether, or
when, those busing orders would come to an end. In the spring,
the Court announced it would hear a case from Oklahoma City
which raised just that question. It was the first significant school
desegregation case the Court had heard in a decade.

From the time of statehood in 1907, the Oklahoma City
schools were segregated by law. Finally, in 1963, a federal
judge declared the system in violation of the Constitution and
ordered an end to segregation. At first, the district assigned
the children to the school nearest their home, but this "neighborhood school plan" did nothing to eliminate the vestiges of

segregation. Black and white children lived in different areas and as a result, still attended different schools. In 1972, the judge ordered cross-town busing to bring about desegregation.

Five years later, the same judge declared that the school district had achieved "substantial compliance" with his desegregation order and was now entitled to operate "without the continual constitutional supervision" of the court. In 1984, the school board chose to take advantage of its new freedom. It ended busing for children up to grade five. Older students were still bused, however.

Lawyers for the NAACP Legal Defense Fund protested. The school board's move re-created segregation, they exclaimed. Half of the 63 elementary schools became more than 90 percent white or 90 percent black after busing ended, they noted. The judge refused to restart the busing, but a federal appeals court in Denver ruled that the case must be reopened. Because segregation still existed, the Oklahoma City school board had not met its "affirmative duty" to eliminate "the vestiges" of the old system, the appeals court said on a 2–1 vote.

The case of *Board of Education of Oklahoma City* v. *Dowell* spotlighted a profound point of dispute in the law that began with Earl Warren's opinion in *Brown* v. *Board of Education* in 1954. Did the Constitution demand racial integration because one-race schools are "inherently unequal," as Warren put it, or did it simply demand that school districts stop segregating? If it was the former, busing should continue in Oklahoma City because it was the only way to maintain integration. However, if the latter view were correct, the case should be over and busing ended. Certainly, the Oklahoma City school board was not segregating its students and had not done so for nearly 30 years. Thurgood Marshall took the view set forth by Earl Warren. Rehnquist, of course, took the latter view.

By 1990, busing seemed something of an anachronism. It had split communities in the early 1970s and had become a national political issue for a time. The Nixon White House had assigned Assistant Attorney General Rehnquist to draft a proposed constitutional amendment to forbid judges from ordering busing. The amendment died on the vine, but public pressure slowly won out nonetheless. The most extensive forced busing plans were gradually abandoned. Still, the Justice Department and the NAACP LDF counted more than 600 school districts that were still under federal court control.

The Bush administration's solicitor general Kenneth Starr came to the Court on October 2 to argue on behalf of the Oklahoma City school board and its bid to end busing. A sharp exchange with Marshall summed up the dispute.

"General Starr, do I understand you correctly that in Oklahoma City the dismantling was done by putting it on residence rather than race?" Marshall asked. In their briefs, Starr and the school board's attorney had said that the city schools had concentrations of black children in some schools and concentrations of whites in others because of housing patterns, not because of actions of school officials.

"But the poor Afro-American kids were still in the same school. Is that your position?" Marshall asked.

"No," Starr said. The judge allowed the desegregation plan to be dismantled because the school board had complied with it for more than five years.

"Does the school stay the same? Does it still stay a Negro school?" Marshall asked again. Usually, the aging justice sat quietly through the arguments. On the occasions when he asked a question, he often had difficulty making himself heard or understood, but a school segregation case energized him.

"Not by virtue of state action," Starr replied.

"But does it still remain a segregated school?" Marshall continued.

"By virtue of residential segregation, it does," Starr said.

"Then, it's still a segregated school," Marshall said, "and you don't think segregation is unconstitutional!"

"With all respect, Justice Marshall, that is emphatically not our position," said Starr. The solicitor general had a mild, almost syrupy manner as an advocate, but he reared up to fight when pushed. "Our position is that any form of state-imposed segregation runs plainly afoul of the equal protection clause."

Despite Starr's protestations, Marshall was right in one sense. The solicitor general did not think a "segregated school" was unconstitutional if the segregation resulted from housing patterns. Neighborhoods were divided among blacks and whites in every city in America. A school board could not impose segregation, Starr argued, but housing patterns could cause the same result.

Julius Chambers, the general counsel for the NAACP LDF, argued for maintaining busing but ran into sharp questions from Scalia, Rehnquist, and Kennedy. According to Chambers, the housing patterns in the city were caused in part by the old system of segregation. Therefore, the busing cannot end until the city itself is integrated.

"Well," said O'Connor, "if 100 years from now in Oklahoma City there were still residential patterns [showing concentrations of blacks and whites], does this order have to remain in effect all that time and on into the next centuries?"

Chambers said that his position was that all vestiges of the segregation must be eliminated.

"So your answer is 'Yes,' " O'Connor snapped.

The justices were left again with a stark choice. If busing were ended, the schools would go back to the old pattern of separation by race. However, if they said that busing must continue until a city's housing is thoroughly integrated, court-ordered busing would have to continue for decades more.

When votes were counted, the chief justice had a majority, but a slim one. The appeals court ruling would have reinstated busing indefinitely in Oklahoma City. Five justices—Rehnquist, White, O'Connor, Scalia, and Kennedy—voted to reverse that ruling, but they were not agreed on a broad opinion that would end all busing orders. White, who in the 1970s had joined liberal decisions in favor of desegregation, did not want to sweep aside the Court's earlier precedents. He would go along with the narrowly worded opinion that freed school districts that had fully complied with the judge's desegregation order. It required a delicately worded opinion, so Rehnquist took on the task. The chief justice wanted to make clear that the era of court-ordered forced busing must come to an end.

The nation's business leaders wanted to bring another era to an end—the era of soaring liability verdicts. Since the mid-1970s, courts had been awarding "punitive damages" in ever larger amounts. Then, the largest punitive verdict upheld in a product liability case was $250,000. The ceiling was blown off in 1978, though, when a California jury handed down a $125 million punitive verdict against the Ford Motor Company. Because of a defectively designed gasoline tank, the Ford Pinto could explode when hit from the rear. In the normal lawsuits that follow an auto accident, persons who are injured by another driver might sue, seeking payment for their actual losses—medical bills and the cost of auto repairs. Their attorneys may also seek damages for the injured party's "pain and suffering." This figure is more difficult to calculate but nonetheless is compensation for the accident. Punitive damages are

different. They are intended to punish the wrongdoer. In a
sense, they are more akin to a criminal fine than to paying a
person for losses. The amount depends almost entirely on the
jury. How much will it take to punish a big company, which,
it was alleged, tried to save money at the expense of the lives
of motorists?

The makers of autos, airplanes, household appliances, new
vaccines, and medical equipment were among those who
feared—and despised—punitive damages. Claims for actual
damages could be estimated and covered by insurance. Perhaps
it would take $50,000 to fully compensate a person severely
injured by a new product, but the jury might also tack on a
$5,000,000 punitive award to send a message to the corpo-
ration. Punitive damages were a wild card.

Probably the hardest hit were insurers. Here's a typical
case: An insurance company refused to pay a $5,000 claim to
a policyholder for the accidental loss of a limb. The man had
had his leg amputated because, according to him, he hurt it in
an accident. The doctors for the insurer, however, said the
amputation was brought on by a preexisting circulatory problem. When the aggrieved policyholder sued the Chicago-based
insurance company in an Alabama court, not only did he win
the $5,000, but also the jury added on a $1,000,000 punitive
verdict to punish the company for allegedly trying to cheat the
policyholder. Often, the plaintiff's attorney made full use of
the home-court advantage. A remarkable number of closing
arguments said, in effect, "Let's send a message that the people
of Alabama or Arkansas or Arizona . . . won't put up with this
kind of treatment from a big company in New York or Chicago
or Los Angeles."

Corporate America was not the only loser in punitive damages cases. The Hare Krishnas and the Church of Scientology
suffered punitive damage verdicts of more than $20 million
each when former adherents contended they had been brain-
washed and deceived. In 1989, a Los Angeles jury awarded
$22 million in punitive damages and for "emotional distress"
to the male former lover of the late Rock Hudson. The late
actor's estate was punished because Hudson had failed to reveal
to his lover that he had AIDS.

For at least five years, attorneys for business had been
appealing punitive verdicts and urging the Court to act. Their
message was that the system was out of control and was hurting
American business. Something must be done. Were these pu-

nitive awards somehow unconstitutional? If so, could they be reined in?

The business attorneys posed two theories as to why these damage awards violated the Constitution. First, they suggested that huge punitive verdicts violated the Eighth Amendment and its ban on "excessive fines." The amendment says in total: "Excessive bail shall not be required, nor excessive fines imposed, nor cruel and unusual punishments inflicted." Because punitive damages are similar to criminal fines, they should be struck down if they are greatly in excess of the maximum fines imposed by the state. For example, a state law may say that a business fraud can result in a fine up to $50,000. By this standard, it would then be unconstitutionally "excessive" for a jury to impose a $5,000,000 punitive verdict for a business fraud.

The second theory focused on the clause in the Fifth and Fourteenth Amendments saying that no person may be "deprived of . . . property without due process of law." This means, the attorneys argued, that first, a person or company must be warned in advance that particular conduct is wrong; second, it must be warned that the conduct may result in a fine; and third, the fine must have an upper limit. The insurance company, for example, could contend that it had no warning that a dispute over a $5,000 claim could result in a $1,000,000 punishment imposed by a state court.

Take this example as an illustration: A motorist from New York City drives through a small town. The signs say "Speed Limit—25" and "No U-Turns." She has been warned. However, when another driver pulls sharply in front of her, she reflexively honks her horn. A police officer then arrests her. "We don't like to hear car horns. They are loud, obnoxious, and disturb the peace," the officer says. Is there a law against blowing horns? Well, not specifically so. "We see it as malevolent conduct behind the wheel," the officer says and then takes the motorist before a judge and reports that this out-of-state resident honked her horn while driving through town in an expensive Jaguar. The judge asks the clerk to check the price of a new Jaguar. A few minutes later, the judge pronounces punishment: The motorist must pay a fine of $2,500. If the car had been old and beat-up, a $25 fine would have sufficed, but it takes a lot more to send a message to wealthy out-of-state drivers, the judge explains. Has the motorist been deprived of her money "without due process of law"? Yes, the corporate attorneys assert, because she had no warning that her conduct could result in such a large fine. However, the court officials might counter that she had been arrested according to proper procedures, informed of what she had done wrong, and fined based on her personal wealth—and that is due process of law.

The Court considered both theories, but in two different cases, the second of which was heard in the fall of 1990. In June of 1989, on the same day the Court ruled that the execution of juveniles or mentally retarded killers did not violate the Eighth Amendment, it also ruled that million-dollar punitive damage verdicts do not violate the Eighth Amendment's ban on "excessive fines." Why not? Because the amendment applies only to criminal cases, not to civil suits, the Court said on a 7–2 vote. It was intended to limit government prosecutors, not private parties suing each other, Blackmun said for the majority. The ruling upheld a $6,000,000 punitive damage verdict against Browning-Ferris Industries of Houston. It had been sued in Burlington, Vermont, for "predatory" price cutting, which cost a local company $51,000 in losses.

The Court added, however, that it would consider the "due process of law" issue in another case. That case, *Pacific Mutual Insurance Company* v. *Haslip*, came before the Court on October 3, 1990. For big business, it was the major case of the year, possibly of the decade.

In 1981, Lemmie Ruffin, Jr., sold insurance for both Pacific Mutual, which provided life insurance policies, and the Union Fidelity Life Insurance, which provided health coverage. He worked out of a Pacific Mutual office in Birmingham, Alabama. In August, he sold a combined life and health policy to Cleopatra Haslip and other city employees of Roosevelt City, Alabama. The premiums were deducted from their paychecks and sent to Ruffin. However, he "misappropriated" the money, as the court record delicately put it, and Union Fidelity sent Ruffin a notice canceling their health insurance. The employees knew nothing of this.

On January 23, 1982, Haslip was hospitalized for a kidney infection and ran up a $2,500 bill. Much to her surprise, she was told her health insurance had been canceled. In May, she and other city employees sued Ruffin and Pacific Mutual for fraud and deceit. Because he was considered an employee of Pacific Mutual, Ruffin was dropped from the suit and the California-based insurance company was held responsible, even though it did not sell health insurance in the first place. The

THE RUSH TO THE RIGHT 371

case was not tried until 1987, but the jury handed down a whopping verdict: $1,040,000 for Haslip, most of it in punitive damages. The other three employees were awarded amounts ranging between $10,000 and $15,000. Pacific Mutual appealed, but Alabama's highest court upheld the verdict on a 5–2 vote, noting that punitive damages were commonly used to punish wanton wrongdoing.

Did this verdict violate Pacific Mutual's right to "due process of law"? Yes, answered most of corporate America. Without adequate warning, the company had been socked with a huge, punishing fine for a fraud that it had not perpetrated. Punitive damages should be declared unconstitutional, they said, or perhaps *caps* (upper limits) should be put on them. For example, if $50,000 is the maximum state fine for fraud, then $50,000 should be the maximum punitive damage verdict for fraud. Pacific Mutual's lawyers also argued that juries should be given specific guidance in setting a damage amount. Currently, jurors simply pick an amount out of the air, they alleged.

The Consumers Union and the state attorney generals filed briefs urging the Court to uphold the current system. A jury of 12 men and women should be permitted to hear the evidence and set a punishment that fits the offense. Big business can only be kept in line with big punishments, they contended.

The Court's conservatives were faced with a dilemma. The business lawyers had made a strong case. Rehnquist, Scalia, and O'Connor had already voiced concern over "skyrocketing" damage awards and the seemingly unlimited power of juries to impose them. The editorial page of the *Wall Street Journal*—a voice of conservatism—had no doubts that these multimillion-dollar verdicts "mock due process" and should be declared unconstitutional.

Yet for years, Rehnquist and his fellow conservatives had preached "judicial restraint." The Constitution does not solve all problems, and the Court should not meddle in state matters, they had insisted. If the Constitution allows states to put juveniles to death, to make abortion a crime, and to send homosexuals to jail because no specific language in the Constitution prohibits such laws, how can the Constitution be said to forbid juries from imposing big fines on corporations?

For the first third of the twentieth century, the Court was a friend of business. It struck down minimum wage and maximum hour laws and much of Franklin Roosevelt's New Deal, on the theory that the government could not interfere with a person's supposed constitutional "right to contract." After 1937, however, when Roosevelt began to replace the "nine old men," the Court shifted abruptly and thereafter gave the government a free hand to regulate the economy.

The mistakes of the nine old men became the abiding lessons learned by the next generation of lawyers and law students. For liberals such as William O. Douglas, the lesson was that the Court should enforce civil liberties and civil rights, not economic and property rights. However, nothing in the Constitution or its history necessarily endorses such a distinction. Meanwhile, young conservatives such as William H. Rehnquist drew a different, but powerful, lesson: The Court goes wrong when it tries to do too much. Better to err by doing too little and leaving most decisions to the elected branches of government, Rehnquist believed.

As a result of that lesson, the Rehnquist Court repeatedly disappointed business. It refused to strike down local rent-control laws, state regulations of business, or the federal antiracketeering law known as RICO, for the Racketeer Influenced and Corrupt Organizations Act. In each instance, Rehnquist gave the same answer he had given to the Cruzans and to the death penalty foes: Take your pleas to the elected officials. Lawmakers in some states had indeed put caps on punitive damages. The Alabama legislature, for example, enacted a $250,000 limit on punitive damages, but too late to help Pacific Mutual. Lawmakers in the state capitals or in Congress could outlaw punitive damages entirely, but the Court under Rehnquist was not going to invoke the "due process of law" clause to do the same on its own.

The October 3 argument in *Pacific Mutual* v. *Haslip* turned out to be uneventful. The justices seemed already to have made up their minds. When the votes were counted, only Sandra O'Connor favored striking down the Alabama jury verdict as unconstitutional. The more liberal members of the Court, Thurgood Marshall and Harry Blackmun, were certainly not going to lead the move to strike down a damage award won by a black woman against a huge insurance company.

On Tuesday, October 9, Souter stood on the Court steps sporting a big grin. He looked transformed from the shell-shocked nominee of late July. No longer the rural hermit and "stealth candidate," as he had been labeled during the summer, he was now fully confirmed by the Senate and sworn in as the ninth justice. He had had little time to get settled in Washington, however. Clerks and other Court employees had joked that the bookish bachelor might rent a room in the Library of Congress, next door to the Supreme Court. Instead, Souter found a small apartment a few miles away, near the waterfront, in the southwest section of the city, but he did not have a bank account established yet. When asked whether he had an employer who could be a reference for him, he was obliged to put down, "William Rehnquist, chief justice." He was still having some difficulty driving to work, he admitted. Though a map of Washington shows a city laid out in a neat, grid pattern, the District of Columbia has an extraordinary number of one-way streets that lead to dead ends, he reported.

Though he may not have been one to seek attention for himself, his arrival had not gone unnoticed around the city. In its "Style" section, the *Washington Post* ran a large story and numerous photos of "Washington's Most Eligible Bachelors." It began, "He's a bookworm who looks like Pat Paulsen [a comedian on the 1960s-era Smothers Brothers show]. His idea of excitement is a long hike in the woods. He does impressions, for God's sake. He wears extremely bad ties. . . . Okay, so he's no Tom Cruise," but the new justice of the Supreme Court is a bachelor. "That makes him a hot ticket, the catch of the day, a Power Date. In short, Washington's idea of Extremely Eligible." Next to a photo of Souter was the Court's phone number. The new justice was amused and pleased to learn that the Court's operators received 275 phone calls in response to the article. He was chagrined, however, to learn that they had not kept any of the callers' phone numbers.

As he smiled for the photographers, Souter said he was looking forward to getting to work. With only one clerk so far and a less than thorough grounding in federal law, the new justice had hundreds of briefs waiting for him in his chambers. On Wednesday, his second day on the bench, the Court would hear one case that could affect working women across the nation. The Court also was set to hear a criminal case that brought about an even bigger change in the law.

The case of *Auto Workers Union* v. *Johnson Controls Incorporated* had been called by one judge "the most important sex discrimination case in any court since 1964." It represented a clash between two fundamental interests: the rights of working women versus the health of their children.

The case began in 1978, when Johnson Controls of Milwaukee purchased 14 plants that make auto batteries. Because lead is a necessary primary ingredient in batteries, its workers are exposed to lead in the air.

The same year, Congress passed the Pregnancy Discrimination Act. It was intended to overturn Rehnquist's opinion for the Court declaring that a company's refusal to pay disability benefits for a female employee having a baby was *not* gender discrimination, even though the company covered all other health-related disabilities. Congress then amended the law to say that employers may not discriminate against women because of "pregnancy, child-birth or related medical conditions." Pregnant women "shall be treated the same for all employment-related purposes . . . as other persons not so affected but similar in their ability or inability to work," the law said. The House and Senate, in their reports on the new law, said that it will force employers to consider only a woman's "ability to work. . . . Employers will no longer be permitted to force women who become pregnant to stop working regardless of their ability to continue."

Meanwhile, Johnson Controls was grappling with the problem of lead in its plants. Lead is a known hazard for the reproductive systems of men and women. Elevated lead levels in the blood have been associated with spontaneous abortions and genetic defects in children. However, the exact risk is not clear. After studying the issue in depth, the Occupational Safety and Health Administration (OSHA) in 1978 said that it found "no basis whatsoever" for excluding all women from areas where they would be exposed to lead. However, it recommended that both men and women who wish to have children should avoid jobs that expose them to lead beforehand.

Based on that advice, Johnson Controls in 1978 discouraged women of childbearing age from taking jobs in the plants, and it warned them of the dangers. Women workers were required to sign a statement making it clear that they understood the risks of lead exposure. Despite its warnings, however, six female employees became pregnant while working around lead, and one baby showed a high level of lead in his blood.

In 1982, the company announced a new policy. Women "who are pregnant or capable of bearing children" were to be excluded from jobs that could expose them to lead. The exclusion covered women who were up to 50 years old, were divorced, or were living alone. The only exceptions were for women who could prove through a doctor's certificate that they were sterilized or otherwise unable to become pregnant. The policy was "designed to prevent unborn children and their mothers from suffering the adverse affects of lead exposure."

In 1984, a group of women workers filed suit against the policy, contending that it violated the federal laws forbidding discrimination based on gender or pregnancy. They were backed by their union, the United Auto, Aerospace and Agricultural Implement Workers of America, as well as by women's rights groups. Several other industrial giants, including Union Carbide, DuPont, General Motors, and Gulf Oil, were said to have similar "fetal protection" policies. If the principle were upheld that women could be excluded from jobs because of the possible effect on a future fetus, the impact could cut across the economy. One study estimated that 20 million working women could be affected, including those who worked in hospitals, on airplanes, and behind computers.

The women fared poorly in the lower courts. Without even holding a trial on the dispute, a federal judge in Milwaukee ruled that the Johnson Controls policy was legal. To the surprise of women's rights advocates, the federal appeals court in Chicago did the same on a 7–4 vote. It described the "fetal protection policy [as] reasonably necessary to industrial safety." The rulings relied on an exception written into the federal job-discrimination laws known as the "bona fide occupational qualification defense." It allows discrimination "in those certain instances" where an employee's age, religion, or gender results in him or her not having the "qualification reasonably necessary to the normal operation of that particular business or enterprise." It can be illustrated with a simple example. Discrimination against workers simply because they are old is forbidden, but an airline could certainly refuse to hire a 70-year-old pilot who has poor eyesight or slow reflexive responses. In that instance, quick reflexes and keen eyesight are "[qualifications] reasonably necessary to the normal operation of that particular business."

Can a woman's ability to bear healthy children be a "qualification reasonably necessary" for working in a battery plant? Yes, said the appeals court majority, because the lead can do real harm to "third parties"—that is, a fetus. The Bush administration agreed partially and filed a friend-of-the-court brief in the case. It recommended that the Court overturn the appeals court ruling because it was too broad. Because the policy upheld the exclusion of women who had no thought of getting pregnant and ignored men entirely, the company should have to justify it during a trial, the brief said. However, the Administration also argued that companies can exclude women from jobs based on "a concern with direct harm to third parties"— again, meaning a fetus.

When the case of *Auto Workers* v. *Johnson Controls* came before the Court on October 10, the justices had already made up their minds that the appeals court ruling would be overturned. Two of the brightest and best-respected appellate judges, Frank Easterbrook and Richard Posner, both Reagan appointees, had dissented from the Chicago court's ruling. In addition, the Bush administration favored a reversal. However, the justices had yet to determine the rationale for reversing the Johnson Controls policy—because it was too broad, or because it was fundamentally illegal? Does federal law allow employers to limit job opportunities for women because of the potential impact on a fetus, or does the law require that employers consider only a woman's ability to do the job?

Attorneys for the Bush administration and Judge Posner spoke for allowing employers to exclude women, as a last resort. The "normal operation" of a business implies the normal, safe operation of a business, they contended, and a battery plant cannot be operated safely with fertile women working there, they reasoned. The risk was too great that women could unintentionally expose a developing fetus to toxic lead. Therefore, the company can say that women of childbearing age do not have the "occupational qualification" to work in "that particular business."

On the other side were the American Civil Liberties Union, the auto workers union, and Judge Easterbrook. They said that an "occupational qualification" in this instance is "the ability to make batteries," as Easterbrook put it. If women can lift a battery or adjust a valve, they are as qualified as the men who are there. The Pregnancy Discrimination Act says quite clearly that female employees "shall be treated the same" as men, without regard to pregnancy or their childbearing ability.

Lead "poisons the fetus and causes permanent brain damage," said Milwaukee attorney Stanley Jaspan, representing Johnson Controls before the Supreme Court. His statement might have prompted a double take. Usually, corporate attorneys minimize the workplace risks faced by their employees. Not Jaspan. His job was to portray the battery factories as hellishly dangerous. No women of any age would want to be nearby.

This argument perturbed O'Connor, however. "It seems to me you are not coming to grips with the Pregnancy Discrimination Act," she said. "Your policy applies to women who are not pregnant and can perform the work."

Antonin Scalia chimed in that Johnson Controls was turning the antidiscrimination act "into a dead letter." "That was always the justification for discriminating against pregnant women. That they shouldn't work extra long hours because it would be bad for the fetus. To allow that kind of exception is to make [the law] into a farce," he told Jaspan.

On the other hand, Scalia also sharply questioned the union's attorney, Marsha Berzon. "How many deformities is too many?" he asked at one point. Scalia's vote would be crucial. If O'Connor voted for the women's rights position, the chief justice would need both Scalia and Souter to form a majority.

When the justices gathered Friday morning to vote on the "fetal protection" case, the seats had been rearranged at the conference table. Following William Brennan's retirement, Byron White became the senior justice and took the seat at the far end of the table opposite Rehnquist. As David Souter's first week came to an end, he felt that he had been hit by a "tidal wave." He had had little time to read the briefs or digest the arguments. He had sat silently on the bench throughout the first week of arguments. Nonetheless, he would now have to vote—and possibly decide—eight cases, including dense disputes over banking and securities law, attorneys' fees in civil rights cases, and federal regulation of pensions.

Still, the fetal protection case posed a stark and simple question: Who decides about the risks facing a fetus—the working woman or her employer?

Rehnquist and White agreed that women could be excluded from a dangerous workplace to protect their offspring. Neither could be said to be a supporter of women's rights. Both voted against the right to abortion in *Roe* v. *Wade* in 1973. Both had said in 1976 that companies did *not* violate the federal gender-discrimination laws when they excluded pregnant women from disability benefits. In 1987, they said that it *did* violate the federal laws against gender discrimination for California to require employers to give four weeks of unpaid leave to women recovering from pregnancy. Now, they concluded that those same federal laws against gender and pregnancy discrimination did *not* forbid employers from excluding women workers to protect their offspring.

Marshall, Blackmun, and Stevens disagreed. They said that federal law left these choices to women, not employers. If women can do the job, they cannot be excluded. Sandra Day O'Connor agreed with them. The Pregnancy Discrimination Act settled the matter in her view. Now, it was up to the last two Reagan appointees—Scalia and Kennedy—and to Souter.

Scalia cast the fifth vote to rule for the women employees. Whether the law was wise or not, it was nonetheless clear. The Pregnancy Discrimination Act said unmistakably that employers can consider only their "ability or inability to work," Scalia said, not their ability to become pregnant or the effect on a fetus. In 1987, Scalia had split with Rehnquist and White in the California pregnancy leave case, and he did so again to form a majority in the *Johnson Controls* case. Kennedy sided with Rehnquist, but Souter cast his vote with Scalia and the others.

All nine justices agreed that the appeals court decision must be reversed, but they split 6–3 on the reasons why. Rehnquist, White, and Kennedy said that they would allow "a sex-specific fetal protection policy" if employers could show that their workplaces were too dangerous for women of childbearing age. The majority ruled that such exclusionary policies are illegal. The opinion, fittingly enough, was assigned to Blackmun, the champion of rights for women.

During the same week, the case of an unsavory character named Oreste Fulminante prompted the Court to reconsider the law on forced confessions. For a century, the justices had strictly insisted that the Constitution forbids any use of a compelled confession during a criminal trial. If this rule was violated, the defendant was entitled to a new trial. In the spring, however, the Court had agreed to hear an appeal filed by Arizona prosecutors, who suggested carving out a new exception to the old rule.

The case had begun on September 14, 1982, when Fulminante called police in Mesa, Arizona, to report the disappearance of his 11-year-old stepdaughter. Two days later, her body was found in the desert. She had been shot in the head at close range by a large-caliber gun and also had strangulation marks on her neck. Fulminante became an immediate suspect.

He had quarreled with the young girl and had recently purchased a .357-caliber revolver with an interchangeable barrel. Moreover, he had five previous felony convictions on his record and had served several prison terms. Still, police lacked enough evidence to charge him with the crime, and he soon left the state.

During the next year, Fulminante was sent to a federal prison in upstate New York on a firearms conviction. Serving a brief sentence in the same prison was Anthony Sarivola, a former Mafia man and current FBI informant. His bureau contact told him to learn more about rumors that Fulminante was a "child killer." Because Fulminante was only 5 feet 3 inches tall and weighed 118 pounds, he was frightened by other inmates, who did not take kindly to child killers. During an evening stroll around the prison grounds, Sarivola told Fulminante he could arrange protection for him, but only if he told him the truth. After initially denying the rumors, Fulminante finally confessed that he had killed his stepdaughter. He said that he had strangled her and shot her in the head. When the two were released from prison weeks later, he repeated the confession to Sarivola's wife, Donna.

Based on this evidence, Fulminante was indicted in Arizona. He objected to the use of the confession, but the trial judge allowed it to be introduced as evidence. He was found guilty and sentenced to death. On appeal, however, the Arizona Supreme Court ruled that the circumstances surrounding his confession were "extremely coercive" because Fulminante feared for his life. Because the confession was not voluntary, it should not have been used at his trial, the state judges said. The Sixth Amendment says, "no person shall be compelled in any criminal case to be a witness against himself." Since 1897, the Supreme Court had interpreted that amendment to permit only the use of voluntary confessions at trial. Because the use of a coerced confession meant an automatic reversal of the conviction, the Arizona court—with apparent reluctance—reversed Fulminante's conviction and said that he must be tried again.

In his appeal to the U.S. Supreme Court, the Arizona attorney general raised two questions. First, was this confession truly involuntary? The informant did not force a confession out of Fulminante, who confessed on his own and for his own reasons. Second, even if the confession was judged to be coerced, couldn't it be considered a "harmless error" because Fulminante also voluntarily confessed to Donna Sarivola? Since 1967, the Court had said that some mistakes at trials could be ignored if they were minor and had no impact on the outcome. For example, if a judge misstated one element of the law when instructing the jury, that misstatement could be a harmless error and did not automatically require that the conviction be reversed. Similarly, if a prosecutor made reference to the fact that the defendant did not testify in her or his own behalf, that, too, was a mistake. Defendants have a right to remain silent, and their silence cannot be used against them. The prosecutor's comment, however, could be considered a harmless error. Nonetheless, in its 1967 ruling in *Chapman* v. *California*, the justices cited several examples of errors that could never be deemed harmless. One of them was the use of a coerced confession during the trial.

This was certainly not a new issue for Rehnquist. Nearly four decades before, he had faced it as a 27-year-old law clerk. In the spring of 1952, the Court received an appeal from three New York men who said that a confession had been beaten out of them by police. Harry Stein and two friends were picked up at their homes in the Bronx for questioning. They were suspects in the robbery and murder of a *Reader's Digest* delivery truck driver near Pleasantville, New York. The police had traced a rented truck to Stein and his cohorts. Over the next two days, the three were held separately and incommunicado. When a prison doctor saw them afterward, one suspect had broken ribs and all three had bruises and abrasions. The police, however, had obtained from them signed statements, up to seven pages long, admitting their roles in the crime. At their trial, their lawyers said the three had been subjected to brutalities reminiscent of the "Elizabethan age." The defendants did not take the witness stand, however, and the police denied using violence. They were found guilty and sentenced to death. A New York appeals court upheld the convictions.

As a clerk for Justice Jackson, young Rehnquist was assigned to read the appeal petitions and recommend whether the cases should be heard or dismissed. The Stein case presented only a "factual question" as to whether the men were beaten, Rehnquist wrote in his memo to the justice, which is contained among Jackson's papers in the Library of Congress. "This Court does not sit merely to correct error or review evidence, whether the case is capital or otherwise," he concluded. He typed below: "DENY whr."

Four justices—William O. Douglas, Hugo Black, Felix Frankfurter, and Stanley Reed—voted to hear the case, however. It was argued on December 18, 1952. In a four-page memo, Rehnquist then suggested to Jackson that the Court adopt the "harmless error" rule for coerced confessions. These three defendants are seeking to have their convictions reversed "even though they are guilty as sin," he began. Other evidence in the record, including testimony from accomplices and the license plate checks, demonstrated that the three had committed the crimes. Why not simply declare a new rule that coerced confessions can be a harmless error if there is other, ample evidence of guilt?

He concluded, "The purpose of federal review of state courts is to guarantee defendants therein a fair trial, not to discipline state police officers. If no evidence has been admitted at the trial which had substantially prejudiced [the] defendant, he has had a fair trial, and this Court's inquiry is at an end. The recent eagerness of this Court to seize upon coerced confessions as grounds for reversal is reflected in the trial below. The defendants, instead of attempting to prove their innocence, devoted their time to proving [that] the confessions were coerced. The ivory tower jurisprudence of the Murphy-Rutledge era [in the 1940s] has weakened local law enforcement, and if this case is an indication has saved few innocent men. It has been a boon to smart criminal lawyers, and has supplied this court with a number of cases. Let's hope it has come to an end. WHR"

It did not come to an end, at least not in June 1953. Justice Jackson delivered the opinion for the Court in *Stein v. New York* and upheld the convictions, but he did not adopt the harmless error rule. Instead, he restated the doctrine that a coerced confession would demand a reversal. "A forced confession is a false foundation for any conviction," he wrote. In this case, however, the New York court of appeals had carefully examined the record and concluded that these confessions were not coerced. In such a situation, the Court must defer to the state judge's factual conclusions, he concluded. Douglas, Black, and Frankfurter wrote dissents, saying that in their view, the Constitution absolutely forbids "secret confinement and police bludgeoning." Nonetheless, the old rule stood that if the Court found a confession to have been coerced, it reversed the conviction and ordered a new trial. The rule still stood on the afternoon of October 10, 1990, when the Court heard arguments in *Arizona* v. *Fulminante.*

There was no question as to how Chief Justice Rehnquist would view Fulminante's appeal. Here was a child killer, "guilty as sin," trying to have his conviction reversed on a technicality. The question was, How would the other members of the Court see it? Souter would be voting on his first case involving the meaning of the Constitution, not just a federal law, as in the fetal protection case. Like Kennedy in the *Patterson* case in February 1988, Souter had had little time to prepare. He would have to rely somewhat on guidance from his new colleagues.

Was Fulminante's confession coerced? Rehnquist said no. The next to vote was the senior justice, Byron White. He disagreed with Rehnquist. It was a close call, White concluded, but Arizona's highest court showed that Fulminante talked to Sarivola under duress. "We normally give great deference to the factual findings of the state court," said White. He could have cited *Stein* v. *New York* as precedent. He voted to say the confession was coerced.

Then, the discussion moved around the conference table in order of seniority. Thurgood Marshall agreed with White that the confession was coerced. Blackmun and Stevens agreed, too. O'Connor sided with Rehnquist, but Scalia agreed with White that it could *not* be considered a voluntary confession, giving White a majority. Kennedy agreed with the chief justice, as did the newest justice, David Souter. The vote stood 5–4: The confession was coerced.

The second question then was, can such a confession be a harmless error? Rehnquist said yes. This was a "trial error," just like other trial errors, and should be analyzed for its impact on the fairness of the outcome. If other trial errors can be considered harmless, so can this one, he argued. White disagreed again. The rule against coerced confessions stood as one of the pillars of the criminal justice system, he insisted. Marshall, Blackmun, and Stevens agreed with White, but O'Connor, Scalia, and Kennedy agreed with Rehnquist. The deciding vote was Souter's, and he, too, agreed with Rehnquist. Now, the vote stood 5–4 to apply the harmless error rule for the first time to a coerced confession.

Still, the justices had yet to decide Fulminante's case. Was the use of the confession in *his* case harmless? Yes, said Rehnquist, because of his second confession to Donna. White disagreed, because the confession to Donna was suspect, too. He was suspicious of criminals who became paid informers. Nothing was mentioned of Fulminante's second confession until a year after Sarivola reported the prison confession and only after the former Mafia man came under tough questioning. White did not think it was reliable. Once again, Marshall, Blackmun, and Stevens joined with White. O'Connor and Scalia sided with Rehnquist, but Kennedy balked. A reported confession to the crime makes an "indelible impact" on a jury, Kennedy contended. "Apart, perhaps, from a videotape of the crime, one would have difficulty finding evidence more damaging to a criminal defendant's plea of innocence," he said. Souter did not cast a recorded vote on the last issue, but the outcome was now set. By a 5–3 margin, the Court ruled that the use of Fulminante's confession was not harmless. Therefore, his conviction was reversed, and a new trial was ordered. Both White and Rehnquist went to work drafting different portions of the *Fulminante* decision.

The case of *Rust* v. *Sullivan* became the biggest of the term and the only abortion dispute. It began, appropriately enough, with Ronald Reagan and a committed conservative who served as his domestic policy adviser. By 1987, Reagan's power was waning. The Iran–Contra scandal had tarnished his public standing and emboldened Democrats on Capitol Hill. No longer could the president rely on his popularity to push through new legislation, but Reagan retained control over the federal bureaucracy. With an executive order, he could change policies throughout the government and without the need to get the approval of Congress.

"On Mondays, we would all sit around the table [with Reagan] and talk about issues," said Gary Bauer, Reagan's domestic policy adviser in 1987 and 1988. "He was particularly concerned about fulfilling all the campaign promises he had made." Abortion stood high on the list. Reagan had promised to protect "innocent human life" and had failed—in Congress and in the Supreme Court.

"It was something he really cared about. He would write it into his speeches if we left it out," Bauer said. "He wanted to make sure no federal funds were used, directly or indirectly, for abortion."

Bauer found a prime target for carrying out Reagan's directive. The U.S. Department of Health and Human Services

(HHS) spent about $200 million per year to subsidize "family planning clinics" for poor women and teenagers. In 1970, Congress had created Title X of the Public Health Service Act to provide these women with contraceptives, pregnancy tests, and advice about family planning. The clinics were visited by nearly five million women per year.

From the beginning, Congress decreed, "None of the funds . . . shall be used in programs where abortion is a method of family planning." Throughout the Nixon, Ford, Carter, and Reagan administrations, this had been interpreted to mean that subsidized clinics may neither provide abortions nor "promote or encourage" abortion. However, doctors, nurses, and counselors were told that they should tell pregnant patients of all their options. A "mere referral" of the patient to an abortion clinic was permitted, federal officials noted.

Bauer, however, wondered why the federal government should be facilitating the killing of unborn children by sending pregnant women to abortion doctors. Why should an Administration committed to the "sanctity of innocent human life" allow such a program to continue? With Reagan's backing, he set out to see that it was changed.

On February 2, 1988, the Administration announced a new set of regulations for the family planning clinics. Now, the doctors and nurses were told that they "may not provide counseling concerning the use of abortion . . . or provide referral for abortion." If a patient was diagnosed as pregnant, she "must be referred for appropriate prenatal" care so as to "promote the welfare of the mother and the unborn child." The clinics' staffs were advised that they may *not* mention abortion as an option. They could give pregnant patients a list of doctors, hospitals, or other clinics for further care, but the list may not include facilities "whose principal business" is abortion. For poor women and teenagers, that eliminated the clinics that provided affordable abortions.

The ACLU and the Planned Parenthood Federation immediately challenged the new rules in court. They said that this "gag rule" violated the terms of the law, stifled the free speech of doctors and their patients, and infringed on the woman's right to abortion. A lawsuit was filed in New York City on behalf of Dr. Irving Rust, a clinic director, against Secretary of Health and Human Services Otis Bowen. Dr. Louis Sullivan became secretary in the Bush administration and inherited the lawsuit. The federal appeals courts split on the issue: The circuit courts based in Boston and Denver struck down the regulations as unconstitutional, while the New York–based court upheld them. The Supreme Court agreed to hear arguments in *Rust* v. *Sullivan* on October 30.

Harvard law professor Laurence H. Tribe, a scholar of the U.S. Constitution, adviser to Senate Democrats, and all-purpose commentator on the Supreme Court, agreed to represent Dr. Rust and his patients. Over the previous decade, Tribe had become a controversial figure. Conservatives and Senate Republicans would never forgive him for, among other transgressions, leading the opposition to Judge Bork's nomination to the Court. As an advocate in the Court, however, Tribe was exceptional. He was quick, attuned to the justices' questions, and, of course, possessed of an encyclopedic knowledge of U.S. constitutional law. Some attorneys, especially those making their first appearance, try to deliver a speech. They treat the justices' questions as distractions. Others try so hard to thoroughly answer the questions that they lose track of their argument. Tribe was particularly good at using the justice's questions to his own advantage. He would furnish a tidbit of information in response to an inquiry and then use it to launch into a key point of his argument.

He faced an uphill battle in the *Rust* case, though, especially since the departure of William Brennan. The Court rarely ruled that a government agency's regulations violate the intent of Congress. If members of Congress disagree with regulations that are intended to carry out the law, they can simply revise the law to make their intent clear. Why should the Court do it for them? In addition, the justices had said already that the government need not subsidize abortion in any way. So, why would the government's refusal to pay for "referrals" to abortion clinics violate the woman's right to choose abortion?

Tribe decided to concentrate on the free speech rights of doctors and their patients. This struck at the heart of what seemed wrong with the regulations. Can the government "gag" doctors and force them to tell their patients only part of the truth? Could the government try to save money through the Medicare program by requiring that doctors not mention to elderly patients with heart disease the option of costly bypass surgery?

"We depend on our doctors to tell us the whole truth," Tribe began, "whoever is paying the medical bill, the patient or the government, whether he is in a Title X clinic or in the

Bethesda Naval Hospital." The mention of "Bethesda Naval" was a typical Tribe touch. Why not bring the argument home to the justices who, in all likelihood, will go there for a checkup or as a patient?

Though patients think they can trust doctors and nurses, the government instead "has set a trap for the unwary," Tribe continued. The clinic doctors, nurses, and counselors are told that they must "omit all information about one legally available option." Meanwhile, they also "must" steer a pregnant teenager to prenatal care for her "unborn child." If confronted with the similar situation in a hospital or clinic, "I would suppose that most of us would conclude the government had used its bargaining power to betray a rather basic trust," Tribe said.

Tribe's free-speech argument also had a built-in weakness, however. The speech at issue was not truly free because the government was paying part of the tab. Before, the Court had made clear that the government can control how its money is spent, even when it intrudes on free speech or "academic freedom." For example, public school teachers do not have a constitutional right to teach the virtues of communism, rather than capitalism, in their classrooms. The school board that pays their salaries can also prescribe what will be taught. Still, it is commonly thought that some professionals are exempt from this requirement. Artists, for example, have asserted loudly that the National Endowment for the Arts cannot restrict works that are "offensive" or "obscene" simply because they are subsidized by the government.

To Rehnquist, such pleas made little sense. Why would anyone have a constitutional right to take the government's money and then deliver the opposite message than the one that the government wanted to convey?

"Is it peculiar to the medical situation here?" the chief justice asked Tribe. Surely, the secretary of state or the president can hire a press spokesperson who "is not free to say, 'Look, I want to tell you reporters everything I know.' " Isn't it true, Rehnquist asked, that the government hires employees who then must say what the top officials want said?

"Absolutely, Mr. Chief Justice," Tribe said. It is true that some people are hired "as mouthpieces for the state." No one suspects that Presidential Press Secretary Marlin Fitzwater is saying exactly what he wants to say. Rather, he is saying what President Bush wants to have said, and everyone understands that.

"Other people serve as professionals in whom people place their trust. That's at the other end of the spectrum," Tribe said, prompting laughter in the courtroom. This argument cut close to home for some attorneys. Where, for example, might government attorneys stand on a spectrum that ranges from honest professionals to paid "mouthpieces"?

Tribe pressed his point, nonetheless. "The people in Title X clinics look like doctors. They are dressed like doctors. They act like doctors. Therefore, when they speak like doctors," he said, the patients have a right to expect the full truth, not a prerecorded message from the government.

When Tribe used up his 30 minutes, the solicitor general rose to defend the regulations on behalf of the Bush administration. He stressed that the family planning clinics had a limited purpose.

"It is not Medicaid. It is not community health services," Starr said. The family planning clinics are not there to provide all-purpose medical care. Rather, they are there for "facilitating or preventing pregnancy, not terminating it," he said. They can help to prevent pregnancies among women who do not want to become pregnant and assist women who do want to become pregnant. Anything else—including abortion—goes beyond the purpose of Title X, he insisted.

The justices wanted to talk about doctors and medical judgments, however. Rarely did the Court's conservatives sharply question the solicitor general, but the bow-tied Stevens took up the task with enthusiasm. Suppose a clinic doctor examines a woman who is pregnant, Stevens suggested, and determines she should have an abortion. "It's not an emergency, but [abortion] is the better of two options from a purely medical viewpoint." What should the doctor do?

He cannot advise her to get an abortion, Starr responded, but he can urge her to see another doctor. Once she tests pregnant, the purpose of the Title X program "is to maintain the status quo."

"The status quo is that she's pregnant," Stevens shot back. "She doesn't need advice to stay pregnant."

Starr apologized for an "infelicitous" phrasing but repeated his view that once a woman is tested as pregnant, she will have graduated from the family planning clinics. She must go elsewhere for help.

Through his first weeks on the Court, Souter had sat silently at the end of the bench. Now, however, speaking deliberately and with his distinctive New England accent, he took up Stevens's point.

"Well, suppose the Title X physician in the course of his consulting exam concludes that the woman is pregnant and in fact is in some imminent danger to her health. Can he refer her to a hospital for an abortion?"

Yes and no, Starr replied. He can refer her to a hospital for emergency care, but he cannot refer her for an abortion.

What if she faces "an imminent health risk?" Souter continued. The woman may have high blood pressure or a heart condition that would make a pregnancy extremely dangerous. If an abortion is advisable, why can't he tell her so? "Why does that violate the statute or the regs?" he inquired.

Starr held his ground: The family planning clinics are not intended to handle all medical problems, he argued, and they are surely not intended to recommend abortion. Secretary Sullivan is simply enforcing the law as Congress wrote it, he insisted.

Souter sounded unconvinced. "Isn't he going one step further?" he continued. "I think you are telling us that in that circumstance, simply because it is outside the object of Title X, the physician cannot perform his normal professional responsibility. You are telling us that the secretary in effect may preclude professional speech."

This had been Tribe's point exactly. The government could refuse to fund or encourage abortion, but it could not "censor" what doctors told their patients. The American Medical Association had filed a brief pointing out that doctors could be sued for malpractice if they failed to tell a pregnant woman with heart trouble, for example, that carrying a baby to term could be dangerous and that an abortion should be considered.

As the argument ended, the outcome looked to depend on O'Connor and Souter. The chief justice could count on White, Scalia, and Kennedy. He needed one more vote for a majority, but both O'Connor and Souter sounded skeptical of the government's argument.

The case of *Ronald Harmelin* v. *Michigan* did not pose an issue of legal complexity. It raised a straightforward question of justice and fairness. Does the Constitution require that the punishment fit the crime? The Eighth Amendment forbids the use of "cruel and unusual punishment," and those words had been interpreted to mean that the punishment must generally fit the offense. For example, while a life prison term was not in itself cruel and unusual punishment, it would be deemed so for a parking violation. However, the new wave of stiff sentences for drug crimes forced the Court to reconsider whether these punishments were cruel and unusual.

In 1963, Harmelin served with the Air Force as an honor guard at the funeral of President John F. Kennedy. Two decades later, he had sunk far. He was a cocaine addict, a pool hustler, and a part-time drug dealer, "purely small time," he says. In the early morning of May 12, 1986, he became a big-time dealer, at least in the eyes of the law.

About 5 A.M., two Oak Park, Michigan, police officers spotted a car enter the parking lot of a motel and then leave a few moments later. When the 1977 Ford Torino did not come to a full stop at a red light before entering the road, the officers flashed their lights. The car pulled over, and Harmelin got out. As he was being patted down, he told the officers he had a gun strapped to his ankle but also had a permit to carry it. He did not, however, have a permit to carry the marijuana cigarettes they found in his pocket. Harmelin was arrested and his car impounded. In its trunk, police found a gym bag with $2,900 in cash and 673 grams of pure cocaine, more than 1½ pounds. The cocaine was said to have a street value of more than $60,000.

Harmelin was convicted of drug possession, but his sentence for his first offense came as a shock: life in prison without the possibility of parole. His attorney described it as "death in prison." Harmelin had run afoul of the nation's stiffest sentence for drug possession.

To crack down on drug kingpins, Michigan lawmakers had mandated a life sentence for anyone caught possessing more than 1½ pounds of cocaine or heroin. It did not matter why the defendant had the drugs—Harmelin says he was "doing a favor for a friend" by delivering the cocaine to a dealer near his apartment. Nor did it matter whether the conviction was his first or his tenth. Because Michigan has no death penalty, Harmelin could have gunned down a dozen persons on the street—including the two officers who stopped him—and received no harsher treatment from the Michigan courts.

His appeal, filed from his prison cell, noted that "Ronnie had absolutely no criminal record, [had] harmed no one, did not display viciousness [or] an inability to reform," yet he was imprisoned like an ax murderer for "possessing a substance one can buy freely and legally on the streets of Peru." His appeal arrived at the Court on April 2, 1990.

Since the early 1970s, the justices had relied almost exclusively on the clerks to screen the appeal petitions. There were simply too many to keep up with, at least if the justices also wanted to read the briefs and write opinions in the cases currently being decided. To spread the workload among the clerks, the justices set up a "pool" system whereby the petitions were divided among seven of the nine chambers (not including Brennan or Stevens). For each appeal, a single clerk was assigned to read it, write a memo summarizing the case, and recommend whether it should be heard. These memos were then circulated around the building. Usually, the justices looked through the petitions themselves in the small percentage of cases that were recommended for review. (On average, the Court agreed to hear about three percent of the appeals.)

Stevens, predictably, had his own system. His clerks scanned the petitions and recommended the ones the justice should read. During the previous 33 terms, Brennan, alone among his colleagues, reviewed all the appeal petitions himself. He represented the last of a great tradition. A civil rights plaintiff whose case was thrown out of court, a Death Row inmate who was facing execution, or a hard-luck prisoner such as Harmelin could count on the fact that at least one justice of the Supreme Court would personally read the appeal. Brennan knew what he was looking for, and he could go through the appeals more quickly than his young clerks. Also, Harmelin's was just the kind of case he was looking for. Just a few weeks after his appeal arrived, the Court had announced that it would hear the case of *Harmelin* v. *Michigan.* However, unfortunately for Harmelin, Brennan was no longer on the bench when the case actually came before the Court on November 5, 1990.

Nonetheless, Brennan and Lewis Powell had left behind one precedent that would help him. In 1983, the Court—on a 5–4 vote—overturned a life sentence given a petty criminal whose sixth conviction arose from bouncing a $100 check. This punishment does not fit the crime, the narrow majority said in *Solem* v. *Helm.* That ruling overturned a 1977 opinion written by Rehnquist declaring that the Constitution does not demand that the punishment fit the crime. By 1983, Blackmun had switched sides, giving the liberals a slim majority. The five-member majority had ruled that the Constitution demands that a criminal's sentence "be proportionate" to the severity of the crime. Harmelin's attorney relied on the *Solem* v. *Helm* precedent, but would the Rehnquist Court abide by it?

Carla J. Johnson, a Detroit lawyer, volunteered to represent Harmelin. She had also defended him in the Michigan courts. "I felt so strongly about his case, I took it for free," she said. From his prison cell, Harmelin had filed what is known as a "pauper's petition." Usually, the Court requires that those who file appeals pay a $300 fee and submit 40 copies of printed briefs, which can cost several thousand dollars. Hiring a top-flight law firm to prepare the appeal can raise the cost to more than $30,000.

From prisoners and the poor, however, the Court will accept a single copy of a petition, along with a photocopy of the lower-court opinion they want to challenge. Each term, a dozen or more "pauper's petitions" are granted a review, many of them in death-penalty cases. Then, the justices ask an attorney to represent the petitioner by filing briefs and making an oral argument. The Court pays the attorney's expenses— travel and printing—but does not pay for the lawyer's work. It is an honor enough, apparently, to appear in the Supreme Court.

For Carla Johnson, it was her first such honor. Facing the justices, she stressed that the Michigan law was intended to nab drug kingpins, but mostly it snares "first-time offenders." The kingpins are usually too smart to carry drugs themselves. They rely on "mules" to do it for them. Juveniles who do not know the law are recruited. As Harmelin put it in one interview, the law mostly snares "idiots like myself."

"Michigan is way out of line with every state in the Union," Johnson said. "What are you going to do next, cut off their arms?" She geared her argument in part to Scalia's opinion in the juvenile death penalty case. There, Scalia had said this severe punishment was not "cruel and unusual" because a few other states would allow the execution of a 16-year-old. In this case, however, no other state would impose life imprisonment without parole for drug possession, Johnson pointed out.

Scalia was unmoved. "Maybe Michigan has a bigger problem with drugs," he said. "Isn't a state entitled to feel more deeply about a problem that can cause a loss of human life? Why can't they say, 'By George, we're going to put a stop to it!'? Why is that wrong?"

Because this punishment is "grossly disproportionate" to the crime, she responded. Harmelin is not a rapist, a murderer, or even a thief, yet he is being punished more harshly than persons convicted of those crimes in Michigan. Also, according to *Solem* v. *Helm*, such a grossly disproportionate punishment is unconstitutional, she insisted.

Rehnquist leaned forward to his microphone and patiently waited for attorney Johnson to finish her point.

"Well, Ms. Johnson, *Solem* v. *Helm* was a 5–4 decision," the chief justice intoned, and it essentially overturned an earlier 5–4 decision on the same subject. "Do you think the Court has reached equilibrium on this issue, or do you think more changes might take place?" he asked, to laughter in the courtroom.

She had run into realpolitik Supreme Court style. Yes, *Solem* v. *Helm* was a clear precedent, but the chief justice disagreed with it, and the votes may have changed since then. Johnson groped for an answer and then responded directly. "I don't think the Court should treat stare decisis too cavalierly," she told Rehnquist.

Oakland County prosecutor Richard Thompson cast doubt on the notion that Harmelin was an innocent dupe. The 672 grams of cocaine is a lot. "That is the equivalent of 1,200 hits on the street," he said. Moreover, when Harmelin was arrested, he also had with him a beeper and a coded address book, besides the cash and pistol. "This is a guy who knew what he was doing," the prosecutor said. He said he suspected Harmelin was probably "a major supplier to mid-level dealers."

The Bush administration also filed a brief in support of Michigan. The case played on two favorite themes of the Administration and the Rehnquist Court: getting tough on crime and deferring to the decisions of state legislatures. Michigan lawmakers are entitled to conclude that the "distribution of drugs is not a victimless crime, but is in fact equivalent to a violent assault both on the users of the drugs and on others who suffer the consequences," the Administration brief said.

Nonetheless, Stevens challenged the argument that Harmelin can be considered a drug dealer. He was convicted only of drug possession. Under the Michigan law, that alone is enough to trigger the life prison term. "Suppose a grandmother is keeping a suitcase for her grandson, who is the 'mule,' and it contains cocaine. He's gone for the weekend. She keeps it for him. Life without parole?" he asked the Michigan prosecutor.

No, not necessarily, because that may not be considered "possession" because she did not know of the cocaine, Thompson replied.

Stevens continued. "Ok, the grandson says, 'I hate to tell you this grandmother, it's cocaine in there. Keep it for me for the weekend,' " he said. Will that trigger the law?

Not necessarily, he responded again. The prosecutor has some "discretion" on whether to bring charges. However, once the charges are brought, judges and the court system have no discretion. Anyone found guilty of possession of the large amount of cocaine must be sentenced to life in prison. No exceptions.

For the Court, Harmelin's case posed another stark choice. Does the Constitution put *any* limits on the increasingly stiff penalties in the war on drugs? Is it cruel and unusual punishment to impose life in prison without parole for first-time drug possession? Must the punishment fit the crime, or can a state use stiff penalties to send a message that it will not tolerate drugs? To judge by their questions, the chief justice could count on O'Connor, Scalia, and Kennedy. Marshall, Blackmun, and Stevens were likely to vote to reverse the sentence. The outcome then depended on White and Souter.

Because the makeup of the Court had changed again, in the fall, the justices agreed to sit for another formal photo. The chief justice was flanked by the two remaining holdovers from the Warren Court, Byron White and Thurgood Marshall. Sitting at the ends were Harry Blackmun and John Paul Stevens. Standing across the back row were Reagan's appointees: Anthony Kennedy, Sandra O'Connor, and Antonin Scalia; next to him stood the new arrival, David Souter. The photographers were brought in in shifts and given five minutes to set up and snap their photos. As one group left the room and a second was getting ready, a pair of fingers emerged from a black robe and perched above the stern visage of Byron White. Behind him only the faintest of smiles crossed the face of Sandra O'Connor.

Already, Souter had been impressed by O'Connor and comforted by the reports of her early experiences on the Court. Like him, she had come from a state court and confided that it took her several years to be fully familiar with the breadth of federal legal issues that come before the Court. With hard work, O'Connor had mastered the terrain by now. Still, Souter admitted to being perplexed when told there "is no Miller Time with Sandra O'Connor." Having avoided television for years, he had never heard the phrase "Miller Time."

In January, the Court considered whether nude dancing deserved protection under the Constitution as a form of free expression. Brennan's opinion in the flag-burning case had made it clear that the First Amendment protected expressive acts, as well as words. Not all expressive acts, however, even political ones, could be shielded from regulation. Assassinating the president expressed a political thought, but the perpetrator would be prosecuted nonetheless. How could the Court draw a line that would protect some acts of expression but not all of them?

Nude dancing in night spots, like burning a flag in a public square, offended many but harmed no one and therefore should be protected from prosecution, its advocates contended. A federal appeals court in Chicago agreed with that argument. Relying in part on the flag-burning decision, it ruled that Indiana officials may not ban all-nude dancing under the state's public indecency law. This measure, similar to that in most states, makes it a crime to "knowingly and intentionally, in a public place . . . appear in a state of nudity." Under this law, a person can be arrested for being nude in a park, on a beach, or on the street. In addition, however, Indiana prosecutors decided also to enforce the antinudity law in private night spots and theaters where dancers appeared nude.

The inclusion of theaters was crucial. In 1972, the Court—in a Rehnquist opinion—ruled that states could use their powers under the Twenty-first Amendment, which repealed Prohibition, to forbid nude or "topless" dancing in bars or other establishments that served alcohol. However, the theaters in Indiana that offered nude dancing did not serve alcohol. So, Indiana prosecutors fell back on their public indecency law. It provided for, as one straight-faced prosecutor put it, a "blanket" ban on nude dancing. In South Bend, the Glen Theatre featured nude dancers who appeared in glass booths in front of paying customers. The theater and two dancers, Gayle Marie Sutro and Carla Johnson, filed a suit in a federal court, challenging the authority of county prosecutor Michael Barnes to enforce the no-nudity law. (Needless to say, this is not the same Carla Johnson who represented Ronald Harmelin.)

A federal judge upheld the state, ruling that "the type of dancing these plaintiffs wish to perform is not expressive activity protected by the Constitution of the United States." However, the Chicago-based appeals court disagreed, on a 7–4 vote. Dancing on stage is "inherently expressive," the court said. This "go-go dancing" conveys a message of "eroticism and sensuality," it said. The state courts in Indiana had suggested that an opera with nudity would be protected as free expression, but not go-go dancing. The U.S. appeals court said it was not going to uphold a distinction between "high" art and "low" entertainment. The state could regulate nude dancing—for example, to keep out minors—but it could not ban it entirely, the appeals court ruled.

The Supreme Court heard the state's appeal on January 8, 1991. The stakes went far beyond go-go dancing in South Bend. State and local governments filed briefs on behalf of Indiana, arguing that if the appeals court decision were upheld, they could not enforce their public indecency laws against any persons who contend that their conduct is "expressive." Meanwhile, artistic groups joined the case on behalf of the nude dancers. If the state can enforce its total ban on nudity in private establishments, the operation of art galleries, plays, operas, and movies could be threatened, they complained.

The hour-long argument in *Barnes* v. *Glen Theatre* contained both high art and low entertainment.

Indiana deputy attorney general Wayne Uhl said that the state wanted to ban nudity, not dancing. He relied on Scalia's opinion in the peyote case: The state's public indecency law was a general law against nudity, not a measure intended to forbid free expression. So, it should be upheld, he argued, even though it has the effect of banning some types of expression.

Even Scalia sounded skeptical of this argument, however. What about opera? The state says you can "sing in an opera without your clothes," Scalia said. "Why opera, but not go-go dancing? Is that the good-taste clause of the Constitution?"

Opera is different because it delivers "a particularized message," Uhl said. Go-go dancing has no message.

Is that so because the dancers aren't good enough? Kennedy wondered. If they were high-quality dancers, would it then be expressive?

"No," Uhl said. Dancing is just not expressive.

"So you're saying," Stevens interjected, "it would be permissible to pass a statute prohibiting tap dancing?"

"Yes," Uhl said.

"Could a state prohibit rock music?" O'Connor asked.

"No," the state attorney replied.

"How is it that music is protected, but not dance?" she inquired.

Because rock music conveys a message, but dance does not, Uhl responded.

O'Connor, who had raised three teenagers, looked unconvinced. "So you think rock music conveys an artistic message?" she asked.

The state attorney was now reeling. He decided to back down a bit. "Well, dance might be communication, but it might not be, either," he said. It depends on the kind of dancing. "We would resist defining dancing so broadly as to include what I'm doing here today."

Yes. "Song and dance," White grumbled.

The Indiana state attorney then returned to his theme that the go-go dancers do not convey a particular, artistic message. "At least one of the dancers said [in a court affidavit] that [the] only reason she dances nude is to make money."

"That's why Dickens wrote his books, too," Scalia countered.

Souter then joined in. He noted that the dancers had put forth a "medium-is-the-message argument." Nudity is essential to conveying their erotic message, they say.

The dancers can perform nearly nude, the Indiana attorney replied. All the law requires is that they "wear pasties and a G-string." These minor items of required clothing, he deadpanned, are "narrowly tailored" to further the state's interest in protecting public morals.

Bruce Ennis, a Washington, D.C., attorney who specializes in First Amendment cases, rose to defend the dancers. "Performance dance, like music, is one of the oldest forms of human communication and is inherently expressive of emotions and ideas," he said.

In response, however, Rehnquist and Scalia both noted that Indiana law bans nudity, not dancing. Why does that trigger the First Amendment? they wondered.

Kennedy then asked what became known as the "adults-only car wash" question. Suppose the owner of a car wash wants to attract more customers and he "hires a woman and says, 'Now, you sit there nude in this glass cage.'" Is that protected under the Constitution?

No, unless "it is a performance dance," Ennis responded.

"Well, suppose he said, 'I've heard the arguments in the Supreme Court and you have to dance,' " Kennedy continued. "And she says, 'I can't dance.' And he says, 'Just wander around when the music starts.' Is that a performance dance?"

"Yes," Ennis said. The First Amendment would protect such a performance, although it could be regulated, he added.

Ennis was pushing the First Amendment argument far, way too far for the chief justice.

"I suppose they have murder laws in Indiana which prevent people from killing people, whether in the course of dancing or not," he said. Could that raise a First Amendment issue?

"Yes," Ennis said. Like any First Amendment case, however, the outcome would depend on the state's interest and whether any message was being communicated.

"Well, what if the dancer wanted to do a kind of Annie Oakley dance in the course of which she fired off a revolver at various targets around the room," Rehnquist continued. "And the dancer says, 'Well, I can't really get across the Annie Oakley message without firing off the gun.'" Is that dance routine protected by the First Amendment?

"Yes," Ennis said, although the state's interest would easily outweigh the right to free expression in that instance. Though the examples sounded absurd, Ennis did not want to back away entirely and agree that some types of expression are due no First Amendment protection. That, after all, was Indiana's position.

The hour-long argument had been a free-for-all. The First Amendment and free speech issues split the Court in unpredictable ways, as the flag-burning case had demonstrated. In that case, Scalia and Kennedy had cast the key votes to protect the flag burners, but both had said that they were most interested in shielding politically oriented expressions. Without William Brennan, no one was left in the conference room who had been a persistent and persuasive advocate for free expression.

In mid-January, the public spotlight was far from the Supreme Court. President Bush had set January 16 as the deadline for Iraq's Saddam Hussein to withdraw from Kuwait. As the hours ticked away, a huge fleet of bombers and fighter planes were preparing to attack Baghdad. Unperturbed, the justices took the bench on January 15 and Rehnquist announced that he would deliver the Court's opinion in *Board of Education of Oklahoma City* v. *Dowell,* the school desegregation case.

Despite his narrow majority, Rehnquist used the decision to send a message to the nation's judges. "From the very beginning, federal supervision of local school systems was intended as a temporary measure," he said. Desegregation decrees "are not intended to operate in perpetuity. Dissolving a desegregation decree . . . recognizes . . . the important values of local control of public school systems." If a school board "had complied in good faith with the desegregation decree" and if the "vestiges of past discrimination had been eliminated to the extent practicable," then the case is over and busing should end, Rehnquist proclaimed. His definition of the "vestiges" of past segregation did not include current housing patterns. Rather, the trial judge should assess the school board's compliance by looking "not only at student assignments, but to every facet of school operations—faculty, staff, transportation, extra-curricular activities and facilities." If discrimination in these school operations has ended, so should the court's supervision of the school system, the chief justice concluded. His opinion was signed by White, O'Connor, Scalia, and Kennedy.

Because the decision was released as the nation was about to go to war, it gained relatively little attention. Rehnquist had written an opinion that laid the groundwork for dismantling the school desegregation decrees of the past 25 years. Thurgood Marshall, who made his name fighting school segregation, certainly knew the significance of the decision. Without pressure from the courts to desegregate, the schools in many areas of the nation would return to being divided by race. Though government-imposed segregation was gone and would not return, Marshall cared about the practical reality, not just the legal distinctions, and for millions of African-American schoolchildren, segregation would continue to be the daily reality. His dissent in the Oklahoma City case, however, drew only Harry Blackmun and John Paul Stevens. Because the case was heard before Souter took his seat, he did not participate in the ruling.

The next week, the students of the Howard University School of Law in Washington, D.C., asked Marshall to attend a ceremonial unveiling of a bust of the school's most famous student. It had been 58 years since Marshall had left Howard and had gone on to his legendary career in the law. Now, 82 years old and in declining health, he returned in something of a gloomy mood. "In many facets of life, we are going backwards as a race of people and a nation," he told the predominantly black audience. "Progress has slowed down. Indeed, it might have stopped."

Nonetheless, the ceremony cheered Marshall, too. At one point, as the students applauded, the aging justice clasped his hands over his head like a victorious prizefighter. School officials had not publicized the event but had sent invitations to members of the Court. Three of them—Rehnquist, Scalia, and Stevens—sent back regrets, saying that they were unable to attend because of schedule conflicts or out-of-town trips. The Court had just begun a three-week winter recess. Nonetheless, as the ceremony was about to begin, other justices began to arrive one by one. Byron White, Harry Blackmun, Sandra O'Connor, Anthony Kennedy, and David Souter all came to the stage to join Marshall. The surprise gathering prompted a quip from Marshall. "We have enough justices to decide a case," he announced.

Though the justices expected only to witness the ceremony, school officials asked that they say a few words impromptu. The usually reticent David Souter went first. During his confirmation hearings, he had told friends that if asked by the senators which justice he had most admired, he would have replied, "Thurgood Marshall." Souter told the Howard students that he considered Marshall "a prophet for our times." O'Connor called Marshall a "living legend," and Blackmun praised "Thurgood's character, integrity, and unceasing commitment to equality." Kennedy said listening to Marshall around the conference table had been "the most memorable thing about my years" on the Court. Byron White, who had served the longest with Marshall, stressed the impact of his stories. They "leave an aftertaste, a lasting reminder of this nation's regretful past. I shall always remember his stories," White said. No one could remember when so many justices had gathered for such an event, and their comments certainly told of Marshall's unique influence, one that was not always apparent in the written opinions.

Marshall had seen American life differently, and he did not let the other justices forget what he had seen. During the bicentennial celebration of the Constitution, the justices had been asked to meet once in Philadelphia to commemorate the

events of 1787. Marshall said he would go only if the com-
memoration were authentic. "I'll wear the knee breeches and
serve the coffee," he announced. The idea was promptly
dropped.

He also delivered a widely quoted speech that threw cold
water on the idea that the framers of the Constitution were
divinely inspired men who delivered a perfect plan for the
government. "We the People no longer enslave, but the credit
does not belong to the Framers," Marshall said. "It belongs to
those who refused to acquiesce in outdated notions of 'liberty,'
'justice,' and 'equality.' " It took the Civil War, the Fourteenth
Amendment, and the Supreme Court of the twentieth century,
he said, to make the U.S. Constitution the widely admired document it is today. Rejecting what he called the "blind pilgrim-
age to the shrine of the original document," Marshall stressed
his belief that "the true miracle was not the birth of the Constitution, but its life." No one but Thurgood Marshall could
have delivered so powerful a rejection of the Reagan administration's doctrine of "original intent."

By the spring of 1991, however, Marshall and his wife
were wondering how long he could continue. Simply getting
around had become ever more painful and difficult. During the
previous summer, he had journeyed to the American Bar Association meeting in Chicago to accept an award but fell while
leaving a restaurant. He was flown back to Washington, D.C.,
where he spent several days recovering in a hospital. At the
Court, Marshall often arrived out of breath just minutes before
the justices took the bench at 10 A.M. His legs were failing, as
was his eyesight. In March, however, he attended a preview
showing of an ABC-TV miniseries, "Separate but Equal," in
which actor Sidney Poitier played attorney Thurgood Marshall
in the *Brown* v. *Board of Education* case. Marshall greeted Poitier as "my twin brother." The tall, dark, and elegant Poitier
resembled the broad and pale Marshall not at all, other than
that both were African-Americans. Asked his reaction to Poitier's film performance before the Supreme Court, Marshall replied, "He was better than me."

On March 4, Blackmun delivered the Court's opinion in
Pacific Mutual v. *Haslip*, a stinging defeat for big business. The
million-dollar punitive damage verdict does not violate the
Constitution because the company was given "due process of
law," he said. Blackmun conceded that "unlimited jury dis-

cretion" might "invite extreme results that jar one's constitutional sensibilities." However, the $1,000,000 verdict in this $2,500 case was less than jarring, he explained, because the Alabama jury had acted "within reasonable constraints." What did that mean? It meant, apparently, that the judge had adequately instructed the jury before it began its deliberations and carefully scrutinized the fairness of the verdict afterward. Scalia refused to sign the opinion because he considered it fuzzy. Because punitive damages have a long history dating to colonial days, "I would end the suspense and categorically affirm their validity," he said. By a 7–1 margin, with only O'Connor dissenting (again, Souter had not been seated by the time of the argument), the Court had upheld the imposition of huge punitive verdicts on American corporations. The ruling spoke loudly that the Rehnquist Court, while conservative, was no ally of American business.

Two weeks later, Blackmun delivered another rebuke to American industry, this time outlawing the use of "fetal protection policies" that excluded women from jobs. Where he had hedged somewhat in the punitive damages case, Blackmun spoke with force and firmness in favor of women's rights.

"Congress indicated that the employer may take into account only the woman's ability to do her job. Fertile women, as far as appears in the record, participate in the manufacture of batteries as efficiently as anyone else," he said. "Decisions about the welfare of future children must be left to the parents who conceive, bear, support and raise them rather than the employers who hire those parents." He concluded with a jab at the male judges in Milwaukee and Chicago who had upheld the fetal protection policy without even examining the evidence in a trial. Like employers, judges have no business deciding "whether a woman's reproductive role is more important to herself and her family than her economic role. Congress has left this choice to the woman as hers to make," Blackmun said. David Souter, whom women's rights advocates had feared as a potential right-to-life advocate, supplied the fifth vote for Blackmun's opinion. Scalia filed a short concurring opinion coming to the same conclusion. In dissent were White, Rehnquist, and Kennedy.

Usually, on decision days, the author of a majority opinion reads a segment from the bench, but the scene in the courtroom gives no hint of the true dispute among the justices. March 26 was different. Rehnquist began by announcing that he and By-

ron White would take turns reading portions of the decision
in *Arizona* v. *Fulminante,* the coerced confessions case. "This
is another kettle of fish," White grumbled as he began. It had
been nearly a decade since he had read a dissent from the
bench, but he sharply denounced Rehnquist's contribution to
the opinion.

"Today, a majority of the Court, without any justification,
overrules a vast body of precedent without a word and in so
doing dislodges one of the fundamental tenets of our criminal
justice system," White said. "Our prior cases have indicated
that there are some constitutional rights so basic to a fair trial
that their infraction can never be treated as harmless error."
Trials are a forum for finding the truth, he proclaimed, but
Americans will not tolerate police tactics that "wring a confession out of the accused. . . . Ours is an accusatorial and not an
inquisitorial system, a system in which the state must establish
guilt by evidence independently and freely secured and may
not by coercion prove its charge against any accused out of his
own mouth," he said.

It was a remarkable performance for White. Since taking
his seat in 1962, he had been a hard-liner on crime. He dissented in the 1966 *Miranda* case and in many of the Warren
Court rulings expanding the rights of crime suspects. White
usually stuck with precedents, however, even those he had
originally disputed. The rule against coerced confessions had
stood since 1897 and had been a pillar of U.S. constitutional
law. He saw no need to knock it down now. On the bench,
White often sat back in his chair and chatted or joked with the
chief justice. As he finished, however, he did not look to be in
a mood for speaking to Rehnquist.

Rehnquist's explanation from the bench was brief. His
written opinion justifying the new rule was not much longer:
six pages. Mostly, he cited cases in which the harmless error
rule had been used before, a list taken directly from the Justice
Department's brief in the case. In his early years on the Court,
Rehnquist had been considered its best writer. He stated his
views sharply, and his work was enlivened by literary and historical allusions, puns, and analogies. In recent years, however,
his writing had become bland. He stated his conclusion, strung
together a few quotes from earlier decisions, and signed off.
Rehnquist no longer made much of an effort to explain his views
or to persuade the reader of their correctness. His writing now
read as the work of a jurist who had five votes and did not need

to persuade anyone that he was right. In the Supreme Court, if you have five votes, you are right. In this case, Souter—in his first week on the bench—provided Rehnquist with his fifth vote.

"The harmless-error doctrine is essential to preserve the 'principle that the central purpose of a criminal trial is to decide the factual question of the defendant's guilt or innocence,' " Rehnquist said, quoting a 1986 opinion. From now on, appeals courts, when confronted with evidence of a coerced confession, should decide whether its use was "harmless beyond a reasonable doubt." If it was, the conviction should stand. If not, it should be reversed. The opinion did not make a distinction between a confession beaten out of a suspect by police and one in which a suspect such as Fulminante has been subtly pressed into confessing. It had taken Rehnquist nearly 40 years, but he had finally rewritten the law on coerced confessions.

In April of 1991, the justices took up the major death penalty case of the term. It gave Rehnquist a chance to reverse an irksome ruling that came during his first year as chief justice.

On Saturday morning, June 27, 1987, the banner headline across the top of the *Memphis Commercial Appeal* had read, "Powell Retires from Supreme Court." The subhead noted, "Justice often cast the deciding vote." Just two weeks before his retirement, Lewis Powell had indeed cast the deciding vote to rule that the family of a murder victim may not speak at the killer's sentencing hearing. The jury must focus on the murderers and their crimes, not the crime's impact on the survivors. A survivor's testimony is "irrelevant" when deciding the fate of a murderer, Powell opined for the 5–4 majority in *Booth* v. *Maryland*.

In the spring of 1987, during Rehnquist's first term as chief justice, Associate Justice Powell had cast the deciding vote to rule that statistical evidence of racial bias did not invalidate the capital punishment system. The *Booth* case raised another matter—fairness in the sentencing of individuals. If the family of the victim can testify, punishments may be handed out unequally, Powell feared. The victim from a large and prominent family would probably be well represented. The victimized convenience store clerk who is single may have no one to speak for the victim. Better to keep the focus only on the murderer and his crime, not the unforeseen impact on the survivors.

Rehnquist thought the ruling was both wrong and dreadfully unfair. Murderers' families can come to court and describe for the jury kind persons who love puppies and little children. Why can't the victims' families say something about their lost loved ones? Rehnquist vowed to overturn the *Booth* decision, and ironically, a gruesome crime on the day after Powell's retirement gave Rehnquist his chance.

Pervis Tyrone Payne, age 20, had spent most of that hot Saturday riding around the Memphis area with a friend, drinking beer and injecting cocaine. About 3 P.M., he stopped by his girlfriend's apartment to see whether she had returned from an out-of-town trip. She had not. Payne had with him a gym bag and three cans of malt liquor.

Across the hall lived Charisse Christopher, a 28-year-old mother, along with her 2-year-old daughter, Lacie, and her 3-year-old son, Nicholas. Somehow, Payne gained entry to Christopher's apartment and apparently drank more beer at her table. Her neighbor heard Charisse shouting, "Get out! Get out!" Then came what another neighbor called "a bloodcurdling scream." Payne had picked up a butcher knife and began stabbing the woman—41 times in all. Blood covered the walls and the floor. Two-year-old Lacie was stabbed in the chest, abdomen, back, and head. Payne stabbed the knife all the way through three-year-old Nicholas. Miraculously, he survived. His mother and sister died.

The first police officer on the scene encountered Payne coming down the steps. He was covered in blood. "I'm the complainant," Payne said. When the officer asked, "What's going on up there?" Payne struck him with his gym bag and fled. His tennis shoes fell from the gym bag to the ground. The empty beer cans with his fingerprints were found in the bloody apartment, and so was his baseball cap.

Payne was found hiding a few blocks away but denied any involvement. "Man, I ain't killed no woman," he told the arresting officers. A jury disagreed, and he was found guilty of two counts of murder.

At his sentencing hearing, his mother, father, and a family friend testified that he was a kind, caring person. They said that Payne did not drink or use drugs.

The prosecutor put on the witness stand Mary Zvolanek, Charisse Christopher's mother, who was now raising her grandson Nicholas. "He cries for his mom. He doesn't seem to understand why she doesn't come home. And he cries for his sister

Lacie," she told the jurors. They were also shown a videotape of the bloody crime scene. In her closing argument, the prosecutor concentrated on the crime's impact on young Nicholas. Nothing can be done, she said, to ease the pain of the families—either the Paynes or the Zvolaneks—and nothing can be done to bring back the murder victims. "But there is something that you can do for Nicholas," she told the jurors. "Somewhere down the road Nicholas is going to grow up, hopefully. He's going to want to know what happened. . . . He is going to want to know what type of justice was done. With your verdict, you will provide the answer." The jury sentenced Payne to death.

The Tennessee Supreme Court upheld the conviction and the death sentence. Though the grandmother's testimony and the prosecutor's statements may have violated the *Booth* ruling, the state judges said that this was a "harmless error . . . beyond reasonable doubt." In fact, the Tennessee judges agreed entirely with Rehnquist and thought that the *Booth* decision was abominable. "It is an affront to the civilized members of the human race," they wrote in their opinion, to allow this murderer to "parade" witnesses in his favor before the jury, while forbidding any testimony about the victim or her survivors.

Normally, the Court would have ignored Payne's appeal. His sentence had been upheld, and all but Marshall among the justices probably agreed with that result. The conservatives supported capital punishment and disagreed with the *Booth* ruling. Even the moderate liberals, such as Stevens and Blackmun, would uphold death sentences. If anyone was a good candidate for a death sentence, Payne surely was. However, Payne's appeal arrived at just the right time for the chief justice. In January, the Court had heard arguments in an Ohio case with an eye toward overturning the *Booth* ruling. To their dismay, the conservatives discovered the ruling turned on Ohio law, not the Constitution. In a brief order, the Ohio case was dismissed.

Rehnquist was miffed. He thought he had five votes to overturn the *Booth* ruling but no case that raised the issue. However, on the long list of pending appeals, the clerks spotted Payne's petition. His court-appointed lawyer had stressed in his appeal the "inflammatory" actions of the prosecutor, citing especially the bloody videotape shown to the jury. At another moment, the prosecutor had stabbed a knife through a drawing of Nicholas. In addition to challenging those actions, however, the appeal also said that the prosecutor had ignored the *Booth* ruling.

On Friday, February 15, 1991, the Court had issued a brief order. It had granted a review of the appeal filed by Pervis Tyrone Payne. The attorneys on both sides were told to focus on this question: "Whether *Booth* v. *Maryland* and *South Carolina* v. *Gathers* [a Brennan opinion applying the *Booth* ruling to prosecutors] should be overruled?" Because it was nearing the end of the term, the attorneys could not be given the normal time to prepare their briefs. Not, that is, if the *Booth* ruling were to be overturned in 1991—so, their time was cut in half. The oral argument was set for April 24, the last day for spring arguments.

Stevens filed a dissent to the order, which was joined by Marshall and Blackmun. It is "unwise and unnecessary" for the Court to rush to judgment on the *Booth* issue, especially in a case that did not turn on the *Booth* ruling, Stevens argued. Marshall did not bother speaking out, but he knew what was coming. The conservative "clique" was in charge at the Court, he complained, and it did not matter much what he or Blackmun and Stevens had to say. The majority had no interest in Payne's case or in the issues it raised. They simply wanted a vehicle for overturning the *Booth* ruling.

Payne's court-appointed lawyer, J. Brooke Lathram of Memphis, was put in an odd spot. His first job was to win a new sentencing hearing for Payne. Yet, he had been called upon to defend the *Booth* ruling, even though it did not actually affect Payne's case.

The prosecutor deliberately inflamed the jury, he argued, to gain the death sentence. She practically "demanded Payne's execution for Nicholas' sake," Lathram told the justices. She also used the videotape of the bloody apartment and the stabbing of the drawing to rouse the emotions of the jurors, he contended.

"Is a prosecutor forbidden any poetic license at all?" Rehnquist asked. "In a closing argument, any lawyer is going to get into a few rhapsodies of sorts. That's the way people argue cases to juries," he asserted.

Payne's case looked hopeless. Lathram then turned to his defense of the *Booth* ruling. If a sentencing hearing focuses on the victim and her family, it will create a bias toward the prominent and the affluent, he suggested. The killer of a "reprobate" may be spared simply because his victim happened to be socially insignificant.

From the far right side of the bench, Souter picked up on Lathram's point. "Isn't the real problem a kind of second-tier, equality-before-the-law argument? That society is placing different values on [different] victims?" he asked.

"I think that's correct, Your Honor," Lathram said. "It injects an arbitrary factor."

"The valuation itself is an arbitrary factor because it is insupportable," Souter said, musing aloud. Once again, as in the abortion clinic case, Souter had hit the heart of the matter. If Souter refused to overturn *Booth*, Rehnquist might not have five votes after all.

Tennessee Attorney General Charles Burson said that the *Booth* case was "wrongly decided" and should be overruled. Convicted criminals should pay for their crimes based on "the full extent of the harm done," he said, and that includes the crime's impact on the survivors. "That information should not be precluded from the jury," he said.

Marshall sat glumly, gazing at the state attorney over the glasses that had sunk down on his nose. "What more did you need!" he said in a thick voice. "The jury was shown pictures of the dead bodies. The blood all over the place. Everything that could be photographed. And practically no defense. What in the world did you need more evidence for?" he asked.

Marshall's questions, though infrequent, were blunt and to the point. In a few words, he had shown why the Payne case was not a good test of the *Booth* ruling. The Memphis jury almost certainly would have sent Payne to Death Row regardless of the few comments about Nicholas.

The crime's impact on little Nicholas "was relevant, probative evidence," the Tennessee attorney general replied.

"What more did you need?" Marshall said again. "Can you imagine any jury not convicting?"

"I think they needed at least a characterization of the victim as a unique human being," he said.

"You seem to assume that some people are unique and others are not," Stevens noted.

Then, it was Souter's turn again. "You are saying it is valid to value the victims differently?" he asked.

"Yes," Burson replied. A presidential assassin can be punished more harshly than a barroom killer, although both committed one murder. "Taking the life of the president creates more societal harm," he said, and, therefore, can be punished more severely.

Attorney General Dick Thornburgh, the man who had helped to choose Souter, came to give the Justice Department's endorsement to overturning the *Booth* ruling. A killer should be "held morally accountable for the full extent of the harm caused by his or her criminal acts," he said.

Once again, the outcome of the case would depend on White and Souter. White had dissented in the *Booth* case but often upheld precedents he initially disagreed with, and Souter sounded concerned about injecting a new kind of inequality into the sentencing system. The outcome would be known soon, as there were only two months left in the term.

As the term neared an end, the justices grew weary and testy. As the cases piled up and the time to resolve them began to run out, the pressure grew. Scores of opinions in the most difficult cases were still pending. Minor disagreements festered into major disputes. Tempers grew short. Irritations grew into anger.

In May, however, Rehnquist seemed unaffected. Around the Court, he was in an especially chipper mood. No longer was he caught up in minor disputes, writing dissents, lambasting his colleagues. He was in charge now. He not only presided over the Court but also controlled its decisions. Kennedy's arrival in 1988 had given him a narrow 5–4 majority in most cases. Now, Souter had provided a margin of comfort.

Through much of the term, the new justice had been swamped by the work, uncertain of his course. He worked nonstop, from eight in the morning until nine at night, stopping only for his lunch of an apple and yogurt. In the evenings, he jogged a few miles and then read some more. He spent his weekends and holidays at the Court, too. Like the justices of the nineteenth century, Souter wanted to write his own opinions, and with pen and paper. He wanted to rely on neither clerks nor computers.

He was delighted to see his anonymity return. A good sign of this came during a return trip to Concord. In a supermarket parking lot, an aged man glared at him and said, "You look like that lawyer." Accustomed to being recognized now in public, Souter replied, "Well, I am." The old man looked him over again. "The hell you are," he said, turning to walk into the supermarket.

At the Court, Souter admitted he had to practically pinch himself to remind himself he was indeed a justice of the Supreme Court. The work load had been heavy, and his writing moved slowly. The chief justice had reason to be pleased with the new justice, though. In the big cases, Souter had sided with Rehnquist when it counted.

On May 23, the chief justice announced that he would deliver the opinion of the Court in *Rust* v. *Sullivan*, the abortion clinic case. Because of Souter, Rehnquist had a five-vote majority. During the argument in late October, the new justice sounded troubled by the government rules because they "preclude professional speech" by doctors. Based on Solicitor General Starr's comments, Souter asked him whether, when faced with a pregnant patient with heart trouble or high blood pressure, the doctor cannot advise a woman to consider an abortion. The government attorney responded that the doctor could not. The law and regulations did not permit clinic personnel to advise patients to get an abortion for any reason, Starr had asserted.

Rehnquist worked around the problem neatly. He drafted an opinion that ignored Starr's response and concluded instead that nothing in the law or regulations would forbid that doctor from advising that patient to get an abortion: "On their face, we do not read the regulations to bar abortion referral or counseling in such circumstances . . . of a woman whose pregnancy places her life in imminent peril," Rehnquist wrote. "Abortion counseling as a 'method of family planning' is prohibited, and it does not seem that a medically necessitated abortion in such circumstances would be the equivalent of its use as a 'method of family planning.' Neither [the law] nor the specific restrictions of the regulations would apply," he wrote.

With those few lines, the chief justice had simply defined away the problem. Despite what the solicitor general seemed to say, the regulations do permit a doctor to recommend abortion for a woman who faces a medical danger, Rehnquist had declared. With that resolved, Souter signed on to the chief's opinion, along with White, Scalia, and Kennedy. Marshall, Blackmun, Stevens, and O'Connor dissented.

Tribe and the ACLU attorneys had raised three objections in the *Rust* case: The regulations exceed the law, they stifle free speech, and they infringe on the woman's right to abortion.

In a 27-page opinion, Rehnquist disposed of all three challenges.

First, the law itself is "ambiguous." Congress said abortion must not be "a method of family planning," but it did not say whether clinics could refer patients to abortion clinics. Therefore, because the law is not clear, "we customarily defer to the expertise of the agency." In reality, the regulations had less do with "expertise" at the U.S. Department of Health and Human Services than with the wishes of Ronald Reagan and Gary Bauer. Nonetheless, the Court usually upheld government regulations and would do so again, Rehnquist declared.

Second, doctors who take the government subsidies do not have a free-speech right to recommend abortion in direct defiance of the government's wishes. "The Government can, without violating the Constitution, selectively fund a program to encourage certain activities it believes to be in the public interest, without at the same time funding an alternate program which seeks to deal with the problem in another way," Rehnquist said. "This is not the case of the Government 'suppressing a dangerous idea,' but of a prohibition on [a] project grantee or its employees from engaging in activities outside its scope. . . . When Congress established a National Endowment for Democracy to encourage other countries to adopt democratic principles, it was not constitutionally required to fund a program to encourage competing lines of political philosophy such as Communism and Fascism. . . . when the government appropriates public funds to establish a program it is entitled to define the limits of that program."

Do doctors have a special free-speech right to speak honestly to their patients? "We need not resolve that question here," Rehnquist wrote, "because [these] regulations do not significantly impinge on the doctor–patient relationship." Because the program does not provide "post-conception medical advice" or abortion, "a doctor's silence with regard to abortion cannot reasonably be thought to mislead a client into thinking that the doctor does not consider abortion an appropriate option for her," he wrote. If doctors are in doubt, they may explain their silence by telling the woman that "abortion is simply beyond the scope of the program." A poor and pregnant teenager can presumably figure out the rest on her own.

Third, the government has not violated a woman's right to choose abortion. "The Government has no affirmative duty to commit any resources to facilitating abortions," he said, and it "may validly choose to fund childbirth over abortion."

Sandra O'Connor had voted to strike down the regulations as violating the intent of Congress. For 17 years, the law had been interpreted to mean that the clinics could tell their patients the full truth, and that meant telling them of abortion as an option. The Reagan administration's new regulations—the "gag rule"—were not what Congress intended, she had concluded.

The 5–4 ruling in *Rust* v. *Sullivan* prompted another round of denunciations of the Court on Capitol Hill and by abortion rights activists.

"Today this nation saw the true impact of the realignment of the Supreme Court by Presidents Reagan and Bush," said Kate Michelman, executive director of NARAL. "Any hope that Justice Souter would respect our fundamental right to privacy and right to choose expired this morning."

Said Representative Les AuCoin (D, Oregon), "Burning a flag is protected free speech, but advising a woman in a federally funded family planning clinic of her option to choose abortion is not? Maybe the Reagan/Bush Supreme Court sees the logic in that, but it escapes me entirely," he said, vowing along with other congressional Democrats to overturn the ruling through new legislation.

(It should be noted the free-speech principle was not entirely understood in Congress, either. Several versions of a new bill required doctors to tell women of all their options, including abortion. In this regard, what of the physician who is morally opposed to abortion? Presumably, if it is unconstitutional to forbid a doctor from mentioning abortion, it is also unconstitutional to require that he or she *must* mention abortion.)

Still, the "gag rule" was strongly opposed by the vast majority of the members of Congress. The Court's willingness to uphold it raised a troubling prospect, one first raised two years earlier by the series of civil rights rulings. The Constitution gives Congress the sole power to make the laws. The president's duty is to "take care that the Laws be faithfully executed." The Court's duty is to enforce the laws. Yet in this instance, as in the civil rights cases, the Republican White House and the Republican-dominated Court combined to uphold a version of the law that was fundamentally at odds with the view of the Democratic Congress. In the civil rights case, in 1990, George Bush vetoed a measure overwhelmingly approved in Congress, designed to correct what lawmakers saw as the Court's misinterpretations of the statutes. In the Senate, the Democrats came up one vote short of the two-thirds margin needed to override Bush's veto. In that situation, who is making the laws?

The same process seemed to be at work as the Court rewrote the law of habeas corpus. In medieval England, a judge could issue a *writ of habeas corpus*—literally, to "have the body"—so that a prisoner could be brought from a dungeon before the court for a trial. The Great Writ gave prisoners their day in court. The king could not lock up prisoners and throw away the key without giving them a chance to defend themselves. In the United States, habeas corpus has become, instead, a second-chance system for persons who have been convicted of crimes. In 1867, two years after the Civil War, Congress passed the Habeas Corpus Act to give inmates in state prisons a right to seek justice in a federal court. If they believed their rights under the U.S. Constitution had been violated, they could petition a federal judge to hear their pleas. If the judge agreed, the judge could void their convictions and release them. The law fit the thinking of the time: The rights of a U.S. citizen stood over and above the authority of the states and their courts.

Despite this law, it took the Warren Court of the 1960s to make this vision a reality. In a series of liberal rulings, several of which were written by Brennan, the Court made it easier for state inmates to transfer their cases into a federal court. At the same time, the Court was greatly expanding the meaning of the constitutional rights such as the right against self-incrimination or unreasonable searches. The result was that more and more inmates could win release through what Rehnquist and others called "technicalities."

For inmates on Death Row, the habeas corpus system extended a lifeline. The numbers told the tale: More than 2,200 inmates sat on Death Rows around the country, yet only about two dozen of those inmates were executed each year. Nearly all the rest had various habeas corpus appeals pending in the courts.

Rehnquist had become determined to change the system. It was chaotic, wasteful, and an abuse of the people's right to have the laws enforced, he contended in series of speeches. These inmates had been given lawyers, were tried before juries, and appealed their convictions through state courts. Each also could then file an appeal to the Supreme Court—most of which were quickly rejected. That should be the end of the matter, Rehnquist asserted. Justice has been done, and the punishment should proceed.

Rehnquist was especially upset by inmates who strung out their cases by filing one habeas corpus petition after another. He wanted the law changed to give these inmates a one-time shot. Afterward, these cases would be final and the courthouse doors closed. At Rehnquist's request, retired justice Powell headed a committee of federal judges who studied the system and recommended just that to Congress. When an inmate's conviction was upheld by the highest state court, the inmate would then have six months to file one habeas corpus petition raising as many issues as the petitioner desired. Once this petition was considered, however, and disposed of by the federal courts, the case would be over. The state governor could then sign the death warrant of the convict, who could make no eleventh-hour pleas to the federal courts.

Congress refused to write this rule into law, however. What if new evidence emerges suggesting that the inmate was innocent? What if it comes to light later that an informer lied during the trial? The Democrats did not want to see the courthouse door slammed shut. During the summer of 1990, the House and Senate considered a new crime bill but failed to adopt the Rehnquist–Powell proposal on habeas corpus.

Without hesitation then, Rehnquist and his fellow justices wrote the same rule into law in the spring of 1991. The ruling came when Warren McCleskey, the Georgia inmate who had killed a police officer, filed a second habeas corpus petition, which reached the Court. He contended that his rights were violated in 1981 when police, prior to his trial, arranged to place an informer in his cell. Because he had then invoked his right to remain silent, the police could not question him more or arrange for someone to do it for them. In 1981, however, McCleskey's lawyers knew nothing of this arrangement. Rather, they say they learned of it only when Fulton County police turned over confidential documents on the case in 1987, six years after McCleskey's trial. When they learned what the police had done, they filed a new writ of habeas corpus before a federal judge in Atlanta, who ruled that the case had merit.

On a 6–3 vote, the Rehnquist Court ruled that the writ should have been dismissed without a hearing. It is an "abuse of the writ" to wait so long to file such a claim, the Court opined. All such claims must be filed immediately after the conviction, the justices ruled in *McCleskey* v. *Zant*. The courthouse door would now be closed to a second habeas corpus petition, except in those rare instances where inmates have strong evidence that they are innocent.

In dissent, Marshall slammed the "Court's activism in fashioning its new rule" in defiance of Congress. "The majority today exercises legislative power not properly belonging to this Court," he said. Blackmun and Stevens joined him in dissent.

Despite the *McCleskey* ruling, the Court majority promised it would look differently on a case in which an inmate might indeed be innocent. That promise was then called into question by a second ruling on habeas corpus law filed a few weeks later. Ronald Coleman, a Virginia coal miner, had been convicted of murdering his sister-in-law. He claimed he was innocent and had evidence to show he was with friends miles away at the time of the murder.

His lawyers, however, bungled in filing his appeal in the Virginia courts. Some 29 days after a court clerk had stamped his conviction final, his lawyer filed an appeal. Actually, this filing, in October 1986, came 33 days after the judge had signed an order making the conviction final. Under Virginia law, a lawyer must file an appeal within 30 days of the time a *judge* issues a final order. Because Coleman's appeal was said to have been late, the state judges refused to consider it. Turned away by the state courts, Coleman's lawyer then filed a writ of habeas corpus with a federal judge asking to have his claims heard. However, on a 6–3 vote, the Supreme Court ruled in June that federal judges should not hear his claims.

"This is a case about federalism. It concerns the respect that federal courts owe the States and the States' procedural rules," O'Connor began her opinion in *Coleman* v. *Virginia*. "Federalism" is known more commonly as "states' rights," and O'Connor believes in states' rights. A former state judge, she has seen no reason why federal judges have to look over the shoulder of state judges. The Virginia judges had dismissed Coleman's case because his lawyer bungled, and the high court would not revive it, O'Connor declared. In the Rehnquist Court, a state's procedural rules could prevail over the rights guaranteed by the U.S. Constitution.

"The Court today continues its crusade to erect petty procedural barriers in the path of any state prisoner seeking review of his federal constitutional claims," said Blackmun in dissent. Marshall and Stevens joined him.

As the Court moved into the last two weeks of June, decisions in 24 cases were still pending, including nude dancing in Indiana, Harmelin's drug possession case, and Payne's death penalty case. Four decisions were handed down on Monday, June 17, seven more on Thursday. Perhaps the most sweeping ruling came in a Florida case involving a new police technique in the war on drugs. At station stopovers in Fort Lauderdale, armed police boarded buses and trains, walked down the aisles, and sought to search the bags of all passengers. On a 6–3 vote, the Court overruled the Florida Supreme Court and said that these searches are legal because "reasonable person[s]" would understand that they are "free to decline the officers' requests" to look through their luggage. Marshall, Blackmun, and Stevens dissented in *Florida* v. *Bostick.*

On Friday, June 21, Rehnquist announced that he would deliver the opinion of the Court in *Barnes* v. *Glen Theatre.* A few minutes before 10 A.M., the summertime tourists had quietly and respectfully filed into the courtroom like visitors to a great cathedral. They then sat with quizzical looks on their faces as the chief justice discoursed on the First Amendment implications of "pasties and a G-string."

Souter had cast the decisive vote. He gave Rehnquist a majority but refused to sign Rehnquist's opinion. Scalia also wrote a separate opinion, although his views closely paralleled Rehnquist's.

First, the chief justice agreed that nude dancing deserved some protection under the Constitution as a form of free expression. He described it as "expressive conduct within the outer perimeters of the First Amendment." However, he asserted that a ban on this kind of free expression can be upheld if it is a "narrowly tailored" restriction designed to protect "societal order and morality," and Indiana's law is just that. The public indecency laws "reflect moral disapproval" of public nudity, he said. Also, the law's "requirement that the dancers wear at least pasties and a G-string is . . . the bare minimum necessary to achieve the state's purpose." O'Connor and Kennedy joined Rehnquist's opinion.

Scalia agreed that "moral opposition to nudity" justifies the law. He disagreed, however, with Rehnquist's assertion that nude dancing deserves some protection under the First Amendment. It does not, Scalia declared, because the Indiana law is directed at conduct, not at free expression.

Souter agreed with Rehnquist that nude dancing deserves some First Amendment protection but disagreed with both Rehnquist and Scalia that "society's moral views" justify the ban. How then can it be justified? The new justice searched through the court record and found a hidden reason. The ban on nude dancing is justified, he concluded, because of the state's interest "in preventing prostitution, sexual assault and other criminal activity" that could be associated with these dance establishments.

White wrote a sharp dissent. The five justices who upheld the Indiana prosecutors did so mostly because they frown on this type of entertainment, he claimed. "While the entertainment afforded by a nude ballet at the Lincoln Center . . . may differ vastly in content (as viewed by judges) or quality (as viewed by critics), it may not differ in substance from the dance viewed by the person who . . . wants some 'entertainment' with his beer or shot of rye," he wrote, quoting a lower-court opinion. Further, the dancing at the Glen Theatre is not "public nudity," he contended. It occurs only in a private establishment closed to all but consenting adult patrons.

That comment prompted an extraordinary exchange between Scalia and White.

Having seen the draft of White's dissent, Scalia jabbed at him in his separate opinion. It does not matter whether the nude dancing took place behind closed doors, he argued. "There is no basis for thinking that our society has ever shared that Thoreauvian 'you may do what you like so long as it does not injure someone else' beau ideal—much less for thinking that it was written into our Constitution," he wrote. "The purpose of Indiana's public nudity law would be violated, I think, if 60,000 [fully] consenting adults crowded into the Hoosierdome to display their genitals to one another, even if there were not an offended innocent in the crowd."

True, White shot back, but "those same 60,000 Hoosiers would be perfectly free to drive to their respective homes all across Indiana and, once there, to parade around, cavort, and revel in the nude for hours in front of relatives and friends." If the state's "interest in morality" justified a total ban on nudity, he asked, why is this not illegal, too?

The 5–4 ruling reversed the appeals court and upheld the Indiana prosecutors. The crucial words in the set of opinions were Souter's. Rehnquist's opinion, if backed by five justices, could have brought about a major change in the law, one that may have threatened artists, galleries, and performers. In Cincinnati, prosecutors had recently sought to close down an art gallery that displayed the sexually explicit photographs of Robert Mapplethorpe. The prosecution was sidetracked when a jury ruled that the photo exhibit was not obscene. What if, instead, the city council had passed a law forbidding the display of nudity or the depiction of homosexual themes? City lawyers might have used this law to shut down the Mapplethorpe exhibit, or at least to insist that particular photos be removed. They could defend such a move as being "narrowly tailored" to protect "societal order and morality." However, because Souter did not agree with Rehnquist's opinion, it did not stand as the law.

The term had been a miserable one for Marshall. Without Brennan, he stood little chance of prevailing in any major case, whether on civil rights, criminal law, the death penalty, or free speech. Before, most of the cases stood 5–4, and there was always a chance that White, O'Connor, or perhaps even Scalia might switch sides. Now, the margin was typically 6–3. Now, a vote switch by White, O'Connor, or one of the others made no difference. Rehnquist still had a conservative majority. The chief justice was in almost complete control.

For months, Marshall's wife and doctor had been urging him to retire. His eyesight was failing, his breathing was labored, and walking demanded a major exertion. Why continue on simply to cast meaningless dissenting votes? By late June, Marshall had made up his mind. June 27, the last day of the term, would be his last day on the bench. Just a year before, his wife had come to the courtroom on the last day of the term to hear Brennan deliver the opinion upholding affirmative action. Now, she was back again, but for quite a different reason.

Brennan showed up, too. He had come downstairs from his chambers when the term had opened on the first Monday in October. Now, he came back to hear the reading of the final decisions. As he entered the room, he looked rejuvenated. He smiled and waved to friends. He shook hands with a procession of lawyers and Court employees who filed past his seat. His head bobbed as he searched for more friends in the audience. He looked to be thoroughly enjoying himself—but not for long.

The chief justice announced that Scalia would deliver the Court's opinion in *Harmelin* v. *Michigan*. By a 5-4 margin, Harmelin had lost. He would remain behind bars for life because of the cocaine he had carried in his trunk. Such a sentence did not violate the Eighth Amendment's ban on cruel and unusual punishment, the majority ruled.

Scalia's opinion was long, historical, and sharp in its conclusions. "We conclude from this examination [of history] that [*Solem* v. *Helm*] was wrong. The Eighth Amendment contains no proportionality guarantee," he said. The punishment need not fit the crime. No matter how severe the punishment for drug possession, the Court would not intervene.

Brennan, his face now frozen, glared at Scalia as he read on. At the other end of the bench, Kennedy turned to O'Connor and shook his head slightly, drawing a nod of recognition from her. Though Scalia spoke with utter confidence, his opinion in reality did not represent the views of the majority. Only Rehnquist had signed it. Once again, Scalia had written a sweeping opinion but did not draw a majority to his views.

Kennedy refused to join Scalia's absolutist opinion. In his second full term, he had split away from Rehnquist and Scalia on occasion. Early in the term, he had written an opinion for the Court overturning a conviction because the suspect's *Miranda* rights were violated. In two rulings, he had insisted that the Constitution forbids any racial discrimination in selecting juries. His separate opinion in the *Harmelin* case reached the same result as Scalia and Rehnquist but wrote a different rule of law. Because of "the pernicious effects of the drug epidemic in this country," Michigan lawmakers can impose a life sentence for drug possession, he agreed. Nonetheless, the Constitution demands that the Court consider whether such sentences are "grossly disproportionate" to the crime. This one is not, he concluded, but a truly "extreme" sentence can be declared unconstitutional. O'Connor and Souter joined Kennedy's opinion.

Once again, White, the hard-liner on crime, found himself dissenting, along with Marshall, Blackmun, and Stevens. Life in prison for a first-time conviction for drug possession *is* cruel and unusual punishment, he declared.

Rehnquist said that he would deliver the opinion in the death penalty case of *Payne* v. *Tennessee*, the final decision of the term. He quickly summarized the brutal murder and the testimony on behalf of young Nicholas, the one survivor: "We are now of the view that a State may properly conclude that for the jury to assess meaningfully the defendant's moral culpability and blameworthiness," he said, "it should have before it at the sentencing phase evidence of the specific harm caused by the defendant." The *Booth* ruling of 1987 turns the "victim into a faceless stranger" and "deprives the state of the full moral force of its evidence," he said. The *Booth* and the *Gathers* cases "were wrongly decided, and should be, and now are, overruled," Rehnquist said.

What about precedent and the doctrine of stare decisis? For supporters of constitutional rights, including the right to abortion, Rehnquist's words were direct and chilling. "Stare decisis is not an inexorable command. It is . . . not a mechanical formula of adherence to the latest decision," he said. Precedent is most important in cases involving "property and contract rights," less so in matters of individual rights, he suggested. If five members of the Court think a past decision is "unworkable and badly reasoned," they will not hesitate to overrule it, Rehnquist declared. White, O'Connor, Scalia, Kennedy, and Souter joined the opinion of the chief justice.

As Rehnquist read on, Marshall sat grimly next to him. He gazed out toward the audience, determinedly ignoring what was being said. In his written dissent, however, he sounded off.

"Power, not reason, is the new currency of this Court's decisions," Marshall said. "In dispatching Booth and Gathers to their graves, today's majority suggests that an even more extensive upheaval of this Court's precedents may be in store. The majority today sends a clear signal that scores of established constitutional liberties are now ripe for reconsideration."

Surely, Marshall was correct. The decisions in the coerced confession case, as well as in *Payne* v. *Tennessee,* showed that the chief justice would move quickly and aggressively to overturn precedents that he opposed. If at least four other justices agreed, the precedents would fall. However, Marshall's defense of stare decisis rang hollow, too. The liberals, when in the majority, also threw out precedents that they had opposed. Marshall had dissented every time a death penalty was upheld, ignoring the Court's precedents to the contrary. With five votes, he certainly would have dismissed the precedents and ruled capital punishment unconstitutional.

The last of the opinions was read, and Rehnquist nodded toward the marshal, who promptly banged his gavel and announced that the "honorable Court" was now adjourned until the first Monday in October. Nothing was said of a pending retirement. Indeed, the chief justice did not know that another change was imminent.

The justices were due to gather in the conference room once more to dispose of the pending appeals. Marshall waited until then to break the news. His many vows to serve out his "life term" had convinced most that Marshall would never announce his retirement—but those predictions were wrong. He had told Brennan first of the news. At the conference table, he told the others he planned to quit after 24 years. The next week, he would turn 83 years old. His eyesight was failing. So were his legs. His breath came in pained puffs. "I'm old and I'm coming apart," he told reporters the day after his resignation was announced. Perhaps what was most revealing at his last press conference was what went unsaid. Though pressed by reporters, Marshall refused to make a single critical comment about the conservative Court or its chief justice.

Still, his resignation added an exclamation point to the term's end. The last of the Warren Court liberals was gone. Rehnquist and the conservatives had control, and now even the voice of liberalism had vanished.

12

The Thomas Hearings

It was just after 2 P.M. on Thursday afternoon when the phones started ringing at the offices of the Alliance for Justice. George Kassouf, who picked up the first call, confessed that he had not heard the news. Thurgood Marshall, the last of the Warren Court liberals and the only black member of the

Court, had just announced his retirement. Kassouf noted, however, that the alliance was ready. Its small staff had already prepared background reports on the Bush administration's top five or six candidates for the Supreme Court. When Nan Aron, the executive director of the alliance, returned from lunch to hear the news, she offered a prediction: "I bet it's Clarence Thomas."

Aron had come to Washington in 1973 with a law degree and a commitment to fight the good fight for civil rights. She had grown up in New York, graduated from New York's Scarsdale High, and protested the Vietnam War as a student at Oberlin College in Ohio. There, she was arrested for trying to block a U.S. Army recruiter from coming onto campus and campaigned in 1968 for Senator Eugene McCarthy, the first avowed antiwar candidate.

As a law student in Cleveland, she had worked in a legal aid clinic providing free help for the poor. After arriving in Washington, D.C., she went to work as a staff attorney at the U.S. EEOC (Equal Employment Opportunity Commission), the still-young agency charged with enforcing the laws against discrimination in the workplace. There, young 1960s-era lawyers, armed with the power of the federal government, could go to a federal court and take on some of America's major corporations—names such as Hewlett-Packard, General Tire and Rubber, Sears, and Xerox. Through class-action lawsuits, the EEOC forced corporate giants to change the way they hired and promoted blacks, Hispanics, and women. Aron left the EEOC in 1976 to join the National Prison Project of the ACLU, which used class-action lawsuits in the federal courts to force states to improve their treatment of prison inmates.

In the 1980s, the Reagan administration set out to change the rules of the game. No longer would the federal courts be a catalyst for social change as defined by groups such as the ACLU. The White House changed the managers of agencies such as the EEOC, but it had little success in changing the laws in the still Democrat-dominated Congress. Increasingly, the Administration turned its attention to the third branch of government—the federal courts. By the mid-1980s, the civil rights activists in the nation's capital were alarmed. Reagan and Attorney General Edwin Meese were "packing" the courts with conservative ideologues, they warned.

During earlier Republican eras, the ideal candidate for a federal judgeship might have been a 55-year-old pillar of the local bar, a lawyer who had gained prominence through years of experience in government and the courts. Under Meese, however, the judicial nominees, especially for the appellate courts, tended to be much younger and less experienced. Some were in their mid-30s. Typically, they made a name for themselves as academics and writers, not through years of court work and government service. While supporters praised these new young judges as stellar intellects, critics labeled them as ideologues.

On Capitol Hill, the Senate Judiciary Committee hardly paused long enough to give them any label. Particularly under committee chair Strom Thurmond, Reagan's judicial nominees won assembly-line approval. After a brief hearing, the judicial nominees gained confirmation to a lifetime seat on the federal bench. Alarmed by this conservative transformation of the federal judiciary, Washington's liberal groups decided to fight back—or at least to throw a wrench into the process. Groups as disparate as the Consumers Union, the NAACP, National Organization for Women, and the National Wildlife Federation feared a court system made up entirely of Ed Meese and Brad Reynolds appointees. They set up a small new organization, with money for only a half dozen staffers, and undertook to gather information on the Administration's judicial nominees. The coalition of civil rights and public interest organizations then vowed to fight those nominees who appeared to be right-wingers. Thus was born the Alliance for Justice, and Nan Aron became its executive director.

The alliance operated a dozen blocks from the White House, out of a cramped office near Dupont Circle that had a decidedly late-1960s atmosphere. Its carpets were torn, the walls scratched. Boxes stood in the halls. Computers were not to be seen. Unlike the slicked-down, white-shirted lawyers of the big downtown Connecticut Avenue and K Street firms, the lawyers for the alliance showed up in casual work clothes and shaggy hair. Nonetheless, they gathered paper relentlessly: legal opinions, speeches, articles, government memos. Upon hearing of potential judicial nominees, they called lawyers from the nominees' hometowns—whether in Buffalo, New York, or in Salt Lake City—and asked about the nominees' reputations. When the nomination finally went to the Senate for confirmation, reporters, civil rights advocates, and even Senate staffers could count on the alliance to have the thickest file of information on the candidate.

Despite the efforts of the alliance, the president's nominees were rarely defeated. During Reagan's eight years in office, he filled 378 judgeships in the three-tiered federal court system. Only three of his nominees were rejected by the Senate: Jefferson B. Sessions of Alabama, who had been nominated as a federal district judge; Bernard Siegan, a San Diego law professor and friend of Attorney General Meese, who was rejected as a federal appeals court judge; and Judge Robert Bork, the failed Supreme Court nominee. By the fall of 1991, Reagan and Bush together had filled 439 of the 837 seats in the federal judiciary. Undaunted by the statistics, the alliance lawyers kept gathering information. They made sure that none of the president's nominees got a free ride.

If Bush indeed was to select Clarence Thomas to fill Thurgood Marshall's seat, the alliance was especially well prepared. It had two full file drawers marked "Clarence Thomas."

Thomas was only 43 years old, a Yale Law School graduate, articulate, forceful—and black. In 1982, Reagan had chosen Thomas to head the EEOC. The post instantly made Thomas one of the most prominent and controversial members of a conservative Administration committed to doing battle with the traditionally liberal civil rights establishment. The job was something of a surprise career move for Thomas. He had come to Washington in 1979, to work for newly elected Senator John Danforth, a Missouri Republican who—as state attorney general—had hired Thomas fresh out of Yale. Danforth had promised Thomas hard work, long hours, and low pay, and best of all, Thomas noted, a chance to work in the fields of energy and the environment. Thomas commented that he did not want to be "coddled" or "typecast" as the office black by being assigned civil rights duties. However, just two years after arriving in Washington, he accepted a post as head of the civil rights division in Reagan's Department of Education. A year later, he became the EEOC chair.

Thomas still resisted being typecast, though. He read everything he could about Abraham Lincoln, Frederick Douglass, and Malcolm X, about the abolitionists' struggle against slavery, the Reconstruction era, and the Fourteenth Amendment, and about the black self-help movement. He admired conservative black economists Thomas Sowell and Walter Williams but distanced himself from Jesse Jackson, Benjamin Hooks of the NAACP, and the Congressional Black Caucus. As he saw it, the civil rights movement of recent years had become hopelessly wedded to the view that race was the cause of all problems and that government was always the solution. Government handouts and "affirmative" preferences did more to make blacks dependent than to liberate them, Thomas observed.

His personal life did not fit a simple pattern, either. He was a teetotaler who joined an evangelical Episcopalian church. He also smoked big cigars, drove a black Corvette, and became an avid weight lifter. He had separated from his first wife, Kathy, in 1981, and later they were divorced, but Thomas kept custody of their son, Jamal. In 1987, he began dating a Republican lawyer, Virginia Lamp, who is white, and five months later they married.

He determined to cut a new path for the EEOC, too. He moved the agency away from large, class-action lawsuits and told its attorneys to pursue individual cases of actual discrimination, not statistical patterns suggesting that blacks or other minorities are being subjected to bias. The Civil Rights Act of 1964 speaks of an "individual" who is a victim of discrimination, not groups, he noted. Advocates for women's rights and for older workers complained that the EEOC was failing to attack gender and age discrimination in the workplace. In 1988, Thomas admitted that the agency's staff had bungled by failing to act on more than 1,000 complaints of age discrimination. Older workers who had entrusted their complaints with the agency learned that its staff had delayed so long that the deadline to file lawsuits against their employers had passed. As a result, their rights to sue had been extinguished.

"This agency was supposed to be an advocate for the workers. Thomas turned it into an adversary," Aron said. "The business community was happy with him. No one else was."

Thomas also seemed to have his eye on much more than the EEOC. He churned out newspaper opinion pieces, sounded off in interviews, and gave dozens of speeches across the country. He denounced "quotas" and racial preferences, advocated black self-help, and complained that the nation's established civil rights leaders did little but "bitch, bitch, bitch, moan and whine." Thomas spoke often and movingly of his own upbringing. As a young child, he had lived in a sharecropper's shack near Savannah, Georgia, which had dirt floors and no running water. However, his grandparents took him in when he was seven years old and sent him to Roman Catholic schools. There, strict but caring nuns prepared him for eventual academic success at Holy Cross College and Yale.

His speeches as EEOC chair were also sprinkled with comments that appealed to the top attorneys of the Reagan–Bush administration. He praised Justice Antonin Scalia's dissent in the 1987 case of *Paul Johnson* v. *Santa Clara County*, which called for outlawing affirmative action in the workplace. In a speech at the Heritage Foundation in Washington, Thomas praised as "splendid" an article by conservative philanthropist Lewis Lehrman that called abortion a "holocaust" and maintained that the Constitution gave fetuses an absolute "right to life." By this interpretation, not only was the *Roe* v. *Wade* decision wrong, but also abortion at any stage of a pregnancy and in every state in the nation was murder. Thomas also called the 1988 case of *Morrison* v. *Olson,* involving the independent counsels the "most important court case since *Brown* v. *Board of Education*" ending segregation. Once again, he praised Scalia's dissent, which had called for striking down the law. Not many Americans would even recognize the case of *Morrison* v. *Olson,* and fewer yet would consider it of vast significance. Still, the top attorneys at the Justice Department and at the White House certainly shared Thomas's view. Because of this law, Ed Meese, Michael Deaver, Oliver North, and John Poindexter, among others, had come under criminal investigation.

To Aron and the alliance staffers, the blizzard of Thomas speeches meant only one thing: He was running for higher office. Certainly, he had made a name for himself at the top levels of the Administration. As vice president, George Bush got to know the outgoing and personable EEOC chair. After moving into the White House, Bush nominated Thomas to be a judge on the U.S. Court of Appeals for the District of Columbia, the same court on which Bork and Scalia had sat. No one in Washington missed the significance of the move: Clarence Thomas was being groomed as the Republican replacement for Thurgood Marshall. This time, the Senate Judiciary Committee took its time and considered the nomination carefully. Democrats Howard Metzenbaum and Paul Simon had wrangled with Thomas during his EEOC tenure. They thought he had been lax, at best, in enforcing antidiscrimination laws, and they were not about to rubber-stamp his confirmation to a lifetime federal judgeship. After months of delay, however, Thomas was approved on a 13–1 vote and donned the black robes of an appeals court judge in the spring of 1990. Fifteen

months later, when word of Marshall's resignation reached the
White House on Thursday afternoon, the president's counsel,
C. Boyden Gray, had the same first thought as Nan Aron: Clar-
ence Thomas.

Bush had scheduled himself to spend the last weekend in
June at his summer home in Kennebunkport, Maine, but he
wanted to move quickly on the nomination. The president did
not want to let the Senate Democrats and the liberal interest
groups pressure him as to who should replace Marshall. The
retiring justice himself weighed in during a Friday morning
press conference, suggesting that the president should not rely
on race in picking his successor if it meant "picking the wrong
Negro." The comment was widely seen as a jab directed at
Thomas.

The president's advisers recognized that another white
male nominee such as David Souter would not do as a replacement for Marshall. For nearly a quarter century, Marshall had
stood as a powerful symbol, the one black member of the nation's heretofore all-white Supreme Court. If Bush sought to
replace him with a conservative white male, he would be
roundly condemned—and his nominee possibly rejected largely
for that reason. Bush told Gray he wanted to take a close look
at a Hispanic candidate for the nomination. Female judges
should be considered, too, and—of course—Clarence Thomas.

The appointment of a Hispanic seemed the politically
smart move. Hispanics made up a large and growing segment
of the electorate in key states such as California, Texas, and
Florida, and they were a potential source of Republican votes.
No Hispanic had ever sat on the Supreme Court; nominating
a Hispanic justice could give Bush a ticket to a huge bloc of
votes. The problem was, Who would he nominate? The White
House simply did not have a distinguished, conservative Hispanic judge who was considered ready for the Supreme Court.
On Saturday, Gray interviewed Judge Emilio Garza, a 43-year-
old Texan who had recently been named to the U.S. appeals
court there but had yet to write a single opinion. Garza had
potential, but he was not ready.

From Kennebunkport, Bush talked with Gray and Thornburgh on a conference call Saturday afternoon. The attorneys
summed up the pluses and minuses for Thomas. On the plus
side, he had a strong Senate supporter in Jack Danforth, a
moderate and well-respected Republican. Warren Rudman had
proved to be a powerful advocate in the Senate for Souter;

Danforth could do the same and could deflect criticism from his protégé. Thomas also had a Southern background. The court had not had a Southerner since Lewis Powell retired, Gray noted. More importantly, as EEOC chair, Thomas had become an expert on the federal antidiscrimination laws. He had immersed himself in the disputes over job quotas and affirmative action. The Supreme Court was wrestling with these same disputes, and "Thomas knew these issues as well as any person in America," Gray said.

On the minus side, Thomas "could use two or three more years" on the appeals court, the president's lawyer observed. Thomas had written only 20 opinions, none of them controversial, and had yet to display the real expertise of an appellate judge. Nonetheless, Gray concluded that he "was ready now."

The other problem was one of appearances. For more than a year, Bush had fought off the Democrats' attempt to overturn the Court's 1989 civil rights decisions, especially the *Wards Cove* v. *Atonio* case, by arguing that a return to the rules of *Griggs* v. *Duke Power* would force employers to use "quotas" in hiring. The legal dispute was complicated and muddy. Much depended on how employers would react to a new set of legal rules. Boyden Gray led the attack on the Democrats' proposal. He argued that if employers could be sued simply because they did not have a high enough percentage of minorities or women and then were forced to prove that their hiring practices were based on a "business necessity," the employers would give up and conclude that they must simply hire more minorities and women. That result did not trouble the congressional Democrats, and their lawyers argued that it was crucial that employers with a mostly white, male work force be required to defend their hiring procedures. Otherwise, employers could, with impunity, violate the federal antidiscrimination laws by using interviews or tests to exclude minorities and women.

By the summer of 1991, the legal dispute had been reduced to a political shouting match. Ted Kennedy and the Democrats said that they were "for civil rights." George Bush and the Republicans said that they were "against quotas." If the president now appointed Clarence Thomas to replace Thurgood Marshall, Bush would look like a hypocrite. After advocating hiring by merit alone and loudly denouncing quotas, he would now appoint the one available black judge to fill the seat of the retiring black justice.

What other good choice was available, though? Bush decided to "stare down" the charges of hypocrisy, one aide commented. He liked Thomas and thought Thomas had a good record. From the president's perspective, Thomas was the best man available for the job. Besides, the Democrats had complained that the Court needed more diversity, someone who had seen America through the eyes of a poor, black person. How could they now criticize the nomination of just such a person? On Sunday, Bush called Thomas and asked him to come to Kennebunkport Monday morning with Boyden Gray and Dick Thornburgh. He indicated that he was nearing a final decision.

On Monday, July 1, the president met alone with Thomas for 20 minutes in the bedroom of his Kennebunkport home, the only place, he noted, where he could get away from the grandchildren. Bush wanted to make sure Thomas was ready to go ahead. The spotlight during the Senate confirmation would be intense. Thomas assured the president that he understood and was ready. They then joined the Bush family on the veranda for a lunch of crabmeat salad.

In midafternoon, the president and Thomas came outside to speak before the cameras. "I am very pleased to announce that I will nominate Judge Clarence Thomas to serve as associate justice of the United States Supreme Court," Bush began. "I believe he'll be a great justice. He is the best person for this position. . . . He's a fiercely independent thinker with an excellent legal mind who believes passionately in equal opportunity for all Americans. Judge Thomas's life is a model for all Americans, and he's earned the right to sit on this nation's highest court."

Thomas, short and thickly built, thanked the president and said he was "honored and humbled" by the nomination. "As a child, I could not dare dream that I would ever see the Supreme Court, not to mention be nominated to it. Indeed, my most vivid childhood memory of the Supreme Court was the 'Impeach Earl Warren' signs which lined Highway 17 near Savannah. I didn't understand who this Earl Warren fellow was, but I knew he was in some kind of trouble." Thomas paused and choked up for a moment as he thanked those who had helped him, "especially my grandparents, my mother, and the nuns, all of whom were adamant that I grow up and make something of myself."

The reaction to the nomination was muted. Both Republicans and Democrats called Bush's pick politically astute. As former education secretary William J. Bennett put it, "What can Ted Kennedy tell Clarence Thomas about equal opportunity in this country?" Thomas had indeed come a long way; his life itself made for a powerful story. Liberals and civil rights advocates who had stressed the importance of promoting blacks cautioned now that it was important to look at the nominee's record and legal views, not just his race. "On civil rights issues, Judge Thomas is closer to Ed Meese than to Thurgood Marshall," said Arthur Kropp, president of People for the American Way.

Nan Aron and the Alliance for Justice put out a brief statement: "President Bush has opted for ideological purity instead of an open-minded vision of justice," she said. During his eight years at EEOC, Thomas "failed to demonstrate a commitment to civil rights and liberties," she said. On Capitol Hill, Utah senator Orrin Hatch predicted an easy confirmation for Thomas. He had already been confirmed four times in the previous ten years, most recently on a 98–2 vote for the appeals court. "This man . . . has had a tough life, but he's made it all the way. Anybody who takes him on in the area of civil rights is taking on the grandson of a sharecropper," Hatch said.

Reporters tracked Thomas's odyssey from Pin Point, Georgia, to Conception Junction, Missouri, to Worcester, Massachusetts, and New Haven, Connecticut, to fill in the details of his life. They learned that Thomas's grandfather Myers Anderson worked his grandson "like a dog," according to a friend. Anderson ran his own business out of the back of his truck, delivering ice in the summer and coal and fuel oil in the winter. They learned that Thomas had intended to become a Roman Catholic priest but was driven away by racism. After high school, he had enrolled in the Immaculate Conception Seminary located in a small town in northeast Missouri. On the night of April 4, 1968, the news reached the seminary that Martin Luther King, Jr., had been shot in Memphis. "Good, I hope the SOB dies," one student called out within earshot of Thomas.

They learned also that Thomas had been drawn to black nationalism and antiwar activism in the late 1960s. As a student at Holy Cross College, he wore combat boots and the leather beret of the Black Panthers. On his dormitory-room wall, he put up a poster of Huey Newton. Thomas was also briefly suspended for his role in blocking a military recruiter from coming onto campus. Nonetheless, he had an excellent academic record and won a scholarship to the Yale Law School. They also learned, however, that he had been admitted under an affirmative action program designed to increase the number of black students at Yale.

Reporters also turned up an array of perplexing quotations from Thomas. "If I ever went to work for the EEOC or anything directly connected with blacks, my career would be irreparably ruined," he told a reporter in 1981, the year before he took the EEOC post. He said that he liked to go to church, but not on Sundays. "I don't like people that much. God is all right. It's the people I don't like," he said in a 1984 interview. When he worked for the Missouri attorney general, he kept in his office a Georgia state flag, which featured the stars and bars of the old Confederacy. In the District of Columbia, where the Washington Redskins are viewed as another Sunday religion of sorts, Thomas told everyone he was a fan of their rival Dallas Cowboys. The news profiles portrayed a complex, still unsettled man.

Only the women's rights groups immediately opposed the nomination. They believed that Bush had chosen Thomas because he could be counted on to vote against *Roe* v. *Wade.* The NAACP leadership was divided by the nomination. In July, Thomas went to work with Boyden Gray and former White House chief of staff Kenneth Duberstein to prepare for his September confirmation hearings.

Nan Aron was frustrated. Thomas had earned his credentials at the EEOC, yet neither the reporters nor the Senate Judiciary Committee and its staff seemed particularly interested in probing his eight-year tenure. Senator Joseph Biden, the committee chair, wanted to engage Thomas in an esoteric discussion about "natural law," she noted. Neither Biden nor his staff paid much attention to how Thomas had handled his job of enforcing real laws—the federal antidiscrimination statutes, she worried. People for the American Way, another liberal group that opposed the nomination, had charged that travel records suggest Thomas made personal trips—for example, to attend board meetings at Holy Cross—but charged them as business trips to EEOC. Aron also said that a former EEOC staffer told her that while the agency was considering a major age discrimination case against Xerox, Thomas lunched with Xerox officials. If true, this suggested a conflict of interest, but no one pursued the story, she complained. "They didn't even want to check it out," Aron said.

Biden and his staff saw it differently. They were considering whether to confirm a Supreme Court justice, not an EEOC director. They concentrated on Thomas's views of constitutional law, not his old travel records and lunch receipts.

Still, Aron and the alliance lawyers kept talking to former EEOC staffers, trying to learn more. They heard from several that Thomas had a short fuse, that he did not tolerate those he considered disloyal. For 17 years, Frank Quinn had been the chief of EEOC's San Francisco office and was nearing retirement. In 1983, however, he complained in a *Newsweek* article that Thomas had blocked lawsuits being initiated by his office. A few weeks later, Quinn learned that Thomas had transferred him to Birmingham, Alabama. Thomas said that the move was part of an executive reorganization, but a federal judge refused to buy that excuse. In response to a suit by Quinn, the judge blocked the transfer, saying that the San Francisco official was the victim of an "overly outraged reaction" by Thomas upset at "the exercise of [Quinn's] First Amendment rights."

Aron had also been told over lunch by another former EEOC staffer—Sukhari Hardnett—that Thomas had displayed a special interest in young, attractive black women in the office. Upset by his attentions, Hardnett said that she tried to stay away from the EEOC chair. In late July, another Washington contact told a more specific story. A female aide to Thomas had left the agency in 1983, he confided, because of sexual harassment. Though no name was given, the woman was said to be teaching law in Oklahoma. Back at the alliance office, Nan Aron and George Kassouf looked through the Directory of the Association of American Law Schools. There were only six women teaching at law schools in Oklahoma. They took down the names and then checked the brief biographies in the back of the book. A University of Oklahoma professor had graduated from Yale Law School. Her work experience, the directory said, included, "Spec. Counsel to Asst. Secy., Dept of Educ., Off. for Civil Rights, DC, 1981–82; Atty. Adviser to Chrm., E.E.O.C., DC, 1982–83." The professor's name was Anita Faye Hill.

This story needs to be thoroughly checked out, too, Aron exclaimed. After all, as head of EEOC, Thomas was the nation's chief law enforcement officer against gender discrimination and sexual harassment in the workplace. If he had sexually harassed a female subordinate, he had blatantly violated the laws he was charged with enforcing. The Judiciary Committee itself, however, had not shown much interest in pursuing such stories. In early August, Aron decided to call staffers who worked for Howard Metzenbaum, the one no-holds-barred Democrat on the committee. He and his staff would go after the facts, she noted. Aron passed on Hill's name and the nature of the accusation and urged that her story be investigated.

In August, President Bush and most of the Senate had left Washington. Their attention was directed toward Moscow, where hard-line Communists had briefly overthrown Mikhail Gorbachev. Thomas busied himself with preparing for the hearings. As Gray and Duberstein saw it, the confirmation process was a high-stakes "game." Thomas could lose by saying too much, but not by saying too little. Any comment on a controversial subject would be used against him by Metzenbaum, Kennedy, and the other opponents. The trick was to answer the questions in a way that did not reveal much. On that score, Souter's performance had been masterful. Thomas would be pushed by the Democrats to talk about abortion and *Roe* v. *Wade*, but practically any answer he provided would only prompt further questions. It was better to sidestep the issue, his advisers suggested.

Thomas could not simply imitate Souter, though. The New Hampshire judge came before the committee as a "blank slate." He had written and said little that provoked controversy. By contrast, Thomas had spent a decade sounding off on legal controversies. That was also not the only difference between the two. Souter had immersed himself in the law and could speak fluently about a vast number of Supreme Court cases. Thomas had not spent years reading cases on religion, free speech, the death penalty, antitrust, search and seizure, or the dozens of other areas of law that occupy the Supreme Court. Thomas was smart, but he had a lot to learn.

In July and August, the American Bar Association (ABA) conducted its own investigation. Nearly 1,000 lawyers and judges were contacted. Three separate panels read all of Thomas's written works. Based on these interviews and analyses, the ABA committee gave Thomas a lukewarm "qualified" rating. This meant that the majority of the committee members believed that Thomas had the basic competence to move up to the Supreme Court. However, it was the lowest rating given any court nominee in at least 30 years. Souter, by contrast, had earned a unanimous "well qualified" rating the year before, even though he was not widely known and had yet to write his first opinion as a federal judge.

The Senate Judiciary Committee hearings opened on Tuesday, September 10, in the historic Senate Caucus Room of the old Russell Building. It was the same room where the Army–McCarthy hearings had been held in 1954, where John F. Kennedy announced he was running for president in 1960, and where both Oliver North and Robert Bork had clashed with Senate panels in 1987. Thomas, beaming and shaking every hand in sight, entered the ornate hearing room on the arm of the old South Carolina senator, Strom Thurmond. The two made for an odd historical pairing. In 1948, the year Thomas was born, Thurmond had run for president as a "states' rights" candidate defending southern segregation.

A national television audience tuned in to see Thomas answer questions, but for the first several hours they saw nothing but the senators reading statements. All 14 members of the committee took a turn in front of the cameras, and then 6 other senators read statements introducing the nominee.

Little more was revealed when Thomas finally was given a chance to speak. Though he had spent a decade in Washington making provocative pronouncements, Thomas insisted that he had no strong views and certainly no "ideology" that would influence his decisions as a justice. He dismissed his many statements on natural law and its role in shaping the Constitution as nothing more than the musings of a "part-time political theorist."

On abortion, Thomas followed precisely the formula that had worked for Anthony Kennedy and David Souter. At first mention of the subject, he told the senators that he believed that the Constitution protected "a right to privacy," including the privacy of married couples. This was the right recognized in *Griswold* v. *Connecticut*, the 1965 ruling on contraceptives that Robert Bork had disputed. Then, also like Kennedy and Souter, once having made this meaningless concession, Thomas said that he could not comment further whether he believed this right to privacy extended to matters involving procreation, childbirth, and abortion. To do so would threaten "my impartiality," he said.

When asked about Lewis Lehrman's controversial article on abortion, which he had called "splendid" in 1987, Thomas replied that he had not in fact read the four-page article. "I think I skimmed it, Senator," he added. When Senator Patrick Leahy (D, Vermont) inquired further, Thomas said, "I have not reread it" in preparation for the hearings.

The *Roe* v. *Wade* ruling was issued on January 22, 1973, when Thomas was a law student at Yale. Thomas was asked, Do you recall your reaction to the decision and whether you discussed it with friends? The judge explained that he was married: "I did not spend a lot of time around the law school doing what other students enjoyed so much, and that is debating all the current cases," he replied. "My schedule was such that I went to classes and generally went to work and went home."

Leahy pressed further. "Have you ever had a discussion of *Roe* v. *Wade*, other than in this room?" he asked.

"If you're asking me whether or not I've ever debated the contents of it, the answer to that is no, Senator."

Outside in the hallways during breaks in the hearings, the Democrats were incredulous. Their frustration had been growing for several years now. Each time, it seemed, the White House selected a candidate for the Supreme Court because the nominee had reliably conservative views. Then, suddenly, when called before the committee, these same nominees had practically no views on the law. They said that they just wanted to be good, impartial judges. Once safely confirmed to the Supreme Court, however, the new justices showed themselves to be rigidly conservative. It was a charade, and the Democrats knew it.

"If it's true [that Thomas has never discussed the *Roe* decision,] he's the only adult in America who can say that," Illinois senator Simon commented.

The president's advisers were frustrated, too. Thomas could speak eloquently and intelligently about the law of employment discrimination and affirmative action, but the Democrats refused to discuss those subjects. "They controlled the agenda," Gray said, not the nominee. Even though Thomas made it clear that he could not in good conscience talk about abortion, the Democrats kept asking anyway. For the Democrats, abortion could be the winning issue with the voters; affirmative action was not.

On Friday, Leahy tried an open-ended question. "Just tell me, to help me know how you think, what would you consider a handful of the most important cases that have been decided by the Supreme Court since you became a law student 20 years ago?" he asked.

Thomas paused. "Senator, to give you a running list, I would have to go back and give it some thought," he replied. He then cited *Roe* v. *Wade* and *Griggs* v. *Duke Power*, the key job discrimination ruling, both of which had been discussed earlier in the hearings.

"Are there some other cases that come to mind in the last 20 years?" Leahy asked. In the senator's view, the question was like asking an avid baseball fan to name some of the best teams over the past 20 years. The answer could turn into a 30-minute monologue.

Thomas hesitated again. "There would be others, Senator. I can't off the top of my head. . . . As you mention them, perhaps I could accord some weight to them. Just not off the top of my head," he said.

"But there are none that sort of stand out that might have been cases that have influenced your thinking?" Leahy inquired.

Thomas then mentioned the *Brown* v. *Board of Education* case of 1954, a landmark to be sure, but not one from the past 20 years. Afterward, Duberstein told reporters that Thomas thought the senator only wanted to hear about cases decided when he was in law school between 1971 and 1974. In fact, those were the years when the Court initiated crosstown school busing in the *Swann* v. *Charlotte-Mecklenburg* case, halted the death penalty in *Furman* v. *Georgia*, set the standard for deciding religion cases in *Lemon* v. *Kurtzman*, set the standard for deciding obscenity cases in *Miller* v. *California*, cleared the way for the publication of the Pentagon Papers in *New York Times* v. *U.S.*, and precipitated Richard Nixon's resignation in the Nixon tapes case, *U.S.* v. *Nixon*.

Thomas displayed a vague recall of recent cases as well. When asked about "fetal protection policies," Thomas said that the EEOC had taken the position that such exclusionary policies could be used only when they were judged to be a "bona fide occupational qualification, and that is ultimately the standard that the Supreme Court adopted." In fact, the Court had rejected that view on a 6–3 vote in the case of *United Auto Workers* v. *Johnson Controls*. Harry Blackmun's majority opinion said that employment policies that exclude women are flatly illegal.

At one point, Biden asked Thomas about his statement that the *Morrison* v. *Olson* decision on independent counsels was the "most important court case since *Brown* v. *Board of*

Education." The appeals court opinion in the case had sparked debate by suggesting that the independent agencies must be brought under the president's control, Biden noted and asked whether the judge agreed with that argument. "I was not involved in that debate and was not aware that there was a relationship or there was a second agenda to *Morrison* v. *Olson,*" Thomas replied. Biden and his staff were perplexed. Thomas had spoken of the *Morrison* case as hugely significant but yet seemed to have hardly given it a moment's thought. When asked about the importance of precedent and the doctrine of "stare decisis," Thomas replied that "I have read somewhere" that someone suggested that precedents should carry more weight in business cases compared to matters of individual rights. Thomas said he disputed that view. He might have been surprised later to learn that the "someplace" was the *Payne* v. *Tennessee* decision issued on June 27, and the someone who voiced that view was Chief Justice Rehnquist.

Thomas's evident unfamiliarity with the Supreme Court's work did not disqualify him as a justice, however. California governor Earl Warren showed up at the Court in the fall of 1953 never having worked a day as a judge and having no knowledge of the cases before the justices. He nonetheless plunged into the work of the Court, and so could Thomas. Still, Thomas's stumbling surprised several wavering committee members, including senators Howell Heflin (D, Alabama), Herbert Kohl (D, Wisconsin), and Biden. They had voted for Souter the previous year and prior to the hearings had expected to do the same for Thomas. However, Thomas's five days of testimony convinced them that at age 43, he was not well prepared to advance to the Supreme Court and had been less than fully honest in his replies.

The six committee Republicans were steadfast in their support for the president's nominee. One Democrat, Dennis DeConcini of Arizona announced that he, too, would support Thomas, but the other Democrats shifted away. When the hearings had begun, most predictions had Thomas winning by a 10-4 or 9-5 margin in the Judiciary Committee. On Friday, September 27, however—three months after Marshall had announced his retirement—the committee split 7-7 on the Thomas nomination. "If he was not willing to answer our questions, I was not willing to vote for him," Leahy said after the committee's vote. Though the committee did not recommend

Thomas for confirmation, it voted nonetheless to send the nomination to the Senate floor.

The divided vote marked a surprising setback for Thomas. No Supreme Court nominee had ever won confirmation without the endorsement of the Senate Judiciary Committee. Nevertheless, most senators were saying that they expected Thomas to prevail by a comfortable margin on the floor. The Southern Democrats, led by Sam Nunn of Georgia and J. Bennett Johnston of Louisiana, held the decisive votes in a close contest. In 1987, when their black constituents overwhelmingly opposed Robert Bork, the southern senators cast the key votes that killed his nomination. This time, however, their black constituents by and large supported Thomas, despite the official opposition of the NAACP and the Congressional Black Caucus.

Now, however, Gray, Duberstein, and Danforth were worried, and not because of the vote count. They, too, had learned the name of Anita Faye Hill. It had taken weeks for her story to be checked out, but during the week of the committee vote, the FBI had furnished reports of an interview with the Oklahoma law professor. Her story, if it leaked out, could blow up and destroy the nomination.

On September 4, an aide to Metzenbaum had called Professor Hill and talked with her about Thomas and gender discrimination. Hill did not mention sexual harassment, and the aide did not ask. Two days later, Ricki Seidman, an investigator who works for Ted Kennedy, called back and asked whether Hill knew of reports of sexual harassment at the EEOC. Hill said that she was not sure she wanted to discuss the matter. For several days, Hill had been talking with friends. Should she come forward and reveal what she knew? The decision was agonizing. Her experience in Washington had been painful, Hill told friends, and she had tried to put it behind her. However, she also said that she felt an obligation to tell the truth about Thomas. She knew James Brudney, a Metzenbaum staffer on the Senate Labor Committee, who had been at Yale when she was there. On Monday, September 9, the day before the televised hearings began, Hill told Brudney her story. Thomas had pressured her to go on dates with him when they worked at the Education Department and later at the EEOC. When she refused, he embarrassed her with vivid descriptions of scenes from pornographic movies, she said.

Hill's life story had echoes of Thomas's. She had grown up in a devout Baptist family, the youngest of 13 children. Her father raised cattle and grew soybeans and peanuts on a small farm near Morris, Oklahoma. His daughter was a quiet achiever, the valedictorian of her high school class. She earned honors at Oklahoma State and graduated from the Yale Law School in 1980. She went to work at a Washington law firm, where a friend introduced her to the new civil rights chief at the Department of Education, Clarence Thomas. Michael Middleton, a lawyer who worked with both Thomas and Hill at the Education Department and later at EEOC, described her as "a real straight-arrow, very proper."

On September 12, Hill repeated her story of Thomas's improper behavior to Harriet Grant, the chief of nominations for the Senate Judiciary Committee. A friend of Hill's, Susan Hoerschner, a judge in California, called the committee to report that Hill had indeed told her of the harassment in 1981. Hill also said, however, that she wanted her story kept confidential. She wanted the senators to know it, but not Thomas. Biden made it clear that he would not spread anonymous accusations. If a charge was going to be lodged against Judge Thomas, he deserved a chance to respond to it, Biden indicated.

Hill then grew more determined to press her case. In the first week of September, she had been reluctant to tell her painful tale. Having now done so with friends and committee staffers, however, she wanted to make sure that the senators knew of it before they voted on Thomas. It still took more calls and more negotiations, but Hill finally agreed to be interviewed by FBI agents. On Monday, September 23, she told her story to FBI agents in Norman, Oklahoma. She also faxed the committee staff a four-page, single-spaced statement detailing her allegations.

Two days later, Gray called Thomas at home to say that a serious new charge had arisen. FBI agents would come out to Thomas's suburban Virginia home to interview him, but Gray said that he could not disclose the nature of the charge. The White House had been criticized for its handling of charges of impropriety lodged against John Tower, President Bush's first nominee as Secretary of Defense. Gray did not want a repeat of that experience. He told Thomas he simply could not say more until the FBI agents had spoken with him.

Thomas was in a rage. The nomination had turned into a torturous ordeal. He began to question whether the job, any job, was worth this. For three months, his life—his every statement—had come under scrutiny. Just when it looked as though he had survived it all, something totally new had come up. He called his wife, Virginia, at the Labor Department. "There's a new charge leveled," he said, and the FBI was on its way to the house to interview him.

The wait seemed interminable. The agents had gotten lost on their way to his house, and Thomas was nearly beside himself with worry when they finally arrived. It only got worse then. Yes, he had known Anita Hill. She had worked for him at the Education Department and at the EEOC. However, the judge vehemently denied that he had ever made improper sexual comments to her or pressured her to accompany him on dates. When his wife arrived home, she found him devastated. Why would Anita Hill, someone whom he had tried to help, come forward with these charges now? he wondered. "I could tell he was killing himself inside, searching to figure out why she would do this," Virginia Thomas said in a later *People* magazine interview. Following the FBI visit, Thomas was unable to sleep or eat. His wife said that he lost 15 pounds. "The Clarence Thomas I had married was nowhere to be found. He was just debilitated beyond anything I have seen in my life," she said.

Meanwhile, the FBI report, which recounted the conflicting stories of Hill's accusations and Thomas's denials, was turned over to Biden and Thurmond on the committee and to the White House. To Gray, it looked like the kind of report that soon would be leaked to the press. He was only partly right; the leak did not come soon. The day before the committee vote, Biden briefed the panel's Democrats on it and said that they were welcome to look at the FBI report. Thurmond was responsible for telling the Republicans, but he mentioned the allegation to only a few colleagues. In his view, Thomas had flatly denied the charges, and that was the end of the matter. The Senate leaders scheduled a vote on Thomas for Tuesday evening, October 8, 11 days after the committee vote.

Most of the news reporters turned their attention to the undecided Democrats. If they cast their votes for Thomas, he could win comfortably with 60–65 votes on the floor. If not, it could be a cliff-hanger. Nonetheless, a few reporters kept pursuing rumors and allegations that had arisen over the summer. Nan Aron knew that there was still one "smoking gun" still undisclosed—Anita Hill's report of sexual harassment. Only the Senate Judiciary Committee members and a few of their staff aides knew of Hill's story. Aron was worried that the report would be covered up, kept secret even from the members of the Senate who were still undecided. By then, however, a few reporters had learned of Hill's story, too.

At the White House, Gray expected each day that Hill's story would appear in the press. As the days were counted off, however, his mood lightened. Maybe their worst fears would not be realized after all. By the weekend, Gray thought it just might be possible that the final Senate vote could come off as scheduled on Tuesday. He was at his Georgetown home Saturday evening when his signal phone beeped. It meant that a call was coming in from the White House switchboard. "I knew then exactly what was coming," he said.

Nina Totenberg of the National Public Radio (NPR) was going on the air with a report detailing Hill's accusations. Timothy Phelps of *Newsday* also had written a story of the allegations, which would appear in the Sunday papers. Totenberg had learned the details of Hill's affidavit and had spoken to the Oklahoma law professor about her story. According to Hill, Thomas often had called her into his office at the Education Department. Rather than discussing work, he would "turn the conversation to discussions about his sexual interests. . . . He spoke about acts he [had] seen in pornographic films, involving such things as women having sex with animals, and films involving group sex or rape scenes." Hill said that she repeatedly told him that she did not want to hear such discussions, but Thomas persisted. He did not physically harass her, nor did he penalize her for her refusal to date him, she noted.

Hill was 25 years old when Thomas moved from the Education Department to the EEOC. Because the alleged harassment had recently ceased, she went with him and took a new job as a special assistant at the EEOC. However, according to Hill, the harassment began again, and in 1983, she checked in to a hospital with what she believed to be stress-related stomach pains. A few months later, she quit the agency and went back to Oklahoma, where she found a job teaching at Oral Roberts University. Clarence Thomas gave her a glowing recommendation. In the NPR report, Senator Paul Simon was quoted as saying Hill's accusations raise "a serious question . . . of credibility" about the Supreme Court nominee. "I think it would be wise to take a serious look" at the charges, he said.

If Thomas had any lingering hopes that the story might prove to be a one-day sensation, Hill dashed them Monday when she held a press conference in Norman, Oklahoma.

"That's it!" Thomas roared when he heard the news. "They can have it! I give up!" he said. He had hit his lowest point. His wife tried to buck him up. "I told him, 'Clarence, don't. Stop that now. Stop,' " she said.

Before the cameras, Hill's manner was quiet, but resolute. She described her experience and answered questions from reporters. Sexual harassment "is an unpleasant issue. It's an ugly issue, and people don't want to deal with it generally, and in particular in this case," she said. She made it clear that she had told her story only because Senate staffers asked her about it. Now, however, she said, "I would like to see the process carried through further," adding that should would be "happy" to tell her full story before the Senate Judiciary Committee.

Overnight, Hill's story blew up in the face of the Senate and its Judiciary Committee. How could the senators have ignored such a powerful—and if true, damning—accusation against the nominee? Millions of women said that they already knew the answer. The Senate was a male club; they just are not sensitive to issues such as sexual harassment. By Tuesday afternoon, however, a majority of the Senate had figured out that the vote had to be delayed. Majority leader George Mitchell and Republican leader Bob Dole agreed to put off the vote for a week. In the meantime, the Senate Judiciary Committee would try to resolve the charges. Thomas had issued a statement welcoming new hearings. "I want to clear my name," he said.

The Thomas versus Hill hearings turned into a TV spectacle. Millions of viewers were gripped by the dramatic clash between the judge and the professor. For 21 hours over three days, the networks broadcast the hearings. The testimony was by turns riveting, appalling, unnerving, and frustrating. Both Thomas and Hill raised a right hand and swore to tell the truth. One of them then looked the American people in the eye—and lied.

The question was, Which one?

Bristling with a raw anger, Thomas "categorically [denied] all of the allegations" made by Hill. He said that he had never asked her for dates, mentioned X-rated films to her, or behaved in an improper manner. He described how they met, how they formed a "cordial and professional" working relationship, and how they parted on friendly terms in 1983. "I have not said or done the things that Anita Hill has alleged. God has gotten

me through the days since September 25, and He is my judge,"
he said.

On the day of his return appearance before the committee,
Thomas had been up until 4:30 A.M. preparing his statement.
He wrote on a pad of paper on the kitchen table. As he finished
a page, his wife typed it up. They had bolstered their spirits
in recent days by inviting several friends over to pray. "They
brought over prayer tapes, and we would read parts of the
Bible. We shut the kitchen blinds and turned on Christian praise
music to survive the worst days," Virginia Thomas reported.
This was "not the normal political battle. It was spiritual warfare. Good versus evil," she added.

After only two hours of sleep Friday morning, Thomas
arrived at the hearing room ready to fight. He spoke deliberately and glared at the senators, several of whom squirmed
noticeably. The thought of Ted Kennedy judging whether Clarence Thomas had engaged in sexual impropriety struck many
as preposterous.

"I have never, in all my life, felt such hurt, such pain,
such agony. My family and I have been done a grave and ir-
reparable injustice," Thomas said. He did not directly accuse
Hill of lying but instead blamed the press and the liberal activists for his awful ordeal. He spoke of "reporters and interest
groups swarming over divorce papers, looking for dirt. Un-
named people starting preposterous and damaging rumors.
Calls all over the country specifically requesting dirt. This is
not American. This is Kafkaesque. It has got to stop. It must
stop for the benefit of future nominees and our country.
Enough is enough."

Sexual harassment did not fit with what was previously
known of Thomas. Dozens of women who had worked at EEOC
came forward to support the former EEOC chairman. The Clarence Thomas they knew was always considerate, proper, and
professional, they insisted. How could it be, they wondered,
that Thomas could repeatedly and grossly harass Anita Hill, yet
no one in the office had heard of it nor had seen any evidence
of such behavior? Office secrets usually don't keep well. It just
did not make sense, they concluded.

Thomas had also played a key role in establishing a strict
Supreme Court standard against sexual harassment. Federal law
clearly prohibited gender discrimination that resulted in a
woman losing a job or a promotion, but there remained some
doubt as to whether it also made illegal sexist behavior that,

while not affecting a woman's job status, nonetheless harassed and offended her. That issue came before the Supreme Court in the spring of 1986, and Thomas traveled to the Justice Department to personally urge the Administration's attorneys to take a strong stand against workplace harassment. Solicitor General Charles Fried said that Thomas compared sexist behavior and its impact on women workers to the plight of a Jewish employee forced to work amidst Nazi memorabilia. Such behavior should be deemed intolerable and illegal, regardless of whether it had a specific "job consequence," he had said. The Justice Department took that position in its legal brief, and the Supreme Court agreed in the case of *Vinson* v. *Meritor Savings*, ruling that the creation of a "hostile environment" for women violated the laws against gender discrimination. If Hill's accusations were true, however, Thomas had violated the standard he later helped to write into law.

After Thomas delivered his powerful, opening denial, Hill was called before the committee. Dressed primly in a blue dress, she looked small and slight sitting alone at the witness table. Once again, she spoke with the calm, resolute demeanor of someone who, though reluctant at first, had decided to tell her full story. Her testimony was graphic. She asserted that Thomas spoke of his own penis and told her of a pornographic film star named "Long Dong Silver." One of the "oddest episodes," she said, involved him holding up a Coke can asking, "Who has put pubic hair on my Coke?" Hill said she regretted having moved with Thomas from the Education Department to the EEOC. "It wasn't as though it happened every day," she said of his offensive talk, "but I went to work during certain periods knowing that it might happen." She also told of a chilling comment that she said Thomas made during a going-away dinner at a restaurant near the office. "He said that if I ever told anyone of his behavior, that it would ruin his career," she said.

Hill spent almost eight hours on the witness stand, answering the senators' questions fully and with considerable detail. She appeared to hesitate only once, when Senator Arlen Specter pressed her to recall a conversation with Democratic staffers. Did she discuss the possibility that Thomas would have to withdraw if she confidentially submitted her allegations? Hill said "no" at first but later said that she was uncertain whether that possibility had been discussed.

Senate committees and TV viewers rarely hear such flatly
contradictory testimony, but jurors in criminal cases do almost
every day. Prosecution witnesses take the stand and accuse a
defendant of criminal behavior. Afterward, the accused takes
the stand to flatly dispute the allegations. Someone is lying.
Trial experts say jurors are swayed by three considerations: the
demeanor of the witnesses, the specificity of their testimony,
and their motivations for telling the truth or a lie.

Both Thomas and Hill made convincing witnesses. He
spoke with anguish and power, she with calm resolution. Hill's
testimony offered far more details, while Thomas offered a general denial. Of course, if Hill's story were a "fantasy," as the
Republican senators suggested, how could Thomas respond but
with a categorical denial? On the other hand, what would be
Hill's motive for inventing such a lurid tale? Why would she
come forward and subject herself to the glare of national television if her relationship with Thomas had been proper and
amiable? Try as they might, Thomas and his supporters could
not offer a plausible motive to explain why the reserved Oklahoma law professor would come forward with dramatically false
testimony.

While Hill testified, Thomas and his wife had gone to their
Virginia home. He stayed downstairs smoking a cigar and talking with a U.S. marshal who had driven them home. His wife
went upstairs to watch the TV. When she recounted Hill's
graphic allegations to her husband, "He just let out this big
howl. He was in shock. He was holding his chest," she said
later. Hill's comments to the committee went well beyond what
she had told the FBI agents the week before. Thomas "looked
shaken. 'I never said those things! Why is she doing this?' " he
asked his wife. Thomas was so tightly wound, so angry, that
his wife feared for his health. "This was killing him. I worried
that his blood pressure would shoot up and he'd have a stroke,"
she said.

On Friday night, an angry Thomas returned to the witness
stand. "I would like to start by saying unequivocally, uncate-
gorically, that I deny each and every single allegation against
me today," he said. "This is a circus. It's a national disgrace
and from my standpoint as a black American . . . it's a high-
tech lynching for uppity blacks." Though he had steered away
from racial politics before, he bluntly asserted now that the
Democrats and the liberal interest groups were seeking to ruin
him because he had broken ranks and joined the conservatives.

"It is a message," he said, "that you will be lynched, destroyed, caricatured by a committee of the U.S. Senate rather than hung from a tree." With his searing testimony, Thomas portrayed himself as the true victim of the encounter with Anita Hill.

He startled Senator Howell Heflin by saying he had not watched any of Hill's testimony. "I have heard enough lies!" he said. Knocked back by the reply, Heflin asked no further questions. The Democrats did not press the judge to rebut the allegations in greater detail.

Thomas returned to the witness stand again Saturday, but the session was dominated by Senator Orrin Hatch. Using a computer scanning of legal opinions, the Justice Department had found a 1988 sexual harassment case from Kansas in which "Long Dong Silver" was mentioned. Hatch suggested that Hill might have found this name there. The story about a pubic hair may have come from the novel *The Exorcist*, the Utah senator suggested. The Republicans stressed that Hill had placed a dozen phone calls to Thomas since moving to Oklahoma. They said that this hardly fits the behavior of a woman who has been grossly harassed.

Before leaving the witness stand, Thomas was asked whether he had had any inkling on July 1 of the ordeal ahead. "I expected it to be bad. I expected to be a sitting duck for the interest groups. I expected them to attempt to kill me. And yes, I even expected personal attempts on my life," he said. "I did not expect this circus."

Because he had blamed the interest groups, rather than Hill, for his final ordeal, Biden asked whether he believed that the interest groups spread Hill's story or actually invented it. "Senator, I believe that someone, some interest group, I don't care who it is, in combination came up with this story and used this process to destroy me," he replied. "I believe that in combination this story was developed or concocted to destroy me." This, too, was a remarkable accusation. While his Republican defenders supposed that Hill had fantasized her account or had a secret, unrequited passion for her former supervisor, the judge seemed to be saying that Washington activists had "concocted" the lurid tale and had persuaded Hill to recount the lie on national television.

While the committee heard from so-called witnesses throughout the day Sunday, none of the "witnesses" had actually witnessed anything that could prove or disprove the competing accounts. Four friends and acquaintances of Hill's testified that she had indeed spoken of harassment during the early 1980s. Four female employees of the EEOC testified that they had observed both Thomas and Hill at work, and they believed Thomas was telling the truth, not Hill. On Sunday evening, more female coworkers offered supporting testimony for Thomas.

During the evening, the committee agreed that it would not hear from Angela Denise Wright, a North Carolina newspaper editor who had worked for Thomas in 1985 and had been fired by him. In a sworn affidavit, she said that Thomas had "consistently pressured me to date him. At one point, Clarence Thomas made comments about my anatomy," she said. He also showed up uninvited one evening at her apartment, she asserted. Sukhari Hardnett also submitted a letter to the committee, saying that she was "amazed and outraged at the 'fatherly ambience' that he is . . . projecting as an image of his office." According to her, "If you were young, black, female and reasonably attractive, you knew full well you were being inspected and auditioned as a female." Neither Hardnett nor Wright claimed that they were sexually harassed by Thomas, but their accounts undercut the notion that Anita Hill was the only woman to have encountered problems with the EEOC chair.

It was nearly 2 A.M. Monday morning when Biden gaveled an end to the special hearings. The senators hoped that the TV hearings would show that they took sexual harassment seriously. Certainly, the topic had gained instant attention from coast to coast. Still, the hearings had brought forth no firm answer to the question as to whether Thomas or Hill was telling the truth. With the testimony delivered into their living room, millions of Americans came to their own conclusions. Most sided with Thomas, according to opinion surveys taken over the weekend. Even though it was impossible to know for sure who was telling the truth, many held that Thomas did not deserve such abuse.

Nan Aron had stayed at the hearings until the end. For most of the time, she talked in the hallways with friends and committee staffers. Though she sympathized with Thomas for the ordeal he had undergone, she did not believe his testimony. "I think he lied," she said.

Throughout the day Tuesday, the senators one by one rose to announce their decisions and to explain their thoughts. Some were angry, some eloquent, and quite a few beset by real uncertainty. A confirmation vote on a Supreme Court justice is so difficult, they believed, because of the unique lifetime tenure that goes with the job. If Thomas were confirmed and served to the same age as Thurgood Marshall, he would not leave the Supreme Court until the year 2030. Despite the grave reservations of many, the deadline for decision had come. At 6 P.M. on October 15, the final tally was 52 in favor, 48 against. Vice President Dan Quayle announced that "Clarence Thomas of Georgia" had been confirmed.

It had been by far the closest confirmation vote for a justice in the twentieth century. As a historical matter, however, some of the Court's most notable justices had also had difficult confirmations. Louis D. Brandeis, the first Jewish nominee, was derided as having socialist sympathies and won confirmation in 1916 only after a long fight and on a 47–22 vote. In 1930, Charles Evans Hughes had been labeled a toady of Wall Street but won approval as chief justice on a 52–26 vote. Just weeks after he won confirmation in 1937, Justice Hugo Black was revealed to have been a member of the Ku Klux Klan. To quell the furor, Black went on radio nationwide, admitted that he had once belonged to the Klan but said that he had quit long before. He then went on to a distinguished 34-year career as one of the Court's leading liberals.

Thomas had stayed at home Tuesday as the Senate debated his fate. When the voting had begun, however, he had gone upstairs to take a shower. His wife came running upstairs to tell him of the result. "You got 52 votes!" she said. "He kind of shrugged. It was the oddest thing. It was like, 'Okay, thanks.' It was as if it didn't matter anymore," she recalled. Finally, it was over. He had survived, but he hardly felt like celebrating.

There was not much celebrating at the Court either. Rehnquist's wife, Nan, had been fading for weeks. On Thursday morning, less than two days after the Senate vote, she died. She was only 62 years old. Nonetheless, the White House went ahead with plans for a very public swearing-in ceremony Friday. Hundreds of Thomas's supporters gathered on the South Lawn for the ceremony. He beamed a broad smile and waved to friends. Byron White, the senior associate justice, substituted for Rehnquist and administered a constitutional oath, the first of two oaths required of federal judges.

On the first of November, Thomas donned the black robes and stepped up to the bench to recite the judicial oath. The courtroom ceremony brought a dignified end to the most raucous confirmation fight in the Court's history. As his wife, Senator Danforth, and an audience of senators, Administration officials, and friends watched, Thomas took his seat at the far-right end of bench. He was the 106th justice of the Supreme Court.

After a brief reception, the chief justice and Thomas took the traditional walk down the marble steps. It was a gray, overcast day, and Rehnquist looked tired and somber. He barely paused at the bottom before turning to walk away. The new justice stood smiling for a moment for the photographers, but he could not entirely escape the confirmation mess. "Down with the male supremacist Court," someone shouted out repeatedly from the street. As he turned to walk back into the building for his first conference session, Thomas was asked how he felt. "Ready to get to work," he said, and briskly walked away.

PART EIGHT
The
1991–1992 Term

13

Crossing the Rubicon

I n the spring of 1992, the Rehnquist Court faced a telling
test. Unquestionably, the conservative justices now held
sway. The old liberals of the Warren era, Justices Brennan and
Marshall, were retired. Indeed, a Democratic president had not
appointed a new member of the Court for a quarter century.
The lone Democrat among the nine justices was Byron White,
and his views often mirrored Rehnquist's.

But what kind of conservatism would this Court practice?
A conservatism that frowned upon novel claims and newly asserted rights, whether from prisoners or property holders, from
gays or street beggars? A conservatism that deferred controversial decisions to the other branches of government? A conservatism that, as its name suggests, preferred to preserve the
status quo?

Or would the new majority push hard toward the right
and roll back the precedents set by a once activist liberal Court?
If earlier rulings that outlawed official school prayers or legalized abortion were seen by the conservatives as flawed, even
fraudulent, would they reverse them?

Before, the answer seemed to depend only on numbers.
Rehnquist and White, for example, had said all along that they
would overturn *Roe* v. *Wade* if three others joined them. In
1989, Scalia said he would do so. Kennedy, while stopping
short of such an outright declaration, nonetheless had signed
on to Rehnquist's opinion in the *Webster* case, which called for
upholding state restrictions on abortion that were "reasonably
designed . . . (for) protecting potential human life." If either

David Souter or Clarence Thomas agreed, the chief justice would have five votes to throw out the right to abortion.

So too in the area of religion. Kennedy upon his arrival had made clear that he believed the liberals had gone too far in excluding religion from public life. When a slim majority voted in 1989 to outlaw the placement of a creche in the Pittsburgh city hall, Kennedy had dissented and called for a major change in the law. Unless the government uses "coercion" to force an unwilling citizen to practice religion or to pay for church activities, the Court should stand aside, he said. "Government policies of accommodation, acknowledgement and support for religion" should be upheld, he asserted. Rehnquist, White, and Scalia joined him in urging such a change. Now, with a vote from Souter or Thomas, Kennedy could wield a new majority.

The Bush administration lawyers certainly understood the arithmetic. Early in 1991, the administration filed a brief with the justices urging that they hear an appeal of a school case from Providence, Rhode Island. The principals of a public school there regularly invited a cleric to deliver an invocation and a benediction as part of the graduation ceremonies. Daniel Weisman, a parent, complained that such an officially sponsored invocation of religion had no place in the public schools. When principal Robert Lee refused to change the practice, Weisman enlisted the help of the ACLU and filed a lawsuit contending that the school had violated the First Amendment's ban on an "establishment of religion." A federal judge in Providence and the U.S. Court of Appeals in Boston agreed with the parent, ruling that any form of officially sponsored prayer was unconstitutional.

The case of *Lee* v. *Weisman* might have ended there, but for Chuck Cooper, the former Rehnquist clerk who had helped make his old boss the chief justice of the United States. In Cooper's view, the lower court opinions striking down the graduation prayers were an outrage. The rabbi who delivered the prayer cited in Weisman's lawsuit barely alluded to religion. "God of the Free, Hope of the Brave," he began, but then veered into words of praise for the nation's political system and its celebration of tolerance, diversity, and freedom. "For the liberty of America, we thank You. May these new graduates grow up to guard it," the rabbi said.

Liberty! Tolerance! Thanks to the liberal rulings of the past, Cooper complained, public-school children did not have the liberty of hearing even a mention of God during a graduation ceremony. Certainly the rabbi's words could not be considered religious indoctrination; they merely invoked the deity to open a solemn ceremony. Cooper also understood the new arithmetic of the high court; after all, he had helped to pick several of the new justices. With that in mind, he prepared an appeal of the Providence school decision and sent it to the Court.

Cooper's efforts also drew the attention of Ken Starr, the solicitor general for the Bush administration. In urging the Court to hear the case, Starr said that the Providence case could be the vehicle for recasting the law on religion as Justice Kennedy had suggested. At a minimum, the public schools should be permitted to "acknowledge our religious heritage," he said. Starr stopped well short of asking the Court to throw out the ban on official prayer in the classrooms, but he did call for a more lenient approach to public invocations of religion. The case of *Lee* v. *Weisman* came up for argument on November 6, just five days after Clarence Thomas took his seat.

But Cooper and Starr ran into unexpectedly stiff questioning—and from a surprising source. Picking up Kennedy's words, Cooper said that the First Amendment is not violated unless a government official uses "coercion" to force someone to participate in a religious ceremony. The words "In God We Trust" on coins or the Court's opening invocation, which includes the phrase "God Save This Honorable Court," express the nation's religious heritage and do not compel anyone to participate in a religious exercise, he said.

Well, then, could a state declare that it has an official church the way it has a state bird or a state flower? O'Connor asked. As in the colonial days, could Maryland say it was a Catholic state and Virginia an Episcopal state?

Yes, Cooper replied, so long as no one is forced to pay taxes to support the church.

O'Connor and Kennedy looked startled. How could an official "establishment of religion" by the state *not* violate the Constitution's ban on "laws respecting an establishment of religion?"

His brow wrinkled, Kennedy seemed troubled. He questioned Cooper's premise that a graduation prayer did not involve "coerced" participation in a religious exercise. Cooper had pointed out that attendance at graduation is voluntary.

Students could stay away and still receive their diplomas, he said.

"In our culture, graduation is a key event in a young person's life," Kennedy told Cooper. "I find it very difficult to accept the proposition that it is not a substantial imposition on a young graduate to say you have your choice: either hear this prayer or absent yourself from graduation."

Starr tried a different approach. Yes, he conceded, some young graduates who disdain religion will hear a religious message, but they can sit silently and ignore it. "You may hear things you don't like and you don't agree with," the administration's attorney said. "That's part of a free society."

A ceremonial mention of God is hardly novel or radical, Starr stressed. The invocation of God is "as old and as enduring as the republic itself. We believe ourself to be one nation under God." He finished strongly, but had he cleared up Kennedy's doubts?

Meanwhile, an even more momentous test case moved toward the Court. In the summer of 1989, Pennsylvania lawmakers had moved quickly to take advantage of the *Webster* decision, which removed the barrier to regulating abortion. The state's new Abortion Control Act said that a pregnant woman must see a doctor and then wait 24 hours before obtaining an abortion. She must also be offered information on fetal development and on alternatives such as adoption. A teenage girl would need the consent of one parent, and a married woman would be required to notify her spouse before she aborted a pregnancy. However, the law did not make abortion a crime. It was signed into law by Governor Robert Casey.

Before the law could go into effect, abortion-rights lawyers filed a suit on behalf of Planned Parenthood of Southeastern Pennsylvania. They said that the law was intended to harass women and should be struck down as unconstitutional.

But what was the constitutional law now on abortion? Was it Rehnquist's plurality opinion in the *Webster* case, which would permit abortion restrictions that were "reasonably designed . . . to protect potential human life"? If so, Pennsylvania's law could stand. And so could an outright ban on abortion, for that matter. Or was it O'Connor's standard, which said that abortion restrictions could stand so long as they did not put "an undue burden" on the woman's right to choose? This seemed to give states some leeway to regulate abortion, but not to ban it. Or was it Blackmun's opinion in *Roe* v. *Wade*,

which said that the state could not put any regulation or restrictions on abortion during the early months of a pregnancy?

Not surprisingly, federal judges were split on how to handle the Pennsylvania law. Initially, a trial judge invoked Blackmun's opinion in *Roe* and struck down the measure entirely.
After all, he noted, Rehnquist did not have five solid votes for
his opinion in the *Webster* case, so Blackmun's version of *Roe*
v. *Wade* remained the law.

But the three-judge panel of the U.S. Court of Appeals in
Philadelphia took a different tack. They looked at the *Webster*
case and concluded that O'Connor's view held the balance,
even though she spoke only for herself. As the fifth, concurring
vote in the *Webster* case, her view was decisive, they said.
Therefore, the Court of Appeals concluded that abortion regulations could stand so long as they did not put an "undue
burden" on pregnant women. Applying that standard, the three
judges upheld most of Pennsylvania's restrictions, such as the
mandatory 24-hour waiting period. However, they voted to
strike down the requirement that the women notify their
spouses. Obviously, most women would tell their spouses, but
the law covered everyone. A woman who was beaten or abused
might fear discussing an abortion with her spouse. A state requirement that she notify her abusive spouse could indeed put
an "undue burden" on her choice, the Court of Appeals said.
Still, everyone knew that this was merely a preliminary decision. The final word would come from the Supreme Court.

In the background could be heard the ticking of the election-year clock. Lawyers for the abortion-rights movement
adopted a surprising legal strategy, one geared mostly to the
fall campaign. In the Supreme Court, they hoped to lose—and
lose big. In doing so, they hoped to energize pro-choice voters
to win big in the fall elections. Certainly they were taking a
bold gamble, but one based on a seemingly realistic assessment
of the Court and the public. Ronald Reagan and George Bush
had sent five new justices to join Rehnquist and White, the
original dissenters in the *Roe* case. Eventually, this new Court
will throw out the right to abortion, they believed, and return
the issue to state legislatures and Congress. If so, why not press
the issue in the Court now so that a loss in the legal arena can
be the catalyst for victory in the political arena? Better to lose
the constitutional right to abortion in 1992, they figured, than
in 1993. In her appeal on behalf of Planned Parenthood, Kathryn Kolbert of the Center for Reproductive Law and Policy,

an independent offshoot of the ACLU, shunned the usual tactic of asking the Court to examine the specifics of the Pennsylvania law. Instead, she asked a simple, blunt question: "Is *Roe* v. *Wade* still the law?"

But Rehnquist wanted no part of this political grandstanding. He always insisted on defining "*Roe* v. *Wade*" narrowly as a decision that struck down a Texas law that criminalized all abortions. That sort of measure was obviously not at issue in the Pennsylvania case. The new state law imposed regulations such as the required 24-hour waiting period, but it did not make abortion a crime. Why not focus on the specifics of the Pennsylvania law and ignore the political grandstanding?

Around the table, the others, including O'Connor and Kennedy, agreed. In late January, the Court announced that it would hear *Casey* v. *Planned Parenthood*, but the order was nearly as surprising as Kolbert's bluntly worded appeal. Typically, the justices agree to rule on the issues raised by the attorneys in their appeal. But the Court's order ignored broad issues raised by Kolbert's petition and indeed did not even mention the words "*Roe* v. *Wade*." Instead, the Court said it would rule on the specific provisions of the Pennsylvania law. It looked as though Rehnquist had prevailed in steering the case toward a narrow resolution, one that would not set off an election-year explosion. If so, the true test of *Roe* v. *Wade* and the right to abortion would not come before 1993.

The oral argument in the Pennsylvania case was set for April 22, the last day for oral arguments during the spring session. Would the justices rule narrowly on whether states could impose 24-hour waiting periods for abortion? Or would they rule more broadly on the right to choose abortion? Once again, the Bush administration raised the stakes. Three weeks before the argument, Starr filed a strongly worded brief that attacked the very notion that women have a constitutional right to terminate a pregnancy.

"*Roe* v. *Wade* was wrongly decided and should be overruled," Starr wrote. "The protection of innocent human life— in and out of the womb—is certainly the most compelling interest that a State can advance. In our view, a State's interest in protecting fetal life throughout pregnancy, as a general matter, outweighs a woman's liberty interest in an abortion."

Starr acknowledged that the Pennsylvania case does not "require reconsideration of *Roe's* actual holding (striking down a criminal ban on abortion)." Rehnquist had said as much.

Nonetheless, "the Court should clarify the standard of review of abortion regulation," Starr asserted.

Lawyers know that the "standard of review" can decide all that follows. It is no "lawyer's quibble over words," Starr noted. For example, in *Roe* v. *Wade*, Blackmun said that women had a "fundamental right" to choose abortion. That standard resulted in judges striking down all manner of abortion regulations. The government cannot infringe an individual's exercise of her fundamental rights.

At the opposite extreme was the anything-goes standard proposed by Solicitor General Starr. It was also the standard favored by Rehnquist. Abortion laws should be upheld so long as they are "rationally related . . . to protecting potential human life," he said. Under this standard, all abortion restrictions could stand, with one possible exception. Rehnquist had noted that it would still be unconstitutional for a state to ban abortions when the mother's life was at stake. It would be irrational, he said, for a state to force a pregnant woman to die in the interest of possibly saving a tiny fetus.

Anyone who thought this was an abstract legal debate could look to Louisiana and Utah. There, state lawmakers had recently enacted measures that would again make nearly all elective abortions a crime. Physicians could be sent to prison for performing such operations. Whether those laws could stand depended on the standard of review set by the Court in the *Casey* case. But if so, how could justices continue to characterize the case as a small dispute over 24-hour waiting periods?

At 10 A.M. on April 22, Kathryn Kolbert stood before the justices and launched into her defense of a woman's right to choose abortion, confident she would lose the case. In their earlier order, the justices said they wanted to examine the specifics of the Pennsylvania law, but Kolbert paid no heed to that directive.

"Whether our Constitution endows Government with the power to force a woman to continue or to end a pregnancy against her will is the central question in this case," she began. "While pregnancy may be a blessed act when planned or wanted, forced pregnancy, like any forced bodily invasion, is an anathema to American values and traditions. In the same way that it would be unacceptable for Government to force a man or a woman to donate bone marrow, or to compel the contribution of a kidney to another, . . . our Constitution protects women against forced pregnancy," she said.

The justices sat silent. They let Kolbert deliver what
sounded like a speech geared to an audience outside the courtroom. Finally, after five minutes had gone by, O'Connor leaned
forward and interrupted.

"Ms. Kolbert, you're arguing the case as though all we
have before us is whether to apply stare decisis and preserve
Roe v. *Wade* in all its aspects," she said. "Nevertheless, we
granted certiorari on some specific questions [concerning the
Pennsylvania law]. Do you plan to address any of those in your
argument?"

"Your Honor, I do," Kolbert replied. "However, the central question in the case is what is the standard that this Court
uses to evaluate the restrictions that are at issue, and therefore
one cannot . . ."

O'Connor interrupted again. "Well, the standard may affect the outcome or it may not," she said, "but at bottom we
still have to deal with specific issues, and I wondered if you
were going to address them."

Once again, it sounded as though O'Connor wanted to
avoid the ultimate issue of whether she supported *Roe* v. *Wade*,
just as she had done in the Webster case. But Kolbert was just
as insistent that she not be sidetracked into arguing only about
a 24-hour waiting period. She plunged back into a discussion
of the importance of women's "reproductive freedom."

Now Kennedy took a turn at narrowing the debate. "I
don't question the importance of your arguing there is a fundamental right, as you have done," he said. "However, there
is a fundamental right to speech," he noted, and the Court had
upheld some limits on picketing, protests, and other infringements on free speech. It is best, Kennedy suggested, "to decide
on a case-by-case basis" the inevitable conflicts between a constitutional right and public regulations. "You have a number of
specific provisions here that I think you should address," Kennedy told the Planned Parenthood lawyer. Still Kolbert refused.
She spoke of the importance of maintaining abortion as a "fundamental right," which would have the effect of sweeping aside
all the state restrictions.

Kennedy cut her off in midsentence. "I am suggesting that
our sustaining these statutory provisions does not necessarily
undercut all of the holding of *Roe* v. *Wade*," he persisted.

The abortion-rights attorney remained unswayed. "It is our position, Your Honor, if this Court were to change the standard (of review) . . . for a less protective standard such as undue burden test or the rational relationship test, . . . that would be the same as overruling *Roe*," Kolbert said.

Having tried and failed to narrow the case, Kennedy seemed perturbed. "Well, if you are going to argue that *Roe* can survive only in its most rigid formulation, that is an election you can make as counsel," he said. "I am suggesting to you that is not the only logical possibility in this case."

It was a puzzling exchange. The lawyers in the front rows of the courtroom glanced at each other with quizzical looks. What was Kennedy getting at? Apparently, like O'Connor, he seemed to be saying that he was not ready to overturn *Roe* v. *Wade* in the Pennsylvania case. But what did that mean? Would he simply vote next year in a case from Utah or Louisiana to overturn "the holding of *Roe*" and the basic right to abortion? If so, Kolbert was right to ignore his plea to focus on specifics. If the Rehnquist Court was going to scrap the right to abortion, she wanted the deed done now, before the voters went to the polls in 1992. But Kennedy's comments hinted at another possibility. Maybe everyone had misjudged his intentions. Perhaps he was ultimately unwilling to overturn *Roe* entirely and to let abortion be made criminal again. If so, the Planned Parenthood lawyers might have badly miscalculated.

Solicitor General Starr took the final 10 minutes of the argument. He pressed the key point of his brief. The Court majority should adopt the standard of review for abortion that Rehnquist had set forth in the *Webster* opinion. "That's the rational basis standard," he said, under which any reasonable restriction designed to protect "potential life" would be constitutional.

Under that standard, Byron White asked, "All of the provisions that are at issue here would be sustained?"

"Exactly," Starr said.

From the left end of the bench came a pointed rejoinder. "And so would a complete prohibition" on abortion, said David Souter.

In his first two years on the bench, the New Hampshire jurist had shown an ability to cut to the heart of the matter during the oral arguments. The Bush administration's attorney preferred to talk about the rather abstract matter of a "standard of review." He didn't want headlines reporting that he had urged the Court to uphold a criminal ban on all abortions.

Starr sought to wriggle away from Souter's question. "A complete prohibition that had no exception for the life of the mother," Starr intoned, "could raise very serious questions . . ."

Souter cut him off. Everyone understood an exception must be made for the woman whose pregnancy could kill her. "Subject to that exception. Subject to that exception," Souter said.

"I think it best not to answer this in the abstract," Starr offered lamely. It was an obvious dodge, one that clearly did not satisfy Souter.

"Well, you're asking the Court to adopt a standard and I think we ought to know where the standard would take us," Souter said.

Pressed, Starr conceded that the "rational basis test would, in fact, allow considerable leeway to the states," but he refused to say that his approach, if adopted, would again permit states to make nearly all abortions a crime.

The white-haired Stevens threw a jab at the government's top attorney. Like Souter, he was also irked by Starr's evasive response.

"That's not really a fair answer," Stevens said. "Under your analysis, there's an interest in preserving fetal life at all times during pregnancy. It's rational under your view. Ergo it follows that a total prohibition, protected by criminal penalties, would be rational."

Starr refused to agree. He wandered off into a discussion of "common law" and his time soon ran out. But the exchange highlighted a key point for those like O'Connor and Kennedy who hoped to avoid a major ruling. If the Court did indeed adopt the "rational basis" standard, the right to abortion would be gone, whether or not the opinion used the words "*Roe* v. *Wade* is hereby overturned."

Two days later, the justices gathered for their regular Friday morning conference to vote on the Pennsylvania case. The discussion moved quickly around the table; with the exception of Souter and Thomas, all of them had been over the subject of abortion before. Initially, they voted on whether to uphold the portions of the Pennsylvania law. No surprise there. Only Blackmun and Stevens, the only remaining advocates of the unqualified right to abortion, voted to sweep aside all the Pennsylvania restrictions. O'Connor was troubled by the requirement that married women tell their husbands about their plans. Since when does the government have the power to tell adults what they must reveal to others? Still, a solid majority favored upholding the provisions of the Pennsylvania law. But on what basis? How should they describe the woman's right and the state's authority? What would be the standard of review? Those questions were not finally decided, but the outline of an opinion seemed clear. Rehnquist thought he had a majority to write a "*Webster*-style" opinion—just as the administration had suggested—that would signal an end to the right to abortion. Blackmun thought the same. *Roe* is dead, he told friends.

For Rehnquist, White, and Scalia, it was an easy case. They had made up their minds long ago that Roe should be reversed. It was only a question of when.They won a fourth vote in Clarence Thomas.

During his confirmation hearings, Thomas squirmed to avoid saying anything about his views on abortion. He sounded foolish in the process, asserting that he had never had time to discuss or debate *Roe* v. *Wade* with anyone in the 18 years since the decision. He certainly had no fixed opinion, he told the Judiciary Committee. But seven months later, his views had apparently crystallized. He agreed to join an opinion either undercutting or overturning *Roe* v. *Wade*.

During his first term, Thomas had shut himself away in the dark chambers of the Court, still badly bruised by his confirmation ordeal. He spoke only with the old friends from his EEOC days and the conservatives of the Bush administration who had championed his cause. He had quit reading newspapers or watching television news.

"He told me the happiest day of his life was when he canceled his subscription to the *Washington Post*," said Clint Bolick, a former EEOC attorney and longtime friend of Thomas's. Even television sitcoms made for a dangerous intrusion into the Thomas household; Hollywood writers had made him into a regular punch line. A proud and dignified man, Thomas seemed to have suffered a terribly cruel fate. He would always be branded as the justice accused of sexual harassment.

But what now? He was firmly ensconced in a lifetime job. Initially, he told reporters at the Court that his goal was to achieve anonymity. "I want to write FERC cases," he joked at one reception. "Maybe a few bankruptcy and tax cases too." The regulatory cases involving oil and gas that emerged from the Federal Energy Regulatory Commission were some of the dullest, most intricate disputes to reach the Court. The author of those opinions could count on being ignored by the press, Thomas said. On the bench, he usually sat quietly, absorbed but hardly ever asking a question.

But when the written decisions began to appear in January, Thomas dropped the guise of timid rookie. Just a few months into the job, he fired off several sharp dissents that urged a major revision in established liberal doctrine. As some of his friends noted, his opinions read like the work of an angry man who would gladly exact some revenge on his liberal critics.

In mid-January, the Court to no one's surprise upheld the conviction of an Illinois child molester named Randall White. He had beed tried for abusing a four-year-old girl who was the daughter of his girlfriend. A baby-sitter had seen him leaving the child's room, and her mother, a police officer, and a doctor all testified as to what the little girl told them soon after the assault. During the trial, the child sat in the courtroom, but she did not take the witness stand to testify against White.

In his appeal to the Supreme Court, White said that his rights under the Sixth Amendment had been violated. This amendment says, "In all criminal prosecutions, the accused shall enjoy the right . . . to be confronted with the witnesses against him." This right developed in England to end the practice of convicting persons based on rumors and hearsay. If a person is to be convicted of a crime, the accuser must accuse him in open court and be cross-examined by a defense lawyer.

But the Supreme Court had never given this clause an absolutist reading. Take, for example, Jones, who is found lying in the street and dying of a stab wound. Before he expires, he says to a police officer: "Smith did it." At his trial, Smith cannot be confronted with his actual accuser; Jones is dead. But the police officer can take the witness stand and testify to what the dying man told him. This is known as a "hearsay exception" to the usual rule requiring direct testimony from accusers. Most state laws allow several similar exceptions. For example, the police officer who arrived at the scene to hear the young girl's instant account of her molestation would also be permitted to testify against the accused molester. In past opinions, however, the Court had seemed to say that an accuser who is available and competent to testify must take the witness stand.

But none of the justices sided with Randall White. Without Brennan and Marshall, no one would declare that White's rights under the Sixth Amendment had been violated. In *White v. Illinois*, the chief justice wrote an opinion that avoided discussing the words of the Sixth Amendment and its reference to "all criminal prosecutions." Rather, Rehnquist said, it has long been understood that some types of "hearsay testimony" are permitted, and White was properly convicted based on such statements, he concluded.

But Clarence Thomas refused to sign on to such a simple solution. He and his clerks wrote a heavily historical 10-page analysis that gave a new twist to the words of the Sixth Amendment. The amendment refers to "the witnesses against" the accused, and that phrase should be read as referring only to persons who take the witness stand, Thomas maintained. Since the four-year-old girl did not take the witness stand, she was *not* a witness against White. Presto! No violation of the Sixth Amendment.

But wait a second. What would be left of the Sixth Amendment if such a dodge were permitted? Persons could be prosecuted again based on rumors and allegations, not on direct testimony by witnesses. Consider this example: Let's say a woman named Anita Hill told friends that a Supreme Court nominee, Clarence Thomas, sexually harassed her years before. But now, Ms. Hill refuses to discuss the matter and will not appear before the Senate Judiciary Committee to voice her accusation and respond to questions from Thomas's supporters. Nonetheless, a parade of her friends come before the Committee with accusations against Thomas based on rumors and on past statements from Hill. Wouldn't that nominee, or anyone else for that matter, believe that his right to confront his accuser had been violated?

A few weeks later, Thomas published a second, surprising dissent, this time in a case involving a prisoner. In 1983, Keith Hudson was an inmate at a Louisiana prison when three guards roughed him up for no apparent reason. With Hudson shackled and handcuffed, they punched him in the stomach, the chest, and the mouth, leaving him with a bruised face and a cracked dental plate. He sued the three officers in a federal court, contending that they had violated the Eighth Amendment's ban on "cruel and unusual punishment." A magistrate heard the evidence from both sides and awarded the inmate $800 in damages. But the U.S. Fifth Circuit Court of Appeals overturned this award and said that the prisoner's rights were not violated because he had not suffered a "significant injury."

But in the Supreme Court, the prisoner won a 7–2 vote. Writing for the majority in *Hudson* v. *McMillan*, O'Connor said that prison guards may use force to put down disruptions or maintain order, but they may not do so "maliciously and sadistically for the very purpose of causing harm." Certainly, guards may not use cattle prods, electric shock, or other forms of torture against prisoners with the excuse that these punishments do not produce a lasting, permanent injury.

Thomas disagreed. The Eighth Amendment was not intended for "protecting inmates from harsh treatment," he wrote. Rather, it limits punishments such as prison sentences, not the day-to-day conditions in prison, he contended. "In my view, a use of force that causes only insignificant harm to a prisoner may be immoral, it may be tortious, it may be criminal," Thomas wrote, "but it is not 'cruel and unusual punishment.' " Scalia joined his dissent. The new justice, who showed so little familiarity with the law during his confirmation hearings, seemed to be trying hard to write broad, abstract, and sweeping opinions. His colleagues were not impressed.

To be sure, there were some exceptions during his first term when Thomas moved away from his hard-line conservative approach. For example, he cast the decisive fifth vote to reverse the conviction of a Nebraska farmer who had purchased child pronography through the mail, but only after U.S. Postal Service inspectors had sent him about a dozen solicitations, letters, and questionnaires. His friends say Thomas has a "libertarian streak." He will rule against the government when it reaches too far to harass or trap an unwary citizen, they say. But conservatives had to be delighted with his first year. He had no qualms in upsetting the liberals or voting to reverse liberal precedents.

With Thomas, Rehnquist had four solid votes in the graduation prayer case and the abortion case. He needed only one vote from the three other Reagan-Bush appointees: Justices O'Connor, Kennedy, and Souter.

But O'Connor was something of a lost cause when it came to overturning popular precedents. Soon after joining the Court, she wrote an opinion saying that the Miranda ruling "strikes a proper balance" between the needs of law enforcement and the rights of the criminal suspect, words that set teeth gnashing among Ed Meese's aides. In 1985, she had derided Rehnquist's call for permitting school prayer. In her view, the government may not appear to "endorse" religion in any manner. And perhaps most important, she refused to join the calls for entirely reversing *Roe* v. *Wade*. Repeatedly, she said she would strike down restrictions that put an "undue burden" on women seeking abortion. In the *Webster* case, Scalia had publicly mocked her views, saying they were "not to be taken seriously." That comment only stiffened O'Connor's backbone. Now, in the face of pressure from the Court's right wing, she was ready to assert her support for the basic right to choose abortion.

And so too was David Souter. In his first year, the quiet and cautious justice had formed something of an alliance with O'Connor. At Thanksgiving, she invited Souter, a bachelor, to join her and her family for a holiday dinner. Both were former state officials—she as a legislator in Arizona and he as an attorney general for New Hampshire—and they often looked at cases in the same way. They both saw themselves as moderate conservatives, but not extremists or ideologues. Like O'Connor, Souter insisted on sticking with precedent, not rewriting the law along the neat, abstract lines preferred by Scalia.

As a Harvard Law student in the early 1960s, Souter idolized Justice John Marshall Harlan, the dignified Wall Street lawyer who became the scholarly conservative of the liberal Warren Court. Harlan saw the law as a wall in which each decision built upon the solid precedent beneath it. Surrounded by activist liberals, he dissented frequently and lectured his colleagues for ignoring precedent. Now, however, the conservatives held sway, but Souter held fast to Harlan's admonition: Stick with the precedent and build from there.

Harlan differed from the Reagan-era conservatives in one other crucial respect. An establishment Republican, Harlan believed that the Constitution broadly protected an individual's "liberty" against intrusions by the government. Where Robert Bork said that the Court should interpret the right to "liberty" based on what the Framers envisioned 200 years ago, Harlan said that the Court should take a modern-day view of individual freedom. In 1961 and 1965, the aging Harlan wrote opinions upholding an individual's right to buy and use contraceptives, despite state laws making such use a crime. His words were cited later in *Roe* v. *Wade* and other decisions bolstering a woman's right to abortion. Like O'Connor, Souter questioned the revolutionary *Roe* v. *Wade* decision when it was handed down in 1973, but it certainly stood as a precedent now. And millions of American women had grown up confident that the

Constitution protected their ultimate freedom to choose abortion. Souter would not vote to revoke that right.

Souter and O'Connor had assumed that Kennedy would join the move to overturn *Roe* v. *Wade* entirely, so they were surprised at what they heard. Kennedy indicated that he would uphold the Pennyslvania regulations but would not join a move to overturn the abortion right entirely. As they left the conference, Rehnquist had assigned himself the opinion writing. A narrowly written opinion could perhaps draw five votes and leave for another day the ultimate decision of whether abortion can be made a crime again. But Souter and O'Connor had another idea. It seemed to them that Kennedy might be closer to their view of the matter than to Rehnquist's.

The judge from Sacramento now stood as the man in the middle. The constitutional right to abortion rested on his shoulders. Rehnquist, White, Scalia, and Thomas were ready to overturn that right. So too were they ready to again permit some forms of prayer in the public schools. Kennedy's instincts were conservative like theirs; he certainly opposed abortion and favored prayer. But like Souter and O'Connor, Kennedy saw himself as a moderate judge, not an ideologue or a right-wing extremist.

Initially, Kennedy had assumed that the Pennsylvania case did not demand a major ruling. He could vote to uphold the state's regulations, such as the 24-hour waiting period, without deciding on the ultimate question of whether to overturn *Roe* v. *Wade*. But Rehnquist's opinion would be read as permitting any reasonable attempt to restrict abortion. It would set off a national uproar, and Kennedy didn't want to be part of that effort. Of course, he could join no one in the Pennsylvania case and simply announce for himself that he concurred in the judgment upholding the regulations. But why? On what basis? He would look foolish if he said nothing. After all, one side in the case said all abortion regulations should be upheld, while the other said all should be struck down. So which is it? What could he say about the right to abortion and the regulatory powers of the state? Where should the line be drawn between valid regulations and unconstitutional restrictions? Kennedy was anguished. He concluded that he had no choice but to decide now: Should the right to abortion stand or be overruled?

He was a Catholic who thought abortion immoral and a conservative jurist who believed the Constitution gave broad powers to the states. Years before, he had referred to the *Roe* decision as "the Dred Scott of our time," an abominable ruling that was as outrageously wrong as the 1857 ruling upholding slavery in every state. His former clerks and friends in the Reagan administration were sure he would vote to overturn the right to abortion.

Yet *Roe* v. *Wade* had been the law for a generation. It had become in recent years the Court's best-known legal precedent. And during his confirmation hearings, Kennedy pledged to the Senate committee that he supported a "marital right to privacy." Unlike Scalia and Rehnquist, Kennedy believed like Justice Harlan that the right to "liberty" guaranteed by the Constitution was broad and evolved. These days, most Americans were convinced that liberty included the ultimate right to choose abortion. Should five justices now upset the nation's established view of the law? That would be seen by most Americans as an extreme decision.

During the past two terms, Kennedy felt himself drawn closer to O'Connor and Souter and away from the rigidity of Scalia. The year before, in the case involving the Michigan drug defendant who had been sentenced to life in prison for cocaine possession, Kennedy had authored a moderate-sounding opinion with Souter and O'Connor. Initially, Scalia had written an opinion that not only upheld the life sentence but declared that the Constitution does not require that the punishment fit the crime. No matter how extreme the punishment, judges should not intervene and declare the sentence an example of "cruel and unusual punishment," Scalia wrote. This went way too far for Kennedy. His opinion, joined by O'Connor and Scalia, said that the Constitution did indeed forbid a punishment that was "grossly disproportionate" to the crime.

Blackmun was surprised one afternoon when Kennedy stopped by to talk. The author of the *Roe* decision had simply assumed Kennedy would join Rehnquist's opinion overruling his 1973 landmark. Many times before, Kennedy had seemed unsure of himself in a close case and in the end had cast his vote with Rehnquist. Blackmun expected a repeat performance. Instead, he found Kennedy going through real soul searching. This was obviously a searing decision for him, Blackmun concluded.

Over the years, Blackmun had kept to himself at the Court and rarely socialized with his colleagues. He dutifully read his mail, however, and often spoke of letters he received. As Kennedy chatted, Blackmun pulled from his desk a few letters that had moved him. They had come from nuns. Despite the official teaching of the Catholic Church, they had written to Blackmun to thank him for upholding the right of a desperate woman to get an abortion.

Rehnquist's draft opinion in the Pennsylvania case had gone around the building in mid-May, but it spoke for only four justices. Blackmun was working on a dissent. But unbeknownst to them, Kennedy had made up his mind. He told O'Connor that he would join an opinion she and Souter were drafting that affirmed the "core" right of a woman to choose abortion. Yes, most of the Pennsylvania regulations could stand, but only because they did not block a woman from obtaining an abortion. The right to abortion would survive, thanks to Ronald Reagan's final appointee.

For months, Kennedy had been on the fence in the graduation prayer case too. At first, he had planned to write an opinion upholding the Rhode Island prayer as a ceremonial invocation that merely acknowledged God but did not subject students to religious indoctrination. But he remained troubled by the choice that would face nonreligious students: Sit through the prayer or stay away from graduation. Kennedy decided that he needed to write that opinion. Though it seemed innocuous, the graduation prayer could not be allowed, he concluded.

Rehnquist and Scalia were stunned. Kennedy had switched sides. The strict ban on religion would remain, and so would the constitutional right to choose abortion. Rehnquist invited Kennedy to go for a morning stroll around the Court one morning in late May, hoping to change his mind. As they walked, the two gestured angrily. Kennedy would not go along with the chief justice this time.

Scalia tried to reason with Kennedy too, but with no success. Kennedy's defection changed everything! Scalia was livid one moment, glum the next. They were one vote short of overturning *Roe* v. *Wade*, and this was their last chance, he complained. With George Bush headed for defeat, Democrat Bill Clinton will fill the next seats with judges who have passed his pro-*Roe* litmus test. *Roe* is fixed forever now, Scalia said. Because of Tony Kennedy, it will never be overturned.

Through much of May, O'Connor, Souter, and Kennedy worked away on an unusual opinion that spoke for the three. Sitting on his black leather couch, Souter wrote out drafts on a legal pad, tore them up, and tried again. All three wanted to do their own writing for this one and not rely on clerks. Souter stressed precedent and its significance for maintaining the Court as a legal body, not a political institution. O'Connor honed in on women's rights and reproductive freedom. Kennedy dwelt on the Constitution's broad protection for "liberty." Working together, they turned out a remarkable 60-page opinion. It offered a more powerfully reasoned defense of the right to abortion than did the original *Roe* v. *Wade* ruling.

Three authors is plenty, but in one sense, the opinion in *Casey* v. *Planned Parenthood* had a fourth as well: Justice John Marshall Harlan. The opinion quoted chunks of Harlan's work in which he urged the Court to uphold the American tradition of individual "freedom from all substantial arbitrary impositions and purposeless restraints. . . . That tradition is a living thing," Harlan had said. Where Robert Bork and Antonin Scalia believed that the scope of individual rights protected by the Constitution was frozen 200 years ago, Harlan said that freedom and liberty could grow and evolve. Souter and Kennedy had now cast their lots with Harlan, not Bork.

When the joint opinion circulated through the building, Blackmun was as surprised as Rehnquist and Scalia. Once again, as in the *Webster* case, he had the pleasing task of revising his draft dissent and making it into a concurring opinion. With him and Stevens joining the essence of the joint opinion, a five-vote majority affirmed the basic right to choose abortion.

"Now, just as so many expected the darkness to fall, the flame has grown bright," Blackmun wrote. "Make no mistake about it, the joint opinion of Justices O'Connor, Kennedy, and Souter is an act of personal courage and constitutional principle."

But Kennedy remained anxious and brooding. He knew that many of his longtime friends would feel betrayed. They had pushed for his nomination and worked for his confirmation in the Senate because they believed he was an experienced, solidly conservative jurist, not one who would sway to the left. They were in for a shock. On June 24, he read from the bench his majority opinion outlawing the graduation prayer in Providence on the grounds that it is an officially sponsored religious ceremony. Scalia mocked Kennedy's opinion as "senseless" and a "jurisprudential disaster." But from his viewpoint, the worst was yet to come.

On June 29, the Court announced that the last decisions of the term would be released, and Kennedy invited a reporter from the *California Lawyer* to stop by for an interview. For several years, the magazine had tried to speak to Kennedy in preparation for a planned profile of the Sacramento native. On this, the most momentous day of his career, he decided he would speak to the reporter. Kennedy's chambers overlook the marble plaza in front of the Court where, on that morning, photographers, cameramen, reporters, and abortion demonstrators had gathered in anticipiation of the Court's announcement. Kennedy, standing before the tall window and gazing out at the throng, knew they were in for a surprise. "Sometimes you don't know if you're Caesar about to cross the Rubicon, or Captain Queeq cutting your own tow line," he mused.

Within the Court, Kennedy's uncertainty had made him the butt of jokes by the conservative law clerks. During the farewell party a few days before the term ended, the clerks had put on skits in which they played the roles of various justices. When the Kennedy character was introduced, they played the theme song from the old television show about a playful dolphin, "Flipper."

But in the courtroom, Kennedy sounded assured as the justices took turns reading portions of the opinion. The scene was dramatic. Rehnquist, as chief justice, spoke first. But rather than read the majority opinion, he announced that the opinion in *Casey* v. *Planned Parenthood* would be delivered by O'Connor, Kennedy, and Souter.

O'Connor began by noting that the Justice Department under presidents Reagan and Bush had asked the Court to overturn *Roe* v. *Wade* on five previous occasions. This case made it six times. Before, O'Connor had withheld stating her view, but now, she said, the doubts must end.

"The essential holding of *Roe* v. *Wade* should be retained and once again reaffirmed," she said. "Some of us as individuals find abortion offensive to our most basic principles of morality, but that cannot control our decision. Our obligation is to define the liberty of all, not to mandate our own moral code. . . . The destiny of the woman must be shaped to a large extent on her own conception of her spiritual imperatives and her place in society."

Next, Kennedy spoke of the Constitution's guarantee of individual liberty. Matters such as marriage and childbearing "involve the most intimate and personal choices a person may make in a lifetime." They are "central to the liberty protected by the Fourteenth Amendment," he said.

Souter than spoke of the Court's obligation to follow its precedents, even those that have provoked bitter controversy. "An entire generation has come of age" since *Roe* was decided, he said. To overturn it now would undermine "the legitimacy of the Court."

Outside, before the justices had finished reading, women's rights leaders were already calling the ruling a "devastating loss." The first news stories also emphasized that most of the Pennsylvania regulations had been upheld by the Court, suggesting that abortion could be further restricted. But those who heard the justices deliver the opinion, as well as those who had a chance to read it in full, knew the story was different. Five Republican justices had combined to stand firm behind the right to abortion. Three were appointees of Reagan and Bush, but they had indeed crossed the Rubicon. There was no going back now.

"Each generation must learn anew that the Constitution's written terms embody ideas and aspirations that must survive more ages than one," they wrote in their conclusion to the *Casey* opinion. "We accept our responsibility not to retreat from interpreting the full meaning of the covenant in light of all our precedents. We invoke it once again to define the freedom guaranteed by the Constitution's own promise, the promise of liberty."

Epilogue

The election of Democrat Bill Clinton confirmed what the Court's decision in the Pennsylvania abortion case had signaled: the sharp turn to the right had been halted. In their alliance, Justices O'Connor, Kennedy, and Souter agreed that they would not join a move to overturn well-established legal precedents simply because they were obnoxious to conservatives. And Clinton's victory foreclosed the possibility, at least for several years, that another stridently conservative appointee would join the Rehnquist Court. The landmark rulings of the Warren and Burger Courts will probably survive the Rehnquist Court, despite the best efforts of the chief justice.

But the Court appointees of Ronald Reagan and George Bush are not about to go away simply because a Democrat has moved into the White House. They are there for life. So what had Reagan and Bush wrought?

Between 1986 and 1991, they sent four new justices to the Supreme Court. William Rehnquist, the most conservative of the justices, also was elevated to the position of chief justice. For a body whose members often serve for decades, these years marked a period of rapid change, similar to the first Nixon administration, when four justices were appointed, and to Franklin Roosevelt's second term, when four justices were replaced in three years. By contrast, the 14 years before 1986 had seen only two changes: the arrival of Stevens in 1975 and O'Connor in 1981.

Nixon's four appointees between 1969 and 1972 succeeded in putting the brake on the liberal activism of the Earl

Warren era, especially in the area of criminal rights. Even more profoundly, FDR's new appointees ended the Court's rock-ribbed protection of big business. From then on, the government could regulate the economy and protect the welfare of workers.

By comparison, the impact of the Reagan-Bush appointees seems quite limited. The Rehnquist Court has given the government more power to regulate abortion, to carry out the death penalty, to permit more acceptance of religion, and to restrict affirmative action. But each of these changes comes at the margin. So far, Rehnquist and Scalia have failed to win a majority to change the law dramatically. Kennedy's bold defection from the right wing in 1992, along with Souter's middle-of-the-road course, split apart what once looked to be a solid conservative coalition.

The new alliance of O'Connor, Souter, and Kennedy seemed to go beyond even questions of legal precedent. Perhaps the explanation lies with some principle of physics. Recall that Thurgood Marshall, the most liberal member of the Court, retired in 1991 and was replaced by Clarence Thomas, who quickly joined the most conservative justices. Yet the Court as a whole seemed more liberal with Thomas than with Marshall. It was as though as more weight was piled onto the right wing of the Court, the moderate conservatives leaned left to preserve the balance.

Certainly, some conservatives have reason to be doubly disappointed. Not only is the Court majority not inclined to reverse liberal precedents, but they also have been unwilling to move aggressively to defend private property or big business. Throughout the Reagan-Bush years, the editorial page of the *Wall Street Journal* applauded the Court for exercising "judicial restraint" in refusing to strike down death sentences, drug-testing programs, or other tough "war on drugs" measures. Instead, however, the *Journal* urged the Court to use its power to strike down laws that displeased conservatives. For example, its editors recommended that the Rehnquist Court declare unconstitutional the independent counsel law that bedeviled the upper echelon of the Reagan administration, the antiracketeering law known as RICO that proved troublesome for some Wall Street financiers, and rent-control laws that anger property owners everywhere. In each instance, the Court refused. This in itself is no surprise, however. Rehnquist and his colleagues are progovernment conservatives, not Chamber of

Commerce advocates. Across the board, they tend to uphold government measures and reject claims of individual rights, whether they come from criminal defendants or developers. If you don't like a state death penalty law, a federal drug-testing law, or a city rent-control law, Rehnquist is likely to offer the same response in all three cases: Take your complaint to the elected officials of the government, not to the courts.

In these areas, Rehnquist has put his stamp on the Court and the law. Under this affable but solidly conservative chief justice, the Court has seen its first duty as upholding the will of the majority and the rules of the government, not the constitutional rights of individuals. Those who challenge the government in the Supreme Court are likely to come out on the losing end: Sergeant James Stanley, the ex-serviceman who wanted to sue the Army for having secretly administered LSD to him; Warren McCleskey, the Georgia murderer who contended that the capital punishment system was racially biased; Nancy Cruzan, the comatose Missouri woman whose family sought for her the right to die; Ronald Harmelin, the Michigan drug criminal who believed that a life term in prison for a first-offense conviction of drug possession was "cruel and unusual punishment"; and Dr. Irving Rust, the New York physician who believed that doctors have a right to discuss abortion with their patients.

The winners before the new Court are usually prosecutors and government officials: William Webster, the Missouri attorney general who won the authority to forbid abortions in public hospitals; Michael Barnes, the Indiana prosecutor who won the power to forbid nude performers in private clubs; U.S. Customs Commissioner William Von Raab, who won the authority to require employees to undergo drug tests; U.S. drug enforcement agents, who established their authority to cross international borders to kidnap suspects and seize drug evidence for use in American courts; and Minnesota lawmakers, who won the power to compel teenage girls to come before a judge when they seek abortions. In this sense, the Court has indeed moved to the right. The justices tend to view skeptically new claims of individual rights, whether from a Sergeant Stanley or a Nancy Cruzan, while they are inclined to uphold new claims of government power, whether it is the authority to test employees for drugs or the power to cross international borders in pursuit of suspects.

But there is one obvious exception to this rule: claims involving free speech. The First Amendment remains robust even in the Rehnquist Court. Who would have thought that Larry Flynt, the porno publisher, and Gregory Johnson, the flag burner, would win their cases in a "conservative" Court? Somehow, the Constitution's guarantee that government may not abridge the freedom of speech has transcended most partisan splits. In 1989, many conservatives were angered when the Court struck down the laws against flag burning. But in 1992, it was the liberals' turn to be dismayed when the Court struck down laws against cross burning. In both cases, the principle was the same: The government cannot punish individuals simply because they have conveyed a loathsome message.

But civil rights claims are quite another matter. Repeatedly, the more conservative Court has rejected discrimination claims filed by blacks, Latinos, and other minorities. Typically, these cases are based on federal antidiscrimination laws rather than on the U.S. Constitution. Congress could once rely on the Court to vigorously enforce its civil rights laws, but no more. In recent years, the reverse has been true. In dozens of decisions, the Court gave a narrow, technical reading of the law that seemed to thwart its purpose. For example, the Civil Rights Act of 1964 bars employers from discriminating against employees because of their race or gender. But in *Patterson* v. *McLean Credit*, the justices ruled that a supervisor's "racial harassment" of an employee did not violate this law because she was not actually fired. In the view of many in Congress, the Rehnquist Court has displayed an uncanny knack for misinterpreting federal laws.

In 1989, after the series of rulings restricting the scope of the antidiscrimination laws, a solid majority in the House and Senate voiced support for writing a new law to overturn the Court's decisions. The Congressional action marked an extraordinary repudiation of the conservative Court. Lawmakers voted to overturn seven separate civil rights decisions. The new legislation, for example, said that an employee who suffers racial harassment on the job can sue for damages, overturning the *Patterson* decision. Workers who are victimized by an unfair seniority system can sue their employers when they are harmed. This change overturned *Lorance* v. *AT&T*, the 1989 decision that told women workers that the deadline had passed for them to sue. Employers whose work force is disproportionately white and male may again bear the burden of proving that their hiring standards are fair. This provision overturned the *Wards Cove* v. *Atonio* decision of 1989.

For nearly two years, President Bush blocked the broad civil rights legislation, deriding it as a "quota bill." As a candidate for the Senate in 1964, Bush had also opposed the original civil rights legislation guaranteeing nondiscrimination in the workplace. This time, he said he would support a new civil rights bill if he could be certain it did not cause quotas. In the summer of 1990, he vetoed the legislation, and the Senate fell one vote short of the needed two-thirds majority to override the veto.

But the grueling fight over the Clarence Thomas nomination seemed to strengthen the pro–civil rights forces in Congress. A group of moderate Republicans, led by Senator Danforth, Thomas's key sponsor, continued to press for the passage of the broad civil rights measure. With the votes lined up in both the House and the Senate to override a second veto, President Bush suddenly had a change of heart. He declared that the new bill would not cause quotas after all, and therefore he could sign it. On October 30, 1991, two weeks after Clarence Thomas won his narrow confirmation, the Senate gave final approval to the new civil rights bill on a 93–5 vote. A week later, the House of Representatives did the same on a 381–38 vote. It had taken two years, but seven civil rights decisions of the Rehnquist Court no longer stood as the law.

That hard-won congressional victory carried an even broader message. In the decades after World War II, the Supreme Court had made its mark as the leading protector of civil rights and civil liberties. Where the justices led, Congress, the President, and the nation followed. But under Rehnquist, the Court has abandoned that role. Now, the justices tend to tilt in favor of the government and against individual rights. When called upon to enforce civil rights statutes, the Court regularly limits the scope of the law. Groups seeking greater rights, whether women, homosexuals, or others, have learned that the Court is no longer their ally. They now turn to Congress or to their state governments, almost anywhere but the federal judiciary. Appealing to the elected officials, they can succeed even where they failed at first in the Court. The new civil rights law dramatically underscored that transformation of responsibility. The protection of civil rights had indeed moved across First Street, from the Supreme Court to Congress.

Index